DATE DUE

The Cultural Lives of Capital Pu

DATE DUE

THE CULTURAL LIVES OF LAW

A series edited by Austin Sarat

The Cultural Lives of Capital Punishment

Comparative Perspectives

Edited by

AUSTIN SARAT

CHRISTIAN BOULANGER

STANFORD UNIVERSITY PRESS

Stanford, California 2005

Stanford University Press
Stanford, California
© 2005 by the Board of Trustees of the
Leland Stanford Junior University

Library of Congress Cataloging-in-Publication Data

The cultural lives of capital punishment : comparative perspectives /
edited by Austin Sarat and Christian Boulanger.
    p. cm.
  Includes bibliographical references and index.
  ISBN 0-8047-5233-8 (cloth : alk. paper) —
  ISBN 0-8047-5234-6 (pbk. : alk. paper)
    1. Capital punishment—Cross-cultural studies. I. Sarat, Austin.
II. Boulanger, Christian.
HV8694.C77 2005
364.66—dc22

                                               2005003157

Printed in the United States of America on acid-free, archival-
quality paper

Original Printing 2005
Last figure below indicates year of this printing:
14 13 12 11 10 09 08 07 06 05

Typeset at Stanford University Press in 10/14.5 Minion

To my children—Lauren, Emily, Benjamin—with love and hope (AS)

This book is also dedicated to the memory of Clay Peterson and Johnny Martinez

Johnny Martinez, 29, was executed in May 2002, by lethal injection in Huntsville, Texas, USA. He was sentenced for the robbery and murder, in July 1993, of Clay Peterson, a clerk at a convenience store in Corpus Christi. There is strong evidence that his legal representation in the critical early stages of the trial was inadequate. Despite the fact that Johnny had turned himself over to the police shortly after the crime and had been remorseful ever since, the State believed that he was a danger to society. After Johnny Martinez killed Clay Peterson, the State, in the name of the People, killed Johnny Martinez. He was pronounced dead at 6:30 p.m, May 22, 2002.

Acknowledgments

This book is the result of a genuine collaboration, one of those special occasions in academic life when one feels oneself part of a real community of scholars. For helping to forge that community we thank our very talented group of contributors who have generously shared their work with us. We would also like to acknowledge the Law & Society Association for providing an intellectual space in which our work could be nourished. We are grateful to Amherst College for providing support and to Amanda Moran, our editor at Stanford University Press, for her interest in, and enouragement of, our project.

Contents

Contributors

SANGMIN BAE recently received her Ph.D. in political science from Purdue University and currently teaches at Butler University. Her research focuses on human rights norms and international relations theory. Her most recent article on capital punishment abolition in South Africa was published in the *International Journal of Human Rights*.

CHRISTIAN BOULANGER teaches sociolegal seminars at the Otto-Suhr-Institute for Political Science, Department of Political and Social Sciences, Free University, Berlin. He is the editor (with V. Heyes and Ph. Hanfling) of *Zur Aktualität der Todesstrafe* [On the topicality of capital punishment] (Berlin: Berlin Verlag Arno Spitz, 2nd ed. 2002)]. His academic interests include comparative research on capital punishment and legal transformation and judicial review in postcommunist and postauthoritarian countries.

JULIA ECKERT is senior researcher at the Max Planck Institute for Social Anthropology in Halle, Germany. She works on questions of legal anthropology, conflict theory, and anthropology of the state and democracy in South and Central Asia. Her current research project focuses on "Citizenship, Security and Democracy in India."

AGATA FIJALKOWSKI received her Ph.D. in Law from the University of London and is lecturer-in-law at Lancaster University, United Kingdom. Her research focuses on the legal transformation in postcommunist countries, as well as the criminal justice area, which includes the abolition of capital punishment in the postcommunist states.

EVI GIRLING, D.Phil. (1993) in social anthropology, Oxford University (Linacre College), M.Phil. (1988) in social anthropology, Oxford University (Linacre College), and BSc in biomedical engineering (1986) Duke University, is currently a lecturer in criminology at Keele University, England. She is the co-author (with Ian Loader and Richard Sparks) of *Crime and Social Order in Middle England* (London: Routledge, 2000). Her publications to date have focused on the sociology of sensibilities toward crime and punishment, children's talk about punishment, and on European efforts to abolish the death penalty.

VIRGIL K. Y. HO is associate professor of history at the Hong Kong University of Science and Technology. He is the co-author (with Göran Aijmer) of *Cantonese Society in a Time of Change* (Hong Kong: Chinese University Press of Hong Kong, 2000). He is the author of a number of historical articles, including "Butchering Fish and Executing Criminals: Public Executions and the Meanings of Violence in Late-Imperial China," in Göran Aijmer and Jon Abbink, eds., *Meanings of Violence: A Cross Cultural Perspective* (Oxford: Berg, 2000).

DAVID T. JOHNSON is associate professor of sociology and adjunct professor of law at the University of Hawaii. He is the author of *The Japanese Way of Justice: Prosecuting Crime in Japan* (Oxford: Oxford University Press, 2002). In 2003–4, he received a Fulbright grant to do death penalty research in Japan and East Asia.

BOTAGOZ KASSYMBEKOVA studied International Relations and Sociology at the American University–Central Asia and Cultural and Social History the University of Essex. She is also a senior editor of the *Essex Human Rights Review* and a co-founder of the Amnesty International Kyrgyzstan youth group. She is currently a research fellow at Freie Universität Berlin studying the social history of guilt in Germany and the question of Russian "Germans'" immigration. Her research interests include Soviet history and social, cultural, legal, and political changes in the post-Soviet states.

SHAI J. LAVI is a member of the Tel-Aviv University Law Faculty. He is the author of *The Modern Art of Dying: The History of Euthanasia in the United States* (Princeton, N.J.: Princeton University Press, forthcoming 2005). He received a Fulbright scholarship and is a member of the young scholars group at the Israeli Academy of Sciences and Humanities.

JÜRGEN MARTSCHUKAT is Heisenberg professor of the "Deutsche For-schungsgemeinschaft" and teaches history at the University of Hamburg, Ger-many. He is the author of *Inszeniertes Töten: Eine Geschichte der Todesstrafe vom 17. bis zum 19. Jahrhundert* [Performances of execution in Germany] (Cologne: Böhlau, 2000) and *Die Geschichte der Todesstrafe in Nordamerika: Von der Kolo-nialzeit bis zur Gegenwart* [The history of capital punishment in North Amer-ica] (Munich: Beck, 2002) and co-editor of *Geschichtswissenschaft und perfor-mative turn: Ritual, Inszenierung und Performanz vom Mittelalter bis zur Neuzeit* [Historiography and performative turn] (Cologne: Böhlau, 2003).

ALFRED OEHLERS is an associate professor in the Faculty of Business, Auck-land University of Technology, New Zealand, where he teaches courses in inter-national business and political economy. His research focuses on processes of economic, social, and political change in Southeast Asia, and most particularly, Singapore and Burma.

JUDITH RANDLE is a Ph.D. student in the Jurisprudence and Social Policy program (Boalt Hall School of Law) at the University of California, Berkeley. Her research interests include capital punishment, crime victims' rights, and legal responses to child abuse.

JUDITH MENDELSOHN ROOD, Ph.D. (1993) in modern Middle Eastern his-tory, University of Chicago, M.A. (1982) in Arabic studies, Georgetown Univer-sity, and B.A. (1980) in history, New College, Sarasota, is associate professor of history and chair of the Department of History, Government, and Social Sci-ence at Biola University in La Mirada, California. She is the author of *Sacred Law in the Holy City: The Khedival Challenge to the Ottomans as Seen from Jerusalem, 1829–1841* (Leiden: Brill, 2004), which analyzes the Muslim commu-nity's political and socioeconomic role in Jerusalem under Ottoman adminis-tration during the 1830s from a natural law perspective, using the archives of the Islamic court.

AUSTIN SARAT is William Nelson Cromwell Professor of Jurisprudence and Political Science at Amherst College. He is former president of the Law & Soci-ety Association and of the Association for the Study of Law, Culture, and the Humanities. He is author of *When the State Kills: Capital Punishment and the American Condition* (Princeton, N.J.: Princeton University Press, 2001), and

Mercy on Trial: What It Means to Stop an Execution (Princeton, N.J.: Princeton University Press, forthcoming, 2005).

NICOLE TARULEVICZ teaches Asian and twentieth-century world history at the University of Melbourne, Australia. Her research interests include constructions of Singapore's national past and future. She has been a visiting scholar in the History Department of the National University of Singapore and has also served as an editor of *Melbourne Historical Journal.*

PATRICK TIMMONS is assistant professor of Latin American history at Augusta State University, Georgia. He is the organizer of the April 2004 Binational Conference, "The Death Penalty and Mexico-U.S. Relations" at the Mexican Center, University of Texas at Austin and curator of the exhibit, "La Última Pena: Five Centuries of Capital Punishment in Mexico" at the Benson Latin American Collection, University of Texas at Austin.

LOUISE TYLER is an independent scholar. Her main area of focus is the synthesis of popular culture (cinema) with political rhetoric.

The Cultural Lives of Capital Punishment

CHAPTER ONE

Putting Culture into the Picture

Toward a Comparative Analysis of State Killing

CHRISTIAN BOULANGER AND AUSTIN SARAT

Introduction

How do the ways we think and feel about the world around us affect the existence and administration of the death penalty? And what role does capital punishment play in defining our political and cultural identity? In this book, we argue that in order to understand the death penalty, we need to know more about the "cultural lives"—past and present—of the state's ultimate sanction. A second claim is that this "cultural voyage" should be undertaken comparatively: we need to look beyond the United States and see how capital punishment "lives" or "dies" in the rest of the world, how images of state killing are produced and consumed elsewhere, how they are reflected, back and forth, in the emerging international judicial and political discourse on the penalty of death and its abolition.[1]

What do we mean by the cultural life of capital punishment? First of all, for the purpose of this introduction, we refer to capital punishment, or the death penalty, as legally administered state killing, used as a punishment in response to a crime.[2] By "cultural lives" we mean capital punishment's embeddedness in discourses and symbolic practices in specific times and places. To talk about the penalty of death having, not only one, but several "lives" is not a simple pun. We argue that, after centuries in which capital punishment was a completely normal and self-evident part of criminal punishment, it has taken on a life of its own in various arenas, which goes far beyond the limits of the penal sphere. We further claim that, even though it is important to consider political (Neumeyer 2004) and socioeconomic (Simon 1997) factors that shape the existence of capital punishment across geographic and social spaces, it is its cultural life that deserves more attention.

As David Garland (1990) has argued, punishment and culture are connected in two ways: culture gives punishment meaning and legitimacy and shapes its practice through cultural "sensibilities" and "mentalities." On the other hand, punishment itself defines cultural and sociopolitical identities and provides vivid symbols in cultural battles. Punishment lives in culture as a set of images, as a marvelous spectacle of condemnation. The semiotics of punishment is all around us, not just in the architecture of the prison, or the speech made by a judge as she sends someone to the penal colony, but in both "high" and "popular" culture iconography, in novels, television, and film. Punishment has traditionally been one of the great subjects of cultural production, suggesting the powerful allure of the fall and of our prospects for redemption. But perhaps the word "our" is inaccurate here since Durkheim (1984 [1893]) and Mead (1918), among others, remind us that it is through practices of punishment that cultural boundaries are drawn, that solidarity is created through acts of marking difference between self and other, through disidentification as much as imagined connection.

And what is true of punishment in general is certainly true of those instances in which the punishment is death. Traditionally, public execution was one of the great spectacles of power and an instruction in the mysteries of responsibility and retribution. Even the privatization of execution has not ended the pedagogy of the scaffold. Execution itself, the moment of state killing, is today an occasion for rich symbolization, for the production of public images of evil or of an unruly freedom whose only containment is in a state-imposed death, and for fictive re-creations of the scene of death in popular culture. Yet all of this may miss the deepest cultural significance of state killing. As Baudrillard (1993: 169) suggests, in regard to capital punishment, "the thought of the right (hysterical reaction) and the thought of the left (rational humanism) are both equally removed from the symbolic configuration where crime, madness and death are modalities of exchange."

It is a commonplace to state that the United States is alone among Western industrialized nations in executing its citizens. Usually, analysis focuses on "American exceptionalism," comparing the new with the old world (Steiker 2002; Moravcsik 2001; Poveda 2000). From a global perspective, however, the United States is not exceptional. Little more than a fourth of the world's population lives in countries that have completely abolished the death penalty. Most U.S.-American death-penalty proponents hesitate to cite states like the Democratic Republic of Congo, Iran, Saudi Arabia, China, or North Korea as examples of countries which are also executing their citizens. However, there is at least one more industrialized democracy, Japan, and other politically respectable states such as India, South Korea, Taiwan, and Singapore in which capital punishment is still applied.

On the other hand, the European Union proudly proclaims itself to be "death-penalty-free" and has succeeded in talking (and sometimes coercing) almost the whole of Eastern Europe into abolition (Fijalkowski 2001; Frankowski 1996). In the territory of Russia and the former Soviet states in Central Asia, Turkmenistan alone has abolished the death penalty completely, although Russia, Kazakhstan, and Kyrgyzstan have moratoria in place. The African continent presents a mixed picture, with nine fully and fourteen de facto abolitionist states and twenty-seven states with the death penalty.[3] Asia is, with the exception of a few small nations, an "abolition-free zone."[4] Equally, no state in the Middle East—except the de facto abolitionist Israel—has decided to abandon judicially authorized state killing.

Abolitionists in Europe like to point out that the death penalty is unacceptable in a "civilized society."[5] In addition, the Council of Europe has expressed its "firm conviction that capital punishment, therefore, has no place in civilised, democratic societies governed by the rule of law" (Council of Europe and Wohlwend 1999). European Court of Human Rights Justice Jan de Meyer put it simply when he said that "[Capital] punishment is not consistent with the present state of European civilisation" (*Soering v United Kingdom* 1989: 439). Some believe that a "civilizing process" leads inexorably to rejection of legalized state killing.[6] Europe, in this view, is a step ahead of the United States, which, along with the rest of the world, sooner or later will catch up. The optimistic view of the globalization of penality is that the differences between countries will be leveled out in an abolitionist direction.[7] As the chapters in this volume suggest, this idea is inadequate to explain what has happened in abolitionist countries and might be misleading when thinking about the global process of abolition. We argue that a closer look is needed at structures and processes on the national and subnational levels.

In recent years, there have been several publications which have looked comparatively into global processes of abolition (Hodgkinson and Rutherford 1996; Schabas 1997; Hood 2002; Boulanger et al. 2002; Reicher 2003; Hodgkinson and Schabas 2004). At the same time, there has been little systematic research on the determinants of the death penalty on a global scale, and most of it is concerned with the question of abolition (Greenberg and West 2001; Neumayer 2004). In comparative perspective, there are a variety of methodologies which one can employ to understand capital punishment. We think that comparative analyses are best served by methodological eclecticism, which combines insights from various approaches (Kohli et al. 1995). In what follows, we discuss previous research and highlight some aspects that we consider important for a comparative cultural research agenda on capital punishment.

Deadly Significant Relationships? Data-Driven Research

That there can be no simple explanation for global variation seems clear. The number of possible factors that differentiate abolitionist from retentionist states is potentially infinite. This, of course, has not kept comparativists from trying to solve the puzzle on the aggregate level. They have collected data on various independent variables to determine how the dependent variable, the (non)existence of capital punishment, can be explained (e.g., Greenberg and West 2001; Neumayer 2004). Among the factors so far studied are:

Crime rates. That state punitivism cannot be explained as a simple response to crime has been a commonplace in analyses of punishment for a long time. This is confirmed by statistical analyses which show that crime rates, punitive attitudes, and policy responses are, if at all, only marginally correlated (Savelsberg 2000, Greenberg and West 2001). This, of course, doesn't mean that crime rates are not important,[8] but only that they do not translate directly into penal policy. For this reason, what has to be studied are the conditions under which high crime rates do result in extreme sentencing, including the death penalty, and when it does not.

Socioeconomic indicators. There is no clear statistical relationship between a country's socioeconomic development and its use or non-use of the death penalty (Greenberg and West 2001, Neumayer 2004). This might be surprising, especially to theorists who think of the abolition of capital punishment as the product of the sociocultural process of "civilization."

Regime type. The more authoritarian a country is, the more it is likely to have the death penalty. Of 194 independent countries rated by Freedom House in 2003, 71 of 90 countries classified as "Free" were abolitionist (de jure or de facto), about 80 percent, versus 19 which were classified retentionist. For "Partly Free" countries, the ratio is 33 (62 percent) abolitionist to 20 retentionist. On the other hand, of the 48 countries rated as "Not Free" three-fourths (36) had the death penalty on the books and had executed someone in the last ten years, compared with 12 abolitionist countries.[9] These data make it clear that there is a relationship between democracy and respect for human rights on one side, and abolition on the other. But with the United States as the world's largest stable democracy and supporter both of human rights *and* of capital punishment, this correlation again leaves us puzzled about American "exceptionalism" within the "Western world."

Religion seems to matter (Hood 2001). Almost all of the states with a majority of Muslims, and certainly all of those claiming to adhere to Shari'ah law, have the death penalty. As Neumayer has pointed out, however, such numerical evidence might be misleading. He suggests that "the lack of democracy, the lack of political incentives, and the fact that most Muslim countries are located in regions with very few abolitionist countries might be more important explanations than Islam itself" (2004: 29). Most states in which Christians (and especially Catholics) are the majority do not execute their citizens (Greenberg and West 2001). Again, the United States stands out. Today, the United States is, together with Belarus, the only majority Christian country with executions. There is evidence from the United States that Evangelical Christians show stronger support for the death penalty than members of other religious groups (Grasmick et al. 1993; Green 2000). Finally, states which have declared themselves to be "atheist," such as the previously communist countries, and those who claim to be so today have not shown any special inclination toward abolition.[10] The same is true for Asian countries where a numerical majority of citizens are Buddhist, even though it has been argued that the "compassionate element" in Buddhism favors abolition (Horigan 1996).

As these various data show, the relationship between religion and the death penalty, on an aggregate basis, is ambiguous. What we need are accounts of how religious beliefs translate into public policy in particular times at particular places. Religion is obviously a part of culture, but, as Geertz has argued (1973: 14) "culture is not a power, something to which social events, behaviors, institutions, or processes can be causally attributed; it is a context."[11] Statistical data on the number of adherents to a particular religion do not necessarily help us explain differences between countries.

Public opinion. How popular is the death penalty and how is its popularity related to abolitionism? In the United States, the answer seems easy. Capital punishment is popular all over the country. Even though support has waned somewhat over the last few years, probably under the influence of growing media attention to miscarriages of justice, over 60 percent of respondents still support it (PollingReport.com 2004; Gross 1998; Cook 1998). However, the aggregate picture is, as always, somewhat misleading, since support varies by state, and so does the application of capital punishment (Norrander 2000; Zimring 2003). International comparisons blur the picture even further: In Canada, opinion polls indicated over 70 percent support for the death penalty during the 1980s and 1990s. In the UK in 1995, when the issue of reinstating the death penalty was debated and subsequently defeated in Parliament, 76 percent of British respondents supported the death penalty, and support remains high, even if it has declined recently (Death Penalty Information Center 2004). While in Western Europe support is currently around 30 percent, it has been consistently higher in Eastern Europe.[12] We know much less about the rest of the world, where there is little research on the topic, but the few figures available show general support of capital punishment.[13]

As various observers have noted, public opinion "appears to follow national political decisions—and, even then, only slowly—rather than leading it" (Moravcsik 2001). In Germany, for example, at the time of abolition in 1948, support for capital punishment was higher than it is in the United States today (Savelsberg 2000: 191). Looking at survey figures we have no way of knowing how deeply rooted support is. Moreover, surveys often don't tell us much about the reasons for support at particular times and places, and how likely is it that these motives will lose their force.

Comparative data-driven approaches are valuable as they can help us to identify factors that might escape the attention of single-case studies. However, they have a number of shortcomings. Explanations that rely on factors at the aggregate level will necessarily miss crucial historical processes and national and regional peculiarities. They run the ever-present risk of "concept misformation" (Sartori 1970) which occurs when abstract concepts are operationalized without knowledge of the context. And finally, they have a hard time accounting for the processes in which structural conditions are mediated by actors, institutions, and historical contingencies.[14] This is why they need to be coupled with medium-range theories which allow for closer examination of individual cases.

The Big, but Not Complete Picture: Theory-Driven Approaches

Most theoretical accounts of the death penalty deploy theories which concern particular countries (such as the United States) or comparative pairs (such as the United States versus Europe). We discuss three types of approaches: national political economy, institutional factors, and the dynamics of regional integration.[15]

National Political Economy

"Materialist" theories explain differences between countries in terms of material interests of individuals and groups. Earlier, Marxian-inspired theories argued that punishment was an instrument of the ruling class used to defend its dominant position.[16] Today, rational choice analyses have taken their place, albeit mostly with a different (or no) normative commitment. They argue that the choice of punishments can be explained by the "demand" for them in the political market.[17] Classes, powerful social groups, or political entrepreneurs are the protagonists in the explanatory framework of these approaches. Some think that the demand for harsher policies is exogenously caused by factors such as crime rates and public insecurity. Others argue plausibly that some of this demand is caused by political actors themselves, who cleverly use the topic to advance their own political careers (Zimring and Hawkins 1986), radicalizing punitive discourses as an effect. Still others do integrate "cultural" factors (mainly from opinion research), arguing that politicians act strategically in exploiting public sentiment to advance their agenda.

Even though we are skeptical regarding purely instrumentalist accounts, we agree that the question "who benefits" from the existence of the death penalty is an important one.[18] Jonathan Simon (1997), for example, has highlighted the neo-liberal agenda of the "conservative revolution" which characteristically combines "lower taxes and the death penalty." In his account, the death penalty in the United States has served a symbolic, not a directly "economic," function. Neo-liberal reform of the welfare state generated insecurity and resentment and undermined confidence in the state's capacity to provide security and legitimacy through welfare and regulation, a capacity that was associated with the modern decline of the death penalty. In response, the "tough on crime" rhetoric associated with support of capital punishment has been used to deflect discontentment and mobilize consent (see also Garland 2001).

It is certainly true that capital punishment can serve as a distraction from socioeconomic insecurities, and in this way, can accompany the decline of the welfare state. However, this is but one of multiple functions capital punishment can serve and is certainly not restricted to "neo-liberal" projects. It could serve the same function in any type of regime. It is not surprising that in the most "neo-liberal" country in Western Europe, Great Britain, we find some of the most vocal supporters of a re-introduction of the death penalty in Europe.[19] However, abolition in Britain survived "free votes" in Parliament even during Margaret Thatcher's reign, and the Tories have not used the death penalty recently as a serious campaign issue (Hodgkinson 1996). More than just the interests of political actors seem to be at stake. One important analytical strategy is to look at the impact of institutions.

Legal-Institutional Factors and Democratic Governance

Recently, "new institutionalist" approaches have emphasized the need to study institutionalized agency, institutional differences, and historical conjectures (Koelble 1995; Hall and Taylor 1996; Thelen 1999). For our purposes, this means looking at how elite strategies and institutional arrangements have worked together in history to produce abolitionist and retentionist outcomes. For example, American penal law federalism is unparalleled in Europe. Congress cannot abolish the death penalty for the whole country even if it wanted to do so, making abolition a slow and incremental process rather than a once-and-for-all event.[20] As Zimring and Hawkins (1986) have shown, the tension between the right of states to choose criminal penalties and federal oversight has led to a situation where capital punishment became a symbol for much larger struggles between the center and the periphery.

In addition, Zimring, Hawkins, and Kamin (2001) have argued that the more democratic penal policy making is, the more it is prone to be driven by punitivism, with the irrational and emotional motives often found among death penalty supporters. Their empirical case is "three-strikes-and-you're-out" legislation in California, but their hypothesis can be extended to capital punishment on a global scale. As one observer put it, "Basically, Europe doesn't have the death penalty because its political systems are less democratic, or at least more insulated from populist impulses, than the U.S. government" (Marshall 2000). One has to be careful not to confuse "democracy" with "public participation in penal policy making." The theory that nondemocratic societies are less punitive because they are more shielded from public pressure has little to it. Throughout history, most authoritarian states, including socialist, have used the death penalty liberally. This is not surprising since penal policy is a domain especially suitable for symbolic politics. Being "tough on crime" can be popular in any regime type.

The argument of Zimring and his colleagues, however, is more nuanced. They refer to popular participation in the penal policy-making process. The comparison between the United States and Europe, in this regard, is instructive. Observers have pointed out that American institutions are more "porous" and open to popular demands than European political structures. They expose many officials, particularly judges, to electoral competition for positions which in Europe are staffed by career bureaucrats or disciplined party politicians (Savelsberg 2000; Steiker 2002). Additionally, U.S. states allow penal policy to be made through referenda, such as the Californian "three-strikes" initiative. This would be unthinkable in most of Europe.[21]

How can this hypothesis be extended beyond the comparison between Europe and the United States? It seems safe to argue that less democratic states (in the participatory sense) seem to have an easier time abolishing capital punishment, since they can expect less resistance by a population overwhelmingly supportive of it. But neither the motivation nor the timing of abolition seems to have any necessary relationship with regime types.[22]

An important "institutional" factor in abolitionist outcomes is judicial abolition. It has so far taken place in Hungary, Ukraine, Latvia, South Africa, and

Albania, with Russia's constitutional court imposing a moratorium (Schabas 1996; Fijalkowski 2002). In each country, a strong majority of the populace supported capital punishment when the courts abolished it. This is not much different from countries in which it was abolished by parliamentary decision. But it certainly creates a greater legitimacy problem. It is no coincidence that all countries in which judicial abolition occurred had experienced a regime change beforehand. They had left behind regimes in which frequent human rights violations had occurred. In the aftermath, institutions which could claim a particular commitment to human rights had more influence than they would normally have had.[23] This has led to an interesting international development in which courts start citing each other's case law on judicial abolition. So far, the U.S. Supreme Court has remained split over the question whether foreign court jurisprudence is relevant to American cases.[24]

The Dynamics of Regional Integration

But there is another, maybe more important, reason for the abolitionist activism of these constitutional courts, namely the dynamics of regional integration. Abolition in Eastern and Southeastern Europe cannot be explained without looking at the fact that international organizations such as the Council of Europe and the European Union have made abolition a criterion of membership, and have actively promoted abolition in Western and Eastern Europe (Council of Europe 1999, 2004). Populations in postcommunist countries overwhelmingly support the death penalty, and it seems safe to say that most governments in the area abolished it less because of the "human rights appeal" of abolitionism and more because of anticipated benefits of compliance with European norms (Manacorda 2003; Fawn 2001). Turkey is a good example of a country that abolished capital punishment for no other reason than to remove obstacles on its way to EU membership.

In the rest of the world, such incentive structures just do not exist. Even if a numerical majority of states within the United Nations are now abolitionist, there is no economic benefit for others to join that majority, and little advantage in terms of "prestige," as long as economically and politically powerful nations such as the United States and Japan still retain the penalty. In Africa and Asia, no international institutions exist which act as forcefully as the Council of Europe and the EU in promoting abolitionism.[25] Interestingly in this regard is Latin America, where abolition has occurred without any regional initiative.

Thus all Latin American states except Guatemala and Belize had abolished the death penalty by 2001.[26]

But the international politics of the death penalty goes beyond the dynamics of regional integration. As Zimring (2003: chap. 2) has pointed out, the death penalty has become a human rights issue, although only recently. There are repeated efforts in the United Nations to promote abolition or at least restrict the use of capital punishment. The European Union and the Council of Europe have hosted abolitionist events and started initiatives to reach countries outside their immediate geographical orbit.[27] The Council of Europe has even warned that it would withdraw the observer status of Japan and the United States if these countries did not take any positive steps toward abolition (Council of Europe 2001). So far, of course, this has achieved little, and not just because in most cases the federal government is the wrong addressee for such calls.

The Cultural Life of Punishment

Thus far we have argued that when trying to account for global variation in capital punishment regimes, we have to pay attention to political economy and institutional dynamics, on both the national and the international level. At the same time, we think that these accounts are incomplete. Institutional rules and individual interests cannot be separated from the cultural context in which they are embedded. Institutions are not "just there." They are the result of historical developments and struggles and are influenced by their political, social, and cultural environments as much as they shape them.

David Garland has forcefully made this argument about the institutions of punishment. According to him, punishment is a social institution "composed of the interlinked processes of law-making, conviction, sentencing, and the administration of penalties. It involves discursive frameworks of authority and condemnation, ritual procedures of imposing punishment, a repertoire of penal sanctions, institutions and agencies for the enforcement of sanctions and a rhetoric of symbols, figures, and images by means of which the penal process is represented to its various audiences" (Garland 1990: 17). Reviewing a century of sociolegal theorizing on punishment, Garland concludes that most theorists have neglected the role of culture in punishment. However, as he points out, punishment is not only shaped by cultural processes, it is itself a cultural agent.

He reminds us that we should attend to the "cultural role" of legal practices, and to their ability to "create social meaning and thus shape social worlds," and that among those practices none is more important than how we punish (Garland 1991: 191).

Punishment, Garland (1990: 248) tells us, "helps shape the overarching culture and contribute[s] to the generation and regeneration of its terms." Punishment is a set of signifying practices that "teaches, clarifies, dramatizes and authoritatively enacts some of the most basic moral-political categories and distinctions which help shape our symbolic universe" (252). Punishment teaches us how to think about categories like intention, responsibility, and injury, and it models the socially appropriate ways of responding to injury done to us. Moreover, it exemplifies relations of power and reminds us of the pervasiveness of vulnerability and pain. Most powerfully, "penality highlights the characteristics of the normal self by policing its failures and pathologies and spelling out more precisely what one is expected minimally to be" (1991: 210).

Penality, for Garland, is a complex cultural process. Individual penal institutions, such as capital punishment, therefore cannot be viewed in isolation from other punitive practices in a society. Ideas about guilt, shame, retribution, and just punishment are reflected, for example, in sentencing schemes, prison conditions, legislative proposals, election campaigns, movie plots, or attitudes toward prison labor. There is no simple causation at work, instead, culture and punishment are mutually interdependent.

The Rise of the Cultural

So what is this "culture" of which Garland speaks? Everywhere it seems culture is in ascendance. More and more social groups are claiming to have distinctive cultures and are demanding recognition of their cultural distinctiveness. Identity politics has merged with cultural politics so that to have an identity one must now also have a culture.[28] As a result, it sometimes seems as if almost every ethnic, religious, or social group seeks to have its "culture" recognized, and for precisely this reason the cultural itself has become a subject of political life to a greater extent than in the past.

The backlash against the proliferation of cultures and identities, and what is called the "politics of recognition" (Taylor 1994), has been vehement. Politicians proclaim "culture wars" in an effort to reassert both the meaning and centrality of certain allegedly transcendent human values (Whitehead 1994). Debates about the meaning and significance of culture become arguments about "civilization" itself in which acknowledgment of cultural pluralism and its accompanying decanonization of the "sacred" texts of the Western tradition is treated as undermining national unity, national purpose, and the meaning of being a citizen.[29] Political contests are increasingly fought over values and symbols, with different parties advancing different cultural programs (Caplow and Simon 1999; Wattenberg 1995).

With the decline of ideology as an organizing force in international relations, culture seems to provide another vantage point from which to understand new polarities (Huntington 1996). In addition, the cachet of the cultural is increasingly resonant in public policy where traditional goals like reducing crime and poverty are giving way to cultural goals like reducing fear of crime and eliminating the culture of dependency. The cultural is the implicit and explicit space of intervention for popular new strategies like "community policing" (Lyons 1999) and "workfare" (Rose 1995) that promise to improve objective problems by altering the attitudes and experiences of the subjects of policing and welfare. Government and other formal organizations believe that it is essential to have cultural strategies in order to more effectively govern their employees and customers and to influence their broader popular image. The twentieth century familiarized us with the idea of propaganda and the fact that political forces had to utilize mass communication to realize their power. Today, however, the cultural has become more than a supplement or a delivery vehicle; it is quite literally where the action is.[30]

The ascendance of the cultural comes paradoxically at a time when scholars increasingly have begun to contest the concept of culture and recognize its troubling vagueness. Talking about culture at the start of the twenty-first century means venturing into a field where there are almost as many definitions of the term as there are discussions of it,[31] and where inside as well as outside the academy arguments rage.[32] In recent years, as we noted above, these arguments have come to play a progressively more visible role in national life, and culture wars are also being fought within universities (Graff 1987). There the history, meaning, and utility of culture as a category of analysis in the humanities and social sciences are all up for grabs.[33] Where once the analysis of culture could neatly be assigned to the respective disciplines of anthropology or literature, today the study of culture refuses disciplinary cabining and forges new interdisciplinary connections.[34] Thus we should resist the temptation to treat the "culture wars" over academic curricula and arts and museum programming as penumbras of some deeper social conflict; they represent their own very real conflict.

Traditionally the study of culture was the study of "'that complex whole which includes knowledge, belief, art, morals, law, custom, and any other capabilities and habits acquired by man as a member of society'" (Edward Tylor cited in Greenblatt 1990: 225). This definition, in addition to being hopelessly vague and inclusive, treats culture as a thing existing outside of ongoing local practices and social relations. In addition, by treating culture as "capabilities and habits acquired," culture was made into a set of timeless resources to be internalized in the "civilizing" process through which persons were made social. Finally, culture was identified as containing a kind of inclusive integrity, parts combining into a "whole."

This conception of culture still has its defenders and may even be on the rise as a political knowledge.[35] Today, however, within the academy critiques of the traditional, unified, reified, civilizing idea of culture abound.[36] It is now indeed almost imperative to write, to quote Lila Abu-Lughod's influential essay, "against culture" (1991: 137) or, in the face of these critiques, to "forget culture" (Brightman 1995). Thus during the course of a suit filed by the Mashpee Indians of Cape Cod in 1977, James Clifford examined the way culture stood up in a context where the very idea of cultural authenticity was on trial. Culture, he said,

> was too closely tied to assumptions of organic form and development. In the eighteenth century culture meant simply "a tending toward natural growth." By the end of the nineteenth century the word could be applied not only to gardens and well-developed individuals but to whole societies. . . . [T]he term culture retained its bias toward wholeness, continuity, and growth. Indian culture in Mashpee might be made of unexpected everyday elements, but it had in the last analysis to cohere, its elements fitting together like parts of a body. The culture concept accommodates internal diversity and an "organic" division of roles but not sharp contradictions, mutations, or emergences. . . . This cornerstone of the anthropological discipline proved to be vulnerable under cross-examination. (Clifford 1988: 338, 323)

Culture, Clifford concluded, is "a deeply compromised idea. . . . Twentieth-century identities no longer presuppose continuous cultures or traditions" (10).

Or, as Luhrmann observed, the concept of culture is "more unsettled than it has been for forty years" (1973: 1058).

Culture, Law, and Capital Punishment

Yet in this unsettled time, studies of law and of punishment have taken up cultural analysis. In the last thirty years, however, first with the development of critical legal studies, then with the growth of the law and literature movement, and finally with the growing attention to legal consciousness and legal ideology in sociolegal studies, legal scholars have come to attend to the cultural lives of law (Silbey 1992; Macaulay 1987; Chase 1986, 1994). Fueled in part by Clifford Geertz's description of law as "a distinctive manner of imagining the real" (1983: 184), they have begun to be attentive to the imaginative life of the law and the way law lives in our imagination. Law, as Geertz suggested, is not "a mere technical add-on to a morally (or immorally) finished society, it is, along of course with a whole range of other *cultural realities*, . . . an active part of it" (218). Treating law as a cultural reality means looking at the material structure of law to see it in play and at play, as signs and symbols, fantasies and phantasms.[37] These views are echoed by Robert Cover, who investigated law's role in creating our "normative universe": "Once understood in the context of the narratives that give it meaning, law becomes not merely a system of rules to be observed, but a world in which we live" (1992: 95–96). As he continues, "In this normative world, law and narrative are inseparably related. Every prescription is insistent in its demand to be located in discourse—to be supplied with history and destiny, beginning and end, explanation and purpose" (26). For research on capital punishment, this requires examining the narratives and discourses of capital punishment in one's own society. As Zimring and Hawkins noted in 1986:

> [the] extensive ethnographic literature on ritual and symbolism focuses mainly on "primitive" societies, tending to overlook the collective ceremonials and focal rituals of large and complex modern societies. Our own twentieth-century institutions and practices, in which what Durkheim called the "collective consciousness" is expressed, have been largely ignored. But it seems likely that the symbolic significance of death penalty legislation, the ritual nature of the murder trial, and the incantatory of the death sentence constitute a large part of the appeal for supporters of the death penalty. (1986: 11)

As they point out, we need to write ethnographies of the death penalty in Western societies as much as we need to study what the punishment of death means in societies that we consider "exotic" or "foreign."

The death penalty process displays many features of a communal ritual,[38] and ritual and symbolism are, as we know, intrinsic parts of modern politics. Many studies have interpreted capital punishment accordingly (e.g., Stolz 1983). Most, however, follow Foucault in concentrating on the instrumental, political aspects of this symbolism, and neglect the question why it finds an audience in the first place. Even fewer studies exist which investigate if, why, and how the symbolic appeal of legalized state killing varies across time and space. Capital punishment has its supporters in each and every country, and the call for the hangman will always find supporters—the question remains what cultural factors contribute to the appeal of the rhetoric of death and, in this way, determine its political utility, its "cultural uses," as David Garland (2002) has phrased it.

But, again, how can we make the concept of culture analytically useful in this respect? Culture is about the meanings we attribute to the symbols, signs, texts, utterances, and behaviors that make up our world, and the corresponding symbols, signs, texts, and utterances that we produce and the behaviors we display in that process of attribution. Culture is not static—it is constantly produced and reproduced and continually changing. In other words, culture consists of recurring, yet contested, patterns in what people think, say, feel, and do at a particular time and place—our mentalities, discourses, sensibilities, and behaviors.[39]

Culture from Above—Culture from Below

The concept of "national character" has luckily and deservedly gone out of fashion. But there is a danger that the notion of "culture" might be used in similar ways. That is why one of the first things cultural analyses have to do is to disentangle the "cultures" of different groups in society. This requires attention to differences between ethnic groups in pluralist societies on one hand, and class and social status on the other.[40]

Cultural production is always entangled with power and can therefore never be separated from power relations and structures of authority. Max Weber (1994), for example, argued that ideologically structured institutions, run by elites, have a profound influence on the human beings subjected to their authority. Weber did not use the world "culture" as a theoretical concept—he was more interested in "worldviews" expressed in religious doctrines and the resulting behavior enforced by religious authorities. Others theorists like Pareto, Michels, or C. Wright Mills remind us that—even in democracies—elites have a larger impact on all spheres of life, including the penal sphere, than the "ordinary population." Elite culture becomes an important subject of study. Law is produced and adjudicated by a small part of the population which has access to legal training and political posts, and legal policy—even if it responds to popular pressure—remains an almost exclusive domain of political and legal elites. How this segment of the population thinks and feels (in Garland's words, their "mentalities" and "sensibilities") has important ramifications for law and punishment. This will influence the way capital punishment is used—or not used—as a political instrument.

Joachim Savelsberg (2000) has taken up this theme in a comparative analysis of the religious foundations of state punishment in the United States and Germany. According to him, in the United States, strong puritan conceptions of good and evil, together with religiously legitimated distrust of state institutions, have produced a punitive, and "democratic," notion of punishment. In contrast, in Germany, Lutheran theology fostered trust in the state and its responsibility for punishment. This made it easier for "enlightened" reformers in the state bureaucracy to enforce penal reform, even against popular will. But as Savelsberg warns us, this cultural context is a background condition and not an explanation. "Lutheran culture" did nothing to abolish the death penalty until 1949—quite the contrary.

Looking at elites only would obviously not be sufficient to understand the cultural lives of capital punishment. They are themselves subjected to the sensibilities and mentalities contained in popular culture. To be sure, this is where regime differences come in. As argued before, it is certainly easier to circumvent popular sentiment when state institutions are strong and isolated from the large and unorganized mass of citizens. In authoritarian states, public opinion matters even less. Yet it is always the case that even though elites might feel differently about penal sanctions than the general population, they cannot escape popular reactions to the rise of crime, loss of security, and the ways the image of "the criminal" is created and re-created in the media, in movies, literature, or on the Internet (Sharrett 1999; Lipschultz and Hilt 2002; Lynch 2002). In addition, elites have little control over the results of their strategies to accommodate (or offend) public sensibilities about capital punishment. Popular culture has a life of its own, replete with alternative sources of value, resistances, and unforeseen resonances in which the public accommodates itself to, or criticizes, the regime of state killing.

Comparative Perspectives

We began this introduction by discussing the difficulties of relying on aggregate data to help us understand the global differences in penal regimes. The chapters in this book present a complex picture, written from a variety of perspectives. While this makes comparison more difficult, it also opens space for further study and introduces perspectives that would have been otherwise lost. It is our conviction that there is no single theoretical paradigm, and no definite set of independent variables which can account for the various lives of the ultimate penalty across time and space. Moreover, it is impossible to fit a representative sample of case studies of countries with the death penalty in a volume like this, to say nothing of a systematic comparison of abolitionist and retentionist countries. It is also quite difficult to find analytic material about capital punishment in countries outside the United States, since a corresponding depth of research just does not exist. Nonetheless, the chapters that follow sensitize us to the variety of ways that capital punishment interacts with, and is constitutive of, culture.

Civilization and Punishment: Self and Other in Europe and the Americas

The first part of the book consists of six chapters which focus on Germany, Mexico, Poland, the United States, and Europe. They show the centrality of the concept of "civilization" in the debate surrounding capital punishment. Across time and space, the authors argue, death penalty opponents have rallied around images of progress and modernity and tried to distinguish themselves from supporters who are variously described as "barbaric," "backward," "uncivilized," and so on. But this concept has not only been used *against* capital punishment, it also has been central in the discourse of those who, rather than abolish capital punishment, have tried to introduce new execution methods as an expression of a modern, civilized, "progressive" penal system. In addition, the chapters in this part explore various ways that punishment is tied into definitions of "self" and "other," in other words, how the way we punish defines the borders between "us" and "them."

Jürgen Martschukat takes us to nineteenth-century Germany, where executions were widespread and common (Evans 1996). He describes penal reform in mid-nineteenth-century Hamburg, where authorities tried to reestablish executions which had been abandoned previously because the violence of earlier executions offended the sensibilities of authorities. Martschukat shows how reforms moved executions from public view to behind prison walls, where only the "supposedly most advanced and rational members of the civic society" would be allowed as witnesses.

This mirrors what Foucault has described for France. Foucault himself attributes this development to a shift in technologies of power which are merely couched in a language of "humanization" of penal practices (Foucault 1995). While Spierenburg (1984) and Elias (1994 [1939]) see in this development an expression of the process of civilization—the privatization of disturbing events, accompanied by a rationalization, demystification, and deritualization of execution—Martschukat turns this relationship around. It is not some historical force which pushes the penal policy-making elite along its way to more humane, more "civilized" penal order. Rather, these elites actively create their fantasies of "civilization" not just—as Foucault argued—to better discipline the bodies of the underprivileged (although of course the subjection of the lower strata has always been part of the politics of capital punishment and recognized as such by them). One cannot, Martschukat suggests, understand changes in capital punishment if we do not take into account how penal practices are used to define "the spirit of the age and the moral constitution of our century." A second argument concerns the removal of ritualistic performance that the move out of the public into the "privacy" of the prison allegedly entailed. According to Martschukat, executions behind prison walls "were still spectacles and definitely ritualistic . . . . the new form of execution partook in the definition of how a civilized society behaved and presented itself."

Patrick Timmons takes as his point of departure a recent incident in U.S.-Mexican relations: the outrage caused in Mexico by the decision of Texas authorities to execute a Mexican national, who had not been informed of his right to contact a consulate. In response, the Mexican government protested vehemently, and Mexican President Vicente Fox Quesada even canceled a visit with his U.S. counterpart George W. Bush. For Timmons, this incident illustrates one of the ways "capital punishment defines cultural difference in the modern world."

In Mexico, there have been no executions since 1937, but the constitution still provides for the death penalty. Neither Americans nor Mexicans know much about the source of this de facto abolitionism which has its roots in the mid-nineteenth century. Exploring the "epistemology of Mexican abolitionism," Timmons provides us with a vivid picture of regime change and constitution-making after the breakdown of the authoritarian and repressive regime of General Antonio López de Santa Anna. Similar to cases like Germany and Italy a century later, this situation provided the new Mexican political elite the chance to reflect on the abuse of capital punishment in the previous regime. Timmons shows how legislators looked at the past and the future: they had experienced imprisonment and the threat of execution; some of their friends or allies had even been executed. They also feared that, should their political enemies return to power, they could again be threatened with death. These memories and fears were, however, not the only factors pushing the deputies toward abolition.

Timmons suggests that Mexican liberals saw themselves as the heirs of European enlightenment, engaged in bringing to Mexico "true civilization." But why, he asks, did the Mexican liberal elite not do away completely with capital punishment? The answer lies in their belief that civilizing progress would push Mexican society toward abolition. In the meantime, an ultimate punishment was necessary, restricted to a few categories of crimes, "political" offences exempted. While not explaining Mexico's current stance on capital punishment, Timmons argues, these events help us understand how a country so close to the "world's execution capital" chose a different path.

Moving north, the chapter by Judith Randle examines an aspect of the cultural life of capital punishment in the United States which has, so far, received only limited attention.[41] She is interested in the ways that capital punishment has become part of identity politics and how abolitionism has taken up regional identities to advance its case. She interprets capital punishment as a "cultural artefact" that incorporates other cultural characteristics of a nation that employs it. Before arguing that local identities matter, she reviews characteristics of "American" culture that favor the existence of the death penalty: most important, she argues, is the individualistic paradigm which sees crime as the free choice of a person who has to take full responsibility for her deeds, together with the clear separation between "good" and "evil" which permeates American culture. At the same time, American state legislatures do not want to be associated with cruel forms of punishment and have therefore overwhelmingly opted for the "medicalized" procedure of lethal injection. Randle argues that executions do not evoke disgust, but are perceived as "carefully regulated, relatively painless undertakings" by a majority of Americans.

But after all, there are some American states which *have* abolished capital punishment, calling into question *any* general argument about "the" Americans. As Randle points out, there is not only a different approach to abolition as such, but also an enormous difference among states which retain the punishment. In both, there is a visible north-south divide. Southern states have always had harsher capital punishment statutes than northern states, and they have been slower to change them. Overall, Randle argues, the evolution of the death penalty in America "really began as the evolution of the *Northern* death penalty," implying that "American exceptionalism" is really a "Southern exceptionalism."[42]

Randle looks at the history of slavery and racism, focusing in particular on discursive struggles over the definition of the penal identity of the states. Not only was the concept of "abolitionism" taken over from the antislavery movement, the argumentative framework of abolition, portraying the "North" as more advanced and civilized as opposed to the "barbaric" South, was taken over as well. In the fragmented history of capital punishment in the United States, Randle shows us that anti-Southern ideology has played a significant role.

The "civilized self" and "barbaric other" are also the subject of the chapter by Evi Girling. She takes us across the Atlantic right into the cultural battle over the definition of what and what is not "European." European institutions, she argues, have made the call for abolition of capital punishment a cornerstone in their quest to establish a distinctive European identity. Furthermore, a "very vocal and evangelical European voice gained prominence on the international stage," making the abolition of the death penalty one of the central missions of European foreign policy. Twenty years after Protocol No. 6 to the Convention for the Protection of Human Rights and Fundamental Freedoms found that an "evolution . . . has occurred in several member States" which "expresses a general tendency in favour of abolition of the death penalty" (Council of Europe 1983), the Charter of Fundamental Rights of the European Union states in its Article 2 simply that "No one shall be condemned to the death penalty, or executed" (European Union 2000).

Girling explores the "cultural peculiarities of abolitionism in Europe" and also its cultural uses. In order to establish Europe as a "community of sentiment," European institutions, and also pro-European politicians, intellectuals, and nongovernmental organizations have started to weave "narratives of identity" around the topic of the death penalty. Capital punishment emerges as one way of distinguishing the European self from the American "Other" (Blinken 2001). Europeans, as Girling claims, see America as a kind of "Europe gone adrift" and hope for its eventual recovery. A human rights approach to capital punishment also means that European institutions and nongovernmental institutions do not regard the practice as an internal matter for the United States alone—quite the contrary, they communicate with American death row inmates, protest their executions, and so forth. For Girling, analysis of the transatlantic struggle over the death penalty reveals a different "clash of civilizations" than the one Samuel Huntington envisions.

The next chapter takes a different perspective on the European–American cultural divide. Louise Tyler uses three films, one American, one French, one Dutch, to provide a reading of the cultural dynamics of state violence in which the debate about capital punishment is located. She claims that film helps to "regenerate" culture and reinforces "the socially appropriate methods of punishing" that are found in any society. Films about state violence in general and the death penalty in particular present a self–other dynamic in which viewers are encouraged to separate themselves from criminal others. Of particular importance here is Tyler's claim that popular culture helps to "normalize" the use of violence against socially defined others. Films that are not explicitly about capital punishment help prepare the way for it. "Others" are identified, labeled as irreducibly evil, and subject to a violent response. State violence is legitimated; evil is conquered and the culture is left reassured that punishing transgressors with death is a natural response.

Tyler's chapter considers how European films get remade for American audiences, and how they are fit into a distinctively American mythology about violence and its place in systems of punishment. Film interpolates its viewers to identify with a heroic struggle of good versus evil, to distance themselves from the criminal other, and to respond violently. Thus, for Tyler, popular culture is an enormously significant, though often unappreciated, factor in explaining the prospects for abolition or the reproduction and maintenance of systems of state killing.

In the last chapter in the first part of this book, we travel to Poland. Sociologist Agata Fijalkowski discusses the past and the present of capital punishment in Poland, where a moratorium was put in place in 1986 and the punishment disappeared from the books in a 1998 criminal law reform. Public opinion in Poland is strongly supportive of capital punishment, but within the elite the decision to abolish it was fueled by two developments. First, as Fijalkowski shows, there was considerable resistance to capital punishment by legal scholars early in Poland's modern history, which also carried over into reformist thinking during communist times. But not only liberal academics, also the "Solidarity" Labour union, which was at the forefront of the struggle for democracy, opposed capital punishment. More important is the second consideration: access to European institutions was not possible unless the punishment was abolished. In Poland, the process of penal policy making took place without the participation of, and even against the wishes of, the population.

Fijalkowski also makes creative use of Zimring's (2003) and Sarat's (2001) thoughts on the role of capital punishment in the image of "the state": Polish society, having been occupied by foreign powers and regimes alien to its own conceptions of statehood, has always been suspicious of authorities, but, at the same time, has been longing for a strong Polish state. As Fijalkowski notes, Polish society is struggling with all sorts of challenges: the breakdown of old ways of living under the communist regimes, the loss of social control and safety nets, and the corresponding rise in crime. Not surprisingly, politicians step out of the "European consensus" and run on "tough on crime" and pro-capital punishment platforms, without, however, being able to break into the establishment. Yet this dissonance cannot destabilize Polish abolitionism, at least for now, since European integration is still a high priority in the population, leading to a grudging acceptance of the disappearance of death sentences. Fijalkowski also discusses the role of the Catholic Church's stance on capital punishment in a strongly Catholic and punitive society: She explains that the church in Poland does not necessarily share the pope's attitudes and that anti-abolitionist politicians can easily refer to earlier pronouncements of the church favorable to capital punishment. Fijalkowski ends her chapter with reflections on the "long-term consequence of the paternalistic stance" Polish authorities have taken in the case of death penalty abolition. Will capital punishment remain a ghost haunting the Polish cultural and political landscape for years to come? And what, she asks, does the paternalistic stance imply for the future of Polish democracy?

State Killing and State Violence in Central and South Asia and the Middle East

The second part of our volume takes us to the Middle East and Central and South Asia, a highly heterogeneous area in terms of cultures, historical influences, and geopolitical orientations. What unites them for our purpose could be described as the presence and/or the memory of violence and the role death and capital punishment have played in forging this memory. A second commonality is that the death penalty in all of the cases surveyed is *not* the most important form of state killing. Instead, death comes in many other forms.

Kyrgyzstan is a "postcommunist" country like Poland, but unlike Poland, it endured seventy years of direct, and at times murderous, Soviet rule. What, Botagoz Kassymbekova asks, are we to make of a country like Kyrgyzstan, where "penal practice may be very remote from the 'cultural forms' relating to punishment that are circulating more generally in contemporary society"? What if images of punishment are overshadowed by the pervading presence of death unrelated to legal procedures? Kassymbekova draws our attention to the many ways people can die at the hands of the state, and suggests that this state killing, not capital punishment, is more relevant for contemporary Kyrgyz society: people are shot on the streets while protesting, die or commit suicide in the army, die from lack of hygiene in hospitals or because of a lack of medical services—all phenomena for which the state is directly or indirectly responsible.

Central Asian nations are mostly ruled by authoritarian leaders. Yet there are three abolitionist countries, Turkmenistan, Azerbaijan, and Armenia, in the region[43] and Kyrgyzstan's President Askar Akaev implemented a moratorium in 1998. One could assume that the Stalinist purges that took place in the 1930s, resulting in thousands of death sentences and executions, may have contributed to the rejection of state killing, as in other countries where gross human rights violations have contributed to the abolition of the death penalty. But as Kassymbekova explains, the moratorium had nothing to do with reverberations of the past in Kyrgyz public imagination. Rather, the reason was simply to please Western donor states and organizations.

The past is not, as one could think, remembered as cruel and horrible, and the death penalty does not evoke feelings of horror. Contemporary Kyrgyz society suffers from great social turmoil and inequality, economic backwardness, and a dramatic rise of crime. This has led many people to be nostalgic for an imagined Soviet past where life was safe and relatively egalitarian. Capital punishment becomes an instrument of equality in this respect—it targets perpetrators of violent crime coming from low social strata as well as the corrupt cadre-turned-capitalist; it hit workers as well as high-ranking officials during the Stalinist purges. The author worries: "If the violent, crude past state killings are not questioned by the people, how can a less violent contemporary government be?"

In India the death penalty is well established, if limited to "the rarest of rare cases." As Julia Eckert shows in her chapter, however, state killing often does not come as a result of a court decision. Instead, many people die in systematic so-called encounter killings, "the colloquial term for the (civilian) deaths that result from what in official nomenclature is termed an exchange of fire." These "encounters" are the equivalents of extra-judicial executions. The Indian public displays a deep ambivalence toward such arbitrary use of public force, Eckert explains. "In their contradictory treatment in public debate, in conspiracy theories, in the Bollywood films and in police lore we find the double life of the killing state: he is at once the vigilante, saving the nation from doom, and the outlaw who thrives on the destruction that threatens the nation." On the one hand, many approve of this practice, because the official legal system is seen as inefficient and unable to deal with corruption, mafia, and the criminalization of politics. "Courageous" police officers, who take on crime by engaging in encounter killings, become heroes in the popular mind. On the other hand, as much as they yearn for order and security, most Indians do not like the idea of weakening the rule of law.

The state has restricted its use of the death penalty and applies it in highly symbolic ways—but this is not enough for a population subjected to violent crime, threats of terrorism, and political corruption. Indian society has lost hope "for the promises of development ideology." No longer are education and social progress seen as the way to eradicate crime along with its sources. In particular, the radical Hindu right has turned to counter-violence, a strategy that echoes developments in the international scene. Social inclusion is replaced by the eradication of the Other. The global "wars on terror" and Hindu nationalism threaten to tip the balance toward the authoritarian dream of order and away from respect for the law. There is practically no "cultural life" of the death penalty, Eckert's chapter shows us, since there is almost no public discussion of capital punishment. In contrast, encounter killings have captured public imagination.

The next two chapters contrast Israel and Palestine, two places with a long and sad history of killing and violence. It might be a surprise to many that Israel does not have the death penalty for ordinary crimes and, in the remaining cases, has so far executed only one person, Adolf Eichmann. Military rule in the occupied territories allows for capital punishment, but no one has ever been executed in a regular procedure. Legal scholar Shai Lavi explains in his chapter that this restraint has nothing to do with a respect for human life that so often is quoted by abolitionists as a prime reason for ending capital punishment. Rather, he claims, the peculiarity of the Israeli case consists of the "sanctity of death": the fear that executing terrorists will backfire. Employing a phenomenological approach, Lavi distinguishes between "punishment, violence, vengeance, and revenge," which he combines with the concepts of justice and justifiability.

Politicians and military officials show little concern over the deaths of Palestinians in combat situations or—as recent events show—over the planned extrajudicial execution of religious extremists. But they do not want to afford the enemy the theatrical spectacle of judicial procedure and execution. Lavi argues that much of the hesitation to use capital punishment against Palestinians convicted of capital crimes, including the planning and carrying out of terrorist attacks, comes from a historical incident which he analyzes in its context: the "execution," by members of a radical Jewish underground organization, of two British soldiers in response to the execution of other members of this organization. Shai argues that this memory was, and still is, alive in Israeli decision makers' memory, that today, "among the primary reasons still given for opposing the death penalty for terrorists is the risk of drawing punishment into a cycle of revenge and of turning terrorists into martyrs." Adolf Eichmann thus remains the exception to a rule, which tells us, Lavi argues, much about the nature of the "presence-absence" of the death penalty in Israel.

Judith Mendelsohn Rood's chapter on Palestine describes how Palestinians are threatened with death from several sides. On one hand, they can become victims of military raids by the occupying powers—as terrorist targets, insurgents, or uninvolved bystanders. On the other, they might be "sentenced to death" by non- or quasi-government entities, such as radical Islamic groups, for being "traitors."

In addition, the Palestinian National Authority also has the death penalty on the books. Having been stripped of most of its power by occupying forces and radical groups, the right to execute is, as Rood argues, one of the remaining symbols of its governance. Contrary to what many believe, the death penalty in Palestine is not based on religious law, but on the vestiges of colonial British law, used mainly by military courts to punish "collaboration with the enemy." Rood explores the history of Islamic thought and shows that Islamic law does not, as a matter of course, require the death penalty. Instead, sacred Islamic texts can legitimately be interpreted to leave strict punishments "only in theory to demonstrate the wisdom and mercy of the restraints put on the exercise of those penalties." She ends in an emphatic critique of the Palestinian "culture of death" and its accompanying violence.

Paternal States, "Asian Values," and Visions of Social Order: Capital Punishment in East and Southeast Asia

The third and last part of this book focuses on East and Southeast Asia, on Japan, China, South Korea, and Singapore. In an area allegedly united by special "Asian Values," we find only a single abolitionist country, Cambodia.[44]

David T. Johnson analyses the case of Japan, the other major democracy with capital punishment next to the United States. As Johnson points out, Japan executes with considerably less enthusiasm: since the early 1980s, on average only around three death row inmates have been executed per year. He shows how executions are shrouded in "secrecy and silence," hiding them from public attention and scrutiny. There is only limited debate about capital punishment and public opinion polls reveal relatively high levels of support. But, as Johnson notes, the state has adopted a deliberate policy to "keep the public uninformed about how, when, and why it kills." Japanese officials insist that this system of secret executions is the "most humane form" of the death penalty, avoiding shame and loss of face for the inmates. Johnson interprets this policy to be aimed at killing "socially before killing physically."

Johnson argues that whether or not telling the inmate in advance is more humane, secret execution is certainly not an adequate practice in a democracy ruled by law. The executed more often than not seem to be chosen strategically—to respond to crimes which happened around the time of the execution but with which the inmate obviously was not connected. He goes on to suggest that "In effect, 'killing secretly' instead of 'killing softly' is the state's main legitimation strategy"—and offers a powerful critique of this practice. Unlike the United States where law promises fairness and rationality—a promise that is repeatedly broken in spectacular and extremely unsettling ways (Liebman et al. 2000)—in Japan capital punishment law hardly makes any promises at all. Most of the death penalty process is in the hands of the unchecked administration. The practice of capital punishment in Japan is indicative of a political culture where bureaucratic authorities more often than not make decisions without public debate and personal accountability.

Moving to the Asian mainland, the chapter by Virgil K. Y. Ho analyzes the situation in China. Although reports about the very large number of executions in China abound (e.g., Amnesty International 1997), there are very few analytical studies of capital punishment in China. Thus Ho's chapter stands out in several respects. First, he looks at official discourses on the death penalty. Second, he uses interviews and surveys to better understand popular feeling about state killing. His analysis reveals a number of important peculiarities. At least in official rhetoric, the death penalty is portrayed as a "necessary evil." In stark contrast to conservatives in the United States who call for the expansion of capital punishment, Chinese officials maintain that even though China cannot abolish capital punishment at the moment, its use should be minimized. The official line is that "keeping capital punishment is not an end in itself, but a means to its eventual abolishment." This seems a cynical statement to make, given that China executes more people than the rest of the world taken together. But progovernment scholars and bureaucrats express the firm belief that the death penalty is a necessary tool of social control. Their aim is not revenge, they claim. Rather, they believe that capital punishment "brings progress to and helps civilize the country."

Compared to Japan, China's execution practice is obviously very public:

Convicts are exhibited in public places, such as sport stadiums, in mass meetings organized by the state, before they are taken to their execution which also takes place before an audience. But, as Ho points out, this publicity is very selective: Chinese authorities make sure to discuss only criminals "of the most horrific and wicked type," human "trash," which need to be disposed of. The executions of petty criminals, in contrast, which could evoke any kind of sympathy go unreported. However, as Ho found out, there is little need to legitimate capital punishment in the eyes of the population. It is unnecessary to convince the people because few people have any doubts to begin with. Ho's respondents overwhelmingly share their government's belief in the social utility of capital punishment and in its deterrent effect. Most display great trust in the ability of the justice system to prevent miscarriages of justice. Capital punishment, Ho concludes, is "popularly perceived and justified in the name of history, tradition, and Chinese culture."

From China, we move on to Singapore, a small but influential island-state in Southeast Asia known for its draconian penal system and the world's highest execution rate relative to its population size. Alfred Oehlers and Nicole Tarulevicz explore this "theme park with a death sentence," as it has been called. They argue that, even though the death penalty is not used against political opponents, it is highly political in nature, being "an integral part of a wider effort to enforce a culture of developmentalism designed to underpin a postcolonial project of nation building." It serves as a powerful symbol in defining the borders between the true Singaporean citizen and criminal outsiders, who need to be eliminated from society.

Singapore's postindependence history is characterized by steady economic growth, orchestrated by a "developmental" state: the government was involved in all aspects of economic, social, and cultural policy making. This strategy has resulted in Southeast Asia's richest, socially stable nation in which several ethnic groups peacefully coexist. At the same time, as Oehlers and Tarulevicz point out, it has fostered a culture in which the individual is expected to subordinate him- or herself to the larger community. It also has led to a definition of "Singaporeanness" which is highly exclusive and intolerant of deviance.

The authors show how a "culture of developmentalism" ties in with the social construction of criminality in Singapore. Crime is not just the breaking of law, it is seen as "ingratitude" and an assault on, or rebellion against, the social order, disqualifying offenders from the right to participate in the noble aim of building a prosperous and efficient Singaporean society. Punishment, on the other hand, tends to be retributive and is intended to inflict pain—physical or emotional—on the transgressor. This is epitomized by the presence, amid glitzy modern skyscrapers and high-tech business, of the ancient practice of caning. Capital punishment also plays its role in the culture of developmentalism, Oehlers and Tarulevicz explain, using as an example the offence of drug smuggling and the 1995 execution of a Filipino guest worker. The spectacle of prosecution and sentencing of drug dealers and murderers, the authors argue, serves not only to punish the guilty, but also to provide public commentaries "on how Singaporeans were substantially different from Others."

The final chapter takes up South Korea, where, as Sangmin Bae argues, the Asian retentionist status quo today is being challenged. Unlike other countries in Asia, a sizable anticapital punishment movement exists and finds support among political elites. Former president Dae-Jung Kim, a Roman Catholic and once a death row inmate, put in place a moratorium on executions and publicly called for an end of capital punishment. In addition, a group of legislators have been drafting abolitionist legislation. Politicians such as these have rejected the view put forward by other leaders in the region who claim that particularly "Asian values" exist and who have disputed the universal validity of human rights. How can this difference be explained?

Bae points to the deeply religious nature of abolitionism in South Korea. Even though there are well-developed and active civil society groups supporting democracy and human rights, capital punishment is not on the agenda of these groups. Instead, religious groups, particularly the Roman Catholic Church, are leading the abolitionist movement. In Korea, unlike Japan, the subject of capital punishment is publicly debated and support has dropped dramatically in recent years.

Despite these developments, Bae explains, there are several factors which stand in the way of total abolition. On a cultural level, state killing finds legitimation in Confucian images of the state as father figure who has power over life and death. Korea is also lacking the "peer pressure" that helped European countries to overcome the popularity of the death penalty. Bae also cites the legacies of authoritarian law that pervade social and political life. Finally, she points out that the democratic successes of recent years owe much to the toleration of conservative forces which work in the background of South Korean politics and which are hostile to the idea of giving up state killing. Nonetheless, as Bae concludes, abolition might come from unexpected directions: the Korean Supreme Court has recently showed some unprecedented activism in death penalty cases. And, despite the lack of regional human rights dynamics, abolition might be brought about by regional rivalry for international prestige between South Korea and Japan.

Conclusion

Taken together the chapters in this book point to several conclusions:

Methodological pluralism and cultural analysis. Our contributors make clear that there are many different ways in which the phenomenon of capital punishment needs to be investigated. The chapters of Martschukat, Lavi, Timmons, Randle, and Rood show the need for historical depth. Other authors have drawn our attention to images of state killing, punishment, and civilization in official discourses (Girling, Ho, Oehlers/Tarulevicz), cinema (Tyler, Eckert), and the popular mind (Kassymbekova, Ho). Their interpretive analyses, we believe, advance our knowledge in ways purely theory-driven comparative studies cannot. That said, our aim is not a "cultural orthodoxy." Given the obvious lack of research, we welcome and encourage any type of study that looks beyond the United States and explores the history and present of the ultimate penalty around the world.

The cultural uses of capital punishment. The chapters in this book indicate that the death penalty is not a neutral cultural entity that exists—or not—for its own sake, expressing timeless cultural values. The death penalty always serves purposes which often are completely unrelated to its alleged function of crime control. That is why analyses of the political economy of capital punishment continue to be very important. The Japanese practice of "justification by association" that David Johnson describes, for example, reminds us of the symbolic message the death penalty sends—not so much to offenders, but rather to the public at large. What is interesting from our point is not so much that these policies are merely symbolic and do nothing about crime.[45] We would like to see more studies on how the symbolic politics of capital punishment are embedded in local culture.

On the other hand, death penalty abolition—as in the case of Europe—cannot be simply understood as the advancement of civilization. Abolitionism can also serve other purposes than simply doing away with the death penalty, as we have seen in Evi Girling's chapter on European identity politics, or as Judith Randle argued about the discursive opposition between the "North" and the "South" in the United States.[46]

But again, to understand the various uses of the death penalty in purely instrumental terms would be to misunderstand the constitutive character of penality. Penal identity, "cultural uses" of punishment, and policy choices are entangled in ways that require a close look and careful analyses.

Democracy, civilization, and the death penalty. The chapters in this book confirm our initial hypothesis that the relationship between the death penalty, abolition, and democracy is an ambiguous one. We have seen that stable democracies like the United States retain capital punishment while authoritarian states like Turkmenistan and Kyrgyzstan experiment with abolition. On the other hand, new democracies like Poland abolish it despite high levels of support. Increased levels of democratization might not always bring a country's population closer to abolition. "Democratic optimism," that is, the hope that sooner or later people will be visited by an abolitionist *Weltgeist*, might not be enough. On the other hand, the movement of regimes away from authoritarianism to the community of democratic nations might prompt democratic governments to consider abolition irrespective of popular feeling.

From a normative standpoint, we think that capital punishment degrades and corrupts democracy by offering politicians a "simple solution to complex problems" (Sarat 2001: 247). Yet elite-driven abolition seems, from the perspective of democratic theory, highly problematic (Fawn 2001), no matter whether abolition comes through the initiative of a parliamentary vanguard or a constitutional court. This dilemma needs to receive more attention than it currently does. Off-handedly dismissing popular support simply as "uninformed" and "irrational" hurts, we believe, the abolitionist cause and is intellectually unsatisfying.

A similar point concerns the relationship between "civilization" and capital punishment upon which several chapters touch. Particularly in European abolitionist discourse, the binary opposition between "civilized" and "uncivilized" criminal justice systems is conjured up all too often and all too easily. While this might be a powerful rhetoric, it only works as a "conversation stopper." It is fur-

ther empirically incorrect, since abolition seems to be rooted in European societies much less than the claim implies. Lastly, it seems like a perpetuation of
colonialist discourse to establish moral hierarchies between whole societies
based on their "civilizational progress."

Normative engagement and cultural analysis. As Paul Schiff Berman (2002)
has rightly pointed out, cultural analysis is not just playful postmodern reflection without real-world use. Cultural analysis helps us to understand "what is
going on" and allows abolitionists to adapt their strategies. Looking through the
Web sites of European anti–death penalty groups, for example, does not suggest
that they know much of American cultural dispositions. Cultural stereotypes,
such as that of a "nation of cowboys," abound. Additionally, little do European
abolitionists know about the ways their arguments are received by American
death penalty supporters. We do not have to go to places like the Middle East or
South Asia in order to find different "webs of significance" in which state killing
exists. Trying to understand discourses and practices that shape phenomena
does not lead one to give up on normative engagement. Both David Johnson
and Judith M. Rood, for example, combine analysis with trenchant critique of
the situations observed.

Looking at the death penalty is not enough. David Garland has argued that it
might be misleading to single out capital punishment for analysis because
much of what is found to be special about the death penalty might in fact be related to the larger punitive culture. Many of the things that make the American
death penalty unique, Garland argues, also apply to the practice of harsh punishments. On a normative level, Garland worries that moving from universalist
moral arguments to contextualist cultural ones will not allow analysts to distinguish between capital punishment and other punishments, such as life imprisonment (Garland 2002). Garland is right that one should not forget the institutional and penal environment in which capital punishment exists.[47] But as
the chapters of this book demonstrate, there *is* something unique about the
death penalty that has no parallel in imprisonment practices, and sometimes
operates completely independently of it: the moral outrage capital punishment
is able to affect and the international human rights politics that target capital
punishment.[48]

Moreover, we have seen that state killing is not limited to capital punishment. It might well be that, given international pressures, many governments

will find it more convenient to shed the legal restraints that govern the death penalty. Instead, they tolerate "encounter killings" or resort to "preemptive" executions. The relationship between capital punishment and other forms of state killing, it seems to us, needs further attention by sociolegal scholars.

Abolitionist perspective. At the moment, it looks like a peak in global abolition of capital punishment has been reached. Any further development is likely to be slow. As we argued at the beginning of this chapter, the postwar and post–cold war increase in abolition activity was due mainly to regional human rights regimes and integration dynamics. We might be able to expect some more developments on the judicial front, although outright judicial abolition is unlikely at least in the United States and Japan.[49] In addition, the scope of capital punishment might be reduced, even in such cases as China. What is clear is that the death penalty lives many different lives and dies many different deaths. Like globalization in general, the globalization of the discourses on state killing should not blind us to the very local nature of punishment. There might be universal reasons against capital punishment—and we believe that there are— but the struggle against the penalty of death must be fought again and again in each different culture in ways that acknowledge and respect capital punishment's distinctive cultural lives.

Notes

1. We use the word "abolitionism" and "abolitionist" to refer to the abolition of capital punishment. In contrast, we use "retentionism" and "retentionist" to refer to the ideas which support the legal institution of capital punishment and countries where it is still practiced. Historically, "abolitionism" has been used to describe the abolition of slavery. Note the difference between de jure abolitionist, which refers to the deletion of the death penalty from the legal code, and de facto abolitionist, which refers to states which have the death penalty on the books, but either do not condemn people to death or do not carry out executions. Amnesty International has proposed a standard to call a country de facto abolitionist when it has not executed anybody for at least ten years. One special case is where a *moratorium* exists. Finally, states can abolish the death penalty for *all* crimes, or only for crimes committed during peace times.

2. As opposed to state killing in a more general sense (i.e., cases in which the state kills intentionally or unintentionally, without judicial process, such as through extra-judicial executions or warfare).

3. Abolitionist: Angola, Cape Verde, Cote d'Ivoire, Guinea-Bissau, Mauritius, Mo-

zambique, Namibia, Senegal, and South Africa. De facto abolitionist (i.e., no executions in the past ten years): Algeria, Benin, Burkina Faso, Congo (Republic), Gambia, Kenya, Madagascar, Mali, Mauritania, Niger, Senegal, Togo, Tonga, Tunisia. See Amnesty International 2005.

4. Zimring 2003: 37. Cambodia, Timor-Leste, Bhutan, and Nepal are fully abolitionist, Brunei Darussalam, Papua New Guinea and Sri Lanka de facto. See Amnesty International 2005.

5. Try Google.com with "civilized society" and "death penalty" for sources. See Rohatyn (2001), and as a response to the "civilization argument," O'Sullivan (2004).

6. For a review of this argument, see Whitman (2003). The hope is that the "advance of civilization" will lead all nations sooner or later to realize the backwardness of capital punishment and move toward abolition. The theoretical assumption behind this view is that there is a macro-sociological process resulting in the refinement and humanization of the methods of and types of punishment. See Spierenburg's (1984) application of Norbert Elias's "civilizing Process" (1994 [1939]) to the sphere of punishment. For critiques of Spierenburg, see Garland (1990: 225–37) and Evans (1996: 873–912).

7. One is reminded of modernization theory which predicted that sooner or later economic development would produce similar socioeconomic and cultural outcomes in all corners of the world (Parsons 1964).

8. David Garland has pointed out how, after long periods of relative moderation in criminal punishment, the rise in crime in the 1970s and 1980s contributed to an atmosphere of fear and punitivism, resulting in the reemergence of harsher penalties, including the death penalty. See Garland (2002).

9. This is our calculation. Data source: Amnesty International (2003); Freedom House (2003). The numbers do not reflect the actual number of executions, which would have to be factored in for a more adequate comparison. See here Greenberg and West (2001).

10. It hardly needs mentioning that there is no necessary relationship between the religious (non)affiliation of the political regime, and that of the population, as the case of communist Poland shows. See the chapter by Fijalkowski in this volume.

11. The widely cited quote goes on: "something within which they can be intelligibly—that is, thickly—described." Today, the notion of "thick description" has been criticized and largely abandoned within anthropology. At the time, it was an advance over essentialist accounts of culture. For critiques of Geertzian notions of culture, see Clifford (1988).

12. Recent polls have found 42 percent support in France; 40 percent in Belgium; 31 percent in Germany; 28 percent in Italy; and 19 percent in Spain. See Krause (2000a). In the postcommunist countries surveyed in 2002, "the absolute majority of respondents do think that death penalty should exist in their country. This group is biggest in Russia

(78.7 percent) and smallest in the Czech Republic (56.1 percent). On the other side, Hungary has the biggest group of death penalty opponents (31.5 percent), while this group is the smallest in Lithuania (15 percent)." Central European Opinion Research Group Foundation (2002).

13.   Gallup International published the following figures: North America 66 percent, South East Asia 63 percent, Eastern Europe 60 percent, Africa 54 percent, Latin America 37 percent, Western Europe 34 percent. See Gallup International (2000).

14.   For an example of historical contingency, see below, note 20. To be fair, studies such as Neumayer (2004) and Greenberg and West (2001) do try to include variables on political leadership. Both point out, for example, that chances of abolition rise with the existence of a left-wing government. All their conclusions are probabilistic rather than explanatory. Our interest, however, does not lie in prediction. Rather, our aim is to understand what was and what is going on in specific times and places.

15.   There are, of course many other ways to differentiate the theoretical landscape, and we do not include all of the theories around. For a discussion of "materialist," "functional," and "conflict" theories of capital punishment, see Greenberg and West (2001).

16.   Rusche and Kirchheimer (1939) argued that imprisonment allowed the capitalist state to get rid of the unemployed. Cf. Garland (1990: chap. 5).

17.   See for a critical review Cameron (1993).

18.   We will revisit the "cultural uses" of the death penalty later in this introduction.

19.   Britain abolished the death penalty in 1965, even before France, but that was still in "socialist" times. For British death penalty support, see Krause (2000a, 2000b) and "Davis Backs the Death Penalty for Serial Killers," *The Independent*, November 11, 2003.

20.   To be sure, the Supreme Court would be in a position to end executions. Some even argue that the fact that capital punishment still survives in the United States is simply the result of a "historical accident." According to Carol Steiker (2002), for example, had the *Furman vs. Georgia* decision been argued on different grounds, capital punishment would have been ended. However, the uproar and resistance the Supreme Court decision generated—in contrast to the results of judicial abolition in countries like Hungary or South Africa—seems to indicate that there is more to American capital punishment than a wrongly argued decision. We will come back to judicial abolition in a moment.

21.   On the question of participation in the penal policy making, see Johnstone (2000).

22.   For example, the socialist German Democratic Republic abolished the death penalty in 1987, the authoritarian president of Kyrgyzstan has been continuing a moratorium since 1998 (see the chapter by Kassymbekova in this book).

23.   The South African Court's decision has not gone unchallenged. See African National Congress (1995).

24. Compare Justice Stephen Breyer's (2003) comments with the public statements and the angry dissents by Justice Antonin Scalia (quoted in Gearan [2004]).

25. The death penalty is also an issue in regional human rights mechanisms, see Schabas (1997).

26. See Amnesty International (2005). It would be interesting to find out what relationship exists between the regime changes and abolitionism on the Latin American continent.

27. See European Union (2002, 2004) and Evi Girling's chapter in this volume. The EU and the Council of Europe have hosted an abolitionist conference and have organized seminars with Japanese legislators, urging them to follow the European example.

28. "[Q]uestions of culture . . . quickly become anguished questions of identity" (Scott 1995: 3).

29. For a discussion of these debates, see Hunter (1991).

30. The recent advertising campaign for the new dollar coin in the United States is a noteworthy example of this. Who would have thought that you would need to advertise money, but in recognizing that even currency must be given "currency," the Treasury Department discovered how much the cultural has become embedded in the economic and the political.

31. An earlier version of the following pages appeared in Sarat and Kearns (1998). Although we acknowledge the difficulty of disciplining the concept of culture, we do not agree with those who believe it to be analytically useless. Exemplifying such claims are the following: "Like 'ideology' (to which, as a concept, it is closely allied) 'culture' is a term that is repeatedly used without meaning much of anything at all, a vague gesture toward a dimly perceived ethos" (Greenblatt 1990: 225). Or, as Mary Douglas has said about the concept of culture, "[N]ever was such a fluffy notion at large . . . since singing angels blew the planets across the medieval sky or ether filled in the gaps of Newton's universe" (1975: 886).

32. As Renato Rosaldo puts it, "These days questions of culture seem to touch a nerve" (1989: ix).

33. "The recent critics of culture in no respect comprise an internally homogeneous block, and the objections currently in play represent a complex skein of partially discrete, partially convergent influences from political economy, modernist and postmodernist anthropologies, varieties of feminist writing, cultural studies, and diverse other sources" (Brightman 1995: 509).

34. Annette Weiner (1995: 15) notes about the discipline of anthropology and its relation to the idea of culture that "Today . . . 'culture' is increasingly a prized intellectual commodity, aggressively appropriated by other disciplines as an organizing principle."

35. The fashionableness in recent years of speculating about the cultural deficits of the poor and the role of liberalism in worsening them speaks to this.

36. For a particularly useful summary of these critiques, see Brightman (1995: 509).

37. For a general discussion of the materiality of cultural life, see Williams (1980).

38. Zimring and Hawkins mention the similarity of capital punishment and the rain dance among African tribes (1986: 14), both in its symbolic significance and its actual effects—the difference being of course that rituals in premodern, stateless societies differ fundamentally in rules and mechanisms from those in the modern state, which has a monopoly of power, rational bureaucracies, and mass medias and publics.

39. Another way to conceptualize culture has been proposed by Ann Swidler (1986). For Swidler, culture can be thought of as a "'tool kit' of symbols, stories, rituals, and world-views, which people may use in varying configurations to solve different kinds of problems" (273).

40. Too many "political culture" studies based on survey research ignore this fact and produce misleading results about a country's "culture."

41. On the legal and political aspect of abolitionist federalism, see Galliher et al. (2002).

42. Steiker (2002). See Zimring (2003) for the argument that these disparities can be attributed to different histories of racism in various parts of the country. Zimring points to the fact that the current rate of execution is correlated to the number of lynching incidents at the beginning of the century.

43. Turkmenistan and Azerbaijan are abolitionist de jure, Armenia de facto.

44. As far as we can tell, no studies exist of why and how capital punishment was abolished in Cambodia. It can be speculated that abolition has something to do with previous gross human rights abuses under the Khmer Rouge regime and the massive involvement of foreign actors in the nation-building experiment after 1993.

45. This argument is already well established in the literature, see for example Zimring and Hawkins (1986).

46. Another interesting research area concerns the extradition of suspects who might be threatened with a death sentence—such as suspected terrorists—from countries which do not have the death penalty to the United States. See, for example, Clarke (2003).

47. In a practical sense, abolitionists who focus exclusively on the death penalty tend to forget that the next-most lenient punishment, life imprisonment, does not necessarily mean more humane treatment. Think of prison conditions in Russia, for example.

48. Interestingly, there is nothing comparable to the global anti–death penalty activism concerning the millions of inmates who languish in inhuman, cruel, and degrading conditions of imprisonment. For a global view on imprisonment, see van Zyl Smit and Dünkel (2001).

49. For an optimistic scenario in the case of the United States, see Steiker and Steiker (2003).

References

Abu-Lughod, Lila (1991) "Writing Against Culture," in Richard G. Fox, ed., *Recapturing Anthropology: Working in the Present*. Santa Fe: School of American Research Press.

African National Congress (1995) "Statement on Death Penalty Referendum Calls," http://www.anc.org.za/ancdocs/pr/1995/pr1127b.html (accessed March 13, 2004).

Amnesty International (1997) "The Death Penalty in China: Breaking Records, Breaking Rules." http://web.amnesty.org/library/Index/ENGASA170381997?open&of=ENG-393 (accessed January 27, 2005).

Amnesty International (2003) "The Death Penalty: List of Abolitionist and Retentionist Countries," http://web.amnesty.org/web/web.nsf/print/deathpenalty-countries-eng (accessed January 18, 2004).

Amnesty International (2005) "The Death Penalty: List of Abolitionist and Retentionist Countries," http://web.amnesty.org/pages/deathpenalty-countries-eng (accessed 30 January 2005).

Baudrillard, Jean (1993) *Symbolic Exchange and Death*. London: Sage.

Berman, Paul Schiff (2002) "The Cultural Life of Capital Punishment: Surveying the Benefits of a Cultural Analysis of Law," 102 *Columbia Law Review* 1129.

Blinken, Antony (2001) "The False Crisis Over the Atlantic," 80 *Foreign Affairs* 35–48.

Boulanger, Christian, Vera Heyes, and Philip Hanfling, eds. (2002) *Zur Aktualität der Todesstrafe. Interdisziplinäre und globale Perspektiven* (2. Aufl). Berlin: Berlin Verlag Arno Spitz.

Breyer, Stephen (2003) "The Supreme Court and the New International Law." Presented at the 2003 American Society of International Law Annual Meeting, Washington, DC, http://www.aclu.org/hrc/JudgesPlenary.pdf (accessed June 20, 2004).

Brightman, Robert (1995) "Forget Culture: Replacement, Transcendence, Reflexification," 10 *Cultural Anthropology* 509–46.

Cameron, Samuel (1993) "The Demand for Capital Punishment," 13 *International Review of Law and Economics* 47–59.

Caplow, Theodore, and Jonathan Simon (1999) "Understanding Prison Policy and Population Trends," in Michael Tonry and Joan Petersilia, eds., *Prisons Crime & Justice: A Review of Research*, vol. 26. Chicago: University of Chicago Press.

Central European Opinion Research Group Foundation (2002) "CEORG June 2002 Omnibus Survey," http://www.ceorg-europe.org/research/2002_06.html (accessed March 13, 2004).

Chase, Anthony (1986) "Toward a Legal Theory of Popular Culture," 1986 *Wisconsin Law Review* 527.

Chase, Anthony (1994) "Historical Reconstruction in Popular Legal and Political Culture," 24 *Seton Hall Law Review* 1969.

Clarke, Alan C. (2003) "Justice in a Changed World. Terrorism, Extradition, and the Death Penalty," 29 *William Mitchell Law Review* 783–808.

Clifford, James (1988) *The Predicament of Culture: Twentieth-Century Ethnography, Literature, and Art*. Cambridge, MA: Harvard University Press.

Cook, Kimberly J. (1998) *Divided Passions: Public Opinion on Abortion and the Death Penalty*. Boston: Northeastern University Press.

Council of Europe (1983) "Protocol No. 6 to the Convention for the Protection of Human Rights and Fundamental Freedoms concerning the abolition of the death penalty," http://conventions.coe.int/Treaty/en/Treaties/Html/114.htm.

Council of Europe (2001) "Abolition of the Death Penalty in Council of Europe Observer States," http://assembly.coe.int/documents/adoptedtext/ta01/eres1253.htm (accessed October 11, 2002).

Council of Europe, ed. (1999) *The Death Penalty Abolition in Europe*. Strasbourg: Council of Europe Publishing.

Council of Europe, ed. (2004) *Death Penalty—Beyond Abolition*. Strassbourg: Council of Europe Publishing.

Council of Europe, and Renate Wohlwend (1999) "Europe: A Death Penalty-Free Continent," http://www.coe.int/T/E/Communication_and_Research/Press/Theme_Files/Death_penalty/e_rap_ap1.asp#TopOfPage (accessed October 11, 2002).

Cover, Robert M. (1992) "Nomos and Narrative," in Martha Minow, Michael Ryan, and Austin Sarat, eds., *Narrative, Violence, and the Law*. Ann Arbor: University of Michigan Press.

Death Penalty Information Center (2004) "Summaries of Recent Poll Findings," http://www.deathpenaltyinfo.org/article.php?scid=23&did=210#Harris1203 (accessed March 13, 2004).

Douglas, Mary (1975) "The Self-Completing Animal," *Times Literary Supplement* (8 August) 225.

Durkheim, Emile (1984 [1893]) *The Division of Labor in Society*. Translated by W. D. Halls. New York: Free Press.

Elias, Norbert (1994 [1939]) *The Civilizing Process: The History of Manners and State Formation and Civilization*. Translated by Edmund Jephcott. Cambridge, MA: Blackwell.

European Union (2000) "Charter of Fundamental Rights of the European Union," http://www.europarl.eu.int/charter/pdf/text_en.pdf, incorporated into: European Union (2003), "Draft Treaty Establishing a Constitution for Europe," http://european-convention.eu.int/docs/Treaty/cv00850.en03.pdf.

European Union (2002) "The EU's Human Rights and Democratisation Policy—Abolition of the Death Penalty," http://europa.eu.int/comm/external_relations/human_rights/adp/index.htm (accessed March 14, 2004).

European Union (2004) "European Union and the Death Penalty (Capital Punishment)," http://www.eurunion.org/legislat/deathpenalty/deathpenhome.htm (accessed March 14, 2004).

Evans, Richard J. (1996) *Rituals of Retribution: Capital Punishment in Germany, 1600–1987*. Oxford: Oxford University Press.

Fawn, Rick (2001) "Death Penalty as Democratization: Is the Council of Europe Hanging Itself?," 8 *Democratization* 69–96

Fijalkowski, Agata (2001) "Abolition of the Death Penalty in Central and Eastern Europe," 9 *Tilburg Foreign Law Review* 62–83.

Fijalkowski, Agata (2002) "Die Abschaffung der Todesstrafe in Mittel- und Osteuropa," in Christian Boulanger, Vera Heyes, and Philip Hanfling, eds., *Zur Aktualität der Todesstrafe. Interdisziplinäre und globale Perspektiven*. Berlin: Berlin Verlag Arno Spitz.

Foucault, Michel (1995) *Discipline and Punish: The Birth of the Prison*, 2nd. ed. New York: Vintage Books.

Frankowski, Stanislav (1996) "Post-Communist Europe," in Peter Hodgkinson and Andrew Rutherford, eds., *Capital punishment: Global Issues and Prospects*. Winchester: Waterside Press.

Freedom House (2003) "Freedom in the Word—Table of Independent Countries—2003," http://www.freedomhouse.org/research/freeworld/2003/table.pdf (accessed February 29, 2004).

Galliher, John F. et al. (2002) *America without the Death Penalty: States Leading the Way*. Boston: Northeastern University Press.

Gallup International (2000) "Millenium Survey—Findings on Crime and Punishment," http://www.gallup-international.com/ContentFiles/millennium10.asp (accessed 6 March 2004).

Garland, David (1990) *Punishment and Modern Society: A Study in Social Theory. Studies in Crime and Justice*. Oxford, UK: Clarendon Press.

Garland, David (2001) *The Culture of Control. Crime and Social Order in Contemporary Society*. Chicago: University of Chicago Press.

Garland, David (1991) "Punishment and Culture: The Symbolic Dimensions of Criminal Justice," 11 *Studies in Law, Politics, and Society* 191–222.

Garland, David (2002) "The Cultural Uses of Capital Punishment," 4 *Punishment & Society* 459–87.

Gearan, Anne (2004) "Foreign Rulings Not Relevant to High Court, Scalia Says," *Washington Post*, 3 April 2003, p. A07. http://www.washingtonpost.com/wp-dyn/articles/A46356-2004Apr2.html (accessed June 20, 2004).

Geertz, Clifford (1973) "Thick Description: Toward an Interpretive Theory of Culture," in anonymous, ed., *The Interpretation of Cultures*. New York: Harper.

Geertz, Clifford (1983) *Local Knowledge: Further Essays in Interpretative Anthropology*. New York: Basic Books.

Graff, Gerald (1987) *Professing Literature: An Institutional History*. Chicago: University of Chicago Press.

Grasmick, Harold G., J. K. Cochran, Robert J. Bursik, and M'Lou Kimpel (1993) "Religion, Punitive Justice, and Support for the Death Penalty," 10 *Justice Quarterly* 289–324.

Green, Amy (2000) "Death Penalty Popular among Bible Belt Christians," *Associated Press*, March 19. http://www.news-star.com/stories/031900/new_death.shtml.

Greenberg, David F., and Valerie West (2001) "Sitting the Death Penalty." Paper presented at the Law and Society Annual Meeting, Budapest, Hungary.

Greenblatt, Stephen (1990) "Culture," in Frank Lentricchia and Thomas McLaughlin, eds., *Critical Terms for Literary Study*. Chicago: University of Chicago Press.

Gross, Samuel R. (1998) "Update—American Public-Opinion on the Death-Penalty," 83 *Cornell Law Review* 1448–75.

Hall, Peter A., and Rosemary C. R. Taylor (1996) "Political Science and the Three New Institutionalisms," *Political Studies* 936–57.

Hodgkinson, Peter (1996) "The United Kingdom and the European Union," in Peter Hodgkinson and Andrew Rutherford, eds., *Capital Punishment: Global Issues and Prospects*. Winchester: Waterside Press.

Hodgkinson, Peter, and Andrew Rutherford, eds. (1996) *Capital Punishment: Global Issues and Prospects*. Winchester: Waterside Press.

Hodgkinson, Peter, and William A. Schabas, eds. (2004) *Capital Punishment: Strategies for Abolition*. Cambridge, UK: Cambridge University Press.

Hood, Roger (2001) "Capital Punishment—A Global Perspective," 3 *Punishment & Society* 331–54.

Hood, Roger (2002 [1990, 1996]) *The Death Penalty: A World-Wide Perspective*. Oxford: Clarendon.

Horigan, Damien (1996) "Of Compassion and Capital Punishment: A Buddhist Perspective on the Death Penalty," 41 *American Journal of Jurisprudence* 271–89.

Hunter, James Davison, ed. (1991) *Culture Wars: The Struggle to Define America*. New York: Basic Books.

Huntington, Samuel P., ed. (1996) *The Clash of Civilizations and the Remaking of World Order*. New York: Simon & Schuster.

Johnstone, Gerry (2000) "Penal Policy-Making. Elitist, Populist or Participatory?," 2 *Punishment & Society* 161–80.

Koelble, Thomas A. (1995) "The New Institutionalism in Political Science and Sociology," 27 *Comparative Politics* 231–43.

Kohli, Atul, Peter B. Evans, Peter J. Katzenstein, Adam Przeworski, Susanne Hoeber-Rudolph, James C. Scott, and Theda Skocpol (1995) "Symposium: The Role of Theory in Comparative Politics," 48 *World Politics* 1–49.

Krause, Axel (2000a) "Life versus Death," 401 *Europe. The Magazine of the European Union* 6–10. http://www.eurunion.org/magazine/0011/life.htm.

Krause, Axel (2000b) "Two Views of Capital Punishment," 401 *Europe. The Magazine of the European Union* 13. http://www.eurunion.org/magazine/0011/interview.htm.

Liebman, Jeffrey Fagan, and Valerie West (2000) "A Broken System: Error Rates in Capital Cases, 1973–1995." Washington, DC: The Justice Project.

Lipschultz, Jeremy Harris, and Michael L. Hilt (2002) *Crime and Local Television News: Dramatic, Breaking, and Live from the Scene.* Mahwah, NJ: Lawrence Earlbaum Associates.

Luhrmann, Tanya M. (1993) "Review of Hermes' Dilemma and Hamlet's Desire: On the Epistemology of Interpretation," 95 *American Anthropologist* 1053–75.

Lynch, Mona (2002) "Capital Punishment as Moral Imperative: Pro-Death-Penalty Discourse on the Internet," 4 *Punishment & Society* 213–17.

Lyons, William (1999) *The Politics of Community Policing: Rearranging the Power to Punish.* Ann Arbor: University of Michigan Press.

Macaulay, Stewart (1987) "Images of Law in Everyday Life: The Lessons of School, Entertainment, and Spectator Sports," 21 *Law & Society Review* 185–218.

Manacorda, S. (2003) "Restraints on Death Penalty in Europe: A Circular Process," 1 *Journal of International Criminal Justice* 263–83.

Marshall, Joshua Micah (2000) "Death in Venice: Europe's Death-Penalty Elitism," 223 *The New Republic*, 31 July 2000, 12–15. http://www.thenewrepublic.com/073100/marshall073100.html.

Mead, George Herbert (1918) "The Psychology of Punitive Justice," 23 *American Journal of Sociology* 577–602.

Moravcsik, Andrew (2001) "The New Abolitionism: Why Does the U.S. Practice the Death Penalty while Europe Does Not?," 32 *European Studies Newsletter*, http://www.europanet.org/past_newsletters/200109/moravcsik.htm (accessed April 29, 2004).

Neumayer, Eric (2004) "The Political Foundations of the Global Trend Toward Abolition." Unpublished paper, London School of Economics and Political Science, London.

Norrander, Barbara (2000) "The Multi-Layered Impact of Public Opinion on Capital Punishment Implementation in the American States," 53 *Political Research Quarterly* 771–93.

O'Sullivan, John (2002) "Deadly Stakes. The Debate over Capital Punishment," *National Review Online*, 30 August 2002, http://www.nationalreview.com/script/printpage.asp?ref=/jos/jos083002.asp.

Parsons, Talcott (1964) "Evolutionary Universals in Society," 32 *American Sociological Review* 339–57.

PollingReport.com (2004) "Death Penalty," http://pollingreport.com/crime.htm#Death (accessed 13 March 2004).

Poveda, Tony G. (2000) "American Exceptionalism and the Death Penalty," 27 *Social Justice* 252–67.

Reicher, Dieter (2003) *Staat, Schafott und Schuldgefühl. Was Staatsaufbau und Todesstrafe miteinander zu tun haben.* Opladen: Leske and Budrich.

Rohatyn, Felix G. (2001) "America's Deadly Image," *Washington Post* (20 February 2001) 23, http://www.deathpenaltyinfo.org/WPost-Image.html.

Rosaldo, Renato (1989) *Culture and Truth: The Remaking of Social Analysis.* Boston: Beacon Press.

Rose, Nancy Ellen (1995) *Workfare or Fair Work: Women, Welfare, and Government Work Programs.* New Brunswick, NJ: Rutgers University Press.

Rusche, Georg, and Otto Kirchheimer (1939) *Punishment and Social Structure.* New York: Columbia University Press.

Sarat, Austin (2001) *When the State Kills: Capital Punishment and the American Condition.* Princeton, NJ: Princeton University Press.

Sarat, Austin, and Thomas R. Kearns (1998) "The Cultural Lives of Law," in Austin Sarat and Thomas R. Kearns, eds., *Law in the Domains of Culture.* Ann Arbor: University of Michigan Press.

Sartori, Giovanni (1970) "Concept Misformation in Comparative Politics," 64 *American Political Science Review* 1033–53.

Savelsberg, Joachim J. (2000) "Kulturen staatlichen Strafens: USA und Deutschland," in Jürgen Gerhards, ed., *Die Vermessung kultureller Unterschiede. USA und Deutschland im Vergleich.* Opladen: Westdeutscher Verlag.

Schabas, William A. (1996) *The Death Penalty as Cruel Treatment and Torture: Capital Punishment Challenged in the World's Courts.* Boston: Northeastern University Press.

Schabas, William A. (1997) *The Abolition of the Death Penalty in International Law,* 2nd ed. Cambridge, UK: Cambridge University Press.

Scott, Joan (1995) "Multiculturalism and the Politics of Identity," in John Rajchman, ed., *The Identity in Question.* New York: Routledge.

Sharrett, Christopher, ed. (1999) *Mythologies of Violence in Postmodern Media.* Detroit: Wayne State University Press.

Silbey, Susan S. (1992) "Making a Place for a Cultural Analysis of Law," 17 *Law and Social Inquiry* 41.

Simon, Jonathan (1997) "Gewalt, Rache und Risiko. Die Todesstrafe im neoliberalen Staat," 37 *Kölner Zeitschrift für Soziologie und Sozialpsychologie* 279–301.

Soering v United Kingdom, European Court of Human Rights, 7 July 1989, http://hudoc.echr.coe.int/Hudoc1doc%5CHEJUD%5Csift%5C204.txt.

Spierenburg, Petrus Cornelis (1984) *The Spectacle of Suffering: Executions and the Evolu-*

tion of Repression: From a Preindustrial Metropolis to the European Experience. Cambridge, UK: Cambridge University Press.

Steiker, Carol (2002) "Capital Punishment and American Exceptionalism," 81 *Oregon Law Review* 97–130.

Steiker, Carol, and Steiker, Jordan (2003) "Abolition in Our Time," 1 *Ohio State Journal of Criminal Law* 323–43.

Stolz, Barbara Ann (1983) "Congress and Capital Punishment: An Exercise in Symbolic Politics," 5 *Law & Policy Quarterly* 157–80.

Swidler, Ann (1986) "Culture in Action: Symbols and Strategies," 51 *American Sociological Review* 273–86.

Taylor, Charles (1994) *Charles Taylor, Multiculturalism: Examining the Politics of Recognition*. Princeton, NJ: Princeton University Press.

Thelen, Kathleen (1999) "Historical Institutionalism in Comparative Politics," 2 *Annual Review of Political Science* 369–404.

van Zyl Smit, Dirk, and Frieder Dünkel, eds. (2001) *Imprisonment Today and Tomorrow. International Perspectives on Prisoners' Rights and Prison Conditions*. The Hague: Kluwer Law International.

Wattenberg, Ben J. (1995) *Values Matter Most*. New York: Free Press.

Weber, Max (1994) *Sociological Writings. Edited by Wolf Heydebrand*. New York: Continuum.

Weiner, Annette (1995) "Culture and Our Discontents," 97 *American Anthropologist* 14–20.

Whitehead, Fred, ed. (1994) *Culture Wars: Opposing Viewpoints*. San Diego, CA: Greenhaven Press.

Whitman, James Q. (2003) *Harsh Justice: Criminal Punishment and the Widening Divide between America and Europe*. New York: Oxford University Press.

Williams, Raymond (1980) *Problems in Materialism and Culture: Selected Essays*. London: Verso.

Zimring, Franklin E. (2003) *The Contradictions of American Capital Punishment*. New York: Oxford University Press.

Zimring, Franklin E., and Gordon Hawkins (1986) *Capital Punishment and the American Agenda*. Cambridge: Cambridge University Press.

Zimring, Franklin E., Gordon Hawkins, and Sam Kamin, eds. (2001) *Punishment and Democracy: Three Strikes and You're Out in California*. Chicago: Chicago University Press.

PART I

Civilization and Punishment

Self and Other in Europe and the Americas

CHAPTER TWO

Nineteenth-Century Executions as Performances of Law, Death, and Civilization

JÜRGEN MARTSCHUKAT

In 1855, the Heidelberg professor of law Carl Joseph Anton Mittermaier highly recommended a book by the French historian Albert du Boys to the readers of the magazine "Archiv für Criminalrecht." According to Mittermaier, du Boys's historical observations proved, in the most excellent manner, "how inextricably the development of criminal law and the progress of civilization are interconnected" (Mittermaier 1855: 134; du Boys 1854).[1] Like so many of his colleagues, the distinguished German expert on criminal law considered the modifications of the execution procedure—from a public celebration of torture to a secret, serious extinguishing of a human life—a preeminent indicator of the maturation and progression of the state of the Western societies.

Mittermaier and his colleagues understood the changing patterns of the criminal justice system and specifically the modern mode of execution of a death penalty as an expression of a deeper conversion of society as well as of the hearts and the minds of the people: from his point of view, a teleological civilizing process seemed to articulate itself in the transformation of the punishment system—a logic that is tempting and often applied even today. However, in recent years, shifts in cultural theory have led to a substantial change of perspective on the actions of human beings and on their existence in society. A society or a civilization, as Timothy V. Kaufman-Osborn has emphasized in his study on the death penalty, are nothing substantial in themselves, but they only exist as ensembles of powers and techniques, of discourses, rules, and practices (Kaufman-Osborn 2002: 5). Moreover, there is no such thing as an ontological driving force that unfolds its power under the surface of these ensembles. The words and the things do not reflect preexistent meanings or conceptualizations, but they performatively produce and reproduce these meanings (Foucault 2002: 168–69).

Actually, the performance concept is crucial in this reorientation in cultural theory, and in recent years "performance" and "performativity" have become umbrella terms of the cultural studies (Wirth 2002; Martschukat and Patzold 2003: 1–37). In this chapter I will use concepts of performance and performativity to acquire an understanding of how capital punishment and the idea of living in a civilized society are interrelated. This approach will offer a substantial alternative to an understanding of history as a teleological civilizing process that is a driving force toward a less violent society. As a starting point for the thoughts on nineteenth-century executions in Germany, I will give a short conceptual outline of performance theory.[2]

Performance Theory

Going back to John L. Austin's speech act theory from the 1950s, "performance theory" emphasizes that words and language as well as deeds and behavior are not "referential" (i.e., they are not references to or reflections of a preexistent reality). Instead, they are "performative," which means that they exert constructive power, shaping and even producing the world we live in. Of course, to unfold this force, utterances or forms of behavior have to fit into the prevalent cultural configuration—that is to say they have to be woven into a network of so-called "conventions," of meanings, modes of behavior, and institutions. They have to connect to numerous points of reference and links that allow the performative act to make sense and unfold a specific meaning at a certain moment in history (Austin 1962).

With regard to historiography, it is important to note that a history inspired by performance theory does not search for individual human intentions behind historical events or processes. Though the existence of men and women as historical actors and the influence of human agency on history are not denied at all, a performance-historiography argues differently. It does not search for individual intentions behind the actions of supposedly autonomous human subjects. It strives to describe historically specific cultural configurations that make certain thoughts, intentions, and actions possible and appear logical, positive, self-evident—and others illogical and false. To put it differently, these configurations form the conditions of possibility for human actions and intentions (Martschukat and Patzold 2003: 1–37).

Specifically three points must be explained more deeply because they are of major importance for a cultural history of capital punishment. First, this cultural configuration is not "preexisting" in the literal sense of the word. The relationship between performance and configuration is "reflexive." That means, on the one hand, this configuration exists only as a web of countless performances, and on the other hand, performances only make sense and unfold constructive power within this web of practices, meanings, and institutions. The point of sense or non-sense is determined by a logic that only exists within this configuration. Of course, this focus on the constitutive power of words and things within specific historic contexts is not intended to deny that different individuals or social groups have different opportunities to inscribe themselves into the cultural web, according to specific qualifications, criteria of competence and knowledge, or institutional sites from which they speak (Foucault 1972: 50–55).

Second, there is no preexistent, ontological, everlasting entity that gives the world and human existence a stable meaning. However, though this system is unstable in the first place, it can acquire a certain stability through the permanent citation of specific utterances and attitudes. This leads to a compression and cohesion of meanings, and I hereby refer to the elaboration of cultural theorists like Michel Foucault and Judith Butler (Foucault 1972; Dreyfus and Rabinow 1982; Butler 1993, 1997a, 1997c). Thus, seen from the angle of performance-theory, "civilization" is nothing more or less than a historically specific compression of meanings, brought about by the repetitive citation of utterances, attitudes, and behaviors within a culture. From this perspective, a "civilized society," after all, exists only as an ensemble of discourses, rules, practices, institutions, techniques, and performances which define what might be considered "civilized" or "advanced," which sort of behavior and attitude is considered adequate in this society or not, and what might be part of this society or not. Yet, even if entities and concepts like "society" or "civilization" are performatively constructed, they are "real" in the sense that they have serious effects on the lives of human beings and are pervaded by social and power structures.

Third, I will not only look at the performative dimension of language and discourse but also emphasize the importance of cultural performances in this process of reinvocation and reconstitution of meanings. The term "cultural performance" does not only describe performances of play or music, but each and every type of presentation and the related reproduction of cultural conventions. Thus, these might be performances of the arts, particular instances of social ritual (such as wedding or punishment rituals), or forms of behavior in everyday life that constitute for instance gender or ethnic identities (Butler 1997b: 401–17; Fischer-Lichte 2003: 33–54). It is specifically important to note that meaning is generated through the interaction of performance, performers, and audience. That implies that the modification of the execution audience during the nineteenth century significantly changed the structure of the punishment performance and its meaning, which I intend to show on the following pages. Furthermore, the reorganization of the audience is a discursive statement itself that brings forth concepts of how a civilized society was supposed to look and organize itself (Martschukat 2003: 229–54).

Consequently, with regard to the execution procedure and its relationship to the contemporary self-perception of the bourgeois society as civilized, let me repeat the focal point of this chapter: civilization is nothing preordained; civilization per se does not exist. "Civilization" and "civilized society" are performatively constituted, which means they exist only in certain performances and utterances that have to be permanently cited, repeated, and reinvoked to gain stability and acquire the notion of self-evidence.

Concepts of Society and Punishment:
Traditional Dichotomies

A crucial factor in the performative constitution of a "civilized society" in the later eighteenth and early nineteenth centuries was the system of punishment, specifically the way in which a death penalty was executed. To further elaborate on this point, I will take a closer look at the reconfiguration of the execution audience and the transition from public to so-called private executions behind prison walls. I will concentrate on Germany in the first half of the nineteenth century and, in the last part of this chapter, further narrow the focus on the city of Hamburg in northern Germany.

Concerning the historiography of capital punishment, it is interesting to note that for early modern and colonial societies of the sixteenth to eighteenth centuries, a performative quality of execution procedures is widely accepted among historians, even if they hardly ever refer to performance theory explicitly. Moreover, with this interpretation, historians are in accordance with the conceptualization of contemporary early modern scholars who described their death penalty system as theater, for instance as "theater of divine punishment," "theater of hell," or "spectacle of suffering" (Spierenburg 1984; van Dülmen 1985; Döbler 1693–97; Harsdörffer 1975 [1656], to name just a few examples).

What did such an early modern performance look like? Michel Foucault's description, for instance, of the execution of the would-be regicide Robert François Damiens in Paris in March 1757 is well known. Without doubt, Foucault chose an extreme and late example of unusual rigidity to present his argument clearly, and yet, the basic features of early modern public executions are represented by this case (Foucault 1994: 9–12; Karasek 1994). Similarly structured executions were conducted in other European cities until the later eighteenth century. For instance in Hamburg, the so-called "poor sinner" had to walk from the town hall in the center of the city to the place of execution in front of the city gates. On his way to the scaffold, he was accompanied by a spiritual chorus and by a large crowd of men, women, and children who observed and followed the procession. Often, the condemned had to wear specific insignia that signified the type of his misdeed, he had to pass the places of his crimes, and if the crimes had been judged extremely grave, pieces of his flesh were torn from his body with red hot pincers (Martschukat 2000). The rituals in other German states, in France, England, or the British colonies in North America and the Early Republic might have differed in detail, but in their basics they were alike (Foucault 1977; Bée 1983; Spierenburg 1984; Masur 1991; Gatrell 1994; McGowen 1994; Evans 1996; Meranze 1996: 19–54, 87–127; Overath 2001).

What meanings were produced and conveyed by this sort of performance? According to contemporary as well as historiographic interpretations, the condemned exemplified the ultimate consequences of a misguided life and at the same time, of a lack of subordination under the divine order. In the moment of execution, people got to see what an unruly and immoral existence looked like and how it ended. Yet, a confessing and repenting sinner was forgiven by the authorities, so that his soul could go to heaven, and therefore, God's magnanimity was demonstrated in the moment of execution, too. Thus, public executions were not only supposed to teach the lessons of "good" and "bad" and convince the spectators to lead righteous lives, but they were also to be interpreted as ritualized answers to the evil in the world, and as reproductions of the social structure in a divine order.

During the second half of the eighteenth and the early nineteenth centuries, the transcendentally inspired conceptualization of European societies significantly changed. Moreover, the contemporaries believed, and numerous scholars have concurred, that with the enlightenment and the emerging civic society, "reason" and "rationality" occupied center stage and human society entered a path of continuous progress. One of the main arguments is that whereas the premodern social structure was held together through rituals and performances, the modern and civilized society was based on textual communication and a so-called rational discourse. The underlying notion of discourse that is prevalent in this interpretation is very different from the discourse concept evolved from speech act theory. The notion of a "rational discourse" gives no room for the performative quality of enunciations or behaviors, but refers to a systematic and intellectually controlled exchange of arguments leading to the ideal, rational solution for any problem (Kelly 1995). The enlightenment seemed to initiate the heyday of human rationality. This rationality still seems timeless and is dehistoricized, and it often is interpreted as not leaving any room for rituals and performances. For instance, with regard to the punishment system, the British historian Randall McGowen wrote that "here was wrung out of it any trace of the ceremonial and festive. . . . Punishment was no longer an elevated spectacle" (McGowen 1994: 281). Similarly, Michael Madow notes in his article on capital punishment and the public in New York that "executions were progressively stripped of their ritualistic and religious aspects" (Madow 1995: 466). Even Michel Foucault maintains in *Discipline and Punish* that the abolishment of pain on the scaffold meant the end of the punishing drama (Foucault 1994: 17ff).

Relocation of the Execution Procedure
from Public to Private

Later in *Discipline and Punish*, Foucault shifts the perspective. At heart, he maintains that in a rational and bureaucratized society, the execution procedure is a performance, too, which is exactly the reason why it had to be hidden. I would go even further and argue that in the nineteenth century, executions of death penalties behind prison walls were not only performances, but still spectacles and definitely ritualistic—and the hiding and reconfiguration of the audience was a constitutive part of an altered ritual. To be sure, such an execution purported different meanings than in early modern societies, since it presented neither a morally misled life nor divine power nor an either angry or gracious God to the people. Yet, the new form of execution contributed to the definition of how a civilized society had to behave and present itself, rational and humane as it considered itself to be. I maintain that the new form of execution—without a chorus, without red hot pincers, without crowds, and without women and children as spectators—was a performative ritual as well: it was a reinvocation of the specific "truth" of living in a more rational and advanced moment in history. This new society intended to have advanced to a new level of perfection, to have left the times of barbarism, brutality, and seemingly senseless violence behind. It defined itself as no longer being attracted to or fascinated by violent acts. And all of these assumptions were suggested in the moment of the deliberate killing of a fellow human, because, as for instance the German scholar Eberhard Friderich Georgii asked in 1779, "was not the state of the criminal laws a barometer of the developmental state of society?"

Let me flesh this out and take a closer look at history itself. On the following pages, I will analyze the discourse and procedural changes in Germany in the late eighteenth and early nineteenth centuries. Since the 1760s, numerous scholars of law, philosophy, and the state discussed the ambivalent effects of the traditional punishment rituals on an enlightened society. Critics such as the widely read Italian Cesare Beccaria (1966, originally published in 1764), Karl Ferdinand Hommel (1778), Johann Adam Bergk (1798), and numerous others emphasized that punishments that were inflicted with the deliberate intention to cause pain, to destroy the body of the condemned, and to spread fear among the people had negative effects on individual characters of the observers as well as on the community as a whole (for a good overview of the literature, see Kreutziger 1989: 99–125).

Yet, a significant problem was that physical violence was considered to exert a "magnetic attraction" on human beings. This attraction was understood to be "natural," and thus, an execution had to fascinate the audience around the scaffold even by the laws of nature. In 1800, for instance *Das Hannöverische Magazin* summarized the debates of the recent decades by stating that "there exists a general inclination of the human mind to watch closely the tortures of its unhappy fellow creatures who have fallen into the hands of the criminal justice system" (Anonymous 1800: Col. 1401, 1413). Shock and fascination were deemed to go hand in hand, and some critics emphasized that physical violence did not only take hold of the lower classes, but of at least some higher and educated members of the evolving civic society, too. Yet, around 1800, it was only a tiny minority of thinkers who asserted that "every execution is not only a spectacle for the man-in-the-street, but often enough an hour of recreation for the esteemed members of the higher classes" (Sturz 1776; Anonymous 1802, 1806) or, as Bavarian officials skeptically noted, an execution "is nothing more than a dramatic spectacle for both educated and uneducated."[3] According to numerous and loud voices in the contemporary discourse, in contrast to the members of the lower classes, when confronted with deadly violence truly enlightened men were able to hold their emotions in check. Consequently, seen from this angle, the observation of a violent act even provided the opportunity to prove and exercise an advanced sensibility and superior state of civilization.

After all, the esteemed members of the civic society were mostly considered to have overcome a joyful inclination to observe the gruesome death of a fellow creature, an act that was deemed "barbaric," then. There was an understanding that only the uneducated were still fascinated by this sort of performance. On the basis of that assumption, public executions with up to 20,000 people gathering around the scaffold in large and heated crowds signified a dark past that had to be abolished in order to give way to a glorious and shining future. The public presentation of deadly violence was considered not only uncivilized, but opposed to the production of a stable community and the successful governing of the governed. To achieve progress, a government had to set a good example for the governed and refrain from what was deemed excessive violence. And old-style execution performances on stage were considered excessively violent, socially and individually harmful, and likely to sow the seeds of cruelty, crime, and moral decay. After all, the amount or style of publicly performed violence was perceived as "the indicator of the intellectual level of a people and the morality of an age," to quote the German law expert Heinrich Zöpfl (1839: 1).

Nevertheless, after a contentious debate on the abolition of the death penalty in the later eighteenth century, most social theorists and specialists in criminal law had come to the conclusion that for the most serious crimes, like murder and treason, the death penalty was inalienable. Thus, it could not be abolished. This seeming necessity of the death penalty on the one hand, and the derogatory effects of its execution on the other, posed a dilemma that called for a rational solution. One possibility was to render the death of the wrongdoer invisible to the eye of the larger public and to reduce the audience to a strictly limited circle of elite members of the civic society, as Ernst Ferdinand Klein, one of the most prominent and outspoken figures in this debate in Germany, had already proposed in 1804 (Klein 1804a, 1804b). Moreover, Klein recommended that as soon as the terror of the French Revolution and its nearly countless beheadings were forgotten, executions should be conducted with this new machine: the absolutely reliable, calculable, and trustworthy guillotine. This technology, which had made possible the mass executions and the rivers of blood during the reign of terror in France, also promised progress for civilization. The guillotine was not only a technologically advanced symbol of the progressive machine age, but through its rapidity it rendered the act of execution and the moment of death almost invisible.[4] Such executions, carried out in a fraction of a second and, possibly, even divorced from the public realm, would make clear how advanced nineteenth-century society was. Within the conceptual framework of performance theory, such an execution has to be understood as reinvocation of the advancement of society. To state the point more directly, the advanced society consisted of performances like painless and invisible executions.

Since the middle of the 1830s, German scholars and criminal justice administrators looked to the United States as their guiding example. Pennsylvania and New York, the hallmark states of social progress, were the first to transfer the execution behind prison walls (Mackey 1982; Masur 1991: 93ff; Teeters 1991: 756–835; Madow 1995; Martschukat 2002b: 52ff; Banner 2002: 144ff). Contemporary German thinkers in the field of criminal law and political theory, such as Carl Mittermaier (1834, 1836: 6), Carl Hepp (1836: 14), Friedrich Noellner (1845: 68), or Albert Berner (1861: 13), referred to the U.S. example while discussing the situation in Europe and specifically in Germany. In the early 1850s, the transfer of the killing ritual started in several German states, and by 1863 public executions were abolished all over Germany (Evans 1996: 305–21; Martschukat 2000: 185–234; Overath 2001: 182ff).[5]

Let me now shift the perspective from a "long shot" on Europe and Germany to a "close-up" on the city of Hamburg that will reveal more details of how such a performative constitution of a civilized self-definition was accomplished. The criminal code of the city had not been reformed since the early seventeenth century, and around 1800 it still prescribed the premodern style of execution. For a while, experts had complained loudly that the local criminal codes were outdated, insufficient, and not adequate for a modern and civilized society. In the later eighteenth century, writers from Hamburg had continuously complained "that the harsh and brutal laws from the preceding barbaric centuries are bonds that still hold an advancing and progressing society in their tight grip and pose a cruel remnant in this increasingly enlightened and humane [eighteenth] century" (Cranz 1793: 7). After the end of the French occupation of the city-state in 1814, every upcoming execution caused trouble for the local authorities: Wouldn't an execution lead to chaos and moral decay among the population of Hamburg and the surrounding area? Wasn't it simply too uncivilized? Yet, the disturbing and even horrifying experience of the Napoleonic occupation made the French guillotine an unacceptable instrument of execution for the magistrates and most people of Hamburg. Finally, several troublesome old-style beheadings caused such insurmountable problems for the self-definition of the local, enlightened elites and governing class that Hamburg's authorities stopped executing death penalties in 1822 for thirty-four years—until 1856. They did not officially abolish capital punishment, though, and that kept the debate about executions and concepts of civilization alive. Accordingly, an increasingly dense discourse demanded a new criminal code and a different, less visibly violent and physically destructive mode of execution. For instance Carl Wilhelm Asher, a lawyer from Hamburg, purported that "we must not fall behind the progress of the age" (Asher 1828: 6) and his colleague Carl Trummer added that the "old laws had to be enlightened with the torch of progress" (Trummer 1828: 16).

In the early 1840s, Hamburg's authorities finally felt the pressing need to create conditions that would render the execution of a death penalty possible again. In recent years, extraordinary brutal and outrageous crimes had occasionally fueled the public and political demand for a death penalty and its execution. One of these cases was Johann Christoph Pfleging, who in 1841 was accused of having slain and robbed a seventy-two-year-old widow. When a case like this remained without death penalty, the governing thought of themselves as incapable of fulfilling their role as rulers. However, an execution had to be in accordance with and replicate the cultural conventions that had been transformed in the preceding decades. Thus, the supreme judges of the city decided in 1842 that the authorities had to anchor an advanced, new style of execution that would perform "nothing else but the character of civilized justice," and over a quarter century after the end of the traumatic French occupation, the judges proposed to use the guillotine instead of the sword.[6] Yet, this seemed still insufficient, and as a report from April 1842 maintained, further procedural changes were necessary "regarding the time of execution, the transfer of the condemned to the execution site, the ceremonial elements in general as well as the specific visibility of the beheading, so that the execution of a death penalty is no amusing event for the lower classes any more."[7] In the following years, commentators and judges continued to debate Hamburg's old criminal justice system as an invocation of irrationality and cruelty. Only a new criminal code with a different capital punishment system would bring "splendor and blessing" over the city, wrote Supreme Judge Carl August Schlüter (1851: preface, 4ff, 32ff).

Finally, in October 1854, a new law was passed. Most significantly, it excluded the general public from the execution performance—only a specified number of adult male members of the educated classes, mostly office holders, were allowed to observe an execution as witnesses. They represented the (supposedly) most advanced and rational members of the civic society who were deemed capable of overcoming this natural attraction of violence, keeping their emotions under control, and of treating the occasion with the necessary seriousness.[8] At the same time, commentators were impressed by the immense power and advanced technical state of the execution machine. They assumed that it theoretically could cut through numerous necks at once in a fraction of a second.[9]

In January 1855, only three months after the new law had been passed, Hamburg's lower court sentenced the murderer Wilhelm Timm to death. Almost every esteemed citizen shared the opinion that a public beheading with a sword would have brought about the demoralization of the city's population. However, according to the new law, the execution was to be conducted behind the prison walls and with the guillotine, and such an execution would not demoralize, but enhance the state of civilization and development. Even the condemned man, the night before his death, understood this as progress in civilization. When, according to his guard's report, he came to know that he would be executed with a machine in the following morning, he was fascinated by its technology, and he finally remarked calmly, "that's nice, that doesn't hurt"[10]— and the reluctance to inflict pain is of crucial importance to the concept of civilized killing. Witnesses of the execution, such as Senator Martin Hudtwalcker, commented in private notes on the impressive rationality and sobriety of the performance, the central feature of which was the invisibility of the actual beheading even for the handpicked observers in the prison yard: "The machine was erected in a way that the witnesses could hardly see the body of the condemned, and the head, after being suspended from the torso, immediately fell into a bag under the scaffold." The newspapers celebrated the perfection of the style and technique of "a quick and sober execution through a push on a button" that was finally considered adequate for an advanced society and a reinvocation of its paradigms.[11]

Yet, a certain ambivalence pervaded the nineteenth-century news reports on crime and punishment. Whereas on the one hand newspapers celebrated the "advanced" execution procedure and the progress of civilization that was indicated by a supposedly increasing abhorrence of gruesome violence, on the other hand the number and scope of detailed and thrilling reports increased steadily. Since around 1800 a different type of audience had emerged that enjoyed the pleasures of a private and secret consumption of detailed and graphic descriptions of crimes and executions. A certain "pornography of pain and violence" that historian Karen Halttunen diagnosed as the complementary side of eighteenth- and nineteenth-century sensibility and humanitarianism in the United States, permeated German societies, too (Halttunen 1995, 1998; Martschukat 2000: 188–94, 222–34; Martschukat 2001).

Not only newspapers expressed the ambiguities of this relationship between violence and civilization. Commercial travel agencies organized boat trips to carry large crowds down the River Elbe from Hamburg to the neighboring city of Stade where public beheadings were still carried out (Martschukat 2000: 239). Similar mass pilgrimages to execution sites, mostly by train, took place all over Germany. People not only traveled far to watch the last public executions; they climbed rooftops and trees in order to look over the prison walls and catch a glimpse of indoor executions. At the same time, the wealthier members of society paid high prices for tickets to witness the indoor execution spectacle. In some places, on the day of execution hundreds of people flooded the prison yard to see what could still be seen from the moment of death (Evans 1996: 396–404).

Broader Perspectives

However, even if the progress in civilization through mechanical and hidden executions was tainted by a widespread desire for the consumption of violence, most contemporary writers and statesmen were proud of themselves and their times for the so-called advancement of the criminal justice system and the state of their society. The new execution ritual was "corresponding to the spirit of the age and the moral constitution of our century," as the authorities of another German state, in this case Baden, praised themselves for the introduction of indoor executions in the middle of the 1850s.[12] Without doubt, those reformed executions were performative rituals, too, just like the early modern "festivals of violence." But in a system of different conventions they were differently performed and produced different meanings. These new performances of punishment shaped the contemporary understanding of having moved away from the age of an avenging God into a state of higher civilization and rationality. Thus, these new punishments contributed to the consolidation of the concept of civilization and a civilized society, even if this concept showed some fractures. The most destructive moment possible, the deliberate killing of a human being, unfolded constructive power by constituting a new, seemingly advanced state of human existence.

Yet, as I have shown, this transition of the execution procedure is neither proof nor consequence of a teleological civilizing process, neither is it inspired by some ontological force existing under the surface of the things and the words. To the contrary, the relationship between civilization and executions has to be turned around: the perfection of killing techniques produces what is considered to be civilization or a civilized society. To put it clearly, seen from the angle of a capital punishment history, civilization *is* perfect executing. If the concept of modernity and civilization is to be reproduced in the moment of execution, the display of a visibly dying, maimed, and disfigured body has to be avoided, as (among others) Alan Hyde has shown in his book *Bodies of Law* (Hyde 1997: 187ff; Sarat 2001b: 187–208; Kaufman-Osborn 2002: 135–64; Martschukat 2003).

This applies not only to the 1850s and 1860s and the transfer of executions behind prison walls. We can find the same type of argument in the debates about the modification of the gallows, intended to achieve what was considered a technically and humanely advanced execution in the second half of the eighteenth century (Gatrell 1994: 45ff; Kaufman-Osborn 2002: 47–92). Similarly, the introduction of a decapitation machine since the days of the French Revolution was coined by a long and intensive exchange of arguments among execution experts, scientists, and politicians about the form and the weight of the blade, the height of its fall, the smoothness of the machine, and so forth (Arasse 1989; Janes 1991; Martschukat 1997). On the other side of the Atlantic, the statements of the discursive formation were strikingly similar when experts discussed the introduction of the electric chair in the state of New York in the 1880s and 1890s: a more sober, rapid, invisible, painless—in one word, civilized—death of condemned prisoners was to be achieved (Neustadter 1989; Martschukat 2002a, 2003). In the twentieth century, execution technology changed with the introduction of the gas chamber in the 1920s and lethal injection in the 1970s, but the performative constitution of civilization and progress by means of perfected executing was still alive (Sarat 2001b: 60–84; Kaufman-Osborn 2002: 179–214).

Notes

1. Unless otherwise indicated, translations of the quotations from German to English are mine.

2. For a collection of analyses of capital punishment and modern society that refers to performance theory in its various shapes, see Timothy V. Kaufman-Osborn, *From Noose to Needle: Capital Punishment and the Late Liberal State* (2002).

3. Bayerisches Hauptstaatsarchiv München MInn 46136, according to Evans (1996: 309).

4. See, for the cultural history of the guillotine, Arasse (1989); Janes (1991); Martschukat (1997: 45–63, 2000: 113–48). Within this cultural configuration, the question whether the head of the executed person continued to live for a while after the execution was an immensely important and pressing problem that caused unrest among numerous contemporaries; see for these debates Martschukat (1997), Rehwinkel (2000: 151–71); Métraux (2001: 167–86); Borgards (2002: 77–98).

5. England and Austria stopped public executions in 1868 (Thesing 1990; Reicher 2003), France continued to execute publicly until 1939. One reason for this was that the opponents of capital punishment consistently voted against private executions because they maintained that an end of public executions would make the death penalty in general more acceptable.

6. Staatsarchiv Hamburg, 111-1, Senat, Cl. Vii, Lit. Mb, No. 3, Vol. 8, protocoll and comments from the 8 and 11 April 1842.

7. Staatsarchiv Hamburg, 111-1, Senat, Cl. Vii, Lit. Mb, No. 3, Vol. 8, expertise from 8 April 1842.

8. Staatsarchiv Hamburg, 111-1, Senat, Cl. vii, Lit. Mb, No. 3, Vol. 9: "Acta betreffend die Öffentlichkeit bei den Hinrichtungen, sowie die Einführung des Fallbeils, statt aller bisherigen Arten der, nunmehr binnen 8 Tagen nach rechtskräftiger Erkenntnis zu vollstreckenden Todesstrafe; beliebt durch Rat- und Bürgerbeschluß vom 19., publ. den 20 Oct., 1854."

9. See for instance the magazine *Freischütz*, 25 January 1855.

10. Staatsarchiv Hamburg, 111-1, Senat, Cl. Vii, Lit. Mb, No. 3, Vol. 10: Kriminalurteile und Executiones: Report of the police sergeant Böhlers about Wilhelm Timm's last hours.

11. Staatsarchiv Hamburg, 111-1, Senat, Cl. Vii, Lit. Mb, No. 3, Vol. 10: Kriminalurteile und Executiones: Report of the witness Martin Hieronymus Hudtwalcker about Wilhelm Timm's execution on 10 April 1856; see, for the press reports, for instance the *Reform*, 44 (April 12, 1856), or the *Hamburger Nachrichten* (April 11, 1856). On pain, punishment, and civilization, see Sarat 2001a: 1–14.

12. Badisches Generallandesarchiv Karlsruhe 234/6774, 159–61: Grossherzogliche Badische Regierung des Mittel-Rheinkreises to Justizministerium, May 9, 1854, according to Evans (1996: 312).

References

Anonymous (1800) "Ueber die öffentlichen Hinrichtungen und den Einfluß, den sie auf die Moralität des Volks haben," 75–79 *Neues Hannöverisches Magazin* 1393–464.

Anonymous (1802) "Ueber Leibes- und Lebensstrafen überhaupt, besonders in Republiken," 1 *Hamburg und Altona* 156–64.

Anonymous (1806) "Auch Etwas über den am 14ten April dieses Jahres in Hamburg vom Leben zum Tode gebrachten Delinquenten," 5 *Hamburg und Altona* 92–94.

Arasse, Daniel (1989) *The Guillotine and the Terror.* London and New York: Allen Lane/Penguin Press.

Asher, Carl W. (1828) *Rhapsodische Bemerkungen über Criminal-Justiz: Zum Theil mit besonderer Beziehung auf Hamburg.* Hamburg: Meissner.

Austin, John L. (1962) *How to Do Things with Words.* Cambridge, MA: Harvard University Press.

Banner, Stuart (2002) *The Death Penalty: An American History.* Cambridge, MA, and London: Harvard University Press.

Beccaria, Cesare (1966) *Über Verbrechen und Strafen: Nach der Ausgabe von 1766 übersetzt und hg. v. Wilhelm Alff.* Frankfurt/M.: Insel.

Bée, Michel (1983) "Le Spectacle de l'exécution dans la France d'Ancien Régime," 38 *Annales ESC*, 843–62.

Bergk, Johann Adam (1798) *Des Marchese Beccaria's Abhandlung über Verbrechen und Strafen—von neuem aus dem Italiänischen übersetzt: Mit Anmerkungen von Didérot, mit Noten und Abhandlungen vom Uebersetzer, mit den Meinungen der berühmtesten Schriftsteller über die Todesstrafe nebst einer Kritik derselben, ...* Leipzig: Johann Gottlieb Beygang.

Berner, Albert F. (1861) *Abschaffung der Todesstrafe.* Dresden: Boetticher.

Borgards, Roland (2002) "Qualifizierter Tod: Zum Schmerz der Hinrichtung in der Rechtsprechung um 1800," in R. Borgards and J. F. Lehmann, eds., *Diskrete Gebote: Geschichten der Macht um 1800—Festschrift für Heinrich Bosse.* Würzburg: Königshausen & Neumann.

Boys, Albert du (1854) *Histoire du droit criminel des peuples modernes considéré dans ses rapports avec les progrès de la civilisation, depuis la chute de l'Empire romain jusqu'au XIXe Siècle.* Paris: A. Durand.

Butler, Judith (1993) *Bodies that Matter: On the Discursive Limits of "Sex."* New York: Routledge.

Butler, Judith (1997a) *Excitable Speech: A Politics of the Performative.* New York: Routledge.

Butler, Judith (1997b) "Performative Acts and Gender Constitution: An Essay in Phenomenology and Feminist Theory," in K. Conboy, ed., *Writing on the Body: Female Embodiment and Feminist Theory.* New York: Columbia University Press.

Butler, Judith (1997c) *The Psychic Life of Power: Theories in Subjection.* Stanford, CA: Stanford University Press.

Cranz, August F. (1793) *Bemerkungen an das unbefangene und aufgeklärte Hamburgische Publikum—Bey Gelegenheit des Criminal-Prozesses gegen die unglückliche Jüdin Debora Traub.* Hamburg.

Döbler, Jacob (1693–97) *Theatrum Poenarum suppliciorum et executionum criminalium; oder Schauplatz derer Leibes- und Lebens-Strafen, . . . —2 Bde.* Sondershausen and Leipzig: Hof-Buchdrucker Ludwig Heinrich Schönermarck.

Dreyfus, Hubert L., and Paul Rabinow (1982) *Michel Foucault: Beyond Structuralism and Hermeneutics; with an Afterword by and an Interview with Michel Foucault.* Chicago: University of Chicago Press.

Dülmen, Richard van (1985) *Theater des Schreckens: Gerichtspraxis und Strafrituale in der frühen Neuzeit.* München: Beck.

Evans, Richard J. (1996) *Rituals of Retribution: Capital Punishment in Germany, 1600–1987.* Oxford and New York: Oxford University Press.

Fischer-Lichte, Erika (2003) "Performance, Inszenierung, Ritual: Zur Klärung kultur-wissenschaftlicher Schlüsselbegriffe," in J. Martschukat and S. Patzold, eds., *Geschichtswissenschaft und "performative turn": Ritual, Inszenierung, Performanz.* Köln: Böhlau.

Foucault, Michel (1972) *The Archaeology of Knowledge and the Discourse on Language.* New York: Pantheon.

Foucault, Michel (1977) *Discipline and Punish: The Birth of the Prison.* New York: Vintage Books.

Foucault, Michel (1994) *Überwachen und Strafen: Die Geburt des Gefängnisses.* Frankfurt: Suhrkamp.

Foucault, Michel (2002) "Nietzsche, die Genealogie, die Historie (1971)," in *Dits et Ecrits: Schriften in vier Bänden—Band 2: 1970–1975.* Frankfurt/M.: Suhrkamp.

Gatrell, V. A. C. (1994) *The Hanging Tree: Execution and the English People, 1770–1868.* Oxford and New York: Oxford University Press.

Georgii, Eberhard Friedrich (1779) *Versuch einer Beantwortung der Frage: Sind scharfe Gesetze einem Staat vorträglich? Aus was für einem Gesichtspunct sind solche gegen einen jeden unterschiedenen Stand desselben, sowohl in Rücksicht ihrer Ausführung als Würkung zu betrachten?* Stuttgart: Erhard.

Halttunen, Karen (1995) "Humanitarianism and the Pornography of Pain in Anglo-American Culture," 100 *American Historical Review* 303–34.

Halttunen, Karen (1998) *Murder Most Foul: The Killer and the American Gothic Imagination.* Cambridge, MA, and London: Harvard University Press.

Harsdörffer, Georg Philipp (1975 [1656]) *Der Große Schau-Platz jämmerlicher Mord-Geschichte: bestehend in CC. traurigen Begebenheiten, ...* Hildesheim and New York: Olms.

Hepp, Carl T. F. (1836) *Ueber den gegenwärtigen Stand der Streitfrage über die die Zuläs-sigkeit der Todesstrafe.* Tübingen: Osiander.

Hommel, Karl Ferdinand (1778) *Des Herren Marquis von Beccaria unsterbliches Werk von Verbrechen und Strafen (1764). Auf das Neue selbst aus dem Italienischen übersezet mit durchgängigen Anmerkungen des Ordinarius zu Leipzig Herren Hofrath Hommels.* Breslau: Korn.

Hyde, Alan (1997) *Bodies of Law.* Princeton, NJ, and Oxford: Princeton University Press.

Janes, Regina (1991) "Beheadings," 35 *Representations* 21–51.

Karasek, Horst (1994) *Die Vierteilung: Wie dem Königsmörder Damiens 1757 in Paris der Prozeß gemacht wurde.* Berlin: Verlag Klaus Wagenbach.

Kaufman-Osborn, Timothy V. (2002) *From Noose to Needle: Capital Punishment and the Late Liberal State.* Ann Arbor, MI: University of Michigan Press.

Kelly, Michael, ed. (1995) *Critique and Power: Recasting the Foucault/Habermas Debate.* Cambridge, MA, and London: Cambridge University Press.

Klein, Ernst F. (1804a) "Ueber die Hinrichtung der Verbrecher, mit Rücksicht auf den von Troerschen Fall," 5 *Neues Archiv für Criminalrecht* 1–19.

Klein, Ernst F. (1804b) "Nachtrag zu dem im 2ten Stück des Vten Bandes enthaltenen Aufsatz über die Hinrichtung der Verbrecher," 5 *Neues Archiv für Criminalrecht* 152–55.

Kreutziger, Bernd (1989) "Argumente für und wider die Todesstrafe(n): Ein Beitrag zur Beccaria-Rezeption im deutschsprachigen Raum des 18. Jahrhunderts," in G. Deimling, ed., *Cesare Beccaria: Die Anfänge moderner Strafrechtspflege in Europa.* Heidelberg: Kriminalistik-Verlag.

Mackey, Philip English (1982) *Hanging in the Balance: The Anti-Capital Punishment Movement in New York State, 1776–1861.* New York: Garland.

Madow, Michael (1995) "Forbidden Spectacle: Executions, the Public and the Press in Nineteenth-Century New York," 43 *Buffalo Law Review* 461–562.

Martschukat, Jürgen (1997) "Ein schneller Schnitt, ein sanfter Tod? Die Guillotine als Symbol der Aufklärung," in Susanne Krasmann and Sebastian Scheerer, eds., *Die Gewalt in der Kriminologie.* Weinheim: Juventa.

Martschukat, Jürgen (2000) *Inszeniertes Töten: Eine Geschichte der Todesstrafe vom 17. bis zum 19. Jahrhundert.* Köln: Böhlau.

Martschukat, Jürgen (2001) "Der 'Maasstab für die geistige Bildungsstufe eines Volkes und die Moralität eines Zeitalters': Die Todesstrafe in Diskurs und Praxis im 18. und 19. Jahrhundert," 9 *Historische Anthropologie* 1–26.

Martschukat, Jürgen (2002a) "'The Art of Killing by Electricity': The Sublime and the Electric Chair," 89 *Journal of American History* 900–921.

Martschukat, Jürgen (2002b) *Geschichte der Todesstrafe in Nordamerika: Von der Kolonialzeit bis zur Gegenwart.* München: Beck.

Martschukat, Jürgen (2003) "'The duty of society': Todesstrafe als Performance der Modernität in den USA um 1900," in J. Martschukat and S. Patzold, eds., *Geschichtswissenschaft und "performative turn": Ritual, Inszenierung, Performanz.* Köln: Böhlau.

Martschukat, Jürgen, and Steffen Patzold (2003) "Geschichtswissenschaft und ,performative turn': Eine Einführung in Fragestellungen, Konzepte und Literatur," in J. Martschukat and S. Patzold, eds., *Geschichtswissenschaft und "performative turn": Ritual, Inszenierung, Performanz.* Köln: Böhlau.

Masur, Louis P. (1991) *Rites of Execution: Capital Punishment and the Transformation of American Culture, 1776–1865.* Oxford and New York: Oxford University Press.

McGowen, Randall (1994) "Civilizing Punishment. The End of the Public Execution in England," 33 *Journal of British Studies* 257–82.

Meranze, Michael (1996) *Laboratories of Virtue: Punishment, Revolution, and Authority in Philadelphia, 1760–1835.* Chapel Hill, NC, and London: University of North Carolina Press.

Métraux, Alexandre (2001) "Der Todesreigen in der belebten Materie: Xavier Bichat über das vielfache Sterben des Organismus," in Th. Schlich and C. Wiesemann, eds., *Hirntod: Zur Kulturgeschichte der Todesfeststellung.* Frankfurt/M.: Suhrkamp.

Mittermaier, Carl J. A. (1834) "Ueber den neuesten Stand der Ansichten in England, Nordamerika, Frankreich, Italien und Deutschland, betreffend die Aufhebung der Todesstrafe," *Archiv des Criminalrechts/Neue Folge* 1–33, 195–227.

Mittermaier, Carl J. A. (1836) "Ueber die neuesten Fortschritte der Gesetzgebung und Wissenschaft in Europa und Amerika, die Aufhebung der Todesstrafe betreffend," *Archiv des Criminalrechts/Neue Folge* 1–30.

Mittermaier, Carl J. A. (1855) "Rundschau über die neuesten Fortschritte in Bezug auf die Strafgesetzgebung, Geschichte des Strafrechts, Strafrechtswissenschaft, Criminalstatistik, gerichtliche Medizin, Rechtssprüche der obersten Gerichtshöfe über merkwürdige Fragen des Rechts," *Archiv des Criminalrechts /Neue Folge* 124–47.

Neustadter, Roger (1989) "The Deadly Current: The Death Penalty in the Industrial Age," 12 *Journal of American Culture* 79–87.

Noellner, Friedrich (1845) "Die Todesstrafe und die Formen ihrer wissenschaftlichen Vollziehung vom strafrechtlichen und practischen Standpunkte betrachtet," in M. Carriere, *Wissenschaft vom Leben in Beziehung auf die Todesstrafe: Ein philosophisches Votum; mit einem strafrechtlichen Kommentar und vom Standpunkte der Erfahrung abgegebenen Gutachten von Friedrich Noellner.* Darmstadt: Leske.

Overath, Petra (2001) *Tod und Gnade: Die Todesstrafe in Bayern im 19. Jahrhundert.* Köln: Böhlau.

Rehwinkel, Kerstin (2000) "Kopflos, aber lebendig? Konkurrierende Körperkonzepte in der Debatte um den Tod durch Enthauptung im ausgehenden 18. Jahrhundert," in C. Wischermann and S. Haas, eds., *Körper mit Geschichte.* Stuttgart: Steiner.

Reicher, Dieter (2003) *Staat, Schafott und Schuldgefühl: Was Staatsaufbau und Todesstrafe miteinander zu tun haben.* Opladen: Leske and Budrich.

Sarat, Austin (2001a) "Introduction: On Pain and Death as Facts of Legal Life," in A. Sarat, ed., *Pain, Death, and the Law.* Ann Arbor, MI: University of Michigan Press.

Sarat, Austin (2001b) *When the State Kills: Capital Punishment and the American Condition*. Princeton, NJ, and Oxford: Princeton University Press.

Schlüter, Carl A. (1851) *Bemerkungen zum hamburgischen Criminal-Gesetzbuch*. Wiesbaden: Schellenberg.

Spierenburg, Pieter (1984) *A Spectacle of Suffering. Executions and the Evolution of Repression—From a Preindustrial Metropolis to the European Experience*. Cambridge, MA: Cambridge University Press.

Sturz, Helfrich Peter (1776) "Ueber Linguets Vertheidigung der Todesstrafen," December, *Deutsches Museum* 1063–68.

Teeters, Negley K. (1991) "Public Executions in Pennsylvania: 1682–1834 (1960)," in Eric H. Monkonnen, ed., *Crime and Justice in American History: Historical Articles on the Origins and Evolution of American Criminal Justice, Vols. 1, 2: The Colonies and Early Republic*. Westport, CT, and London: Meckler.

Thesing, William B., ed. (1990) *Executions and the British Experience from the 17th to the 20th Century: A Collection of Essays*. Jefferson, NC, and London: McFarland.

Trummer, Carl (1828) *Fremdes Gesetzbuch? Oeffentlichkeit? Geschworenengericht? Todesstrafe? Beiträge zur Strafgesetzgebung unserer neuesten Zeit; auch in besonderer Beziehung auf Hamburg. Zugleich als Gegenschrift der 'rhapsodischen Bemerkungen über Criminal-Justiz'*. Hamburg: Meissner.

Wirth, Uwe, ed. (2002) *Performanz. Zwischen Sprachphilosophie und Kulturwissenschaften*. Frankfurt am Main: Suhrkamp.

Zöpfl, Heinrich (1839) *Denkschrift über die Rechtmäßigkeit und Zweckmäßigkeit der Todesstrafe und deren Abschaffung*. Heidelberg: Winter.

CHAPTER THREE

Seed of Abolition

Experience and Culture in the Desire to End Capital Punishment in Mexico, 1841–1857

PATRICK TIMMONS

Introduction

In August 2002 Mexican President Vicente Fox canceled a visit to U.S. President George W. Bush's ranch in Crawford, Texas. That summer, the two national governments had been battling over water rights in the U.S.-Mexico border region on behalf of water-hungry states such as Chihuahua and Texas. Yet the high drama of Fox's canceled visit emerged not as a result of a natural resource dispute, but because the state of Texas had executed Javier Suárez Medina, convicted of capital murder for the 1988 shooting death of Lawrence Cadena, a Dallas-area narcotics officer. In Austin before the execution, both sides' tempers flared over the Mexican government's allegations that Texas law enforcement had violated Article 36 of the 1963 Vienna Convention on Consular Relations, which provides that when arrested, a foreign national has the right to be informed that he or she has the right to contact their nearest consulate.[1] Several days before Suárez Medina's execution, Charley Wilkison, a spokesman for the Combined Law Enforcement Associations of Texas (CLEAT) expressed outrage at the Mexican government's allegations. "Texas officers face a very violent, often-well-armed public. The sacrifice of these officers is to stand for the rule of law. It's unfortunate that a criminal would be hidden by a foreign government" (Timmons 2002a). In Texas and in Washington, D.C., prosecutors, state offi-

cials, and foreign policy analysts could not comprehend the Mexican government's actions on behalf of one of their nationals who even admitted his guilt.

The diplomatic uproar over Suárez Medina's execution illustrates one of the
ways capital punishment defines cultural difference in the modern world. As
they held out for a possible stay, Mexican officials placed their understandings
of punishment in stark contrast to those elaborated by the United States. In ar-
ticulating such difference, the Mexican government attracted much attention.
Outside the Walls Unit, a state prison in Huntsville, television and print reporters from Mexico and the United States assembled in a large group.[2] Shortly
after witnessing Suárez Medina's death, the victim's son, Lawrence Rudy Cadena—who was married to a Mexican woman—articulated his own disbelief at
Mexico's pronouncements. At a press conference outside the Walls Unit Cadena
asked, "Why is [Mexico] the country of my children, defending a man who
killed their grandfather?"[3] Cadena had been inside the prison when Mexican
officials articulated their rationale. Before Cadena emerged from the death
house, the Mexican Consul-General of Houston Eduardo Ibarrola stated, "We
consider that the death penalty is unnecessary to combat crime, that it is not
useful and that it does not resolve the suffering of the victims" (Timmons
2002b). Suárez Medina's execution thereby enabled Mexican officials to articulate their own definition of "civilization" in the face of U.S. "barbarism."

Around the time of the execution, cultural, political, and diplomatic reasons
drove the Mexican government's actions. The Mexican president's Catholicism
was no secret and it is possible that Fox takes seriously the Vatican's universal
opposition to the death penalty. At the political and diplomatic levels, since the
attacks on the United States of September 2001, the Fox government realized
that Mexico could no longer claim a special relationship with Washington.
During the first eight months of Bush's tenure, the presidents proclaimed their
friendship for each other, suggesting that they might reach new trade, water,
and immigration agreements. In the wake of 9-11, the Bush administration
pushed these concerns to one side, privileging security issues and dismissing
Fox's desire to negotiate new treaties. Washington's newfound policy objectives
dealt a serious blow to Fox's credibility on issues sensitive with the Mexican
public. By canceling the trip because of the execution of a Mexican national in
Texas, Fox articulated how far the special relationship had collapsed and the

lengths to which he would go, internationally at least, to prove that Mexico was trying to clean up its poor human rights record.

For much of the past century, Mexican citizens have experienced significant human rights violations. Hence Fox's promise to improve the country's respect for human rights as part of his campaign platform during the 2000 presidential elections, in which the Mexican people voted to remove the one-party dictatorship of the Partido Revolucionario Institucional (PRI). Given the ongoing indigenous rebellion in Chiapas and the growing concern over murdered women in Ciudad Juárez (to name but two Mexican issues with international prominence), protesting Texas's execution of a Mexican national offered a means to increase Fox's domestic political capital. Indeed, academic observers such as John Bailey of Georgetown University, and Peter Ward of the University of Texas at Austin, summed up Fox's cancellation as either "symbolic politics" or a political maneuver to convey "a message to lower levels of the bureaucracy that he does not control, such as the police" (Timmons 2002d, 2002e). In this way, the Mexican government managed to curry international support when it protested the application of the death penalty on philosophical and moral grounds. The Mexican government submitted a petition supported by nine countries demanding a stay of execution to U.S. authorities.[4]

At the time of Suárez Medina's execution, the Mexican government's representatives attempted to explain their objections to capital punishment. In doing so, they relied upon civilizational arguments. On 13 August 2002, Javier Alejo, Mexico's Consul-General in Austin, said Suárez Medina's case arose because of "a corrupted judicial process [and demonstrated] a lack of respect in every meaning of the phrase. The death penalty represents a primitive philosophy" (Timmons 2002c). Similarly, the Mexican Congress passed resolutions condemning the execution and the alleged violation of international treaty protocols. Sergio Acosta Salazar, a deputy in the Federal Congress, summed up the chamber's feelings when he said, "We're very irritated and angry. We think that the United States ought to have a first world-legal system—not one from the Eighteenth Century" (Timmons 2002a).

This emotive political rhetoric alluded to the culture of abolitionism in Mexico. In all the explanations for the Mexican government's actions, observers readily stated that Mexico was not a death penalty jurisdiction, but no group or

person could go further than that statement to explain why abolitionist sentiment in Mexico might be deeply rooted. According to Amnesty International,
Mexico is a de facto abolitionist country, meaning that while still possible under law, outside of military jurisdiction a death sentence has not been passed
since the 1950s and has not been carried out since the end of World War II.[5] In
one interview in Austin, Consul Alejo himself blurred the distinction between
law and practice, suggesting that in practice Mexico no longer retained the
death penalty. The Fox government drew little attention to the distinction between de facto and de jure abolition at the time of Suárez Medina's execution,
and when questions arose about the government's commitment to full abolition, the administration responded by saying only that they would work with
the Congress to introduce the necessary amendment to the 1917 Constitution's
Article 22 which continues to preserve the legality of capital punishment in
Mexico.[6] That said, the Mexican government's commitment to abolition in the
United States remains strong because it supports the Mexican Capital Legal Assistance Project, headed by Minnesota attorney Sandra Babcock.[7] Mexico's cultural arguments about the retrograde nature of the death penalty in the United
States have since become less prominent in turning to legal measures to save
defendants' lives. The implications of the cultural factors behind de facto abolitionism speak volumes about the depth of hostility to the death penalty in
Mexico and help to explain why the Mexican government devotes significant
resources to helping their nationals condemned in the United States.

Suárez Medina's execution, Lawrence Rudy Cadena's disbelief that the Mexican government would seek to aid his father's killer, and the language of "civilization and barbarism" permeating Mexico's outrage and sustaining its legal
crusade against death sentences in the United States provide suitable points of
departure to ask questions about the cultural life of capital punishment in Mexico, or, as is more appropriate, the cultural life of abolitionism. The remainder
of this chapter examines the death penalty in nineteenth-century Mexico,
which might seem incongruous or spurious, given the contemporary example
outlined above. The argument herein elaborated does not suggest that the current Mexican government's anti–death penalty stance has been determined by
the country's nineteenth-century capital punishment regime. Instead, I argue
that historical analysis of capital punishment in Mexico helps explain the country's long-standing ambivalence toward fatal forms of justice. It is important to

refer to Mexico's ambivalence over the death penalty because although modern abolitionism's roots may be traced to the nineteenth century, the movement succeeded only in outlawing the imposition of death for political crimes. And, notwithstanding the continuation of capital punishment in Mexico through the first half of the twentieth century, the implication is that Mexico has a long history of opposing capital punishment. Given the way the death penalty produced a minor rift in U.S.-Mexican relations in 2002, it would be useful to understand something of the epistemology of Mexican abolitionism.

Nineteenth-Century Experiences of Capital Punishment and Imprisonment

Mexico's independence in 1821 presented the country with significant possibilities and problems. Difficulties arose almost immediately when the new political class failed to construct order out of the postwar chaos. Centralists and federalists disputed the power of the states and federal government, and conservatives and liberals clashed over the extent to which the country should try to extirpate its colonial heritage. Conservatives looked back on the stability once provided by the Spanish crown, while liberals sought to eradicate the colonial heritage, doing away with the legal privileges of the Church, the army, and large landholders. In a disastrous war with the United States, President Antonio López de Santa Anna lost over half of Mexico's territory to the northern neighbor. In a peculiar twist, that stigma could not even prevent Santa Anna from returning for one last presidency from 1853 to 1855. On 9 August 1855, after many months of fighting between Santa Anna's final conservative administration and the forces of its liberal enemies, in the face of the latter's victory, the disgraced leader fled the country.

With the dictatorship in collapse and Santa Anna exiled first to Cuba and then Colombia, the liberal rebels laid claim to the national government in Mexico City. Under the statement of principles articulated to unite dissident liberals against the dictatorship, the 1854 Plan of Ayutla, the new government prepared for a Constitutional Congress.[8] From February 1856 to February 1857 about a hundred deputies gathered in Mexico City to reform the country's fundamental laws. As such, these members—many of whom practiced law or had previous political careers—debated and defined the structure of government vis-à-vis state and federal responsibilities, the role of the Church in public life, and individual rights (Sinkin 1979).

The section on individual rights, which was the first of eight sections in the Constitution, included elaborations of individual rights outlawing torture, illegal imprisonments, and the death penalty, among others. The Congress's drafting committee proposed a death penalty clause that both provided for the abolition of capital punishment for political crimes and made full abolition for ordinary crimes contingent on the construction of a national penitentiary regime.[9] Although the abolition of the death penalty for political crimes was of particular importance to the Congress's members and will be analyzed shortly, the contingent nature of abolition for ordinary crimes remains startling, even to this day. Mexico has been perhaps one of the few countries in the world ever to mandate through fundamental law that the abolition of capital punishment depended upon the construction of penitentiaries.[10] From where did these reforms, such as complete abolition for political crimes and contingent abolition for ordinary ones, come?

Regarding abolition for political crimes, members entered Congress with assumptions and goals drawn from their own experiences. The factors promoting the abolition of capital punishment for political crimes in nineteenth-century Mexico seem similar to historian Louis Masur's analysis of capital punishment in revolutionary America: experience of political conflict sensitized the political class in the way imprisonments and capital punishments had colored politics.[11] During the first thirty years of Mexico's independence from Spain, various governments of differing ideologies (conservative, liberal, centralist, federalist) had used death to eradicate their political opponents, sometimes without recourse to a tribunal that might grant the execution a semblance of legitimacy. Agustín de Iturbide (conservative) and Vicente Guerrero (liberal), both military men and heroes to the Independence movement, were executed by military firing squads.[12] By the 1850s, liberal and conservative newspapers articulated their hostility to capital punishment for political and ordinary crimes. In the 1856–57 Congress, two of Guerrero's relatives, his son-in-law Mariano Riva Palacio and his grandson Vicente Riva Palacio, acted as deputies, living reminders of the relationship between executions and political crimes. This specter of slain leaders and the experience of lengthy civil wars moved the liberals present in the Constitutional Congress to eradicate the legitimacy of executions for political crimes. Unlike our own contemporary societies, Mexico's congressmen in 1856 and 1857 could not "deny the violence" associated with the imposition of punishments (cf. Garland 1990: 243).

Experience of political repression directly contributed to the desire to abolish capital punishment for political crimes.[13] Abolition for political crimes went beyond the troubling images of slain independence fighters and emerged from the liberal generation's experiences under Santa Anna's dictatorship. *Su alteza serenísima* (His Supreme Highness), as the dictator styled himself, suppressed all printed debate about his government with the passing of a press law just after returning to power in 1853. Known as the Ley Lares, the law mandated placing an author's name on their published works. With the threat of incarceration for journalists, editorials hostile to the government ceased. This latest restriction on the freedom of the press sent a number of liberals to retirement in the provinces, and still others went into exile. Santa Anna also suggested that vocal dissent should lead to death. If liberal leaders, such as Melchor Ocampo, Mariano Arista, Benito Juárez, or Eligio Romero were caught, then "they should be shot as soon after they have been apprehended."[14] Santa Anna's final dictatorship threatened the execution of its political enemies, doing so without so much as a reference to legal process.[15]

By 1854, the situation had become so intolerable that prominent supporters of the liberal cause, such as Juan Álvarez, Ignacio Comonfort, Florencio Villareal, Tomás Moreno, Santos Degollado, Luis Ghilardi, and others, rose up in the Rebellion of Ayutla. By way of reaction, the conservative government threatened conspiracy charges against those who distributed the revolution's proclamation, the Plan of Ayutla. The punishment stipulated death. According to the Law of Conspirators, the liberal generation confronted death as the response to political dissidence (Villegas Revueltas 1996: 129). Thus, because Santa Anna's administration threatened imprisonment and execution for political dissidence, during the subsequent Constitutional Congress when given the opportunity many members sought to abolish the death penalty for political crimes.

As much as the liberal Congress may have reflected upon past experiences to shape the abolition of the death penalty for political crimes, this principle could also be articulated by turning toward the future. The most radical liberal sitting in the Congress, the journalist Ignacio Ramírez, spoke out against the death penalty in general. Nothing worthwhile could come, he suggested, from society acting as the vengeful party, piling "corpse upon corpse" (Zarco 1956: 783). In regard to restricting abolition to political crimes, Ramírez hoped that the members would think beyond their own interests, opting for full abolition. Thus, and as the liberal newspaper *El Siglo Diez y Nueve* reiterated on 29 August, the desire for abolition for political crimes was not fueled simply by the horror of past wars. Liberals, Ramírez criticized and *El Siglo* suggested, worried about their own futures. If their government did not hold, then the conservatives might return and charge their liberal opponents with a capital offense. With abolition for political crimes, the liberals, whether moderates or radicals—and members of both liberal persuasions attended the Congress—might protect their lives from future conservative revenge (*El Siglo Diez y Nueve*, 29 August 1856: 4). In other words, two factors seemed to be working together: the principle of future self-interest grounded in the experience of recent history. Estevan Altamirano, editor of the conservative newspaper *La Nación*, summed up this relationship when he explained why the death penalty should be abolished for political crimes: "Revolutions and political changes are so common here that the death penalty should be abolished; political crimes are only crimes according to the opposing side. He who yesterday should have perished on the scaffold is today a national patriot for exactly the same reason as the one that would have cost him his head" (Altamirano 1856: 2–3).

Although everyone in the chamber agreed that they write the abolition of the death penalty for political crimes into the Constitution—the votes in favor of the article totaled seventy-nine with none against—beyond the chamber, not all concurred. Among the press in Mexico City, only the French journalist, René Masson, editor of *Le Trait d'Union*, wrote: "From today, politics offers impunity, grouped under its banner will be evildoers of all sorts. To abolish the death penalty in political matters in a country where politics has always caused disagreement and will continue to cause disagreement is to want to remedy an evil with an even greater evil" (quoted in McGowan 1978: 154–55).

Newspaper editorials from each side of the political divide, conservative and liberal, argued vociferously against Masson. The liberal newspaper *El Siglo* disputed the picture of rampant criminality painted by the French ex-patriot and could not believe that Masson had argued that the Congress failed to recognize the country's needs. *El Siglo*'s editors pointed out that even in the face of armed reaction, such as an uprising in Puebla to the southeast of Mexico City in January 1856, there had not been "one firing squad, nor had it been necessary for the re-establishment of order to spill one drop of blood."[16] The editors at *El Siglo* returned to familiar territory to argue against Masson. "Don't they know," wrote the editor "how Guerrero perished? . . . Don't they know about Mejía's fate? Only the history of our country is enough to make every person of heart and feeling applaud the Christian reform decreed by the Constitutional Congress?" (*El Siglo Diez y Nueve*, 29 August 1856: 4). The conservative newspaper *La Nación* went further still stating that it would be happy to see the penalty abolished from the face of the earth, for all crimes, political and ordinary. "That would have been a huge step," the editors wrote in an article republished in *El Siglo*, "on the path to true civilization when man becomes closer to his creator" (ibid.).

For all this seeming humanitarianism, the issue of stopping the incarceration of political prisoners never reached a head in the Congress. That the Congress's members failed to abolish political crimes *in toto* speaks volumes about their conception of how state power should still control politics. However, this comment is not meant to suggest that liberals had no experience of imprisonment. During the 1840s and 1850s, the new liberal generation came to understand imprisonment much as they understood the death penalty, through experience. This insight is significant because if a particular administration chose not to execute a dissident but instead imprisoned them in a jail, prison, or dungeon, this experience impacted the life of capital punishment for ordinary crimes.

Making the abolition of capital punishment for ordinary crimes contingent upon the construction of a penitentiary regime could be explained through Enlightenment-based understandings of penal reform. In the nineteenth century liberal and conservative members of Mexico's political class maintained a great deal of familiarity with canonical works of the European Enlightenment. Mexican liberals saw themselves as the Enlightenment's heirs. In this regard, literate nineteenth-century Mexicans of the political class were aware of philosopher Cesare Beccaria's assessment of the futility of capital punishment; the Italian reformer favored "permanent penal servitude [where] a single crime gives very many lasting lessons" (Beccaria 1995: 68). But simply because an Enlightenment philosopher advocated penal reform did not make the project relevant to a

Mexico struggling to articulate and define its own modern future. Historians must no longer see Mexico, to name but one example from Latin America, as following in lockstep with European or U.S. understandings of modernity.[17] Instead, analyses should try to stress the ways local experience helped to shape and reshape nonindigenous cultural forms, such as the Enlightenment, and make them significant in a different geographical and historical context. For the purposes of the present analysis, the same point may be applied to philosophical approaches toward punishment. In other words, to understand how Italian influences pertained to Mexican classical liberal penology, we must search out those experiences that fostered reform. In turn, this suggestion leads to the insight that local experiences go a long way in crafting orientation toward punishment. In this way we must turn to those experiences that informed Mexico's cultural life of capital punishment for ordinary crimes in the mid-nineteenth century.

Political repression and imprisonment provided a rapid informal education about prison conditions and capital punishment for ordinary criminals. "The subject of which I speak has affected me personally," wrote the publisher Ignacio Cumplido in January 1841 as he justified why his publishing house devoted a three-part series to prison reform in the widely distributed periodical *El Mosáico Mexicano*.[18] Perhaps the most important publisher of his generation, in the early 1830s, during his mid-twenties, Cumplido collaborated on the newspaper *El Fénix de la Libertad* with the liberal politicians Luis de la Rosa and Mariano Riva Palacio.[19] Cumplido spent thirty-three days in the Acordada prison because, though no monarchist, he published a pamphlet of José María Gutiérrez Estrada who broke press censorship laws by candidly supporting monarchism as a solution to Mexico's political problems.[20] "Since I was in the Acordada I contracted a debt with humanity and wish to repay it. The sufferings in that prison interest me greatly because of the shocking disorder it is in, its state of moral relaxation and the considerable expense needed to conserve it."[21] With this experience as his basis for analysis, and coupled with his own observations from an 1838 visit to Cherry Hill Penitentiary in Philadelphia and Sing-Sing in New York State, Cumplido suggested a series of wide-ranging reforms.[22]

The movement toward prison reform did not remain restricted at the level of Mexico City's elite. The reforming impulse appeared some ten years later in the Estado de México when a local official, Primitivo Martínez wrote to the state's governor, Mariano Riva Palacio, about the public works projects under way in his municipality. Martínez suggested to his superior that he had some materials ready for reconstructing the municipal prison. As soon as Governor Riva Palacio could send him to an engineer "I will communicate my ideas to him with regards to the similarity, in my poor conception, of the Chalco Penitentiary with that of the Panopticon of Philadelphia" (*Primitivo Martínez to Mariano Riva Palacio* 1850). The subordinate even tried to send the governor the Philadelphia Penitentiary's plans and rules. "It is obvious," Martínez continued, "the convenience of an establishment that tends to prevent crimes rather than punishing delinquents, making them miserable, vilely excoriated by society instead of returning to society moralized by work and religion." Local experiences and the use of foreign penitentiaries as models for reform worked their way seamlessly into Cumplido's prescriptions and other's designs for modernizing their prison systems.

Cumplido reinforced his criticism of the Acordada prison with the suggestion that it did nothing to stop recidivism through rehabilitation. The criminal justice system incarcerated a variety of inmates who had committed different crimes, which to Cumplido meant that lesser criminals came into contact with those convicted of grave crimes, making "an evil mass composed of contrary elements, that time makes homogeneous and compact, succumbing virtue to vice, by means of repeated examples of immorality and corruption" (Cumplido 1841: 126). The jailers allowed prisoners to mix and mingle in the central patio. There, Cumplido saw prisoners who did not have decent clothes, making their deformities visible. The publisher blamed the degradation of the inmate on his treatment in prison, rather than blaming crime itself for an inmate's corruption.

Ultimately, reflecting upon prison conditions and inmates enabled the publisher to relate these failures to the persistence of executions for certain ordinary crimes. Cumplido's story of denied rehabilitation found its tragic dramatic rhetorical flourish in the tale of one young man who, though possibly innocent, when incarcerated involved himself with the more famous inmates. Upon release, he continued to commit crimes and returned again to the Acordada. In the end, according to Cumplido, he was taken to the scaffold "as if he were a monster" (Cumplido 1841). Shortly before his execution, Cumplido observed that thoughts beset the condemned, preventing him from listening to the priest at his side. Cumplido recounted the youth's dying words:

> They are going to kill me. I was mostly innocent when they put me in prison for the first time. Some correction and good advice would have convinced me to have left the wayward path. During my time inside, I haven't been taught a trade I could use to sustain myself, and I haven't heard a moral dictum either; crime and vice has constantly been in front of my eyes. . . . Why are they going to kill somebody who needed to be taught to kill? I am the work of the same people who condemn me. (ibid.)

With this scene, Cumplido captured a theme that became a central issue in the struggle for prison reform and the justification for death penalty abolition in nineteenth-century Mexico. The decrepit state of Mexican prisons, especially the Acordada, led a prisoner eventually to the scaffold. Perhaps if a prison rehabilitated, then there would be no need for the death penalty?

The issue of penitentiary reform and the blow it dealt the death penalty emerged again some eight years later in 1849. Doctor and university professor José María Benitez and lawyer Antonio Campos de la Vega published a pamphlet proposing the construction of a penitentiary for the Estado de México.[23] Up until that point, they commented, construction for a new penitentiary could not proceed because of scarce resources, meaning, "citizens could still not enjoy the incalculable benefits of this source, the only cement of the general good" (Benitez and Campos de la Vega 1849). The absence of a house of correction, they continued, meant that no "dyke [existed] for the evil ones." Expressing a sense of patriotic duty toward their descendants, Benitez and Campos de la Vega supported their desire to build a penitentiary because "no security [existed] for the lives and interests of their fellow citizens, public morality was very lax, and there were scandalous murders, robberies, and legal infractions." Consequently, they proposed initiating a system for accepting donations to help construct a new penitentiary where inmates might work to sustain themselves and their families. The pamphlet even included a receipt potential subscribers could complete to prove they had submitted the funds (ibid.: 10). As a result of such efforts, the government of the state, presided over by Mariano Riva Palacio, licensed the subscription advocated by Benitez and Campos de la Vega. One citizen, Manuel Terreros, who referred to himself as the governor's friend, wrote to Riva Palacio on 22 December 1849 to inform him that he had begun to contribute 500 pesos to the penitentiary project. From such donations, a year later, the governor presided over the construction of a new penitentiary, leading some residents of the state to believe that the death penalty might soon be abolished.

During the patriotic celebrations of 15 September 1850, Mariano Navarro, one of Riva Palacio's subordinates from the town of Jilotepec, took up the theme of abolition when he made a speech outside the new penitentiary about how "modern civilization" had worked important reforms on society. Earlier that year, Navarro himself informed the governor of the repairs he was trying to make to Jilotepec's jail.[24] At the celebrations Navarro said that the "character and object of . . . justice, is not in exercising a sterile revenge on the injuries that it receives, but in giving its members a sufficient guarantee of their security" (*El 16 de Setiembre en la capital del Estado de México* 1851: 48). The construction of the new penitentiary precipitated changes in the form of certain punishments. "The philosophers of the last century have fought the law that forces society to impose the death penalty, and since then its reputation has fallen into discredit, as much in practice as in opinion" (ibid.). Enlightenment philosophers, Navarro suggested, as he alluded to Beccaria, had improved the way societies responded to crimes, "removing the need for extreme measures" (ibid.). Navarro suggested that society did have the right to defend itself, but "it did not have the right to exterminate aggressors while no other method exists to prevent the violation of public security, but with the guilty's sacrifice" (ibid.). In other words, if methods existed to protect society without using the death penalty, then such extreme punishments had to be retired.[25] In making this argument, Navarro could then point out the meaning of the new penitentiary standing behind him: "The penitentiary system has established a new era that will become famous in the philosophical history of punishment, and it makes death [as punishment] unnecessary. It confirms the goals of social justice and makes effective the legislative reforms directed towards the variation of the penal systems. Such reforms are incomplete and defective if the success of punishments cannot be assured, especially those that take away freedom" (ibid.: 49).

Enlightenment prescriptions had taken root in Mexico. The strife of the early nineteenth century had horrified members of the political class because they could be tried and executed for dissent. How, then, would the members of the 1856 Congress respond to the penal reformers' proposition that the death penalty should be abolished for all crimes?

Filomeno Mata, a member of the committee that drafted the 1857 Constitution, declared in open debate that during the drafting process he had advocated
for full abolition. But he gave in, he said, to circumstances because he believed
capital punishment formed a current part of Mexico's penal system, and while
the system itself remained unreformed, one of its constituent parts (death as
punishment) could not be suppressed. Thus, without the penitentiary system,
the death penalty should remain for assailants, the arsonist, patricide, aggravated and premeditated murder as well as murder for profit, for grave military
crimes, or piracy "as defined by law" (Zarco 1956: 241).

The issue of legal definitions arose as a matter crucial to the deputies. As presented, the article read that assailants and traitors could be executed. The journalist and politician Francisco Zarco reminded the deputies that Santa Anna
had called liberals traitors and that the leaders of the Ayutla Rebellion had also
been called assailants (*salteadores*). In an attempt to make sure that keeping the
death penalty for such crimes would not result in political executions, Ponciano
Arriaga, who acted as speaker, reformed the article to read, "traitors in foreign
wars" and "highway robbers" (*salteador de caminos*) (ibid.: 785). Beyond these
changes, the original language of the article remained so that if a person murdered another in an aggravated or a premeditated manner or did so for some
sort of gain, capital murder charges could be brought.

By making the death penalty's abolition contingent on the construction of a
penitentiary system, liberals took seriously the notion that people acted crimi-
nally because of individual choices, not from innate traits.[26] The reasons for
abolition seemed clear to Zarco. Capital punishment could not be a timeless institution. Executions instead sprung from society's idea that it could take revenge upon the delinquent (Zarco 1856: 1). Accordingly, vengeance should never
enter a social institution; justice ought to have as its goal the repair of the damage caused and the correction and improvement of the delinquent, argued
Zarco. "None of this," he continued, "could be achieved by offering people the
bloody spectacles that served only to demoralize them" (ibid.). Ramírez argued
in similar tones. "A society full of force and power should not work in the same
way as the offended person; it ought to obtain a reparation, and if it threatens
imposing a penalty it should not do so in the name of revenge, but with the aim
only to correct the delinquent" (ibid.: 2). The criminal individual could be
changed, so the argument went, if the authorities placed him or her in a peni-

tentiary. While many deputies seemed to agree, most recognized that penitentiaries able to reform individuals did not exist throughout the country as a whole. Thus, the contingent death penalty clause represented a means to reconcile future desires with present realities.

Executions would continue, then, until the government constructed a national penitentiary system. Beyond the issue of rehabilitation, the deputies mentioned few details about the definition of a penitentiary system. And Arriaga, who favored the death penalty for the stated ordinary crimes while penitentiaries did not exist, suggested that the Constitution had advanced enough by abolishing death for political crimes (ibid.: 1). Even so, Zarco warned that the abolition of the death penalty would depend on the laziness of builders or the lack of materials. To avoid this situation, a suggestion arose for an amendment that would put a fixed term on the abolition of the death penalty. Or at least suppress the death penalty when penitentiaries appeared in major points around the country. The Congress dismissed both measures because they might create inequality in state legislatures.

When the deputies finally moved to vote on whether the death penalty should be abolished once the government constructed a penitentiary regime, sixty-three deputies voted in favor and sixteen against. This vote reflected the disposition of many nineteenth-century Mexican liberals about the nature of change. By making the abolition of the death penalty contingent upon the construction of a penitentiary regime, liberals affirmed their belief in the general direction of progressive change.[27] This was hardly a blind leap of faith as it rested on the essence of liberalism. An innate belief in progress constituted the liberal mindset (Zarco 1857, quoted in Villegas Revueltas 1996: 149–50). According to historian Jacqueline Covo, Mexican liberals'

> Conception of progress supported their optimistic convictions; born of Christianity and influenced by nineteenth-century doctrines of philosophy and economics, progress was one of the laws of the history of humanity: if truth, justice, democracy and civilization, since the first moments of world evolution are exposed to attacks of error, iniquity, despotism and of tradition it is inevitable the former will triumph. (Covo 1983: 45–48)

Given such faith in progress—that the state of the country would improve over time—it is possible to understand why the deputies, though horrified by the death penalty as it might apply to political crimes, voted on a contingent death penalty clause for ordinary crimes. Over the coming years, while political crimes no longer brought capital charges, prosecutors and judges continued to seek executions for certain ordinary crimes. And, sometimes, but not always, ordinary capital charges would be brought against people who committed crimes with significant political consequences (Canales 2001).

Conclusion

Social scientists and historians have long ignored this history of death penalty abolitionism in nineteenth-century Mexico. At the time of Suárez Medina's execution in 2002, no analyst or member of the Mexican government could accurately explain the underlying historical factors for de facto abolition. Thus, by seeking to tell an ignored story and using a cultural lens, this analysis has sought to provide reasons for the relatively weak life of capital punishment in Mexico. One of modern Mexico's formative constitutional experiments— which relied on personal experience to shape modern laws—helps explain the cultural life of abolitionism south of the Rio Grande. As such, it provides a much-needed historical explanation for why Fox's administration seemed to hold its most important bilateral relationship hostage over a death penalty case. Although violent deaths by extrajudicial means have not been and are not rare in Mexico, the incidence of death sanctioned by law enrages many Mexicans. If, as David Garland has suggested the definition of "'civilization' may be explained as a cultural configuration produced in Western societies by a specific history of social development and organization," the present analysis has attempted to explore the history of legal development in the creation of Mexico's "modern sensibility" toward capital punishment (Garland 1990: 215).

Ultimately, the cultural life of capital punishment in Mexico has been deeply conflicted, or, to use a concept introduced earlier, ambivalent. In the 1850s legislators expressed this ambivalence by failing to do away with the death penalty immediately, settling instead for a contingent death penalty clause. In Garland's terms, this failure to do away with the death penalty represents the incomplete nature of the civilizing process (Garland 1990: 240). Although the government did not construct a penitentiary regime, executions for ordinary crimes continued. By 1900, when Porfirio Díaz's government finally constructed Mexico's first modern penitentiary, questions began to arise about the punishment's continued legitimacy. Given that Díaz relied on the death penalty as a tool of power, Congress worked to reform the death penalty article, striking the language about contingent abolition. This death penalty article found its way into the Revolutionary Constitution of 1917 and has never been changed. Over time, for reasons that are less than clear, the death penalty eventually fell out of favor, either with judges, juries, or state legislators who removed the punishment from their penal codes.[28] The retention of capital punishment in the federal Constitution requires an article all to itself and can only be mentioned by way of conclusion. The retirement of capital punishment has meant that the cultural life of abolition in Mexico has almost come of age, and its roots go back to the mid-nineteenth century. To sustain the cultural life of abolition the Mexican government must introduce a reform of the 1917 Constitution. Without such a reform, full abolition does not exist in Mexico.

Notes

1. For the convention's text, see United Nations Conference on Consular Relations (1963). For Texas's interpretations of this treaty, see Attorney General of Texas (2000).

2. Since 1982, when legal capital punishment returned to Texas, executions in Huntsville have become more regular, rarely attracting the crowds or press interest brought on by the first executions. To attract such attention, it seems the person to be executed must be unusual in some way, as in the case of Karla Faye Tucker, the first woman executed in Texas since the Civil War. See Pickett with Stowers (2002).

3. Cadena's wife is a Mexican national. See Timmons (2002b).

4. Petitioners comprised the governments of Argentina, Chile, El Salvador, Guatemala, Honduras, Peru, Paraguay, Poland, and Uruguay. Suzanne Gamboa, "Mexico Vows to Go to the Supreme Court," *The Argus*, 13 August 2002.

5. For an analysis of the death penalty pronounced in Tabasco State against Alejandro Jiménez Magaña and Román Díaz Castillo on 3 January 1958, and that against Policarpo Asencio Villareal in 1956 (also in Tabasco), see Cano de Ocampo (1991). The doctoral thesis of Everard Meade, a history professor at the University of California San Diego, clarifies when the last executions in civil jurisdiction occurred in Mexico. See Meade (2005).

6. Almost two years after Suárez Medina's death, the government has introduced no such reform and the PRI even led a widely approved nonbinding referendum to bring the death penalty back into the penal code of the Estado de México, one of the country's most populated states situated on the capital's outskirts.

7. For an interview with Babcock after Suárez Medina's execution, see Timmons (2002f). On 5 February 2003 Babcock obtained temporary stays of execution for all Mexican nationals under sentence of death in U.S. penitentiaries through provisional measures pronounced by the UN's judicial body, the World Court. For Mexico's application to the Court, see *Avena and other Mexican Nationals* (2004).

8. For the full text of the Plan de Ayutla, see Tena Ramírez (1964: 492–99).

9. The proposed article read: "For the abolition of the death penalty it remains up to the administrative power to establish quickly a penitentiary regime. In the meantime, the death penalty is abolished for political crimes, and cannot extend itself to other cases except for the traitor to the motherland, the assailant, the highwayman, the arsonist, parent killer and aggravated, premeditated, advantageous homicide" (Zarco 1957: 346).

10. I can find no evidence that contingent abolitionism was written into the constitutions or laws of the jurisdictions within the United States, or, for that matter, of other countries or jurisdictions. For a history of the death penalty in the United States, see Banner (2002); for an analysis of capital punishment from a contemporary global perspective, see Hood (2002).

11. In the 1856–57 Constitutional Congress, members spoke time and time again of Santa Anna's tyranny. According to one early historian, Anselmo de la Portilla, this "could easily be explained by the circumstance that almost all of those who formed the assembly had suffered cruel persecutions" (Portilla 1858: 55). Masur (1989: 55) notes that while fearful of the death penalty, late-eighteenth-century Americans opposed capital punishment once the struggle for independence had ended.

12. Villegas Revueltas (1997: 16). For a nineteenth-century retelling of Iturbide's and Guerrero's executions, see Riva Palacio and Payno (1989).

13. My understanding of experience and its relationship to a cultural form, such as that of abolitionism, is informed by Thompson (1963).

14. Anexo III, "Lista de Desterrados," in Vázquez (1981: 315–17), quoted in Villegas Revueltas (1997: 47).

15. This issue arose on 26 June 1856 when the Constitutional Congress discussed proroguing Santa Anna's dictatorship. Juan Antonio de la Fuente referred to the law as one of the "hateful marks of despotism and sophistry because of all of its distinctions, its rules are lost in the abyss of arbitrariness, charging governors with the verdict and the imposition of punishments without a preliminary hearing without responsibility and without recourse" (Zarco 1956: 411).

16. *El Siglo Diez y Nueve*, 29 August 1856: 4. This statement is slightly disingenuous but cannot be picked apart here. For a fuller analysis of the presence and absence of executions in 1856 Puebla, see Chapter 1 of Timmons (2004).

17. Carlos Aguirre and Ricardo Salvatore (1996: xii) have repackaged the older view

by using the concept "traditional modernity," meaning modern understandings grafted onto a patrimonial social structure.

18. Ignacio Cumplido to Francisco Modesto de Olaguibel, 20 January 1841, in Cumplido (1841: 121). According to María Esther Pérez Salas Cantú, *El Mosáico Mexicano* had a weekly distribution of 1,000 copies with a domestic and foreign subscription base. Many subscribers belonged to the political class, such as the deputy Carlos María de Bustamante, the Supreme Court Justice José María Bocanegra, and General José Joaquín Herrera, permanent inspector of the militia. See Pérez Salas Cantú (2003: 143–45).

19. A decade after the appearance of *El Fénix de la Libertad*, Cumplido initiated *El Siglo Diez y Nueve*, one of the most widely read liberal newspapers of the nineteenth century. See Pérez Salas Cantú (2003: 139).

20. Ignacio Cumplido, "La cárcel de la Acordada en México. Origen de esta prisión, y su estado moral en la actualidad," in Cumplido (1841: 123; Gutiérrez Estrada 1840). In a subsequent pamphlet Cumplido wrote that the publication of Gutiérrez Estrada's work did not mean that he agreed with its contents. Instead, Cumplido suggested that he published impartially a variety of works with conflicting opinions. See Cumplido (1840, quoted in Pérez Salas Cantú 2003: 157).

21. Cumplido to Olaguibel, 20 January 1841, in Cumplido (1841: 121).

22. Cumplido's experience of a Mexican prison, coupled with his visits to U.S. prisons, does not mean that he slavishly followed a U.S. model. Cumplido similarly drew from U.S. and European publishing and printing advances to create one of the most successful publishing houses in nineteenth-century Mexico. See Pérez Salas Cantú (2003: 101–81). Without the Mexican context, of course, his successes would not have existed.

23. For biographical information on Benitez, see *Diccionario Porrúa de historia, biografía y geografía de México* (1995: 419–20). Campos de la Vega seems to have been employed at the state penitentiary. Eight years later in 1857 he represented the Indians of San Miguel in a land complaint with the Hacienda de la Gavia. See "Copia de la cuenta donde se asienta el ingreso y egreso habido desde el 24 de Mayo de 1849 en la Tesorería Particular de los fondos de la Penitenciaría del Estado," document 4029, Mariano Riva Palacio Archives (MRPA), Benson Latin American Collection (BLAC), hereafter MRPA, BLAC, and Ramón de la Sierra to Mariano Riva Palacio, 6 June 1857, document 6635, MRPA, BLAC.

24. See Mariano Navarro to Mariano Riva Palacio, 8 June 1850, document 4268, MRPA, BLAC.

25. In *Punishment and Modern Society*, David Garland (1990: 136) suggests that Michel Foucault interpreted this change in the technology of punishment as evidence of "a deeper change in the character of justice itself." See also Foucault (1978).

26. The contrast attempts to illuminate a difference between the perception of crim-

inality by Mexico's classical liberals and the later understandings of the country's positivist criminologists. In mid nineteenth-century Mexico, liberals in the classic mold suggested that crime was not innate, but by the later years of the century this understanding had been eroded by the influence of positivism whose adherents saw criminal traits as innate and immutable. This interpretation is derived from Piccato (2001) and Speckman Guerra (2002). Positivism's subversion of classical liberal penology only appears when the death penalty is in focus. Carlos Aguirre and Ricardo Salvatore (1996) suggest that positivism doubted the reformation of the criminal but neither they nor their contributor on Mexico Robert Buffington recognize the implications of this shift for the retention of capital punishment. See Buffington (1996: 169–93).

27.　The relationship between prisons and the death penalty means that the latter should not be studied in isolation from the former. I thank Austin Sarat for mentioning this insight at the 2003 Law and Society Association meeting in Pittsburgh.

28.　Laurence Rohlfes (1978) has suggested that the death penalty fell out of favor with judges in the late nineteenth century, as they no longer pronounced capital sentences upon defendants. There is little empirical evidence to back up this claim, however, meaning that this claim should be treated as a hypothesis for further investigation. Unfortunately, Mexico's judicial archives are in a formidable state of disrepair).

References

Aguirre, Carlos, and Ricardo Salvatore, eds. (1996) *The Birth of the Penitentiary in Latin America: Essays on Criminology, Prison Reform, and Social Control, 1830–1940*. Austin, TX: University of Texas Press.

Altamirano, Estevan (1856) "La abolición de la pena de muerte," *La Nación*, 31 August 2–3.

Attorney General of Texas (2000) *Magistrate's Guide to the Vienna Convention on Consular Notifications*. Austin, TX: Office of the Attorney General.

Avena and Other Mexican Nationals (Mexico vs. United States) (2004) International Court of Justice, judgment of March 31. http://www.icj-cij.org/icjwww/idocket/imus/imusframe.htm.

Banner, Stuart (2002) *The Death Penalty: An American History*. Cambridge, MA: Harvard University Press.

Beccaria, Cesare (1995) *On Crimes and Punishments and Other Writings*. Edited by Richard Bellamy and translated by Richard Davies. Cambridge: Cambridge University Press.

Benitez, José María, and Antonio Campos de la Vega (1849) *Solicitud que los ciudadanos Dr. José María Benitez y Antonio Campos de la Vega elevaron al gobierno del Estado im-*

petrando permiso para construir con oblaciones voluntarias una cárcel penitenciaría en esta ciudad. Licencia concedida para este fin por el mismo gobierno y bases a que debe subjetarse la Junta Directiva de la Obra. Toluca: Imprenta de Juan Quijano.

Buffington, Robert M. (1996) "Revolutionary Reform: Capitalist Development, Prison Reform, and Executive Power in Mexico," in C. Aguirre and R. Salvatore, eds., *The Birth of the Penitentiary in Latin America: Essays on Criminology, Prison Reform, and Social Control, 1830–1940.* Austin, TX: University of Texas Press.

Canales, Claudia (2001) *El poeta, el marques y el asesino: historia de un caso judicial.* Mexico: Ediciones Era.

Cano de Ocampo, Guadalupe (1991) *Ensayos de derecho penal. I. Diez mil pesos por un homicidio. II Ultimo case de aplicación de la pena de muerte en Tabasco.* Villahermosa: Universidad Juárez de Ciencias Sociales.

Covo, Jacqueline (1983) *Las ideas de la Reforma en México, 1855–1861.* Mexico: UNAM.

Cumplido, Ignacio (1840) *Manifestación al público del impresor ciudadano Ignacio Cumplido, con motivo de su prisión verificada el 21 de octubre de 1840.* Mexico: Imprenta de Ignacio Cumplido.

Cumplido, Ignacio (1841) *El Mosáico Mexicano* vol. 5. Mexico: Imprenta de Ignacio Cumplido.

Diccionario Porrúa de historia, biografía y geografía de México 6th ed. (1995) Mexico: Editorial Porrúa.

El 16 de Setiembre en la capital del Estado de México (1851). Toluca: Imprenta del Instituto Literario.

Foucault, Michel (1978) *Discipline and Punish: The Birth of the Prison.* Translated by Alan Sheridan. New York: Vintage.

Garland, David (1990) *Punishment and Modern Society: A Study in Social Theory.* Chicago: Chicago University Press.

Gutiérrez Estrada, José María (1840) *Carta dirigida al Excmo. Señor presidente de la república, sobre la necesidad de buscar en una convención el posible remedio de los males que aquejan a la república, y opiniones acerca del mismo asunto.* Mexico: Imprenta de Ignacio Cumplido.

Hood, Roger G. (2002) *The Death Penalty: A World-Wide Perspective* 3rd rev. and update ed. Oxford: Clarendon Press.

Masur, Louis P. (1989) *Rites of Execution: Capital Punishment and the Transformation of American Culture, 1776–1865.* Oxford: Oxford University Press.

McGowan, Gerald (1978) *Prensa y poder, 1857–1857. La revolución de Ayutla. El Congreso Constituyente.* Mexico: El Colegio de México.

Meade, Everard (2005) "Anatomies of Justice and Chaos: Capital Punishment and the Public in Mexico, 1917–1960." Unpublished Ph.D. thesis, University of Chicago.

Pérez Salas Cantú, María Esther (2003) "Los secretos de una empresa exitosa: la imprenta de Ignacio Cumplido," in Laura Suárez de la Torre, ed., *Constructores de un cambio cultural: impresores-editores y libreros en la ciudad de México, 1830–1855*. Mexico: Instituto Mora.

Piccato, Pablo (2001) *City of Suspects: Crime in Mexico City, 1900–1931*. Durham, NC: Duke University Press.

Pickett, Carroll, with Carlton Stowers (2002) *Within These Walls: Memoirs of a Death House Chaplain*. New York: St. Martin's Press.

Portilla, Anselmo de la (1858) *México en 1856 y 1857. Gobierno del General Comonfort*. New York: S. Hallet.

Primitivo Martínez to Mariano Riva Palacio, 16 March 1850, document 3974, Mariano Riva Palacio Archives (MRPA), Benson Latin American Collection (BLAC), General Libraries, University of Texas at Austin.

Riva Palacio, Vicente, and Manuel Payno (1989) *El libro rojo*. Prologue by Carlos Montemayor. Mexico: CONACULTA.

Rohlfes, Laurence J. (1978) *Police and Penal Correction in Mexico City, 1876–1910*. Unpublished Ph.D. thesis, Tulane University.

Sinkin, Richard (1979) *The Mexican Reform, 1855–1876. A Study in Liberal Nation-Building*. Austin, TX: Institute of Latin American Studies.

Speckman Guerra, Elisa (2002) *Crímen y castigo. Legislación penal, interpretaciones de la criminalidad y administración de justicia, Ciudad de México, 1872–1910*. Mexico: El Colegio de México/UNAM.

Tena Ramírez, Felipe (1964) *Leyes fundamentales de México, 1808–1864* 2nd ed. Mexico: Editorial Porrúa.

Thompson, E. P. (1963) *The Making of the English Working Class*. New York: Vintage Books.

Timmons, Patrick (2002a) "Mexican National's Execution Criticized," *The Daily Texan*, 7 August.

Timmons, Patrick (2002b) "Execution Proceeds Despite Opposition," *The Daily Texan*, 15 August.

Timmons, Patrick (2002c) "Mexican National Set to Die Tonight," *The Daily Texan*, 14 August.

Timmons, Patrick (2002d) "Mexican President Cancels Trip," *The Daily Texan*, 16 August.

Timmons, Patrick (2002e) "Fox's Trip Cancellation Questioned," *The Daily Texan*, 26 August.

Timmons, Patrick (2002f) "La abogada de Mexico: Sandra Babcock's Battle Against the Death Penalty," *Texas Observer*, 25 October.

Timmons, Patrick (2004) "The Politics of Punishment and War: Law's Violence during the Mexican Reform, circa 1840–1870." Unpublished Ph.D. thesis, University of Texas at Austin.

United Nations Conference on Consular Relations (1963) *Official Records*. New York: United Nations.

Vázquez, Carmen (1981) *Santa Anna y la encrucijada del Estado: la dictadura, 1853–1855.* Mexico. Cumbre.

Villegas Revueltas, Silvestre (1996) "Francisco Zarco," in Antonia Pi-Suñer Llorens, ed., *En busca de un discurso integrador de la nación, 1848–1884.* Mexico: Universidad Nacional Autónoma de México.

Villegas Revueltas, Silvestre (1997) *El liberalismo moderado en México, 1852–1864.* Mexico: UNAM.

Zarco, Francisco (1856) "Editorial: Crónica parlamentaria," *El Siglo Diez y Nueve*, 26 August: 1.

Zarco, Francisco (1857) "Las leyes y las costumbres. La federación y la libertad de cultos," *El Siglo Diez y Nueve* 30 November 1857. Reprinted in F. Zarco (1989–94) *Obras completas* vol. 8. Mexico: Fundación Jorge L. Tamayo.

Zarco, Francisco (1956) *Historia del Congreso Constituyente [1856–1857].* Mexico: El Colegio de México.

Zarco, Francisco (1957) *Actas oficiales y minutario de decretos del congreso extraordinario constituyente de 1856–1857.* Mexico: El Colegio de México.

CHAPTER FOUR

The Cultural Lives of Capital Punishment
in the United States

JUDITH RANDLE

Punishments as Cultural Artefacts

In the final chapters of *Punishment and Modern Society: A Study in Social Theory*, David Garland concludes that penal theorists expend far too much energy explicating punishment's "hidden social rationality" while neglecting the fundamental role "culture" plays in shaping penal practices (Garland 1990: 193). According to Garland, while penal practices may contain functionalist principles, as sociologists would have it, the psychic constitutions of the individuals equally determine the particular penal practices which manifest in a particular society. For Garland, "culture" is the set of meanings and significances which a human group has assigned to "differences which occur in the natural and social worlds" (200, footnote omitted); it consists of "mentalities," which are the concepts and categories humans use to organize the surrounding environment, and "sensibilities," which are the affects that accompany these mentalities, above all of which is a society's threshold for graphic displays of violence (195).

> These cultural patterns structure the ways in which we think about criminals, providing intellectual frameworks (whether scientific or religious or commonsensical) through which we see these individuals, understand their motivations, and dispose of them as cases. Cultural patterns also structure the ways in which we feel about offenders. . . . The intensity of punishments, the means which are used to inflict pain, and the forms of suffering which are allowed in penal institutions are determined . . . by reference to current mores and sensibilities. (195)

Put simply, how a society makes sense of the surrounding world shapes how it punishes by providing definitions of crime, shaping how citizens feel about crime and criminals, and regulating the psychic boundaries of what are considered to be appropriate punishments. Regarding the latter, Garland stresses that cultural patterns determine what punishments a society will *not* mete out. In particular, corporal punishment has all but been abandoned in the West as such violence offends the psychic repression of instinctual urges that has constituted the process of "civilization" (see also Elias 2000).

Garland also argues that as a social institution, punishment not only reflects but also produces the society and culture within which it is embedded. Penal practices create and re-create mentalities and sensibilities, and mentalities and sensibilities surrounding crime and punishment form the basic moral paradigm of a society that essentially shapes the behavior of its people. Other scholars have asserted and explored the wider implication of Garland's analysis that punishment is not simply a legally sanctioned response to a crime, a means to an end (or more recently, simply an end in itself [see Simon and Feeley 1995]) contained within the boundaries of legal institutions and legal actors. Rather, punishment—and more broadly, the law—inhabits all domains of social life, both within everyday practices and as symbols, representations, images, and messages that are transmitted throughout a culture (Steiner, Bowers, and Sarat 1999). Law and punishment, therefore, are "cultural artefacts."

The American Death Penalty as Cultural Artefact

The United States's unique position among Western nations in its retention of capital punishment poses "cultural" questions such as what within American society keeps the death penalty alive, how capital punishment resides within the American psyche, and what the death penalty does for and to American culture. Capital punishment is, to use Garland's expression, a "cultural artefact"; its practice in the United States reflects and reproduces contemporary American requisites and constructions of the social world, and yet its livelihood exists beyond its actual imposition to occupy deeper social and personal significances. In this section I attempt to uncover these significances.

Any attempt to understand capital punishment in America must begin with its presence as an outlier among Western states. Internationally, over half of the world's countries have abolished the death penalty since World War II on the premises that it violates modern standards of civility as well as a basic right to life with which all people are endowed (Amnesty International 2002; Hood 2001).[1]

The history of the U.S. death penalty helps elucidate its modern existence as well as demonstrates the role broader cultural understandings have always played in U.S. capital punishment. Although capital punishment survives in America, it has always been cloaked in ambiguity as Americans have debated the propriety of such a drastic and historically torturous penalty in a modern, free state. But rather than abolishing the death penalty the United States has generally allayed these misgivings by searching for progressively "civilized" ways of carrying out executions (Banner 2002; Bedau 1997; Denno 1998; Haney 1995, 1997a, 1997b; Lynch 2000; Masur 1989) alongside affording capital defendants greater legal protections to ensure that only those truly deserving of death will be executed (e.g., Acker and Lanier 1998; Steiker and Steiker 1998). Hence, hanging was initially adopted in the 1600s as an alternative to corporal torture; the electric chair came in the 1800s as a quicker, less painful, and more successful (that is, a more certain) alternative to hanging; and the twentieth century witnessed the births of the gas chamber and lethal injection. Meanwhile, Supreme Court decisions in the twentieth century guaranteed capital defendants attorneys (*Powell v. Alabama*, 1932; *Hamilton v. Alabama*, 1961; *Gideon v. Wainwright*, 1963), substantially narrowed the number and type of offenses for which defendants could face the death penalty (e.g., *Gregg v. Georgia*, 1976; *Coker v. Georgia*, 1977; *Eberheart v. Georgia*, 1977), mandated a separate penalty trial during which the defendant could present background factors to mitigate his or her actions (*Gregg*), granted convicted defendants mandatory appeals (*Gregg*), and created guidelines for jurors to follow when choosing between life and death (*Gregg*).

Several aspects of these historic changes are pertinent to Garland's thesis and the death penalty's "cultural" nature. First, these changes in capital punishment reflect broader changes in Western societies during the Enlightenment and post-Enlightenment period. While rises in industrialization, capitalism, standards of living, and rational ways of thinking were "modernizing" and "civilizing" society in general, similar "evolutionary" changes were occurring in the administration of capital punishment. As the threshold for violence lowered, respect for the condemned's comfort increased, executions were made more palpable for the audience, and the legal restrictions on the death penalty increased. Additionally, executions (as well as punishments in general) were eventually moved out of the public sphere to behind prison walls, to be witnessed only by a select few (Banner 2002; Foucault 1977; Haney 1997a). Second, the medicalization of executions and the recent provision of "super due process" rights to capital defendants are arguably two aspects of today's death penalty that make it amenable to modern sensibilities. While lethal injection, the predominant method of execution in the United States, can be compared to the merciful method of euthanizing animals, legal protections garner a feeling of security that only those defendants truly deserving of death will be executed and that even the deserving will have several chances to avoid death (Haney 1995, 1997b).

In addition to the creation of a regulated, "painless" execution process suitable to a "civilized" society, modern understandings of crime and criminals allow the death penalty to flourish in the United States. Despite our apparent need for "civilized" executions, support for the death penalty appears to be partly fueled by a "nasty underbelly" (Lynch 2000: 26) of fear, vengeance, and disregard for criminal lives which is generated by mediated and politicized images of remorseless, incorrigible, mutant evildoers. Such images construct offenders as society's catch-all enemy, and ever-increasingly harsh punishments as both deserved and the only answer to the "crime problem" (Beckett 1997; Beckett and Sasson 2000; Haney 1995, 1997a, 1997b).[2] Similarly, it has been argued that since the 1960s politicians have redefined the criminal justice system as a contributor to the crime problem due to "loopholes" created by due process rights (Beckett 1997; Beckett and Sasson 2000; Bowers, Sandys, and Steiner 1999; Bowers and Steiner 1999; Haney 1995, 1998; Steiner et al. 1999). Surveys consistently show that the majority of U.S. citizens lack faith in the criminal justice system and that these attitudes are related to support for harsher punishments (Beckett 1997; Beckett and Sasson 2000; Haney 1998); calls for harsher punishments seem to be in part a reaction to the perceived failure of the criminal justice system to carry out its duties. Even former capital jurors have admitted to voting to impose the death penalty on a defendant *even though they believed he did not deserve it* because they feared that had they not he would have been paroled from prison after a relatively short period of time (Steiner et al. 1999).

Support for the death penalty also resonates with the historically individualistic paradigm through which Americans perceive human behavior (Haney
1998; Poveda 2000). Partly a derivative of the "American Dream"—that success
comes to anyone who works hard enough—upon which the United States was
founded, and partly due to decontextualized, merciless portrayals of criminals—particularly within law and order politics—Americans believe that criminality stems from individual evil rather than societal conditions that shape individual choices. Capital violence in particular is perceived as the product of
"free and unencumbered evil choices, on the one hand, and monstrously de-
ranged, defective traits on the on the other" (Haney 1998: 352–53). Similarly,
Garland writes that "[i]n its standard tropes and rhetorical invocations, this political discourse relies upon an archaic criminology of the criminal type, the
alien other" which depicts lawbreakers "in ways that are barely human, their
conduct being essentialized as 'evil' or 'wicked' beyond all human understanding" (2001: 135). Thus, for many the death penalty is a "moral imperative": the
only warranted treatment of Evils who prey on Innocents (Lynch 2002).

Finally in tracing the origins of the current "punishment wave" (Haney
1997a), Garland finds that "the policies that have emerged over the last few
decades [including increased use of the death penalty] have their roots in a new
collective experience of crime and insecurity, an experience that is itself structured by the distinctive social, economic, and cultural arrangements of late
modernity" (2001: 139). Beyond the independent contributions of mass media
representations and political rhetoric, Garland identifies structural changes to
society in the last half of the twentieth century which have heightened feelings
of personal insecurity and rendered Americans more responsive to emotional
stratagems, such as real increases in susceptibility to criminal victimization,
structural unemployment, and political instability. The outcome of all these
forces has been that crime has become "an organizing principle of everyday
life" (Garland 2001: 106), not simply a material event but also an acute awareness and emotional status deeply embedded within American consciousness.

Taken all together, the contemporary concept of "capital punishment" which
exists in the minds of today's Americans tends not to evoke the disgust modern
citizens associate with former methods of execution and/or the killing of another human being, while it does contain the comfort—or fear—that condemned inmates will spend many years on death row awaiting appeals and that
many in fact will not be executed. Executions are perceived as carefully regu-

lated, relatively painless undertakings that remain within the boundaries of physical violence, while at the same time satisfying the more primitive, repressed urges of fear and vengeance associated with modern understandings of criminality, and modern insecurity more generally. Consistent with Garland's "cultural artefact" thesis, this version of capital punishment is the product of mentalities and sensibilities that in turn shape what Americans desire, and deem appropriate, as punishment.

America's Death Penalties

Civilization and Regional Identity

As I have shown, America's death penalty has been fundamentally fashioned by the opposition or uneasiness which surrounds it, supporting Garland's assertion that "[p]enal policy is . . . a rich and flexible tradition which has always contained within itself a number of competing themes and elements, principles and counter-principles" (1990: 7). Specifically, Garland addresses how "civilization," as it applies to both penality and culture generally, is a *relational* concept and process, defined and practiced in opposition to that which is defined as "uncivilized": "To say that a penalty is or is not 'civilized' is to measure it against the sensibilities which modern Westerners recognize as their own. 'Civilization' is a generic term conveying a fundamental distinction between the self-conscious refinement of feeling to which modern Western society lays claim, and the harsher, more primitive ways attributed to other peoples" (Garland 1990: 215).

Indeed, recent research has begun to uncover these so-called identity politics involved in European nations' abandonment of capital punishment (Girling, in this volume) and, to a lesser extent, within the United States (Galliher, Koch, Keys, and Guess 2002). In the next sections I show that while antigallows sentiment and activity cannot be dismissed as simple deviations from the norm, neither can the geographical locations from which they have originated be ignored. Regional and conceptual fragmentation have always characterized capital punishment in the United States and, more importantly, have always informed each other. I argue that state analyses reveal sharp historical divisions grounded in identity politics in regions of the United States remarkably similar to those which characterize today's U.S.-West divide, and which provide for capital punishment's divergent cultural lives in the United States.

Disparate Penalties

The tendency to discuss the American death penalty as a national phenomenon overlooks what is in fact a sundry of state policies and practices. Twelve
states and the District of Columbia presently prohibit capital punishment; of
the thirty-nine jurisdictions with capital punishment, two[3] currently have gov-
ernor-imposed moratoriums on executions, six qualify as de facto abolitionist
states,[4] and fourteen have executed five or fewer persons since 1976. The number of inmates on death row in capital punishment states ranges from two in
Wyoming to over six hundred in California, and is a poor predictor of execution rates—as of April 2002, Missouri had executed 57 of 156 persons sentenced
to death since 1976, while California had executed 10 of 744. States also differ on
the number of crimes classified as capital, the minimum age of eligibility for
capital punishment, how death sentences are decided, and the average length of
time prisoners spend on death row (see generally, www.deathpenaltyinfo.org).

Patterned divisions reach back to the founding of the United States and
most conspicuously form a South/non-South divide (Harries and Cheatwood
1997). On the simplest grounds, the Southern states have almost always been
more willing executioners than states in other regions in that they have had
more capital statutes, more death sentences, and more frequent executions. Following the American Revolution the northeastern colonies scaled back their
capital statutes to include only a handful of crimes—usually arson, treason, and
murder. In the coming decades most limited the death penalty to only murder
or murder and treason, and since then twenty-five non-Southern states have
abolished capital punishment at least temporarily within their borders. By contrast, only one Southern state has ever even experimented with abolition,[5]
Southern states retained capital punishment for an assortment of felonies (including some nonviolent) well into the twentieth century,[6] and executions have
become increasingly concentrated in the South over the last two hundred years
(Harries and Cheatwood 1997).

Equally significant in the South/non-South divide are two sets of historically
disparate policies that mark a uniquely Southern death penalty. First, antebellum Southern states had separate, harsher capital statutes for slaves and free
blacks that were absent from non-Southern states and which carried on in
spirit long after the Civil War (Bowers 1984). Prior to the Civil War, a general
rule among Southern states was that a slave could be put to death for any crime

for which a free white could receive three or more years in prison. The crime of rape received special racial attention in Southern states; in Virginia, for example, the rape of a white woman by any black man (free or slave) was a capital offense, while the rape of a black woman by a white man was punishable by ten to twenty years in prison. Further, emancipation did not save African Americans in the South from lopsided treatment at the gallows. Blacks were systematically excluded from sitting on capital juries, capital "trials" of black defendants often lasted less than an hour, and semi- and extra-legal lynchings of African Americans erupted throughout Southern states in the late nineteenth century and continued on in various waves into the 1940s.

Second, Southern states were slower than Northern states to adopt the changes in capital punishment outlined in the previous section. Overall, it is fair to say that the evolution of the death penalty really began as the evolution of the *Northern* death penalty. The arduous movements to abolish capital punishment which punctuated the mid-nineteenth and early twentieth centuries, and which were characterized by deliberate efforts to rid society and citizens' consciousnesses of the "hanging day" ritual, were virtually absent in the Southern states. As a consequence, Southern states lagged behind in their adoption of progressive legislation. Thus, while all Northern states had moved hangings out of town squares and into jail and prison yards by 1860, Southern states made no remarkable efforts at this until fully fifty years later (Bowers 1984). Similarly, to curb the public's "morbid curiosity," most Northern states during this time period passed legislation that gave state actors, rather than local sheriffs, jurisdiction over hangings, severely restricted the number and type of witnesses allowed at hangings, moved hangings from daylight to early morning hours (usually dawn), and prohibited the press from reporting anything about an execution other than it happened (Madow 1995). Again, Southern states eventually adopted most of these measures, but much later than in the North. For example, Southern states started moving to state-imposed executions in 1910, fully two decades after most Northern states already had (Bowers 1984).

Identity Politics in Earlier Eras

Culture, Identity, and Symbolic Legislation

Some earlier efforts to explain the South/non-South divide have attributed a cultural lag in the civilizing process in Southern states (e.g., Zimring 2003).

That is, while citizens outside of the South have naturally abandoned violence as their societies have (also naturally) modernized, Southerners, for various reasons, have not so progressed and consequently have higher thresholds for violence; endorsement of capital punishment is seen as an extension of antiquated or unevolved Southern sensibilities.

Such accounts, and accounts of procedural civilization in Northern states, are at best incomplete because they leave out the relationship between Northern and Southern culture and policy—that is, Garland's analysis of "civilization."[7] "In its rhetorical use," Garland states, "the notion of 'civilized' . . . [is] a bland and ethnocentric way of distinguishing others from ourselves" (Garland 1990: 215). The self-other identity component of "civilization" appears central to lawmaking processes for which "civilization" is significant. "Symbolic legislation," as such processes have been called, designates "negative reference groups" as alleged counterexamples of civilized statehood, thereby highlighting the legislation's moral necessity and celebrating the superior moral quality of the state in which it passes. Capital punishment's function has long been noted as beyond concrete and into the symbolic realm at the personal level (Ellsworth and Ross 1983), and more recently, has been recognized at the state level. Gaylord and Galliher (1994) and Girling (in this volume) have shown that the abolition of capital punishment in the international arena now conveys the message of advancement and superiority in statehood. As a capital punishment state, the United States currently serves as a major negative reference group—a counterexample of uncivilized statehood highlighting the moral necessity of abolishing the death penalty—for those Western countries which have abandoned the death penalty (or are contemplating its abandonment) and receives regular international censure for retaining the "barbaric," "inhumane," and "uncivilized" practice of executing its citizens. Incorporating these so-called identity politics into Garland's framework, it can be said that among Western foreign elites capital punishment has been rendered archaic, offensive to modern sensibilities, and affiliated with inferior civilizations.

The South: "The Headquarters of Cruelty for the World"

Similar developments in the early U.S. death penalty experience are foreshadowed by two aspects of the early capital punishment reform/abolition movements. First, these movements were shrouded in similar claims of moral and civil advancement in light of the "barbarity" of the British (Davis 1957; Masur 1989). From the revolutionary period on, capital punishment was regularly cited as "indecent," "inhumane," "uncivilized," "disgraceful," "brutal," and so on, in contrast to Americans' self-proclamations as "benevolent," "humane," and "enlightened" people. Masur notes that a 1782 execution in New York prompted some prominent Americans to regard the executioners as "[c]ruel murderers" and the execution itself as an "instance of Barbarity . . . the most wanton, unprecedented and inhuman Murder that ever disgraced the arms of a civilized people" (1989: 57). Second, antebellum calls for reform existed within the larger antislavery movement, a movement which was fueled by Northerners' demoralization and demonization of Southern acts and peoples (Glenn 1983; Masur 1989). Within abolition[8] literature, "inhuman," "barbaric," and "uncivilized" were common terms used to describe both slaveholders and their acts, and these words appeared alongside graphic descriptions and photos of tortured, starved, and otherwise maltreated slaves, a strategy designed to further the antislavery cause by shocking and offending Northern readers (Clark 1995; Current 1976; Glenn 1983). Abolitionist writers painted pictures of masters not only as backward and relentlessly cruel but also as enjoying, relishing, the pain they caused African Americans.[9]

Slaveholding was not seen as the only manifestation of the master's immoral and sadistic character, and abolitionists attacked slaveholders "as generally of seared conscience, corrupt hearts, brutal wills, and darkened understanding" (cited in Ginzburg 1988: 64). This image of the primordial slave master was extended to all persons in the South, and many abolitionists assailed Southerners as generally ignorant, dishonest, and impious, and all of their ways as of a foregone era. According to one writer, for example, Southerners perversely "delighted in such barbarous sports as cockfighting and horse racing" (cited in Ginzburg 1988: 123). Ashamed by Southern states of affairs, another abolitionist concluded that they "exceed all the acts of cruelty of the civilized and barbarian world beside. Yes, the twelve slave states of America are the headquarters of cruelty for the world" (cited ibid.: 124). Implicit and explicit in these criticisms was the opposing image of the cultured Northerner: reticent, honest, hardworking, nothing like the "monsters of cruelty and crime" (110) down below.

Southern Degeneracy and Northern Anticapital Punishment Sentiment

In fact, Northern abolitionists took their techniques with them in the fight against capital punishment. Capital punishment was among the slated Southern practices and drew similarly disparaging depictions as it became associated with Southern "blood lust." Additionally, Southern lynchings—especially those sanctioned or ignored by Southern law enforcement—blurred the distinction between legal and extralegal violence, reinforced the connection between slavery and state killing, and outraged Northern "refined" sensibilities until for many Northerners (not only designated reformers), the entire capital punishment institution and concept became fundamentally linked to Southern degeneracy (Galliher et al. 2002; Guess 1999; McGonigal 1998; Stiff 1996).

Authors have recently begun to uncover the direct connection between Southern violence and Northern capital punishment reform, arguing that cultural elites (politicians, members of the news media, clergy) campaigned for reform on the grounds that it would elevate their state's moral standing in relation to Southern decadence and racism. Case studies of the four contiguous Northern states which have been without the death penalty since at least the early twentieth century have revealed that the construction of the South as a negative reference group was an essential component to their early abandonment of the practice (Galliher et al. 2002; Guess 1999; McGonigal 1998; Stiff 1996). Identity politics were largely cultivated in Northern newspapers, which were quick to report, and reprove, incidences of Southern violence and racism during reformist eras. According to Galliher et al., these "comparisons with the South provided a powerful symbol of . . . perceived cultural superiority" (2002: 96).

Southern lynchings played a central role in comparisons following the Civil War and throughout the Progressive Era, rousing endless condemnation of the Southern character and fueling Northern support for abolishing, or maintaining abolition of, capital punishment. For example, an editorial from a Massachusetts newspaper in response to an 1899 Georgia lynching accused the lynchers of "throw[ing] off the restraints and effects of many centuries of progress and stand[ing] forth in the naked savagery of the primitive man," ridiculed their "appetite for blood," and charged sardonically that "this, fellow-citizens, is the quality of the civilization of which you and we boast" (cited in Ginzburg 1988: 19–20).[10]

Likewise, procedural retentions, occasional Northern lynchings, and other public acts of violence incited deprecating comparisons with Southern racism and incivility among Northern elite. Commenting on a series of race riots in 1923 New York, for example, a Chicago race relations commissioner argued that they "had given northern cities a common shame with the communities of the south." The lynchings of three black men in Duluth, Minnesota, in 1920 equally provoked harsh criticism for the "disgrace [brought] upon this common-wealth" (Galliher et al. 2002: 95). In response to the lynchings, "leading newspa-pers throughout the North vilified residents of Duluth for having stained their city's good name and castigated them for being no better than Southern racists" (95).

Regional Assessments and Identity Politics Today

"Ask Most Americans about Capital Punishment . . ."

Today's death penalty concept comprises a regional component anchored in the continuing "anomaly" of the Southern death penalty among the rest of the United States and identity politics aimed at Southerners. On one level, this re-gional component surfaces as an (often uneasy) awareness that capital punish-ment is enjoyed disproportionately in the South. In fact, it is today difficult to come across a discussion in the United States about capital punishment that does not make some reference to Southern dominance, and perhaps abuse, of the practice. As writer Sara Kelly (1998) correctly remarks: "Ask most Americans about capital punishment and . . . you'll likely hear about the hype surrounding the Texas death machine, where 50 men and women have been executed since the beginning of 1997. Or about Florida, where a well-worn electric chair nick-named Old Sparky made the news when flames shot from a condemned man's head."

On another level, the South continues to be a reference point from which non-Southern state elites evaluate their own capital punishment policies and practices. For example, a recent article in the *Maryland Bar Journal* titled "The Florida Death Row Experience: Is It Coming to Maryland?" compared allegedly dire legal representation on the death rows of both Maryland and Florida, warning readers that Maryland would "soon need an effective legal services program for death-sentenced inmates in order to prevent our capital punishment system from becoming like Florida's" (Anonymous 1985: 10). Similarly, Kelly cautions that "the Deep South may soon cede its status as the cradle of capital punishment to Pennsylvania," home of "America's deadliest D.A." (Kelly 1998: 1).

Additionally, identity politics have been present in recent efforts to abolish and reinstate capital punishment in various states. McGonigal argues that Iowa's abolition of the death penalty in 1965 is partially indebted to one of Iowa's leading newspapers, the *Register*, which "devoted considerable space to the depiction of inhuman treatment of African Americans in the South" (1998: 35) in response to the civil rights movement during then-governor Harold Hughes's push to end the death penalty in 1964 and 1965. Selma, Alabama, was specifically targeted "as an example of an area without moral virtue" (19). Ultimately, according to McGonigal, the *Register* conveyed the message that "[b]y abolishing the death penalty, Iowans would be showing mercy and respect for all life in contrast to the frequent executions in the South. . . . Through daily coverage of Southern white violence and poverty-stricken conditions of Southern blacks the *Register* set Iowans apart from their neighbors in Dixie" (36–39).

Similarly, Galliher et al. (2002) argue that efforts to reinstate capital punishment in longtime abolitionist states are regularly defeated amid charges that the death penalty is a "remnant of barbarous times" and that restoration would be a "moral abomination" that would sully the state's record of civility. Racism and racial disparities in the administration of capital punishment, especially in Southern states (whether true or not), as well as the positive correlation between legal and extralegal violence in the South, also continue to be effective reminders among elites in abolitionist states that capital punishment is unjust, ineffective, and part of an earlier era (Galliher et al. 2002; McGonigal 1998).

For example, McGonigal (1998) reports that anti-Southern ideology helped curb reinstatement in Iowa during the 1995 legislative session. One state senator against reinstatement was reported as saying during legislative debates: "Look at the South. You don't think that race doesn't have anything to do with people in jail in the South?" (cited in McGonigal 1998: 59). Koch and Galliher

(1993) also report that leaders and newspapers in Michigan, the longest-running abolitionist state, regularly belittle Southerners and their death penalty. Recounting several 1981 articles in the *Detroit News* aimed at Alabama, Florida, and Virginia, they report that one "columnist pleaded: 'Put away those varnished electric chairs, human gas chambers and cyanide pellets, rifles aimed at hearts, and the latest device—the intravenous "humane" poisoning equipment which looks like it belongs in a Nazi death camp'" (cited in Koch and Galliher 1993: 332). Another mocked Florida demonstrators outside of the Jacksonville prison who purportedly chanted "go Sparky go" and "kill, kill, kill" during an execution (cited in Koch and Galliher 1993: 333–34). According to Koch and Galliher (1993: 335), Michiganites are proud of their status as "the first English-speaking government to abolish capital punishment" and quoted one Detroit attorney during 1985 reinstatement hearings as saying "Why kill when you [Michigan] have shown the world for 149 years that there is an alternative?"

Texas: America's Death Penalty Capital

As the visible leader of executions in the post-*Furman* era, Texas has emerged as particularly symbolic on all levels, withstanding incessant excoriation from all over the United States, even, it appears, from states that retain the death penalty. Modern America's death penalty concept includes statements such as Jesse Jackson's plea at a Pennsylvania rally in the summer of 2000 that "Texas has taken on serial killer proportions" and that "[t]hey're lining people up for the slaughtering pens" (Lewis 2000) and Texas rabbi Samuel Stahl's confessional, "Living in the Death Penalty Capital" (Stahl 1999), and Mike Tolson's (of the *Houston Chronicle*) disparaging article on Harris County's "silver needle society" (Tolson 2001). Likewise among academics the Texas death penalty has been named a "juggernaut . . . a massive inexorable force . . . that crushes whatever is in its path" (Hammel 2002: 107). Far from being mere mockings of "backward Southern Culture," these characterizations reflect and perpetuate the fundamental relational nature of the American capital punishment concept and, consequently, the regional division in actual executions; as in the *Maryland Bar Journal* article, Culver and Boyens (2002) argue that the frequency of executions in Texas has raised concern in California about its own death penalty and helps keep executions in that state at a bare minimum.

Conclusion

I have tried to provide evidence of the regional component embedded in the cultural life of American capital punishment outside of the South, which has been grounded in Garland's notion of "civilization" and supported by recent discussions surrounding identity politics and symbolic legislation. A brief historical examination revealed that while the burgeoning middle-class Northern virtue of self-control spawned disgust at the alleged backwardness of Southern ways, Northerners depended on this backwardness for their elevation. And despite today's comparatively tame execution ritual, the South continues to maintain a presence in the death penalty concept through its legacy of violence (legal and extralegal) and racism and persistently higher rate of executions than elsewhere in the United States. Discussions about the death penalty regularly include regional comparisons, and opponents of the death penalty continue to allege moral superiority in contrast to frequent, race-ridden Southern executions. Warnings that the Southern death penalty is "coming to a state near you" are now being sent. Thus the image of the barbaric Southerner and the cultured Northerner was and continues to be central to the American death penalty concept outside of the South.

Notes

1. Though, undoubtedly, many countries have done so out of political pressure from neighboring countries.

2. In fact, both the "crime problem" and the construction of offenders in this manner are relatively recent phenomena. Evidence of the impact of political rhetoric, television, and film on public attitudes toward crime and punishment has become a relatively mundane topic among researchers; it is broadly accepted that the public's recent outcry for severe sanctions such as increased use of the death penalty has had less to do with the actual incidences of criminal activity than the increased media attention given to these activities since the mid-1960s, the notion beginning in the 1970s that "nothing works" to rehabilitate offenders, and the explosion of crime-oriented television dramas and graphic horror movies over the last several decades (Austin and Irwin 2001; Beckett 1997; Beckett and Sasson 2000).

3. Former Illinois governor Ryan imposed a moratorium in 2000, and former Maryland governor Glendening imposed a moratorium in 2002.

4. Amnesty International defines de facto abolitionist states as those that have cap-

ital punishment statutes but have not carried out an execution in at least ten years (Amnesty International 2002). U.S. de facto abolitionist states and the year of their last execution are as follows, provided by the Death Penalty Information Center (http://www.deathpenaltyinfo.org/article.php?did=121&scid=11) unless otherwise noted: New Hampshire, 1939; Connecticut, 1960; Kansas, 1965; see http://www.kscadp.org/kansas_facts.html; New Jersey, 1963, New York, 1963, South Dakota, 1946; see http://www.state.sd.us/corrections/FAQ_Capital_Punishment.htm).

5. Tennessee abolished capital punishment from 1915 to 1919 (Galliher et al. 2002). It is also worthy of note that Tennessee can be considered a border state, not a full-fledged Southern state.

6. As of January 1972, the following nonlethal felonies were capital offenses in Southern and border states: arson (Arkansas, Georgia, North Carolina, and Virginia); burglary (Alabama, Kentucky, North Carolina, and Virginia); robbery (Alabama, Georgia, Kentucky, Mississippi, Missouri, Oklahoma, Tennessee, Texas, and Virginia); rape (Alabama, Arkansas, Florida, Georgia, Kentucky, Louisiana, Maryland, North Carolina, Oklahoma, Tennessee, Texas, and Virginia); attempted rape (Virginia); possession or use of a sawed-off shotgun in the commission of any crime of violence (Virginia); entering a bank with intent to commit larceny while armed with a dangerous weapon (Virginia); machine-gunning (Florida). By contrast, the following non-Southern, nonborder states retained nonlethal felonies as capital offenses as of January 1972: Arizona (robbery); Nevada (rape). See Bowers (1984).

7. This is not to say that what I present entirely completes the picture of disparate capital punishment policies and practices across the United States. Galliher and his colleagues (2002) and Guess (1999) have shown convincingly that explaining individual state policy demands attention to each state's individual history. Another important criticism of this perspective is that non-Southerners were still savagely killing off Native Americans while criticizing Southerners.

8. Although the bare terms "abolition" and "abolitionist" have been extended to discussions of the anti–death penalty movement, in this context I retain its original meaning referring only to slavery.

9. According to Clark (1995), some of Northern newspapers' favorite techniques were to reprint Southern ads for missing slaves with mangled body parts, scars, and deformities; excerpts from discriminatory and punitive legal codes; and stories of sexual assaults against women.

10. Comments such as these were very common in Northern newspapers. Ginzberg (1988) offers an outstanding collection of Northern reactions to Southern lynchings.

References

Acker, James, and Charles Lanier (1998) "Beyond Human Ability? The Rise and Fall of Death Penalty Legislation," in J. Acker, R. Bohm, and Ch. Lanier, eds., *America's Experiment with Capital Punishment: Reflections on the Past, Present, and Future of the Ultimate Penal Sanction.* Durham, NC: Carolina Academic Press.

Amnesty International (2002) "Facts and Figures on the Death Penalty," http://www.amnesty.org (accessed 9 June 2004).

Anonymous (1985) "The Florida Death Row Experience: Is It Coming to Maryland?," 18 *Maryland Bar Journal* 8.

Austin, James, and John Irwin (2001) *It's about Time: America's Imprisonment Binge* (3rd ed.). Belmont, CA: Wadsworth.

Banner, Stuart (2002) *The Death Penalty: An American History.* Cambridge: Harvard University Press.

Beckett, Katherine (1997) *Making Crime Pay: Law and Order in Contemporary American Politics.* New York: Oxford University Press.

Beckett, Katherine, and Theodore Sasson (2000) *The Politics of Injustice: Crime and Punishment in America.* Thousand Oaks, CA: Pine Forge Press.

Bedau, Hugo Adam (1997) "Background and Developments," in H. A. Bedau, ed., *The Death Penalty in America.* New York: Oxford University Press.

Bowers, William (1984). *Legal Homicide: Death as Punishment in America, 1864–1982.* Boston: Northeastern University Press.

Bowers, William, Marla Sandys, and Benjamin Steiner (1999) "Foreclosed Impartiality in Capital Sentencing: Juror's Predispositions, Guilt-Trial Experience, and Premature Decision Making," 77 *Texas Law Review* 1476–557.

Bowers, William, and Benjamin Steiner (1999) "Death by Default: An Empirical Demonstration of False and Forced Choices in Capital Sentencing," 77 *Texas Law Review* 605–717.

Clark, Elizabeth (1995) "The Sacred Rights of the Weak: Pain, Sympathy, and the Culture of Individual Rights in Antebellum America," 82 *Journal of American History* 463–93.

Coker v. Georgia (1977) 433 U.S. 584.

Culver, John, and Chantel Boyens (2002) "Political Cycles of Life and Death: Capital Punishment as Public Policy in California," 65 *Albany Law Review* 991–1015.

Current, Richard (1976) "Tarheels and Badgers: A Comparative History of Their Reputations," 42 *Journal of Southern History* 3–30.

Davis, David (1957) "The Movement to Abolish Capital Punishment in America, 1787–1861," 63 *American Historical Review* 23–46.

Denno, Deborah (1998) "Execution and the Forgotten Eighth Amendment," in James

Acker, Robert Bohm, and Charles Lanier, eds., *America's Experiment with Capital Punishment: Reflections on the Past, Present, and Future of the Ultimate Penal Sanction*. Durham, NC: Carolina Academic Press.

Eberheart v. Georgia (1977) 433 U.S. 917.

Elias, Norbert (2000) *The Civilizing Process: Sociogenic and Psychogenic Investigations* (rev. ed.). Oxford: Blackwell Publishers.

Ellsworth, Phoebe C., and L. Ross (1983) "Public Opinion and Capital Punishment: A Close Examination of the Views of Abolitionists and Retentionists," 29 *Crime and Delinquency* 116–69.

Foucault, Michel (1977) *Discipline and Punish: The Birth of the Prison*. New York: Pantheon.

Galliher, John, Larry Koch, David Keys, and Teresa Guess (2002) *America without the Death Penalty: States Leading the Way*. Boston: Northeastern University Press.

Garland, David (1990) *Punishment and Modern Society: A Study in Social Theory*. Chicago: University of Chicago Press.

Garland, David (2001) *The Culture of Control. Crime and Social Order in Contemporary Society*. Chicago: University of Chicago Press.

Gaylord, Mark, and John Galliher (1994) "Death Penalty Politics and Symbolic Law in Hong Kong," 22 *International Journal of the Sociology of Law* 19–37.

Gideon v. Wainwright (1963) 372 U.S. 335.

Ginzburg, Ralph (1988) *100 Years of Lynchings*. Baltimore: Black Classic Press.

Glenn, Myra (1983) "The Naval Reform Campaign against Flogging: A Case Study in Changing Attitudes toward Corporal Punishment, 1830–1850," 35 *American Quarterly* 408–25.

Gregg v. Georgia (1976) 428 U.S. 153.

Guess, Teresa (1999) "Ritual Action and Death Penalty Abolition: A Case Study." Unpublished Ph.D. dissertation, University of Missouri, Columbia.

Hamilton v. Alabama (1961) 368 U.S. 52.

Hammel, Andrew (2002) "Jousting with the Juggernaut," in D. Dow and M. Dow, eds., *Machinery of Death: The Reality of America's Death Penalty Regime*. New York: Routledge.

Haney, Craig (1995) "The Social Context of Capital Murder: Social Histories and the Logic of Mitigation," 35 *Santa Clara Law Review* 547–609.

Haney, Craig (1997a) "Psychological Secrecy and the Death Penalty: Observations in the 'Mere Extinguishments of Life'," 16 *Studies in Law, Politics, and Society* 3–69.

Haney, Craig (1997b) "Violence and the Capital Jury: Mechanisms of Moral Disengagement and the Impulse to Condemn to Death," 49 *Stanford Law Review* 1447–86.

Haney, Craig (1998) "Mitigation and the Study of Lives," in J. R. Acker, R. M. Bohm, and

C. S. Lanier eds., *America's Experiment with Capital Punishment: Reflections on the Past, Present, and Future of the Ultimate Penal Sanction*. Durham, NC: Carolina Academic Press.

Harries, Keith, and David Cheatwood (1997) *The Geography of Execution: The Capital Punishment Quagmire in America*. New York: Rowman & Littlefield Publishers.

Hood, Roger (2001) "Capital Punishment: A Global Perspective," 3 *Punishment and Society* 331–54.

Kelly, Sara (1998) "Waiting to Die: The Madness of Life on Pennsylvania's Death Row," *Salon* http://www.salon.com/feature/1998/09/cov_15feature.html.

Koch, Larry, and John Galliher (1993) "Michigan's Continuing Abolition of the Death Penalty and the Conceptual Components of Symbolic Legislation," 2 *Social and Legal Studies,* 323–46.

Lewis, Kate (2000) "Protestors Take Attention Away from Convention," *Indiana Daily Student,* 3 August, http://idsnews.com/news/2000.08.03/region/2000.08.03.protesters.html (accessed 9 June 2004).

Lynch, Mona (2000) "The Disposal of Inmate #85271: Notes on a Routine Execution," 20 *Studies in Law, Politics, and Society* 3–34.

Lynch, Mona (2002) "Capital Punishment as Moral Imperative: Pro-Death-Penalty Discourse on the Internet," 4 *Punishment and Society* 213–36.

Madow, Michael (1995) "Forbidden Spectacle: Executions, the Public, and the Press in Nineteenth Century New York," 43 *Buffalo Law Review,* 461–562.

Masur, Lois (1989) *Rites of Execution: Capital Punishment and the Transformation of American Culture, 1776–1865*. New York: Oxford University Press.

McGonigal, Kate (1998) "Abolition of Capital Punishment in Iowa: Structural Foundations and Triggering Events." Unpublished M.A. thesis, University of Missouri, Columbia.

Poveda, Anthony (2000) "American Exceptionalism and the Death Penalty," 27 *Social Justice* 252–67.

Powell v. Alabama (1932) 287 U.S. 45.

Simon, Jonathan, and Malcolm Feeley (1995) "True Crime: The New Penology and Public Discourse on Crime," in Th. G. Blomberg and S. Cohen, eds., *Punishment and Social Control: Essays in Honor of Sheldon Messinger*. New York: Aldine De Gruyter.

Stahl, Samuel (1999) "Living in the Death Penalty Capital," http://www.bethelsa.org/be_s0507.htm (accessed 9 June 2004).

Steiner, Benjamin, William Bowers, and Austin Sarat (1999) "Folk Knowledge as Legal Action: Death Penalty Judgments and the Tenet of Early Release in a Culture of Mistrust and Punitiveness," 33 *Law and Society Review* 461–508.

Steiker, Carol, and John Steiker (1998) "Judicial Developments in Capital Punishment Law," in James Acker, Robert Bohm, and Charles Lanier, eds., *America's Experiment* with *Clapital Punishment: Reflections on the Past, Present, and Future of the Ultimate Penal Sanction*. Durham, NC: Carolina Academic Press.

Stiff, Katherine (1996) "Un-American Activities in Minnesota: The Continuing Abolition of the Death Penalty." Unpublished M.A. thesis, University of Missouri, Columbia.

Tolson, Mike (2001). "A Deadly Distinction." *Houston Chronicle*, 5 February

Zimring, Franklin E. (2003) *The Contradictions of American Capital Punishment*. Oxford: Oxford University Press.

CHAPTER FIVE

European Identity and the Mission Against the Death Penalty in the United States

EVI GIRLING

The pursuit and successes of the abolition of the death penalty in European politics and culture in the latter half of the twentieth century stand in forlorn juxtaposition with what may be taken to be the main developments in crime control and criminal justice (e.g., Garland 2001; Pratt 2002). Yet whereas the continuing survival of the death penalty in all its archaic, ostentatious, decivilizing, and dyscivilizing resonance constitutes an intellectual puzzle, the processes through which in certain cultural and political contexts such survival or retreat remains effectively beyond political will or imagination have not merited much academic attention—the death of the death penalty was indeed "a death foretold."

There are a number of important contributions documenting the political tide against the death penalty on an international level (e.g., Hood 2002; Schabas 1997; Hodgkinson and Rutherford 1996). These contributions chart the state of affairs and the history of abolitionism in international politics and conjecture as to the possible futures and tactics for successful abolition. Another more recent strand of research has refocused on "the cultural uses of the death penalty" (Garland 2002; Sarat 1999, 2001; Lynch 2002; Kaufman-Osborne 2002) in the United States. This chapter argues that the cultural uses of the death penalty extend beyond the countries firmly in its grip. Europe's stance on the death penalty and the mobilization of its "virtual" citizens to actively pursue the abolition of the death penalty worldwide have captured the imagination of American abolitionists who seek to understand the lessons that the success of the European abolitionist movement holds for America (Zimring 2003). This discussion seeks to go beyond the instrumental question of what lessons European abolitionist politics hold for the United States and other pro–death penalty states and aims to explore the embeddedness of the anti–death penalty position in specifically European symbolic practices and discourses. The focus is on the cultural uses of the death penalty in Europe, which has come to proclaim itself a death penalty–free zone. What are the cultural uses of this ostentatious abolitionism?

The constitution of the reflexive self has played a central role in the concerns of the sociology of punishment (from Foucault to Elias). Penal cultures "hold out specific conceptions of subjectivity and they authorise specific forms of individual identity [defining] notions of what it is to be a person[,] what kinds of persons there are[,] and how such persons and their subjectivities are to be understood" (Garland 1990: 268). Penality thus "provides a basic model for our understanding of other people and for our understanding of ourselves" (ibid.). Penal narratives are both about deviant others and about the not-so-often discussed condition of the "punisher." It is the condition of the punisher that captures the "European" (however elusive and fragile that term may be) community of sentiment—of people who imagine and feel things together (see Appadurai 1990, 1996). European narratives on the death penalty ponder precisely on the punisher's position—the historical inevitability of this position and the paradox of the continuing practice of the death penalty by "cognate others" (e.g., the United States). Christie seems to write both as a criminologist and as a European when, in reflecting on the practice of the death penalty in the United States, he notes: "I am of course also represented by what happens in the USA. It is in a way also part of me that cultural relatives find it acceptable to do such things to so many fellow citizens" (1993: 186).

This chapter seeks to explore the relationship between penal identity and European identity (or what has been called "the engineering of the European soul").[1] This European penal identity has a cosmopolitan disposition and "extend[s] the field of relevance and mutuality [to] embrace distant others as symbolically significant" (Tomlinson 1999: 207). The very vocal European "acknowledgment" (see Cohen 2001) of the death penalty as a moral suffering to be eradicated from the face of the earth is a relatively recent development. It was only in the 1990s when all the core members of the European Union (EU) had abolished the death penalty from their books after a transition from declining use to abolition that a very vocal and evangelical European voice gained prominence on the international stage (see below and also Zimring 2003). Through the last decade of the twentieth century it became increasingly apparent that Europe had ceased to be a "bystander" on the death penalty. Suddenly, the fact that the death penalty was being carried out in other parts of the globe had political and moral implications for Europe.[2] These were not practices in foreign lands, but the people involved were "significant others." How are we to make sense of this erosion of implicatory denial (see Cohen 2001)? In this chapter I examine the links between European narratives of identity and the subjectivities that the current global spectacle and international debate on the present and future of the death penalty help constitute.

Imagining Europe: Europe as a Death Penalty–Free Zone

Much of the international discourse about the fates of capital punishment and about international penal law more generally involves a penal Europe being imagined—an imaginary which has become what has been called "idée forcée" in global penal politics (see Manners 2002, Manners and Whitman 2003). The Council of Europe, the European Union, and their member states have played a very important role in bringing about what has been described as an international sea change in political activity against the death penalty (see Grant 1998), with many of the United Nations proposed resolutions and memoranda concerning the death penalty sponsored by the European Union. The abolitionist movement has become a central plank of European Union policy and international relations (Manners 2002; Manners and Whitman 2003).

The political history of the abolitionist movement in Europe is usually traced in official publications to the very inception of the European institutions in 1943 when the Council of Europe sought to "unite Europe around the shared principles of the rule of law, respect for human rights and pluralist democracy" (Council of Europe 2001b: 7). The European Convention on Human Rights was adopted in 1950 and aimed to act as "a safeguard for all those who find themselves in the territory of Europe" (ibid.). The right to life was the first substantive article, but it was sometime later that the Council of Europe sought to abolish the death penalty. The placing of the abolition of the death penalty at the very moment of the inception of the Council of Europe asserts its perceived position as an essential part of a common heritage and intellectual tradition (see also Council of Europe 2001a). This narrative is repeated relentlessly in European Union and Council of Europe publications and Web sites and has become the "myth of creation" of a European community of sentiment.

Throughout the 1960s increasing numbers of Western European countries abolished the use of the death penalty. In the early phases of the abolition of the death penalty in Europe each European country had its own debates about the death penalty and each country abolished it afresh (see Zimring 2003). As Zimring (2003) observed, this was a period of change without a specifically "European-wide" discourse on abolition. In subsequent decades, however, the death penalty position was declared "not to have a place in a civilized society" (Council of Europe 2001b: 8) and the Parliamentary Assembly drafted Protocol No. 6 to the European Convention on Human Rights which abolished the death penalty in peacetime. Since 1994 one of the conditions for new states to join the Council of Europe was the immediate institution of a moratorium on executions and a commitment to sign and ratify Protocol No. 6 within one to three years. To be part of the European political and cultural fold countries also have to be admitted (and socialized) into a European "community of sentiment" (Appadurai 1996). They have to imagine a death penalty–free continent and feel the horrors of the death penalty together. The European Parliamentary Assembly engaged in sustained campaigning to change public sensibilities in aspiring members and to prod politicians to take the first "courageous steps" toward abolition. The abolitionist discourse gained a higher profile during the last years of the twentieth century where it was brought again to the forefront of European political discourse, albeit on a transnational level.

The turn of the millennium also marked the fiftieth anniversary of the European Convention on Human Rights—the Council of Europe—and proved a symbolic watershed in European abolitionist politics. The Council of Europe and the European Parliament declared Europe's aspiration to celebrate the new millennium as a death penalty–free continent (Council of Europe 1999: 1). Europe as an imagined collective space was defined and promoted by "abhorrence" of the death penalty. After this declaration of a time for work against the practice of the death penalty anywhere in the world, the Council of Europe stepped up its efforts to persuade both aspiring member states and "rogue states" with observer status (the United States and Japan) to abandon this practice.

There were repeated and much publicized pleas (both in the form of demarches and press releases) from the European Commission, the European Parliament, and the EU presidency to the U.S. government and state governors to abolish capital punishment, or failing that, to limit its application in certain cases. These pleas were repeated whenever an execution was due to take place. Death rows were visited by European Union and Council of Europe officials and other European politicians as well as representatives from the European branches of non-governmental human rights, anti–death penalty and religious groups. Several individuals on death row received widespread publicity in the year 2000 (i.e., Juan Raul Garza and Derek Rocco Barnabei). In the case of Barnabei the European Parliament President Nicole Fontaine expressed a "European" bewilderment in an open letter to the people of the United States stating that "Europeans represented by the Parliament cannot understand why the United States is the only major democratic state in the world that carries out the death penalty" (cited in Krause 2000). The persistent publicity surrounding these campaigns was described by those on the receiving end as "a generalized assault on capital punishment by many in this country and foreign countries" (Gwin 2000).

Alongside these political interventions there was a deepening of European grassroots involvement against the practice of the death penalty in the United States. Europe has very well-organized and networked anti–death penalty organizations such as Amnesty International, Hands Off Cain, Together Against the Death Penalty, and the Catholic Movement of the Sant'Egidio. These organizations initiated the Moratorium 2000 campaign which collected 3.2 million signatures presented to the UN in April 2001 to support the UN call for a worldwide moratorium on executions as a step toward ending capital punishment. In June 2001 the first World Congress against the death penalty (organized by the then newly formed French Organization Ensemble Contre la Peine du Mort [Together Against the Death Penalty]) took place in the very home and heart of European institutions—the Council of Europe and the European Parliament buildings. The Congress brought together activists from around Europe along with representatives from the United States, Japan, Russia, and other "target" states. The Congress received extensive backing from both the Council of Europe Parliamentary Assembly (which housed the conference) and the European Parliament. The European Union and the Council of Europe called a special rare joint session of heads of member states to "Solemnly call for a moratorium on the death penalty." This bringing together of the Council of Europe (what has been called the "conscience" of Europe) with its executive and democratic branch affirmed the position of the death penalty in the ideoscape (Appadurai 1990) of the European Union. On the final day of the Congress thousands of demonstrators from all over Europe filled the streets of Strasbourg chanting and displaying placards against the death penalty practice in the United States.

The momentum gained by the 2000 campaigns has not come to an abrupt end. The Italian-based organization Comunità di Sant'Egidio, with the endorsement of the World Coalition against the Death Penalty and Ensemble Contre le Pein du Mort, has launched a World Day against the Death Penalty. The first World Day against the Death Penalty was marked in October 2002 and has now become an annual event in the abolitionist calendar. It features cultural events, vigils, and special ceremonies around key monuments in several European towns and cities.

Europe as a death penalty–free zone has been fiercely protected, even casting its shadows and threatening international co-operation in the war against terror since 2001. EU countries have consistently refused sharing intelligence or extraditing suspects to the United States unless assurances were received that the death penalty would not be imposed. The reporting of the European position on the death penalty has thus become a permanent and unremarked upon feature of the now frequent news reports on requests for the extradition of terrorist subjects to the United States.

The imagining of Europe as a death penalty–free zone therefore takes the form of many collective acts of imagining and collective witnessing (Van Ham 2001). The European Union and the Council of Europe have gradually introduced symbols of Europe's identity (i.e., the flag, the European anthem, etc.). This is an attempt to cultivate what Michael Billig (1995) has called a banal nationalism (or in this instance "europeanism") by inscribing a consciousness of the European Union in public practice and in the everyday lives of its citizens. The "anti–death penalty position," the position of ostentatious abolitionism is such an agent of European consciousness. As discussed above it is (extending

Billig's example) both the flag that is waved fervently[3] but also the flag that "hangs" almost unnoticed outside public buildings (Billig 1995: 38–39)—both a "European mission" and a habitual statement of a "european" position.

Narratives of European abolitionism unify the fates and sensibilities of people and institutions in Europe and claim a reformist and abolitionist penal identity. The narratives present the European position as a natural consequence of the shared values of a territorially and historically cogent community. Spatial cogency is achieved through the EU's frequent and proud declarations to be a death penalty–free zone. Historical cogency rests on a recounting of a primitive and uncivilized past which Europeans share (and which culminated in World War II) (see for example Council of Europe 2001b). The European present and its espousal of an abolitionist stance is presented to be a consequence of Europe's triumph over barbarity and a safeguard for a civilized future in which a death–penalty free world becomes one of Europe's success stories (ibid.). This is an eloquent and persuasive narrative of Europe's stance against the death penalty as a story of people (like the penal reformers of centuries past) "doing good." The European Union's vocal stance against the death penalty fits in with its pursuit of an international role as "promoter of norms"—what Manners (2002) has described as its establishment and entrenchment as a normative power in world politics. The international pursuit of the abolition of the death penalty can be seen as an example of the normative power of the EU (see Girling 2002; Manners 2002), the EU yielding power to define what passes for normal in world politics (Manners 2002). The very existence of the death penalty in the United States, China, Japan, and other jurisdictions in which it is still practiced has been pathologized (ibid.). Yet this was not an aberration to be ignored or to be gazed at as a bystander. The rest of this chapter seeks to explore the discourses of difference and affinity in the European witnessing of and intervention in the moral sufferings of the death penalty across the Atlantic.

Global Spectacles: Witnessing American Executions

America's death rows have increasingly become a global spectacle which "periodically explodes on the world screen" (Dudziak 2000: 50). Especially in the European media the campaign of accusation is "sustained, systematic, organized, and relentless" (Lacorne 2001).[4] Even though the death penalty cases get media attention all around Europe, in some countries like France and Italy the reporting is detailed and intense. The life stories of certain American death-row inmates such as Karla Faye Tucker, Betty Lou Beets, Gary Graham, Odell Barnes, and Mumia Abu-Jamal are thoroughly familiar to readers of French newspapers (ibid.).

George W. Bush's track record as the governor of Texas raised the stakes. He was described as "the world champion executioner" by former French Justice Minister Robert Badinter,[5] and a German Parliamentarian, told a *Washington Post* reporter all that she knew about George W. Bush: "just two things. He is the son of President Bush, and he has sent 150 people to their death in Texas, including the mentally ill" (ibid.). During President Bush's first visits to Europe in the early summer of 2001, the issue of the death penalty was raised by vociferous protesters, European media and European politicians (see Blinken 2001). "An identifiable villain in the White House"[6] made extensive headlines for the abolitionist cause in Europe, bringing unprecedented media scrutiny on Texas executions[7] during the presidential campaign.

The American death rows are not the only site of this global spectacle. Executions are also brought to and fought on European soil. In the first years of the twenty-first century the Colosseum in Rome has become a key symbolic site for European campaigners, bringing home the plight of those condemned to death. The monument to deadly spectacle was illuminated every time a death sentence was commuted anywhere in the world or when a country agreed to denounce the death penalty. Similar events have taken place in cities across Europe since 2002 to mark the World Day against the Death Penalty.

A Matter of Time: All Roads Lead to Abolition?

The European narrative of the inescapable, inevitable appeal of human rights—which necessitated the continuous acts of persuasion described above—may have provided a suitable mission for the European Union but was soon challenged by the global spectacles of capital punishment in the United States. The appeals to state governors and other U.S. officials seemed to fall on deaf ears. The European anti–death penalty organizations enjoy a good relationship with campaigners in the United States, many of whom attended the first World Congress against the Death Penalty but could neither save individual defendants from death row nor change the minds of American politicians.

Michel Taube's book entitled *Lettre ouverte aux Américains pour l'abolition de la peine de mort* (Open Letter to the American People for the Abolition of the Death Penalty) is an impassioned plea to Americans for the abolition of the death penalty, reminding them of the shared values and traditions between the United States, the French, and Europe. The very existence and prevalence of the practice in the United States and the failure of what the Europeans thought would be the inescapable appeal of human rights needed to be explained, to be made sense of. Time yet again (see Neumann [1999]) provided for the European narratives a useful medium through which the difference between the United States and Europe could be articulated. If the death penalty belonged to the past then so did the United States—"In European eyes, America is still a barbaric country, a Wild West that does not know how to police its population and control its judges and sheriffs" (Lacorne 2001: 51).

America's "obsession" with the death penalty was presented as barbarous and primitive. Lacorne described how one French anthropologist offered a cosmological explanation for America's "taste" for the death penalty. "Facing the threat of destruction of their social order, modern Americans, like the Aztecs, are terrified by the prospect of an end to the current cosmic cycle. Only the deaths of countless human beings can generate enough energy to counter the danger" (2001: 52).

This setting of the United States as "out of present," locked in pasts that other countries have left behind, is reinforced by another set of commentaries. These are frequent references to the positioning of the United States with other countries which resist the abolition of the death penalty (e.g., China, Iran, Saudi Arabia, Nigeria). These are societies which are themselves presented to be caught up in time warps—of communism, of third world continents, and of Islamic fundamentalism. Yet in the European pleas and interventions to the United States there is still a discernible feeling that "America is only a kind of Europe gone adrift" (Cebrian 1999: 41), an America which, as is reiterated in every letter and every attempt at persuasion (see for example Taube's open letter), belongs because of its democratic credentials, its culture, and history in the company of "civilized" nations.

Moisi has argued that in gazing toward America "Europeans see themselves.

As individuals, Europeans may be as divided on the issue of death penalty as Americans are, but as a group they cannot accept that the self-proclaimed leader of the civilized world considers the death penalty a normal procedure, left to the sovereign decision of its individual states" (Moisi 2001: 150).

The American reaction to Benetton's "We, on Death Row" campaign which was launched in January 2000 and which featured portraits of death row prisoners (see Girling 2004 and Kraidy and Goeddertz 2002) on some level, as Sarat (2001) has argued, exposes the naivety of "old abolitionist strategies." As I discuss elsewhere (Girling 2004) U.S. citizens refused to call those on the posters and death row "we" and had to look away and efface every trace of the campaign under the condemning eye of the Europeans.

The narrative of inevitable and ultimately consensual progress toward abolition, this folk theory of civilizational abolition, is both fragile and contested. As researchers and commentators have pointed out time and again there remains a base of public support for the death penalty even in the very heart of a "death penalty–free zone" (see Zimring 2003 and Sarat and Boulanger in this volume). In such a context the continuing practice of the death penalty by "cognate others" is troubling for European abolitionists. The future that the Council of Europe and the European Parliament had so painstakingly imagined and guarded—a "civilized future with civilized sanctions"—may not be inevitable after all.

Discourses of Belonging and Citizenship: "Finding One's Self in the Territory of Europe"

Central to European grassroots involvement are the high-profile cases of individuals on death row. Individual cases have captured the imagination of residents of one or other of the member states. Through them "Europe" lives on death row and articulates its right to intervene. This right to intervene goes beyond traditional definitions of citizenship (defined in political terms—such as a matter of membership, obligations, and rights) set out by legal definitions of membership. What is accorded to those condemned to death in the United States is a more informal definition of belonging to / membership in a European community—a form of cultural citizenship (see Stevenson 1999).

These legal provisions for the protection of foreigners facing the death penalty are in the form of legal bars to U.S. extraditions and the Vienna Convention which governs the protection of the rights of foreign nationals on death row (Grant 1998). European Union member countries have been firm in refusing to send prisoners to the United States if there is a risk that they will be charged with a capital offence unless assurances are received that an alternative sentence will be given. Those (Europeans and others) who find themselves in the territory of Europe are fairly well protected against the application of the death penalty in the United States. The protection of "Europeans" who find themselves in the United States and charged with a capital offence is however much more limited. The Vienna Convention enables foreign governments to ensure the safety and fair treatment of their citizens abroad. According to the Convention the consuls provide a "cultural bridge" and help foreign nationals "navigate" hostile, complex, and unfamiliar legal system (see Grant 1998). But who is a citizen or who is a foreigner in a legal system? In the following examples I very briefly discuss three cases which challenged traditional discourses of citizenship, foreignness, and belonging.

The LaGrand brothers were born in Germany of a German mother but had spent their adult life in the United States so there were no cultural or linguistic barriers in their defense. They had not been offered consular advice contrary to the Vienna Convention for the Protection of Foreign Nationals and their execution caused outrage in Germany. In its attempt to save them from execution Germany put forward an argument which claimed that the U.S. system was prejudiced against the poor and therefore the LaGrand brothers (despite their cultural competence) needed the help of an outsider to navigate it (Socolovsky 2000).[8]

Two further instances and claims of citizenship that extend its legal definitions appear in the case of Derek Rocco Barnabei and Joseph O'Dell. Barnabei was the son of an Italian immigrant to the United States but he was not an Italian citizen himself. His death sentence prompted protests by the Italian Olympic team during the opening ceremonies of the Sydney Games in 2000, demonstrations in many Italian towns against the death penalty and calls for clemency by Italian politicians. Web pages were dedicated to saving his life and even in 2005, about 5 years since his execution, there is still a steady trickle of messages from ordinary Italians reflecting on his fate. President Nicole Fontaine of the European Parliament stated that Barnabei's case had "given rise to particularly strong reactions in Europe because there were . . . doubts about his guilt and because, while he is an American citizen, his family originally came from Italy" (cited in Fleishman 2000). The region of Tuscany was a particularly vocal and passionate supporter of his case with ordinary citizens and the local church getting involved in the case.[9] During the first World Congress against the Death Penalty a speaker from Tuscany (Angelo Passaleva, then vice-president of the Tuscany region) remembered the case of Barnabei as a crucial time in the consolidation of the region's sentiment against the death penalty. The language he used to describe the feelings of the Tuscan residents toward Barnabei resurrects another discourse of citizenship and belonging to Europe. The Tuscans, he said, remembered those generations who were forced to emigrate to make their fortunes. They had no choice but to move away from Tuscany which was one of the first places to abolish the death penalty to a country in which their economic misfortune would decades and centuries later prove fatal for their children. Such discourse of belonging could encompass any American of European decent.

The third case is that of Joseph O'Dell who was declared after death to be an honorary citizen of Palermo. There was never any suggestion that O'Dell had Italian links and yet his case became the focus of another high profile, passionate, and poignant European stand against the death penalty. On the day of his execution, as a mark of national mourning, flags were lowered in Palermo and Italians observed a minute's silence. After his execution his body was flown to Palermo and he was buried in a local cemetery (described by Fleishman [2000]—an American journalist—as "reserved for dukes and mafia bosses"). On his tombstone he was described as an honorary citizen of Palermo: "Joseph R. O'Dell 3rd, beloved husband of Lori Urs O'Dell, honorary citizen of Palermo, killed by Virginia, U.S.A., in a merciless and brutal justice system" (cited in Fleishman 2000).

These examples present an interesting juxtaposition between narratives of belonging to Europe and vulnerability to the practice of the death penalty in the United States. In the case of the LaGrand brothers they did not need the consul's help to navigate a foreign culture, but they were still "foreigners" in the American criminal justice system by virtue of their poverty.

The fate of Barnabei brings to the fore the interconnectedness and vulnerability of our globalized world—an interconnectedness that is cast both across space (Barnabei's family has links with Tuscany) and also across time and weaves the story of a fate from which Barnabei could not have escaped. His family had to leave Italy, which is now a safe haven, for an uncertain and precarious future for their children across the Atlantic. Joseph R. O'Dell's honorary citizenship after his death makes him (albeit posthumously) an Italian executed by the United States. The Italians may have been unsuccessful in their attempts to keep O'Dell alive, but after his death they claimed him as one of their own.

Conclusion

I have shown the ways in which the mediascape and ideoscape (Appadurai 1990) of European identity have enabled a "time for work" against the death penalty and tried to chart some of the ways in which "Europeans" extend "the field of relevance of mutuality to embrace a sense of distant others as symbolically 'significant others'" (Tomlinson 1999: 207).

This struggle over the death penalty could indeed be about what Huntingdon (1996) called a "clash of civilizations," of cultural identities. One of the themes of European Commission discourse about European culture has been a sense of vulnerability to dangerous and contaminating foreign influences— what has been described as "fear of Americanization" (see Shore 2000: 52). The "fear of Americanization" is also a motif of Europe's opposition to the death penalty, but beyond what is in some way a catch phrase of cultural politics this "fear of Americanization" is also (in the case of the death penalty) a reflection on other possible "punishing" relationships which "provide(s) a basic model for our understanding of other people and for our understanding of ourselves" (Garland 1990: 298).

This "clash of civilizations" often leads commentators into discussions of pessimistic futures of conflict, war, and fortressing. Yet this "clash of penal civilizations" which underscores the moral tales about the death penalty may also have safeguarded a regional future from "decivilizing episodes" in the field of criminal justice—a field in which the passions and vagaries of the particular moment seem to be the order of the day. The cultural identities at stake are about the "way we punish." The European Parliament and the Council of Europe have symbolically enshrined the death penalty in both domestic and foreign policy. In this pursuit a "european" anti–death penalty position is part of a "banal europeanism." It has not been my aim here to evaluate the effect of the European drive for abolition on the United States. American scholars have already begun to imagine the conditions and the kinds of abolitionist movements that trigger sea changes (and not just tinkering) with citizens' sensibilities (Zimring 2003; Sarat 2001; Kaufman-Osborn 2002). What the European campaigns do is to present "new narrative possibilities" (Sarat 2001: 250) about the death penalty on both the transnational and the global level—new mediascapes and ideoscapes (see Appadurai 1990) in which the death penalty will never again simply be a matter of national sovereignty. "We are all on death row."

Notes

I thank Christian Boulanger and Austin Sarat for their helpful comments, patience, and assistance during the draft preparation process. Any remaining errors are of course my own.

1. Telling compelling stories of "common cultural heritage" and creating a "European consciousness" has proven difficult in many respects (Delanty 1995; Shore 2000). In the European political arena, identity formation and culture building have become "explicit political objectives in the campaign to promote what EU officials call l'idée européene or 'European idea'" (Shore 2000: 26).

2. According to Cohen there are three kinds of denial. Literal denial maintains the position that this is not happening at all. This kind of denial would have been difficult to sustain as the death penalty was openly practiced and debated in most countries even though its "moral sufferings" may not be immediately apparent to onlookers. Interpretive denial maintains that what is happening has a different meaning to you than that apparent to others. For a number of years in European and International Covenants, the right to life was recognized as a human right, but the death penalty itself was not a violation of that right. What was happening was not state killing, something which should offend our democratic and civilized sensibilities, but "justice." In implicatory denial the facts are not denied—yes people do get killed by the state in the name of justice. In this case what is denied or minimized is the psychological, political, and moral implications of remaining a bystander—what happens in the United States and Japan for example has no implications for my psychological, political, and moral state.

3. The mission against the death penalty in part seems to answer the concerns which were being expressed in the 1990s about the general "lack" of a mission; what has been called a lack of a "shared sense of identity and destiny" (Leonard 1998: 22).

4. Given that it is still very difficult to find daily or weekly publications that "openly express a sense of European identity" (see Cebrian 1998), this consensus on the treat-

ment of the death penalty across different national publications is all the more important.

    5. Reported in the *Washington Post*, 18 December 2000.

    6. Chris Stalker—British Branch to Amnesty International. Interview. *Washington Post* 18 December 2000

    7. For example there were individual cases receiving widespread attention in Europe precisely because of their connection with George W. Bush, such as the execution of Johny Paul Penry in November 2000. John Paul Penry's execution also received publicity as a landmark execution—he was the 150th person to be executed in Bush's reign as governor.

    8. Germany maintains that in the United States, "poverty and inadequate counsel are . . . the two 'key variables' determining whether capital punishment is sought, imposed and carried out. . . . Indigent defendants, like the LaGrands, are most likely to have ineffective lawyers and thus are disproportionately likely to receive death sentences" (cited in Socolovsky 2000). Karl and Walter LaGrand were executed in 1999.

    9. Near the time of the execution the *Philadelphia Inquirer* pondered on the absurdity that "[his] execution will most likely warrant only a few paragraphs, maybe accompanied by a mug shot, in American newspapers. But, 6,000 miles away, in Italy, Barnabei is a cause celebre, portrayed as a martyr trapped in an American court system bent more on vengeance than compassion" (cited in Fleishman 2000).

References

America (2001) "Editorial: A Federal Execution," 184, no. 15 *America. The National Catholic Weekly* (5 July) http://www.americamagazine.org.

Appadurai, Arun (1990) "Disjuncture and Difference in the Global Cultural Economy," in Mike Featherstone, ed., *Global Culture: Nationalism, Globalisation and Modernity*. London: Sage.

Appadurai, Arun (1996) *Modernity at Large: Cultural Dimensions of Modernity*. London and Minneapolis: University of Minnesota Press.

Billig, Michael (1995) *Banal Nationalism*. London: Sage Publications.

Blinken, Anthony (2001) "The False Crisis over the Atlantic: With Friends Like This," 80 *Foreign Affairs* 35–49.

Cebrian, Juan Luis (1999) "The Media and European Identity," 16 *NPO: New Perspectives Quarterly* 39–42.

Christie, Nils (1993) *Crime Control as Industry*. London: Routledge.

Cohen, Stan (2001) *States of Denial*. Cambridge: Polity.

Council of Europe, Parliamentary Assembly (1999) "Europe: A Death Penalty Free Continent," Report by Committee on Legal Affairs and Human Rights Doc. 8340 http://assembly.coe.int/documents/adoptedtext/ta01/eres1253.htm (accessed 13 July 2004).

Council of Europe (2001a) "The Council of Europe and the Death Penalty: Death Is not Justice." Report by the Directorate General of Human Rights (December) http://www.coe.int/T/E/Human_rights/deathpen.pdf (accessed 4 June 2004).

Council of Europe (2001b) *The Death Penalty Abolition in Europe.* Strasbourg: Council of Europe Publishing.

Delanty, Gerard (1995) *Inventing Europe: Idea, Identity, Reality.* London: Macmillan.

Dudziak, Mary (2000) "Giving Capital Offense," 7 *Civilization* 50–54.

Fleishman, Jeffrey (2000) "Italians Fight U.S. Use of Death Penalty," *Philadelphia Inquirer* 20 August.

Garland, David (1990) *Punishment and Modern Society.* Oxford: Oxford University Press.

Garland, David (2001) *The Culture of Control; Crime and Social Order in Contemporary Society.* Oxford: Oxford University Press.

Garland, David (2002) "The Cultural Uses of Capital Punishment," 4 *Punishment and Society* 459–87.

Girling, Evi (2002) "'Wir im Todestrakt: Die Todesstrafe in Amerika im Blick der Europäer'" (We, on Death Row: Death Penalty in the US under the European Gaze), in C. Boulanger, V. Heyes, and P. Hanfling, eds., *Zur Aktualität der Todesstrafe. Interdisziplinäre und globale Perspektiven.* Berlin: Berlin Verlag Arno Spitz.

Girling, Evi (2004) "'Looking Death in the Face': The Benetton Death Penalty Campaign," 6 *Punishment and Society* 271–84.

Grant, S. (1998) "A Dialogue of the Deaf? New International Attitudes and the Death Penalty," 17 *Criminal Justice Ethics* 19–32.

Gwin, Paul (2000) "'End Execution' Campaign," 401 *Europe. Magazine of the European Union* 10–12.

Hodgkinson, Paul, and Andrew Rutherford (1996) *Capital Punishment: Global Issues and Prospects.* Winchester: Waterside Press.

Hood, Roger (2002) *The Death Penalty: A Worldwide Perspective.* 3rd ed. Oxford: Oxford University Press.

Huntingdon, Samuel (1996) *The Clash of Civilizations.* New York: Simon and Schuster.

Kaufman-Osborne, Timothy (2002) *From Noose to Needle: Capital Punishment and the Late Liberal State.* Ann Arbor, MI: University of Michigan Press.

Kraidy, Marwan M., and Tamara Goeddertz (2002) "Transnational Advertising and International Relations: US Press Discourses on the Benetton 'We on Death Row' campaign," 25 *Media, Culture and Society* 147–65.

Krause, Axel (2000) "Life versus death," 401 *Europe. Magazine of the European Union* 6–10.

Lacorne, Denis (2001) "The Barbaric Americans" 25 *Wilson Quarterly* 51–54.

Leonard, Mark (1998) "Europe; a Continent in Search of a Mission," 127 *New Statesman* 20–22.

Lynch, Mona (2002) "Capital Punishment as Moral Imperative: Pro-Death-Penalty Discourse on the Internet," 4 *Punishment and Society* 213–36.

Manners, Ian (2002) "Normative Power Europe: A Contradiction in Terms?," 40 *Journal of Common Market Studies* 235–58.

Manners, Ian, and Richard Whitman (2003) "The 'Difference Engine': Constructing and Representing the International Identity of the European Union," 10 *Journal of European Public Policy* 380–404.

Moisi, Dominique (2001) "The Real Crisis Over the Atlantic," 80 *Foreign Affairs* 149–54.

Newmann, Ivor (1999) *Uses of the Other: The East in European Identity Formation.* Manchester: Manchester University Press.

Pratt, John (2002) *Punishment and Civilization—Penal Tolerance and Intolerance in Modern Society.* London: Sage.

Sarat, Austin, ed. (1999) *The Killing State.* Oxford: Oxford University Press.

Sarat, Austin (2001) *When the State Kills: Capital Punishment and the American Condition.* Princeton, NJ: Princeton University Press.

Schabas, William (1997) *The Abolition of the Death Penalty in International Law.* Cambridge, UK: Cambridge University Press.

Shore, Chris (2000) *Building Europe: The Cultural Politics of European Integration.* London: Routledge.

Socolovsky, Jerome (2000) "Angered by Executions, Germany Criticizes U.S. Death Penalty at World Court," *Associated Press* (14 November).

Stevenson, Nick (1999) *The Transformation of the Media. Globalisation, Morality and Ethics.* London: Longman.

Taube, Michel (2000) *Lettre ouverte aux Américans pour l'abolition de la peine de mort.* Paris: L'ecart.

Tomlinson, John (1999) *Globalization and Culture.* Cambridge: Polity Press.

Zimring, Franklin (2003) *The Contradictions of American Capital Punishment.* Oxford: Oxford University Press.

CHAPTER SIX

Crime and Punishment / Self versus Other

The Cultural Life of Capital Punishment in European and American Film

LOUISE TYLER

> It is the nature of mythic symbolism to exaggerate, to read particulars as universals, to treat every conflict as Armageddon, in microcosm. The primary social and political function of the *extraordinary* violence myth is to sanction the *ordinary* violence of oppression and injustice, of brutalities casual or systematic, or the segregation, insult or humiliation of targeted groups.
>
> Richard Slotkin, *Gunfighter Nation*

Introduction

This chapter deals with the comparative cinematic cultural life of crime, punishment, and death, addressing the ways cinema regenerates culture and reinforces the socially appropriate methods of punishing those who transgress the norm. "Regeneration of culture" works through the repetition of symbols, ideals, and iconography within a particular cultural field, allowing them to reach a status of normalcy, and allowing the state to appropriate this way of thinking. The regeneration of culture is a myth-making enterprise. "The ultimate source of myth is the human mind itself, for man is essentially a myth-making animal. He naturally seeks to understand his world in order to control it, and his first act in compassing this end is an act of the mind or imagination" (Slotkin 1973: 7). It is the argument of this chapter that film is a cultural practice which generates, along with notions of just punishment, a mythology of *self* versus *other*, sharply delineating *good* from *evil*. In American cinematic reference, "self" is the idealized image we are encouraged to identify with, while "other" is the antitheses of that image. I argue that this does not hold true for European cinema. The "self" is more nebulous, making identification of self and other in its European form more difficult. The United States relies upon its cultural mythology to reinforce its current philosophy. This becomes problematic when it is realized that this mythology is replete with images of violence and justifications for violence. This justification takes the form of the good guy versus the bad, us versus them, self versus other; where we the self (the idealized image) are always in the right and they the other are punished for their transgression of the right. As Barker notes, "Violence is an arbitrary re-labeling of behaviors, and then also of representations of those behaviors, which in its very act of naming achieves a number of political ends. It excludes many actually harmful behaviors by those in power and authority" (2004). This further normalizes the dichotomy of self versus other, allowing a progression of increasingly violent behavior to be simplified to a process where state-sanctioned death is no longer a violent act but a justification and necessity to quell the violence of the other. The films selected for examination do not directly address the death penalty. They do, however, clearly illuminate how, through state-sanctioned violence, death is normalized as a reaction against the many and brutal transgressions of the easily identifiable other. State-sanctioned death becomes a necessity in order to "make the self safe." In *The Point of No Return* the state "saves" the heroine from death in order to use her as an instrument of death. This is *accepted* because it is the state who is directing against whom the violent action is perpetrated and therefore violence, state-sanctioned death is not seen as existing outside the parameters of a just society. In the American version of *The Vanishing*, evil is easily identifiable, lulling the viewer to not only identify with "the self" but accepting the ultimate death as inevitable and righteous.

In a 1999 American opinion poll, the three most oft-cited reasons in defense of capital punishment were: (1) to expiate particularly heinous crimes; (2) to satisfy the friends and family of the victims of these crimes; and (3) to deter the repetition of such crimes in the future (U.S. Department of Justice 1999). All of these reasons are mirrored in the justification of the use of violence as an end to crime in American films.

To borrow from and paraphrase David Garland, in this particular study punishment is taken to be a process whereby violators of an agreed-upon code of conduct are condemned and sanctioned in accordance to a specified category and procedure. "It involves discursive frameworks of authority and condemnation, ritual procedures of imposing punishment, a repertoire of penal sanctions, institutions and agencies for the enforcement of sanctions and a rhetoric of symbols, figures, and images by means of which the penal process is represented to its various audiences" (Garland 1990: 17). In accordance with this parameter, the process of punishment becomes escalated while the population becomes apathetic to the process, its only interest being the outcome, the elimination of the deviance through any means necessary. Movies that depict capital punishment show the ultimate necessity for those who violate authority. But since this is an argument that cultural regeneration of violence has produced an apathetic response to state-sanctioned violence, it is important to show how a violent response to transgressors is normalized and escalated until each progressive step arrives at the final outcome, apathy and acceptance of state-sanctioned death. Examining films that do not directly deal with the death penalty further illuminates how the myth of violence necessitates the need for an escalation of violence. Violence begets violence and the state in our happy ending mythology becomes the ultimate dispenser of violent actions.

We as a culture learn to accept state sanctioned death, through our introduction and close relationship to the death of the other through popular culture, specifically film. Film reifies the myth of a culture. This myth "appears to be built of three basic structural elements: a protagonist or hero, with whom the human audience is presumed to identify in some way; a universe in which the hero may act, which is presumably a reflection of the audience's conception of the world and the gods; and a narrative, in which the interaction of the hero and universe is described" (Slotkin 1973: 8). It is also a fixture of this universe that there exists "the other," that person who is the antithesis of the hero, the non-hero. The person is as distinguished as the hero, in that we identify him/her immediately by how he or she stands apart from the hero, embodying all the characteristics which are not present within the person of the hero, "the other." As Sarat (1995) noted, "What we know about the way law does death comes in the most highly mediated way as a rumor, a report, an account of the voiceless expression of the body of the condemned. Or it comes in images and representations made available to popular culture." It is through the hyperviolent death of the "other" that we as a culture slowly began to accept the state-mediated death of the "other." The person sentenced to death who we never knew and could not imagine knowing is the two-dimensional figure of our shadowy memories who most often takes shape in the form of our cultural representation of the "bad guy" For we are always asked and forced in the direction to identify with the "good guy," our ideal self; therefore, accepting the punishment of "the other" the "bad man." It is through this role as spectator both cinematically and as the observer of the functioning of state-sanctioned deaths that we find solace in the fact that for our benefit the state systematically carries out death sentences on those who have transgressed the law and were unable to find the lawyer to save their souls. The cinema and our cultural ideology restates that the good guys always prevail and that evil is always punished. We are so accustomed to this discourse that its imagery shapes our beliefs once we step from the cinema. It is not a causal relation but a normalizing relation. "[D]epictions of violent behavior are special: They invoke some of society's most central and guiding values, those which justify the use of force, illuminate the parameters of social order, and demarcate legitimate from illegitimate action" (Slocum 2000). Watching violence does not cause us to perpetrate violence; rather watching an idealized version of state and self allows us accept as "right" and normal processes we do not view and seldom come into contact with. State-sanctioned death is such a process.

Comparing Cinematic Representations of Crime, Punishment, and Death

Viewing these two sets of films *Le Femme Nikita/The Point of No Return* and *The Vanishing/The Vanishing* in their manifestations toward French, Dutch, and American culture will demonstrate the association we have as "self" and "other," as well as how the culture seeks to define and portray transgressor, heroes, crime, and punishment; always succumbing to the ultimate punishment, death. "In order to understand the fiction film, I must both 'take myself' for the character . . . and not take myself for him so that the fiction can be established as symbolic. Similarly, in order to understand the film, I must perceive the photographed object as absent, its photograph as present, and the presence of this absence as signifying" (Metz 1982: 259).

Good versus evil, crime and punishment, capturing and punishing the "bad guys" have all taken on mythic proportions in American iconography. The cultural life of capital punishment exists as an "extraordinary violence myth" and serves to sanction the nonordinary violence hidden under the rubric of justice. As David Garland (1990: 252) has argued, punishment is a set of signifying practices that "teaches, clarifies, dramatizes and authoritatively enacts some of the most basic moral-political categories and distinctions which help shape our moral universe." Our cinematic mythic world signifies certain ideals of good versus bad and in this symbolization naturalizes conceptions of punishment which exceed the bounds of a civilized nation. "Cultural forms create conditions of possibility, they expand the present by informing it with memories of the past and hopes for the future; but they also engender accommodation with prevailing power realities, separating art from life, and internalizing the dominant culture's norms and values as necessary and inevitable" (Lipsitz 2001: 16). Our cultural myths simplify the world into dualities of good versus bad, self versus other, where the bad guys are readily identifiable, deserving of punishment and we expect their demise to come before the final credits roll. American cinema naturalizes the idea of a violent end to those who transgress societal norms. The ideology of American cinema seeps into the conceptions of "real" life where reel life and real life play upon the images of one another. "Ideology is the invisible cement that holds the structure of society together" (Allen 1995: 11). American culture derives this ideology from its cultural icons, most significantly the American cinema. "Cinema is a sign system that produces meaning and in that respect could, like all other social or cultural productions be seen as a language" (Hayward 2000: 321). This language reifies our concepts of crime and punishment, good versus evil, and our concept of self and the other. The particular sign system of cinema when coupled with acts of law and order defines both subtly and overtly ways that are acceptable to punish. In doing so, this language of law and order reinforces the mythical distinction between "good" and "bad"; itself a reference to the difference between self and other. This dual distinction operating with and on itself makes state-sanctioned death sentences in the United States more acceptable because it is embedded within the myth of American culture—state identification of bad is never wrong and death is always referenced to "the other" (see also Munby 1999: 62).

American movies represent a multibillion-dollar-a-year business. The movies not only disseminate culture within the United States but also export particular cultural images. "[T]he real impact of popular culture, then, may not be the direct action it triggers but its power to shape attitudes and perceptions over the long run. . . . These messages have a collective effect, building upon and reconfiguring prior information, and in the end shaping each person's political identity" (Shea 1998: 4). This identity is often shaped in opposition to the other. We know who we are because we know who we are not. This dissemination of popular culture transgresses borders, but it appears to be only a unilateral transformation. American movies account for nearly 60 percent of box office receipts in France, and the figure is 80 percent for Europe as a whole; by contrast foreign-language films represent less than 1 percent of the U.S. box office total.

The films used in this analysis, European films which have been remade in the United States specifically for American audiences, exemplify this dichotomy. *La Femme Nikita* (1991) which was voted number-three best foreign movie of 1991 by the National Board of Review and number eleven on Landmark's Theater favorite foreign film poll, grossed $5,017,971 in the United States, although it was the second-highest grossing film in France; whereas *The Point of No Return* grossed $30,038,362 domestically and was considered a box-office failure. *The Vanishing,* the European version, was voted number two best foreign movie of 1991 by the National Board of Review. The American version of *The Vanishing* grossed $14,543,394 domestically, far outselling its European counterpart. (All numbers are from the Internet Movie Database, http://www.imdb.com/.)

These films were chosen because they comparatively exemplify the difference between self and other, crime and punishment in European and American cinematic products. These films also shape attitudes by crime and punishment via the route of replication. *La Femme Nikita* was remade into a Hong Kong action movie titled *Black Cat*, then remade again in the Hollywood version *The Point of No Return.* It was then disseminated to a broader audience by being remade as the popular cable series *La Femme Nikita. The Vanishing,* remade for American audiences as *The Vanishing,* was reproduced with the same director. The contextual representation of crime and punishment was altered to fit American audiences. *The Vanishing* can also claim genealogy in the television crime series *Without a Trace.* If reproduction is the sincerest form of flattery then both *Le Femme Nikita* and *The Vanishing* can claim to disseminate a particular cultural ideology far after their initial run in the theaters. It is, however, an American version of crime and punishment, self versus other, and not its European counterpart that is reproduced and naturalized. As a cultural set of images, and a pedagogical tool of proper response to crime and punishment, the cinematic image commands front row. Comparative examination of European releases and their Americanized versions sets the sight for production of the difference between self and other and the appropriate response to transgressors.

La Femme Nikita / The Point of No Return

La Femme Nikita, directed by Luc Besson (1991), and its Americanized counterpart *The Point of No Return,* directed by John Bedham (1993), exemplify the difference between self and other and its concurrent notions of crime and punishment. Although the camera angles and dialogue are at times identical, the marking of difference between self and other and the ways of responding to crime contain a nuanced difference. It begins with the marketing of the concepts. The movie posters establish agency (other) versus nonagency (self). The movie poster for *La Femme Nikita* (movie poster used for American distribution) is a visual hue of smoky blues, black, and red. In the middle of the poster horizontally placed is Nikita sitting on the floor, in stiletto heels, short tight black dress, pearls, her legs bent at the knee, holding a silver gun looking out of the frame. Her gaze at something unseen out of the frame "brings us closer to the role of spectator" (Metz 1982: 257). Underneath her name, Nikita, which is boldly displayed in red proclaims "Nikita A New Kind of Lethal Weapon." American audiences before entering the theater are positioned to be the gaze of the spectator, we are admonished from the arrival of the poster before we pay our money that she is dangerous, and this danger, while "wildly seductive and erotic," is a danger we need to view as spectator and not as self. Compare this to the movie poster for *Point of No Return* which literally pulls us into the position of Bridget Fonda. The poster is a composition of whites, reds, and black. Bridget Fonda is identified prominently across the top of the poster, she stands on the right side vertical, her back prominent, her head turned toward the viewer, a very large gun placed in her right arm crossed over her body. She is looking right at you. Inviting you into her world. The two most prominent visual cues are her face lit with eyes staring at the viewer and the gun. Next to her face is the caption: "The Government Gave Her a Choice. Death. Or Life as an Assassin. Now. There's No Turning Back." She is no longer "the lethal weapon" responsible for her actions. The government is responsible. So as spectators we are allowed to position ourselves as self as Bridget Fonda. We have been given a reprieve of the responsibility of our actions before we enter the theater. "[T]he spectator occupies the perceptual point of view of the camera upon the events of the film" (Metz 1982: 49). From the beginning of *La Femme Nikita* our viewing cues signify crime minus punishment, or punishments minus crime. We are cued to a "new kind of lethal weapon," a beautiful female holding a derringer, inviting us to be the spectator of her actions. Bridget Fonda invites the opposite. We are cued to both crime and punishment. We are invited to share the ordeal of Bridget Fonda (the female on the poster only being identified by her name not her character's), and we are absolved of guilt for the crime that has led to the punishment. We were given a choice by the government, the ultimate punishment "death or life as an assassin . . . now there is no turning back." Hence, since absolution is reserved for those with mitigating circumstances we are cued to the fact that this crime was undeserving of the ultimate punishment. Being unaccustomed to putting beautiful white females to death, our cinematic experience allows us to enter the theater comforted in the fact that this crime and punishment scenario is outside the paradigm which we are accustomed to (white female as perpetrator and executor of crime and punishment) while adhering to the standards which make us comfortable (the benevolent government, patriarchal enough to spare the beautiful white female, gave her a chance).

In *La Femme Nikita,* Nikita at the beginning of the film kills without compassion and conscience. Nikita and her friends enter a store after hours to steal. She in cold blood kills a police officer. She is caught, tried, and sentenced for the "willful murders" of her three friends and three law enforcement officers. The court rules: "In reply to the question of mitigating circumstances. The jury has replied in the negative. Therefore, the accused is sentenced according to article 304 . . . to life imprisonment. With a 30 year minimum before parole." After the sentencing, Nikita cries "Motherfuckers!" and is lead away kicking and screaming. She is next seen at night in a solitary cell confined by hand straps. Two gentlemen dressed as doctors prepare a vial. Nikita cries: "You can't do this. I don't want to go like this." And she slowly blacks out. Upon awakening she encounters the following situation:

> Bob: You died on Saturday at 5 pm. The prison doctor confirmed suicide from massive overdose of tranquilizers. You are buried . . . Row 8 Plot 30.
> Nikita: Mister, is this heaven here or not?
> Bob: No . . . but it could turn out to be. I work for the government. We've decided to give you another chance.
> Nikita: What for?
> Bob: To serve your country.
> Nikita: What if I don't want to?
> Bob: Plot 8 Row 30.

She is saved from this state sanctioned death/nondeath by the state and trained to become a killing machine for the state. She becomes "the vehicle through which patriarchal violence literally reproduces itself." It is after her indoctrination for the state, when she is assigned to kill for the state, that she begins to express remorse and is hesitant to kill. In the Americanized version *The Point of No Return* and the American cable series *La Femme Nikita* the difference is slowly mutated. Maggie in *PONR* has more regret for the killings she does for the state and is quicker to become distraught for each killing she perpetrates. Nikita in the television series is in fact wrongly accused of the crime she is said to have committed. In *Point of No Return* Maggie, the Nikita character Americanized, is a junkie, who with her gang of misfits robs a drugstore. The robbery goes wrong, the police show up, and Maggie shoots a police officer in the head. There is more emphasis in the American version on her culpability, since she is strung out on drugs. She is guilty of the crime but there are mitigating circumstances. Maggie is also sentenced to death and finds reprieve from the state. The state-sanctioned order to kill Maggie/Nikita is reasoned as acceptable in both films. The cultural difference is in who is allowed to be responsible for committing the crimes and how their punishment is enforced. In Nikita the spectator is asked to remain just that, a spectator. The other relegated to the role of observer of actions that are outside our realm of acceptance. In *The Point of No Return* we are asked to identify with the Nikita character after she has had all responsibility removed. We can comfortably be in the role of self because the self has been denied responsibility for her acts. Both women commit crimes and both are ostensibly punished for these crimes. Their "punishment," a reprieve from state-sanctioned death, includes the authority to commit murder for the state. These crimes, murder committed for the state, are not, however, considered crimes.

The Vanishing

The Vanishing represents how we are coded to identify the self versus the other and how this identification salves the idea of death being a just punishment for the other. Although there is never the threat of a state-sanctioned death arising in *The Vanishing,* a crime is committed and in the mutated American version the crime is punished by death. We as spectators and quasi-hero stand-in accept the fate of the "bad man" because we are coded to believe this is the only true ending. In synopsis *The Vanishing* is the story of a disappearance of a woman and her boyfriend's relentless search to find her and/or discover what happened.

The Dutch/French version of *The Vanishing* directed by George Gluizer first appeared in 1988. In the European version the transgressor is a college professor, Raymond Lenmore. He is a family man. Telling his wife, "I am perhaps the only French man who has known only one woman," establishing his place in our universe as a loyal husband. His normalcy is reinforced by the daily activities we often glimpse: he picks his daughter up from school, he attends the other daughter's volleyball games, and in his home the radio plays in the background to reassure us of the unremarkable environment which is his daily life. He is at first the self. The narrative scheme and camera angles provide the view of the world from his vantage point as well as the boyfriend's. The boyfriend, Rex Hoffman, exists as another part of the self. He is the man all men can identify with. He is seen as a man who balances himself with both good and bad traits. During their trip, he leaves his clearly frightened girlfriend, Saskia Wagter on the side of the road frantically searching through the car, crying out his name. We see Rex calmly walking away going for gas as in the background we hear her call his name. When he returns and she is not at the car, we clearly see that he is frantic with fear and worry. When he finds her he is remorseful. He professes the inability to know what to do in every situation, while proclaiming his love for her. He is everyman. He is Dutch but speaks French. He loves his girlfriend but is impatient with her. Rex Hoffman is the self most men and women can identify with without proclaiming ancestry in heroism.

Professor Raymond Lenmore kidnaps Saskia Wagter after she and her boyfriend have reconciled and decide to continue their vacation. After the kidnapping we see events as experienced by both Raymond Lenmore and Rex Hoffman. The acquaintance is never outside the realm of the believable. The boyfriend conducts an endless, tireless, three-year search in an attempt to find out what happened to his girlfriend. The professor continues with his daily life absent remorse and apprehension. Finally, the worlds intersect when the professor becomes fascinated with the boyfriend's search. The professor professes to admire the boyfriend's "perseverance" and agrees to meet with the boyfriend and divulge all information. The boyfriend, wanting to discover what happened to his girlfriend, agrees to the professor's demands. These demands are that if he truly wants to know, he experience exactly what she did at the hands of the professor. The boyfriend agrees, is drugged, and buried alive. In the final scene we see the horror on the boyfriend's face from his crypt underground. The fear and the pain both for his demise and for finally understanding what Saskia experienced. This scene is transposed with a view of the professor sitting 100 yards away surrounded by his family, the wife watering the garden, the girls frolicking about the professor, Raymond Lenmore sitting, thinking, getting away with a double homicide. A newspaper covering the story of Rex Hoffman's disappearance sits in the back of the professor's car. Two horrible crimes have been committed, perfect crimes in that the perpetrator had gotten away with both. The professor, as manifested by the final scene, is a visual representation of the devout family man. The viewer is asked to transpose her identification. Either identify with the self as manifested by Rex Hoffman and experience death, or identify with the self/other and experience how it is to inflict death and not suffer the retribution of society. If it is "through practices of punishment that cultural boundaries are drawn, that solidarity is created by marking difference between self and other through disidentification as much as imagined connection" (Boulanger and Sarat in this volume); then the marked difference between the two different vanishing(s) points to the different cultural perceptions and relations to punishment and crime. In the Dutch/French version it is possible to imagine a world where "evil" exists and is not or cannot be reprimanded by the state, a world where evil is not readily identifiable as a trait of the other through tics, idiosyncrasies, and speech patterns. In a telling scene a television commentator states, "In this crowded square in Arles, there is possibly a murderer. You see him without knowing. Simply another face in the crowd." The veracity of this statement is manifested when the Lenmore family, watching television together, is interrupted by a daughter exclaiming, "Look Papa it is us!" Meanwhile Raymond Lenmore sits passively and watches television. In this European version both good and bad coexist, and you cannot tell who is who without the inside view. Raymond Lenmore, explaining to Rex Hoffman why he felt the need to kill, gives two examples of abnormalcy camouflaged within society. In the first instance, describing his own particular case, he states, "A slight abnormality in my personality, not noticeable to those around me. In the medical dictionary you can find me under Sociopath." He has now fully become identified with the other, but he still remains the other with whom we are unknowingly acquainted daily. Here is a man who resembles self, can be self, but is not. His daughter calls him a hero when he saves a small child from drowning. Lemore's reply is, "Of course I am a hero. But you must watch out for heroes. A hero is capable of excess." This is the difference between the two cinematic cultures, the self and other are acquainted daily and their differentiation is not manifested with excess. The hero and the villain in European cinema are often the same. Punishment, therefore, particularly manifested as death to the transgressor of societal norms, is harder to imagine if the person is so easily mistaken for the self. It is within this realm of possibility to imagine oneself transgressing the law, or at the very least identifying the self with the transgressor. In American culture this anomaly cannot exist.

Paraphrasing Justice John Marshall's concurrence in *Furman v. Georgia*, the actions committed by the professor are ugly, vicious, and reprehensible. The question remains then, is death the only viable solution? In the European version the answer is no, for the perpetrator of the acts is never actually caught by the authorities and the "hero" dies at the hands of the villain. In the American version the answer is of course a resounding *yes*—the punishment of death is justice and justification, giving the "hero" peace and making the world a safer place.

In the American version of *The Vanishing* crime and punishment as mirrored by the self and other are Siamese twins. The American version, as well as the Dutch/French version, was directed by George Gluizer. It was released in 1993, starring Kiefer Sutherland as Jeff, the boyfriend, and Jeff Bridges as Barney, the chemistry professor. The basic storyline remains the same. Jeff and Diana Shaver (Sandra Bullock) make a stop at a rest area/gas station. As Jeff refuels the car Diana goes into the store for beer and never returns. As viewers we are placed in the position of Jeff, the frantic and loyal boyfriend. For three years we surmount a tireless search for Diana, eventually attempting to rebuild our lives with another woman; although it is patently clear we are still loyal to the missing Diana. After the passage of three years we are contacted by the chemistry professor, Barney, who informs us/Jeff that he is the one who kidnapped Diana three years ago and he will reveal her fate if Jeff agrees to experience what Diana experienced. Jeff agrees. In this version Jeff of course does not die. He is saved by his loyal Diana replacement, and in turn saves her from Barney. Both then administer retribution upon Barney for his crimes. Jeff is saved, Diana is avenged, and the "bad man" is given the ultimate punishment for his crimes, he dies at the hands of the self/hero and his trusty sidekick.

At the outset there are patently different marketing interpretations between the two versions. The European version has posters with a picture of Saskia shrouded by darkness with a slightly startled look on her face. She is enveloped by the darkness of night, yet she looms large in the forefront. She is the reason for, white female, coded with fear. She is the other whom we want to know, as opposed to the other seemingly enveloped by the darkness whom we know we should fear as she does. She is the one we want to protect, the fear being we may prove incapable of doing so. The poster marketing the American version of the movie contains a fractured picture of the other, Jeff Bridges. We know he is the other because of the way he is coded on the picture. Bridges is backlit, his face dominated by the slightly sinister grin he holds. His picture appears to have been torn and pieced back together. He is a broken man, mentally deficient, clearly the other, one who does stand out in the crowd. We are coded at the outset to set this person apart, that he is broken, not whole. He incites fear and distrust because that is the role of the other in American cinema. The other is the vestibule of fear, giving us a place and a reason for retribution. Since capital punishment, the most final of society's punishments, is almost always reserved

for the easily identifiable other, "the poor, the Negro and members of unpopu-
lar groups" (*Furman v. Georgia* 408 U.S. 238 [1972] Justice Douglas, concurring),
then this white male who is also deserving of the ultimate punishment must
clearly exist outside the established norm. He cannot be allowed to exist as the
sane and unidentifiable family man of the European version. He cannot be seen
as someone who is balancing within the paradigm. It must be clear that his
transgression is a result of "mental defect." As portrayed by Jeff Bridges, Barney
Cousins is an unbalanced maniac, whose hair is constantly unkempt, who talks
with an accent, walks with a limp, and who upon sight would ignite a feeling of
discomfort. He could not blend in a crowded square, he could not be rationally
thought of as a hero because he flouts the American conventions of normality.

Conclusion

Richard Slotkin reiterates through *Regeneration through Violence* (1973) and
Gunfighter Nation (1998): "mass-mediated representations . . . which function
as a public display of the transgression of cultural norms; as such . . . a site at
which one may investigate the relationship of the individual to the culture in
general, as well as the cultural articulation of 'proper behavior.'" Although neither of the *Vanishings* is, strictly speaking, a capital punishment movie, both are
stark interpretations of crime and punishment. And it is through our indoctrination of crime and punishment that we as a culture come to benignly accept
the imposition of capital punishment. The differences between cultural perceptions of self and other, the ability of American culture to reinforce the belief
that the other, easily recognizable, is the instigator of crime and the self also
easily recognizable as the enforcer of crimes fosters a belief that it is a brief skip
from cultural perspectives of crime and punishment to state-sanctioned law
and order remedies in whatever their manifestations may be, including the ultimate punishment, capital punishment.

The view of the other that allows us to rationalize and accept state-sanctioned punishment when viewed through the darkness of the cinema is a view
reinforced not only by the physical difference exhibited by the other but by the
overt actions the other makes of his daily rituals. We realize punishment is just
because it is action that is other directed. As hero and self we cannot physically
resemble the other nor can we imagine committing such extraordinary acts of

violence as manifested by American cinematic villains. These violent acts not only code how necessary it is to punish the perpetrator but also signify how unlike the self the perpetrator must be to commit such atrocities.

"[T]he death penalty, today as in the past, symbolizes the ultimate power of the state, and of the government of society, over the individual citizen" (Koch and Galliher 1993: 333, 327). Capital punishment exists in American movies as a fact, not a process. When the hero dispenses with the bad guy at the end he is acting in defense of our culture and therefore exacting justice upon the transgressor. This act of justice most often results in the loss of life. The bad guy is gone, the hero/state prevails, capital punishment has been exacted. "Violence . . . is not produced by a need to release aggression but by a social imperative to overcome competition, discover kinship by confirming otherness and affirm hierarchies of central versus marginal individuals" (Slocum 2000).

The cinema legitimizes the concept of capital punishment by referencing it to our most basic cultural ideology, good versus bad, where good always prevails. American culture is uncomfortable with ambiguous or unhappy endings. We are unaccustomed to not being able to readily identify the bad guy and for having bad triumph. So we medicate our senses with cultural references that assure us this is not the way of *our* world. Paraphrasing Kintsch (1998), the film spectator works with associated concepts activated and reactivated from long-term memory that mesh with the current perceptual situation. As the spectator thinks, the patterns begin to stabilize, activating those elements that fit together and deactivating those that do not (see also Oakley, forthcoming). This conditioning process filters itself into our daily vocabulary, our daily reference. We now see capital punishment as good versus bad in two-dimensional images. "Capital punishment sacrifices the lives of killers to reassure a culture that would otherwise be perplexed and troubled by the constitutive uncertainty haunting some of its more cherished categories of self-interpretation" (Connolly 1999: 197).

If John Wayne in his many manifestations could err, if Maggie could err, if Kiefer Sutherland could err, then it could mean the state could err. If the Indians, Mexicans, dark-skinned, different-speaking other are not clearly recognized as the bad guy, how are we supposed to identify the evil person when we come into contact with that person daily? We are referred to a particular ideology of who is good and what is bad (although our politically correct minds assure us that there are "some good ones" within the bunch). But she who does not think like us must be deserving of punishment which the state has deemed to be meritorious. "[A] death penalty democratically administered, a death penalty that enlist[s] citizens to do the work of dealing death to other citizens, implicates us all as agents of state killing" (Sarat 1995: 1103).

Capital punishment is state-sanctioned death. The thought of us being in compliance with the death of another individual is so far removed from daily consciousness that our ideal of crime and punishment and self versus other is naturalized via cultural references. Cultural myths have a way of reinterpreting themselves so that they never die. The cinema as a forum for cultural mythology reinforces the veracity of cultural mythology. The acceptance and predominance of cultural mythology via cinematic references is heightened by the seamlessness of the cinema and the positioning gaze. We as spectators become lost in the screen. We see, we idolize, we identify with certain perspectives. This identification allows the mythology to be reinforced while allowing us to reify our positioning relative to the other. In American cinema, for perhaps two hours and forty-five minutes we become the hero. We are positioned to identify with the hero's struggles, with his fight, and inevitably with his triumph over evil. We are vested in ensuring that the bad man pays for his sins. The cultural myth perpetrated by American cinema is that good always wins and evil is readily identifiable and rightly punished. Bad guys get what they deserve and goodness prevails. There are no gray areas and as such we are led to believe that the bad guy always gets what s/he deserves in the end. The happy ending is a cultural icon. We are delivered from evil and how the evil doer meets his demise is irrelevant. Violence begets violence, but in American cinema it is okay for the only way to beat the bad man is with a violent turn that eliminates him and therefore once again makes the world a safe place. "The exaggerations of mythic violence prepared the public mind for the acceptance of a greater license for the use of *force* and *violence* against 'dangerous' social elements" (Slotkin 1998: 191). The exaggeration of mythic violence also allows for a greater demarcation between self and other. This is a radical departure from most foreign cinema. Happy endings are never guaranteed and evil sometimes prevails over good. It is a world where the delineation between us versus them is never so clear-cut. The gaze is often that of the villain as much as it is of the hero. We are forced through the cinematic gaze to see life from the perspective of the other. We are forced to empathize with the object as much as the subject, never assured of who will triumph. The violence while just as exaggerated appears more "real" because our gaze ensures that we may be on the receiving end of the violence. We are both hero and villain. Good and bad are not so readily identifiable, and therefore we cannot bring ourselves to accept the use of force and violence as readily as it may be directed at us as well as the other.

References

Allen, Richard (1995) *Projecting Illusion: Film Spectatorship and the Impression of Reality.* New York: Cambridge University Press.

Barker, Martin (2004) "Violence Redux," in Steven Jay Schneider, ed., *New Hollywood Violence.* Manchester, London: Manchester University Press.

Connolly, William E. (1999) "The Will, Capital Punishment, and Cultural War," in Austin Sarat, ed., *The Killing State: Capital Punishment in Law, Politics, and Culture.* Oxford, England: Oxford University Press.

Garland, David (1990) *Punishment and Modern Society.* Chicago: University of Chicago Press.

Garland, David (2000). *The Culture of Control.* Chicago: University of Chicago Press.

Hayward, Susan (2000) *Cinema Studies*: Key Concepts. New York: Routledge University Press.

Heath, Stephen (1977) "Film Performance," 1 *Cine-tracts: A Journal of Film Communications, Culture and Politics* (Summer).

Furman v. Georgia (1972) 408 U.S. 238.

Kintsch, Walter (1998) *Comprehension: A Paradigm for Cognition.* Cambridge: Cambridge University Press.

Koch, L. W., and Galliher, J. F. (1993) "Michigan's Continuing Abolition of the Death Penalty and the Conceptual Components of Symbolic Legislation," 2 *Social and Legal Studies.*

Lipsitz, George (2001) *Time Passages: Collective Memory and American Pop Culture.* Minneapolis: University of Minnesota Press.

Metz, Christian (1982) *The Imaginary Signifier: Psychoanalysis and the Cinema.* Bloomington: Indiana University Press.

Munby, Jonathan (1999) *Public Enemies Public Heroes: Screening the Gangster from Little Caesar to Touch of Evil.* Chicago: University of Chicago Press.

Oakley, Todd (forthcoming) "Toward a General Theory of Film Spectatorship," 17 *Almen Semiotik.* http://www.cwru.edu/artsci/engl/oakley/TGSF.pdf.

Sarat, Austin (1995) "Violence, Representation, and Responsibility in Capital Trials: The View from the Jury," 70 *Indiana Law Journal* 1103.

Shea, Daniel M. (1998) *Mass Politics: The Politics of Popular Culture.* New York: St. Martin's Press.

Slocum David, J. (2000) "Film Violence and the Institutionalization of the Cinema," *Social Research* (Fall), http://articles.findarticles.com/p/articles/mi_m2267/is_3_67/ai_66888954 (accessed June 20, 2004).

Slotkin, Richard (1973) *Regeneration through Violence: The Mythology of the American Frontier 1600–1860.* Norman: University of Oklahoma Press.

Slotkin, Richard (1998) *Gunfighter Nation: The Myth of the Frontier in Twentieth Century America.* Norman: University of Oklahoma Press.

U.S. Department of Justice (1999) "Capital Punishment 1999," Bureau of Justice Statistics, http://www.ojp.gov/bjs/abstract/cp99.htm (accessed June 19, 2004).

CHAPTER SEVEN

Capital Punishment in Poland

An Aspect of the "Cultural Life" of Death Penalty Discourse

AGATA FIJALKOWSKI

Introduction

This chapter considers Polish attitudes toward punishment. It seeks to contribute to the continuing debate concerning the abolition of the death penalty that is currently taking place in Poland. The chapter will explore how these attitudes have been affected by peculiar Polish traditions, namely, the communist experience, religion, and European enlargement.

In his work on the sociology of punishment, David Garland identifies a cultural aspect in this field. He argues convincingly that socially constructed mentalities and sensibilities have major implications for the way in which offenders are punished (1990: 195). Mentalities and sensibilities refer to the positions taken in respect of, and attitudes toward, punishment. How these have been shaped in Poland calls for an examination of key periods in Polish history, as well as the future, most clearly in the form of European Union (EU) enlargement. Accordingly, key developments in three different periods—prewar, communist, and postcommunist—will be considered.

The chapter will further seek to demonstrate and reaffirm how Łoś's theory of "control mentality" has transformed itself into calls for a stronger state which also includes the reinstatement of capital punishment (Łoś 2002). The death penalty provides one forum in which the state can save face by taking action with clear and popular results (Sarat 2001; Simon 2002; Schiff Berman 2002).

Where punishment is located in the relationship between the state and its citizens reflects a reciprocal relationship, where we experience not only what punishment does for us, but what punishment does to us (Sarat 2001: 23; Garland 1990: 195). What this means for the role of punishment in a society where democracy and the rule of law are relatively nascent notions requires further contemplation and research. This chapter seeks to address some of the underlying issues.

Historical Overview

> Memory has always had political or ideological overtones, but each epoch has found its own meaning in memory.
>
> Hacking (1995: 200).

Scholars who revisit history to search for definitions of punishment often reassemble societal roles, examine the belief system of society, and look at the language that conceptualized reality at the time (Schiff Berman 2002: 1141; Geertz 1983: 182; Foucault 1979: 72–131). These scholars demonstrate the close relationship between law and culture and, significantly, reveal an insight into legal consciousness, which reflects the way that "legality is experienced and understood by ordinary people as they engage, avoid, resist the law and legal meanings" (Schiff Berman 2002: 1141; Ewick and Silbey 1998: 35). An examination of the Polish past and where capital punishment was located within state and societal attitudes may explain Polish views on the matter.

Discussions about the death penalty in Poland began in the Second Polish Republic of 1918, when it began drafting a criminal code for the newly established state. It is important to recall that Poland at this time emerged from over a century of imposed rule on the part of Russian, German, and Austrian powers. Throughout its history, as independent Poland and one existing under externally imposed rule, Poles fought to keep Polish culture, language, and traditions alive. This feat should not be underestimated as it reflects strong internal networks that translated into resistance, which in turn may explain Polish society's natural tendency toward a strong state structure that protects its needs and interests. Zimring has noted that Americans' fear of government and the country's strong due process tradition contradicts the strong support for capital punishment (2002: 42–64, 119–39). The majority of Poles have been, and continue to be, suspicious of the state, as will be seen shortly. Despite differences in historical factors that shaped U.S. and Polish attitudes toward punishment, one can question whether there is a common stance as concerns the role of the state. The state, in carrying out the punishment, might reflect the recognition and respect of society's support of capital punishment, and ultimately reflect the real location of power in the relationship between the state and the citizen, with the society, as capital punishment is being carried out *for* society (Sarat 2001: 23).

The draft criminal code originally did not envisage the death penalty as a punishment. During the Codification Commission's work, discussions with respect to capital punishment centered on the main goals to be achieved by the death penalty; findings from the First World War were quite influential (Zubik 1998: 96; Szumski 1997: 80–90). Experts were divided on the issue, and in the first three drafts of the code the death penalty was not included. By sheer fate it found its place in the 1932 criminal code by one vote (Zubik 1998: 97–198).

When the Soviet authorities began consolidating power in 1944, assuming power in 1946, they retained the 1932 Code, but passed a series of decrees that operated alongside its provisions. Most of these decrees included capital punishment as a penalty (*Dziennik Ustaw* 1946). It was not until the end of the dark period of Stalinism in 1956 that the death penalty discourse returned, as a reaction to its indiscriminate use on the part of the Soviet authorities, in particular the secret services, during this period.

Some brief remarks about the Soviet legal model are required at this point, since this was this model imposed in Poland. Under Lenin, the use of terror was justified on the grounds that coercion and terror were necessary evils of the revolution, particularly during the transition from capitalism to communism. Lenin embarked on a terror campaign against class enemies, defined as anyone who "stubbornly clung to capitalist traditions" (Lenin 1983: 41). In order to achieve this aim quickly and effectively, an autonomous quasi-legal body, the All-Russian Extraordinary Commission for Combating Counter-Revolution and Sabotage (*Cheka*), was created. Revolutionary tribunals worked alongside the *Cheka* and sentenced thousands to death: they were not guided by any legal code, and both organs succeeded in eliminating many of the politically inconvenient. *Cheka* was later transformed into the People's Commissariat for Internal Affairs, or NKVD, under Stalin, who also reshaped the agency several times and at each stage employed mass terror against "socially dangerous" persons (Voslensky 1983: 47; Łoś 1988: 12–13). It is difficult to speak of the existence of any fairness, justice, or transparency; judges were targeted as well (Medvedev 1971). The *Cheka* later evolved into the KGB; the secret services retained their rule of terror over the population, as did the secret services in each of the Central and Eastern European countries where Soviet rule was imposed. The use of terror works alongside a subservient criminal justice apparatus.

Frankowski (1996) succinctly describes the nature of the criminal justice apparatus that operates under communist rule. First, he correctly stresses the instrumental role of criminal law. Second, he considers the way in which severe punishments are believed to be highly effective in controlling criminality. Third, swift criminal proceedings, unhindered by technicalities, are believed to have a substantial deterrent effect. In such a system, the death penalty is used to intimidate the population at large. The way in which criminal measures are applied, such as the death penalty, is not dictated by penal policy measures but rather by political considerations. In other words, the death penalty is primarily a political issue rather than a criminal justice issue.

The discussion is kept alive by inconsistencies that exist in Polish legal literature as concerns the use of the death penalty in the years immediately following the war, namely, to whom it was applied and which bodies were responsible for carrying out the sentences (Zubik 1998: 101).[1] The penalty was used indiscriminately. As noted above, potential political opponents were targeted. It was also used for economic and property crimes, which was, and still is, characteristic of communist regimes (*Dziennik Ustaw* 1950).[2] Similar measures were implemented throughout the region (Fico 1999: 118; Frankowski 1996: 218–20). The discussion draws attention to the series of decrees that were passed between 1944 and 1956, which called for the death penalty in a wide range of offenses. These decrees hid the true intention of the authorities, which was to eliminate all potential opponents to the newly established Soviet regime. The most infamous of these decrees, from 1944 targeting fascist criminals, was used to imprison and execute most of the leaders of the Polish Underground (*Dziennik Ustaw* 1944).[3] The famous *Nila* case illustrates the logic behind the decrees perfectly (Mitera and Zubik 1998: 101).[4]

The manner in which the death penalty was imposed and implemented did not meet any standards of basic procedural rights (Frankowski 1996). Furthermore, capital punishment was imposed outside the formal criminal law appa-ratus. Quasi-legal judicial bodies were created at various levels of military and common courts to hear cases that were fabricated and at which evidence was presented that was procured by use of torture. It is estimated that between 1946 and 1953 between 2,000 and 3,000 death sentences were passed in regular courts and military courts; but the number of people executed outside the regular court system was much higher (Zubik 1998: 99; Szumski 1997: 82). The exact fig-ure of death sentences passed during this period will never be determined, al-though one can be certain that thousands of people were charged and executed for crimes that they had not committed. These aspects of communist rule are being addressed, as more information is being made available in archives and court files, formerly classified as secret (Utrat-Milecki 1996).[5] The discussion initiated in the mid-1950s focused on the need to apply amnesty or abolish the death penalty.

This arbitrary use of punishment drove a further wedge between society and the imposed, ruling power, because of the lack of legitimacy in the authority of rule and in the enacted legal norms. The notion of "us" (*my*) and "them" (*oni*), which characterized communist rule, quite aptly described the relationship, where punishment, a part of the criminal justice process, was a political tool rather than part of penal policy considerations (Frankowski 1996: 218). Its arbi-trary application was determined by the authorities as a "political tactic." It also revealed an inconsistent policy. Nonetheless, underlying the criminal justice system's seeming weakness was its repressive character (Łoś and Zybertowicz 2000).

Kassymbekova (2003), writing about the Kyrgyz experience, aptly observes that in such a system punishment is mystified. Punishment, as used by the Communist Party, was not always clear, rather, what was made clear was where the control of legal norms lay. At the height of Stalinism, marked by show trials throughout the Soviet bloc, the repressive nature of the criminal law and sys-tem was evidenced (Hodos 1987; Piekarska 1995). Kassymbekova's mystification lays in the nature of communist rule itself. Communist rule was imposed by a nondemocratic regime, under the guise of democracy, which was not con-cerned with acceptance or recognition of its legitimacy. For example, the 1936 Stalinist Constitution was a document that comprised a rich catalogue of rights but in practice was empty and came to represent an audacious act of double-speak. The state was concerned with control, and in Poland discipline was exercised by key branches of the criminal justice apparatus, whose motivation was the "normalisation of fear founded on a deliberate destruction of human bonds and sovereignty of the person" (Łoś and Zybertowicz 2000:50; Łoś 1988: 143). Thus, people were viewed as "appendages to the state economy [rather] than as private citizens" (Łoś 1988: 51), whereby the regime's technology of power could be described as "ritualistic, costly and often violent, and its disciplinary techniques were focused on the individual as a concealed enemy, whose potential usefulness lay in dissuading other individuals from joining forces against the party-state" (ibid.). The dissuasion was successful because of the fear that the system generated, a fear that not only represented a fear of the state, but also a fear of one's own friends, colleagues, acquaintances, in general, of one's fellow citizens (Łoś 2002). At one level, recalling Frankowski, it can be argued that the theory of deterrence worked effectively in the system. Yet it must be recalled that the system's effectiveness was viewed as such by society, a belief that influences contemporary notions on punishment, despite identifiable flaws in the communist system's manner of managing crime. The role of capital punishment in this rubric was logical. The regime's headache came with the critique of how the punishment could be consistent with the prevailing ideology whose adherents had significant contributions with respect to abolishing the death penalty.

In the discussions concerning the drafting of the Polish criminal code, capital punishment became the topic of serious debate among the criminal law community. Already in 1956 two prominent criminal lawyers spoke out against capital punishment (Ehrlich 1956; Wolter 1956), and in her 1963 article Maria Ossowska recalled Marxist theory and questioned the reasoning behind the state's decision not to adhere to Marxist thought. A decade later two interesting monographs were written on the subject, both from an abolitionist perspective. The first, from 1966, by the criminal law scholar Marian Cieślak, provided a global overview of the death penalty and argued for its abolition at least during peacetime. Nevertheless, the 1969 Criminal Code retained the death penalty and defined the punishment as an exceptional one. Clemency could only be granted by the Council of State (*Rada Państwa*) (Zubik 1998: 103).[6]

In the second monograph, from 1978, Alicja Grześkowiak[7] argued that the death penalty had no place in a modern, rational penal system, as the deterrent effects of the death sentence were unsubstantiated. Such monographs were mainly written by scholars critiquing the place of capital punishment in a socialist legal framework. In fact, the workers' movement has been opposed to capital punishment throughout history, with the main voices within the movement who called for abolition being from dissidents or intellectuals (Jankovic 1984).

The abolitionist stance in Poland gained momentum with the birth of the Solidarity movement (Zubik 1998). Even though a moratorium was in effect in 1988, one of the reforms that formed part of the negotiation between the government and representatives of the opposition movement Solidarity at the 1989 Round Table Talks was the abolition of capital punishment (ibid.: 105). This was the first time that civil liberties and individual freedoms were discussed openly. The abolition of the death penalty during peacetime was addressed, for example, in 1979, by Jerzy Jasiński,[8] who argued that the utilitarian and the moral positions needed to be distinguished when addressing the death penalty. The debates concerning the death penalty which were occurring in Poland coincided with the discussions that were taking place at the international level, within the United Nations and the Commission on Human Rights, of which key members of the movement were aware.

Yet these voices were contained and perhaps not representative of society's views. The call for recognition of civil liberties ran parallel to the majority support for strict laws and capital punishment, a phenomenon that is echoed in South Korea (Bae 2004). And while the post-Stalinist period did not bring about abolition or a decrease in capital offenses in the region (although the number of executions was quite low when considering the number of capital offenses), it demonstrated a marked change in the implementation of capital punishment. In general, during this period, the number of death sentences that were carried out decreased (Frankowski 1996: 225). Lastly, as the communist regime was visibly weakening, a moratorium was established in 1988. The last executions were carried out in 1986 (Zubik 1998: 106). The moratorium that was established in 1988 was an indefinite one and, in 1995, the last capital sentence was passed but not carried out. Poland seemingly followed the path of eventual abolition of the death penalty after the collapse of communism in 1989.[9]

Current Developments

The road to abolition began when Poland joined the Council of Europe. As of 1994, membership was based on the condition that new members ratify the European Convention on Human Rights (ECHR) and its Sixth Protocol,[10] which the new applicant states dutifully promised to do. This new requirement coincided with the worldwide trend of increasing rates of the abolition of the death penalty or moratoria regarding its use. The mandate of the Council of Europe expresses clear political goals that are shared by the Europe that new members aspired to join. "The Council of Europe was created to unite Europe around the shared principles of the rule of law, respect for human rights and pluralist democracy. This political project aimed to entrench a common philosophy about the type of society that member states want to create, strengthen and defend" (Council of Europe 2001).

An interesting turn of events in the 1990s is described by Girling (2002) as challenging state sovereignty and identity politics in the world and transforming the death penalty into an international relations issue. Capital punishment was now viewed as having no place in a civilized society.

Certainly after signing the European Convention, Poland was under considerable international pressure to ratify Protocol No. 6 and further to abolish the death penalty via legislation. With impending European integration, the motivation was strong. At the same time, resistance was demonstrated on the part of certain political groups. In the April 2000 parliamentary vote, the majority (257 votes) supporting ratification of Protocol No. 6 came from a mix of left- and right-wing parties, such as the Solidarity Electoral Action (*Akcja Wyborcza Solidarność*; AWS), the Democratic Left Alliance (*Sojusz Lewicy Demokratycznej*; SLD); the Polish Peasant's Party and People's Labour Movement Coalition (*PPS-Ruch Ludzi Pracy*); unanimous support came from the Freedom Union Club (*Klub UW*); and two votes came from the Polish People's Coalition (*Polska Strona Ludowa*; PSL). Opposition votes numbered 117, including, *inter alia*, 56 from AWS, 21 from SLD, and 20 from PSL; 33 members abstained ("Znieszenie pryzpieczętowane," *Rzeczpospolita* 2000). The ratification of Protocol No. 6 ended an embarrassingly long ordeal, much longer than the required one- to three-year period.

The abolition of the death penalty in Poland was a protracted process with a somewhat quiet ending, if compared to the manner in which it was considered by its postcommunist counterparts. In Hungary, for example, the Constitutional Court rendered an advisory opinion on the constitutionality of capital punishment in 1990, despite strong support for the punishment. The complaint was initiated by law professors (Uitz 2002). In order to examine the politics surrounding abolition, two sources of law will be examined: the Constitution and the Criminal Code.

The 1997 Constitution gives precedence to international agreements ratified by Parliament over laws (Zoll 1998). Article 38 of the Polish Constitution declares that everyone has a right to life, which can be interpreted as prohibiting the introduction of the death penalty into ordinary legislation. This provision is further supported by Article 40, which forbids the application of corporal punishment: it can be argued that capital punishment could be included in this category. Yet, the prohibition of the death penalty as such is not mentioned in the Constitution, as opposed to, for example, the Romanian case. This can be attributed to the debates that center on the drafting of the document and the subsequent referendum on the Constitution.

Examining developments in the region, most postcommunist countries have abolished the death penalty following a constitutional court ruling, upon petition for an advisory opinion. For example, the Constitutional Courts of Hungary, Lithuania, and Albania have found that the death penalty violates constitutional principles enshrined in the respective documents of these countries (Fijalkowski 2002: 342). The Czech Republic, Slovakia, Slovenia, Croatia, and Romania have abolished capital punishment through legislation (ibid.). Unlike its Hungarian or Lithuanian counterparts, for example, the Polish Constitutional Tribunal has not ruled on the unconstitutionality of the death penalty. It seems unlikely do so, unless Parliament would seek the reinstatement of the death penalty, which is doubtful, despite strong public support (see below). If such a scenario arose, then the Tribunal's ruling would most likely reflect the decisions of its counterparts. The general trend has been to declare capital punishment unconstitutional based on the violation of constitutional provisions concerning the right to human dignity and/or the right to life (Uitz 2002).

Polish scholars see little room for the reintroduction of the death penalty, especially with the combined reading of Articles 38 and 40 (Sarnecki 2000). As international agreements ratified prior to the consent of the Parliament have precedence over laws, Polish criminal legislation inconsistent with such agreements cannot be applied and, further, should be abolished (Article 188(2)). Ratified international agreements should also guide the mode of interpretation of domestic legal provisions. And, to bring this nearer to closure, on 14 April 2000, Poland adopted legislation approving ratification of the Sixth Protocol to the ECHR, amid much controversy. Shortly before the vote in April 2000, one parliamentary member asked whether Protocol No. 6 was part of the law of the European Union ("Zniesienie przypieczętowane," *Rzeczpospolita* 2000). Additionally, Article 30 of the Constitution imposes an obligation on state bodies and on the legislator to protect the dignity of the individual not only against threats on the part of the state but also by other persons. The provisions of Article 3 of the Criminal Code are extended by this constitutional provision; the subject is no longer only a subject of criminal law protection. The provisions are extended to the imposition of punishment and punitive actions by criminal law and the right to respect the dignity of the person must be addressed (Zoll 1998: 90–91). The prohibition on subjecting anyone to torture or inhuman treatment is found in Article 40. The Polish Criminal Code entered into force on 1 January 1998 (*Dziennik Ustaw* 1998).

The drafters of the Criminal Code comprised a small elite of criminal law lawyers in the country, mainly from Jagiellonian University in Cracow. The Law Faculty at Jagiellonian University has excellent academic standing in the country and internationally. Many of the faculty's law graduates have sat on the bench of the Constitutional Tribunal. This group looked to and embraced Western models for inspiration and rejected past arguments calling for abolition (Zoll 1998; Buchała 1998). Drafters defended their abolitionist view on capital punishment, basing it on international norms and European standards that were "forward-looking" and educative and interestingly not mentioning former debates among criminal law scholars, presumably because of the different political ideology those debates were rooted in. Capital punishment was presented as not having a place in civilized society (Nowicka-Włodarczyk 1998). Reasoning put forward by scholars from the 1970s or 1980s did not form a part of the discussion; rather, classical arguments dating to biblical times comprised part of the arguments alongside European developments. The drafters of the Criminal Code introduced "forward-looking" arguments, assessing the need for the punishment, in a future Polish state that is part of Europe. Some judges even actively published in national newspapers, considering the decisions of the Supreme Court on sentencing and, at the same time, educating society about the new criminal law provisions with respect to sentencing (Paprzycki 1999).

The Polish Criminal Code has been widely criticized by society as being too liberal. In polls taken by the leading Polish polling agency, CBOS, two years after the Code came into force, the majority of respondents felt that the criminal law was inadequate in dealing with the rising crime rate. Interestingly, these public views coincide with polls taken in 1996, when respondents supported stricter laws under the former criminal code (CBOS 2000). As regards capital punishment, public opinion was and remains strong. The majority of the population has supported the death penalty for over a decade, with the lowest percentage of supporters in 1989, at 52 percent, rising to 77 percent in 1996 (ibid.). For 2000, 58 percent of respondents polled "definitely" supported the death penalty and 19 percent responded with a "rather yes"; only 8 percent surveyed responded with a "definitely no" (ibid.). Polls taken by the Brussels-based Central European Research Group (CEORG) revealed that 73.6 percent of Poles support the death penalty, alongside 59.8 percent of Hungarians and 56.1 percent of Czechs (CEORG 2002). Strong support for capital punishment is reflected in the Central and East European region.

Thus it is not surprising to see that the majority of the populace also supports stricter laws. These sentiments coincide with the increasing fear of becoming a victim of a crime, which has been revealed in recent surveys. In 2000, for example, in another poll conducted by CBOS, two-thirds of Polish society expressed such fears (CBOS 2000). These fears are prompted by the fact that criminal patterns have changed since the collapse of communism. Although criminal statistics are notoriously difficult to evaluate, especially under the former regime, studies have shown that the number of offenses reported doubled between 1989 and 1999 (Łoś 2002: 180–81). The statistics may reveal another factor about Polish sensibilities—a fear against crime and personal safety, but they may hint at yet another factor—the fear that the strong structures and bonds that have held society together traditionally may be under threat.

Polish resistance against various modes of repression in its tumultuous history has kept Polish society, culture, language, and traditions alive under conditions of oppression.[11] These strategies of resistance were both concrete and symbolic and very much an important part of the Polish strategy for survival during long periods of imposed rule marked by the first partition on the part of Russia that took place in 1795, which resulted in the country's disappearance from maps until 1918; followed eleven years later by German and Soviet occupation from 1939 until 1944; and, finally, communist rule which lasted from 1945 until 1989 (Davies 1982). The collapse of the communist regime has left particular bonds of resistance meaningless and, in its place, new threats, manifested in the rising crime rates, necessitate new strategies and ways of coping. Perhaps these new strategies on the part of Polish society involve retaining the label of "them" as concerns the state apparatus. Alongside this understandable confusion, Polish society is experiencing the consequences of more freedom and responsibility for one's own personal safety. In other words, the collapse of communism has meant a collapse of control safety nets. More significant is the issue of one's vulnerability, which was protected very carefully through various means of conditioning (see below).

Since the collapse of communism, people are clearly fearful of becoming victims. Personal safety was perceived differently under the former regime and, furthermore, the reporting of crime and criminal statistics were strictly controlled by the regime, which meant that only certain crimes were reported, and mostly where crimes were solved and state control reinforced (Łoś 2002: 168–69). This addresses the essence of the totalitarian regime—one which is omnipotent, omnipresent, and which has no space for private freedom. Totalitarian rule presents itself as perfect, not flawless, but as a whole it does not need to be clear about power, thus its mystical nature. Łoś (2002) argues that the way in which crime was reported deprived people of the tools to talk about their fears; instead crime remained a private issue. Indeed, no space was created for criticism; likewise, no space was created for the private citizen. In consequence, a fear of personal safety was created. This personal safety could be extended to the fear of personal liberty that came with the introduction of democratic reforms.

Naturally, the media played a role in the censorship, as it still does today. The rise in crime is accompanied by open reporting. In most news reports, crime coverage is uncensored and, in addition, the criminal justice apparatus is "exposed" in its failures. Although the media tend to focus on the sensational cases of failure, the public is left with a negative general impression of a system that is characterized by chaos and corruption. The public perception that crime is increasing is reinforced this way. Crime control is an issue that is publicly discussed and part of political rhetoric (Łoś 2002: 166–67). Naturally, the feelings of insecurity increase and coincide with calls for stricter crime control.

The current mayor of Warsaw, for example, Lech Kaczyński, won the office with a law and order *(Prawo i Sprawiedliwość)* political campaign that included the vocal support of the death penalty, which Kaczyński views as offering everyone justice in cases where murder is committed (Interview 2001). For him, "the only matter, is the matter of the sentence" (ibid.). Kaczyński has openly supported the death penalty following the recent announcement made by the pope against capital punishment. The announcement was made when Kaczyński was minister of justice. Kaczyński's response to the Vatican was one of ambivalence, and during a radio interview he mused "I am well aware of the [pope's] stand, and of [the Commandments] and it is for this reason that I am a supporter of the death penalty" (ibid.).

In Polish society, which is predominantly Catholic, the stance of the Church is quite significant. The Catholic Church galvanized the opposition and provided a safe haven against the oppressive regime. The position of the Church in Poland with respect to capital punishment has been one characterized by inconsistency to say the least. In 1995, in his "Evangelium Vitae," Pope John Paul II declared that execution is only appropriate "in cases of absolute necessity, in other words, when it would not be possible to defend society. Today, however, as a result of steady improvement in the organisation of the penal system, such cases are rare, if not practically non-existent."

It is important to distinguish between the position of the Vatican and that of the Catholic Church in Poland. Various scholars have speculated as to the Church's position on the subject of capital punishment (Jasiński 1995). On the one hand, it appears that the Church has left the question of capital punishment in the hands of the state, as a matter of legislation, which finds favor among retentionists; on the other hand, it seems to be suggesting that states can do without the death penalty, which leaves room for politicians to maneuver and manipulate public opinion. This is possible because of Polish society's special relationship with the Church in periods of conflict and dissent. The Church has historically supported Polish social and national interests and been at the center of keeping society together in its representation (Titkow 1993: 232). The Church's role has suffered with the collapse of communism and the establishment of a new economic order (Jasiński 1995: 233). Kaczyński's campaign is popular because it aligns itself with the old adage of retribution, where it is absolutely clear that only when "murderers disappeared from world, then I [Kaczyński] would cease supporting the death penalty" (Interview 2001). The campaign also challenges the weaknesses of the criminal law and criminal law system and seems to fit in with the general view that the criminal justice apparatus is in a moribund state, an opinion that is shared by the public. Alongside this, one finds leading legal scholars who openly and publicly support capital punishment.[12]

The requirement posed by the Council of Europe on the new member states to abolish capital punishment was posed amid strong public support for capital punishment. One of the tasks of the European Parliamentary Assembly was to campaign to change public sentiments in the countries and to try to "persuade politicians that they have to lead and not follow public opinion on the matter" (Girling 2002). The elite who drafted the criminal law and have led this argument have not been effective in Poland. It is doubtful that most politicians are convinced as much as led by entry into the European Union.

In his discussion on punishment as a social institution, Garland (1990: 282) describes how social institutions are shaped by both historical and contemporary factors. This includes the key actors involved in penal practice, namely, judges, correctional officers, and state officials. They will carry out their tasks in a wider social context, responding to various social institutions found inside the state and globally (ibid.: 283). Social institutions are dynamic and develop alongside social values and arrangements that come from a variety of sources (ibid.).

Clearly, this is not a new development. France, for example, abolished capital punishment amid great controversy. To take an example closer to Poland, Lithuania went about by petitioning its Constitutional Court to rule on the matter. In its judgment, the Court based its reasoning on studies that showed that capital punishment did not have a deterrent effect. It went on to base its reasoning on various international and European legal instruments, despite the fact that Lithuania had not ratified Protocol No. 6. Gelazis (2002: 400), in examining democracy in the country, aptly observes how state institutions have adopted a paternalistic attitude toward governance, where the political elite make decisions and seek institutional ways to implement them. As a result, public debate occurs after the decision has been taken, which leads to an increased distance between citizens and the decision-making process—the notion of "us and them" prevails. The long-term result is questionable as concerns "circumventing the electorate in terms of the durability of the policy and its implementation" (ibid.). The scenario has been repeated in the Ukraine (Wolczuk 2002).

Several key points must be made about the dissonance between the elite discourse and the values held by the majority of Polish society. As in the United States, the retention of the death penalty is fueled by campaigners who see this as an important symbol. All abolitionist countries have faced the adjustment of attitudes and sensibilities shaped by political processes and social forces (Garland 1990: 246). Whether and how this is possible in Poland requires several questions to be explored. First, the role of punishment has changed. Punishment was used arbitrarily as a means to eliminate and deter political opposition. It was a very important feature of communist rule, which shaped the way in which society viewed punishment and the state. The state's totalitarian rule meant that society had to condition itself concerning its relationship with the state and vice versa; as a result, resistance on at least two fronts was created and sustained. This development is not unique in Polish history which has seen imposed rule throughout the centuries. Second, the collapse of communism led toward European integration, which was and continues to be a priority. Regarding criminal justice, this means that the discourse on criminal law issues is not guided by policy considerations as much as political ones, once again depriving Poles of the tools to legitimize their fears and concerns about crime and punishment. Interestingly, arguments that once were at the forefront of the Solidarity movement were ignored. The due process element of the discourse on civil liberties has been replaced by support for crime control and a strong state. It also is accompanied by the notion of Poland, as a country with a rich history in rights, in which the role of religion was and continues to be prominent. Kaczyński's campaign exemplifies this trend of a strong role of religion in a punitive society. Garland notes that "[p]enal laws and institutions are always proposed, discussed, legislated, and operated within definite cultural codes. They are framed in languages, discourses, and sign systems which embody specific cultural meanings, distinctions, and sentiments, and which must be interpreted and understood if the social meaning and motivations of punishment are to become intelligible" (1990: 198). Łoś's (2002) theory on "control mental-ity" argues that this fear of the state has been transformed into a fear of crime and longing for a stronger state. If we examine Polish attitudes about punish-ment, we see that they reflect structures and relations that have been affected by certain processes. The communist experience forced society to adjust its con-duct to take into account that of the state and its peculiar rule, to such an extent that these attitudes became ingrained and affected relations between members of society. This process eventually becomes "natural," in the sense that it seems right in itself. The ultimate result is that "the individual may cease to be aware of these norms as social conventions [here Garland is referring to Western val-ues] and may even obey them in the absence of other people, so strong are the social conditioning and forces of habit which regulate such conduct" (Garland 1990: 220).

Likewise, this is reflected in the attitudes of the elite that lead the call for the reinstatement of capital punishment. Both society and political elites desire and support the notion of a strong state—and in what better area to conduct this discourse than in capital punishment—the ultimate punishment that is meted out by the strong state.

Concluding Remarks

Social conditioning and forces of habit may be the ways to convince Polish society—and its neighboring counterparts—that capital punishment has no place in a civilized society. Such strong support does not disappear quickly. For Polish society it goes hand-in-hand with the traditional resistance to repression and resistance, as noted above. Moreover, these bonds exemplify the struggle and fight for freedom. It is also linked to religion and the Catholic Church. These factors, the resistance, Catholic Church, and a longing for stricter con-trol, form part of the Polish perception about an ideal state framework, which, if anything, is one that is strong. Traditionally Polish society could be charac-terized as a punitive society; this chapter has identified significant factors which support this thesis, yet it seeks to draw attention to some underlying issues which the attitudes hide.

To return to an earlier point, the mystification of punishment under com-munist rule existed because the punishment, as used by the Communist Party, was not always clear (Kassymbekova 2003). What was made clear was where the control of legal norms lay. At the height of Stalinism, marked by show trials throughout the Soviet bloc, the repressive nature of the criminal law and system was evidenced (Hodos 1987; Piekarska 1995). This tightly controlled system is seemingly in disarray, and society has had to adopt different strategies and ways to cope. Such a relationship, between penal policy decisions and societal attitudes and responses, is not straightforward, especially in a society marked by persistence of conflict and dissent, throughout its history: during the Partition lasting over a century; the prewar period; and communist rule (Greenberg 1980). The development that can be identified now is in some ways the "demystification" of the project. As the system of punishment was mystified under communist rule (Kassymbekova 2003), the abolitionist campaign "demystifies" capital punishment, as being an effective deterrent. Another component of this demystification process is led by the Council of Europe, in particular as concerns the death penalty. In this process the location of the control of legal norms is clear and—as under the former regime—just as far from the views of society.

The present-day discourse about this particular part of the cultural life of punishment masks something else—the perceptions of the meaning of democracy for Polish society. Bauman, in writing about freedom, observed:

> "You can say what you wish. This is a free country." We use and hear this expression too often to pause and think of its meaning; we take it as obvious, self-explanatory, presenting no problem to our, or to our partner's understanding. In a sense, freedom is like the air we breathe. We don't ask what this air is, we do not spend time discussing it, arguing about it, thinking of it. That is, unless we are in a crowded, stuffy room and find breathing difficult. (1988: 1)

In examining the discourse in Poland about capital punishment, one is witnessing Girling's identity politics "in action," led by the politicians on the one hand who are attracted by European integration, and lawyers on the other, who must consider European and international norms in their reasoning. One must ask whether it reaches society and, if so, whether it is in a limited way which leaves society dissatisfied with and disassociated from the discourse, because it is not addressed to society. The long-term consequence of the paternalistic stance as concerns the democratic process is uncertain. Even the future of freedom is not predetermined, even if the seemingly "right" choices are made.

Notes

I thank Antonio Ocaña Pradal and Barbara Mauthe for valuable comments and lively discussions on the subject. I also thank Susan Hirsch, who chaired the panel at the Law and Society Association Meeting, Pittsburgh, PA, USA, June 2003, where this paper was originally presented. This work is based on a general overview of the abolition of capital punishment in Central and Eastern Europe. See Fijalkowski (2002).

1. A special court was created in September 1944 and disbanded 17 October 1946. The Supreme National Tribunal established by the *Decree of 22 January 1946 Concerning Special Courts* sentenced 631 persons to death. A quasi-criminal court was established to hear the cases brought under the August Decree. Recently, details of two cases have been uncovered, which have further fueled the controversy surrounding this dark period; prosecutors have filed charges against the presiding judge in one of the cases, claiming that she adjudicated the case with the full knowledge that the defendant had not committed the crimes he was charged with.

2. Article 9(1) of the Law of 28 October 1950 Concerning the Ban on Possessing Foreign Currency, Gold Coins, Gold or Platinum as well as Making the Punishment Concerning Monetary Crimes More Severe provided for the death penalty as an alternative punishment; in these cases the defendant was found guilty of changing money without the approval of the Monetary Commission.

3. The death penalty was provided as an alternative punishment in the Decree of 22 January 1944 Concerning Responsibility for the September Massacre and Fascist State and as a mandatory sentence in the Decree of 31 August 1944 Concerning the Application of Punishment for the Fascist-Nazi Criminals Guilty of Crimes and Attacks on Civilians and Patriots and Traitors of the Polish Nation.

4. "Nil" was the code name of General Emil Fieldorf, one of the most important leaders of the Polish Home Army, which operated underground during the Second World War. In the early 1950s, he was tried and sentenced to death for conspiring with the Germans during the war by one of the special courts created after the 1944 decree concerning special courts for fascist-Nazi crimes. See Toranska (1987: 328–31) and Piekarska (1995: 25–41).

5. There is also very little known about the state of prisons in Poland during this period.

6. According to statistics, between 1964 and 1969 some thirty-three final death sentences were rendered; between 1970 and 1975 some seventy-eight final death sentences were rendered by courts of regular jurisdiction.

7. Alicja Greśkowiak has been an important spokesperson against capital punishment. She was a member of the Solidarity opposition movement and currently is a professor of law at the Catholic University of Lublin and a member (Marshall) of the Polish Senate.

8. Jerzy Jasiński is an important opponent of capital punishment and a professor of criminology.

9. For an interesting analysis of crime rates and imprisonment in Poland, see Greenberg (1980). See also Krzysztof Kieślowski's film *A Short Film about Killing*, part 5 of the *Dekalog* (10 Commandments) series. The film represents the views of Polish intellectuals concerning capital punishment in the 1980s.

10. Protocol No. 6 to the ECHR, concerning the abolition of the death penalty, adopted by the Council of Europe in 1982, provides for the abolition of the death penalty in peacetime; it states parties may retain the death penalty for crimes "in time of war or of imminent threat of war." Any state party to the ECHR can become party to the Protocol. See also Gross (1996). The Second Optional Protocol to the International Covenant on Civil and Political Rights (ICCPR), aimed at abolition of the death penalty and adopted by the UN General Assembly in 1989, provides for the total abolition of the death penalty but allows state parties to retain the death penalty in time of war if they make a reservation to that effect at the time of ratifying or acceding to the Protocol.

11. See also Titkow (1993).

12. Janusz Kochanowski exemplifies this trend. A law professor and editor of a conservative legal journal *Ius and Lex*, Kochanowski is a supporter of capital punishment.

References

Bae, Sangmin (2003) "Democratic Consolidation in Progress: South Korea on the Road to the Abolition of Capital Punishment." Unpublished paper on file with author.

Bauman, Zymunt (1988) *Freedom*. Milton Keynes: Open University Press.

Buchała, Kazimierz (1998) "Kara śmierci: argumenty za oraz przeciwko tej karze" (Capital Punishment: Arguments for and against the Penalty), in E. Nowicka-Włodarczyk, ed., *Kara śmierci* (25–37). Cracow: Fundacja Międzynarodowej Centrum Rozwoju Demokracji.

CBOS (Centrum Badania Opinii Społecznej/Centre for the Study of Public Opinion) (2000) "Czy w Polsce żyje się bezpiecznie?" (Is Poland Safe?), April. http://www.cbos.pl/ENGLISH/OPINIA/2000/04/3/OPINIA_3.htm.

CEORG (2002) "Central European Research Group Omnibus Survey." June, http://www.ceorg-europe.org.

Cieślak, Marian (1966) "Problemy kary śmierci," 12 *Państwo i Prawo* 833–53.

Council of Europe (2001) "The Council of Europe and the Death Penalty: Death Is Not Justice," October. http://www.coe.int/T/E/Human_rights/deathpen.pdf (accessed 4 June 2004).

Davies, Norman (1982) *God's Playground: A History of Poland,* Vol. 2. *1795 to the Present.* New York: Columbia University Press.

Ehrlich, S. (1956) "Głos przeciw karze śmierci" (A Vote Against the Death Penalty), 28 *Nowa Kultura*.

Ewick, Patricia, and Susan S. Silbey (1998) *The Common Place of Law*. Chicago: University of Chicago Press.

Fico, Robert (1999) "The Death Penalty in Slovakia," in R. Hood et al., eds., *The Death Penalty: Abolition in Europe*. Strasbourg: Council of Europe Publishing.

Fijalkowski, Agata (2002) "Die Abschaffung der Todesstrafe in Mittel- und Osteuropa" (The Abolition of the Death Penalty in Central and Eastern Europe) in C. Boulanger, P. Hanfling, and V. Heyes, eds. *Zur Aktualität der Todesstrafe: Interdisziplinäre und Globale Perspektiven*. Berlin: Berlin Verlag Arno Spitz. (In English [2001] "Abolition of the Death Penalty in Central and Eastern Europe," 9 *Tilburg Foreign Law Review* 62–83.)

Foucault, Michel (1979) *Discipline and Punish: The Birth of the Prison*. New York: Vintage Books.

Frankowski, Stanislaw (1996) "Post-Communist Europe," in P. Hodgkinson and A. Rutherford, eds., *Capital Punishment: Global Issues and Prospects*. Winchester, UK: Waterside Press.

Garland, David (1990) *Punishment and Modern Society: A Study in Social Theory*. Oxford: Clarendon Press.

Geertz, Clifford (1983) *Local Knowledge: Further Essays in Interpretative Anthropology*. New York: Basic Books.

Gelazis, Nida (2002) "Defending Order and Freedom: The Lithuanian Constitutional Court in its First Decade," in W. Sadurski, ed., *Constitutional Justice, East and West*. The Hague: Kluwer Law International.

Girling, Evi (2002) "'Wir, im Todestrakt': Die Todesstrafe in Amerika im Blick der Europäer" ("We, on Death Row" American Death Penalty under the European Gaze), in C. Boulanger, P. Hanfling, and V. Heyes, eds., *Zur Aktualität der Todesstrafe*. Berlin: Berlin Verlag Arno Spitz.

Greenberg, David F. (1980) "Penal Sanctions in Poland: A Test of Alternative Models," 28 *Social Problems* 194–204.

Gross, Aeyal M. (1996) "Reinforcing the New Democracies: The European Convention on Human Rights and the Former Communist Countries—A Study of the Case Law," 7 *European Journal of International Law* 103–11, http://www.ejil.org/journal/Vol7/No1/art5.pdf (accessed June 10, 2004).

Grześkowiak, Alicja (1978) *Kara śmierć, w polskim prawie karnym* (The Death Penalty in Polish Criminal Law). Toruń: Nicholas Copernicus University.

Hacking, Ian (1995) *Rewriting the Soul*. Princeton, NJ: Princeton University Press.

Hodos, George (1987) *Show Trials: Stalinist Purges in Eastern Europe, 1948–1954*. New York: Praeger.

Interview with Lech Kaczyński by Krzysztof Skowroński (12 June 2001), http://www. radio.com.pl/trojka/salon/default.asp?ID=1256.

Jankovic, Ivan (1984) "Socialism and the Death Penalty," 6 *Research in Law, Deviance and Social Control* 109–37.

Jasiński, Jerzy (1995) "Kościół wobec kary śmierć" (The Church with Respect to the Death Penalty), 7 *Państwo i Prawo* 56.

John Paul II, Pope (1995) "Evanglieum Vitae." http://www.vatican.va/holy_father/john_ paul_ii/encyclicals/documents/hf_jp-ii_enc_25031995_evangelium-vitae_en.html.

Kassymbekova, Botagoz (2003) "'Mystified Punishment', Clear Control." Unpublished paper on file with author.

Lenin, Vladimir Illyich Lenin (1983) *The State and Revolution, in Selected Works in Three Volumes*. Vol. 2, 2nd ed. Moscow: Bodley Head.

Łoś, Maria (1988) *Communist Ideology, Law and Crime: A Comparative View of the USSR and Poland*. New York: St Martin's Press.

Łoś, Maria (2002) "Post-Communist Fear of Crime and the Commercialization of Security," 6 *Theoretical Criminology* 165–88.

Łoś, Maria, and Andrzej Zybertowicz (2000) *Privatizing the Police State: The Case of Poland*. Houndmills: Macmillan.

Medvedev, Roy (1971) *Let History Judge: The Origins and Consequences of Stalinism*. New York: Macmillan.

Mitera, Monika, and Marek Zubik, eds. (1998) *Kara śmierć w świetle doświadczeń współczesnych systemów prawnych* (The Death Penalty in Light of the Findings from Contemporary Legal Systems). Warsaw: Helsińska Fundacja Praw Człowieka.

Nowicka-Włodarczyk, Ewa (1998) *Kara śmierci*. Cracow: Fundacja Międzynarodowej Centrum Rozwoju Demokracji.

Ossowska, Maria (1963) "Ogólne refleksie związane z projektem nowego kodeksu karnego" (General Reflections Concerning the Draft Criminal Code), 5–6 *Państwo i Prawo* 900.

Paprzycki, Lech (1999) "Ustawa łagodniejsza, lecz kara surowsza" (A Less Severe Law, a More Severe Punishment), *Rzcezcpospolita*, 21 (May), http://www.rzezczpospolita.pl.

Piekarska, Katarzyna Maria (1995) "Naruszanie zasady jawności w 'sądach tajnych'" (Violation of the Principle of Open Proceedings in the "Secret Courts"), 27 *Studia Iuridica* 25–41.

Sarat, Austin (2001) *When a State Kills: Capital Punishment and the American Condition*. Princeton, NJ: Princeton University Press.

Sarnecki, Paweł (2000) "Opinie: Dopuszczalność kary śmierci w świetle obowiązujących przepisów konstytucyjnych" (Opinion: Retention of the Death Penalty in Light of Constitutional Provisions), 3 *Przegląd Sejmowy* 77–85.

Simon, Jonathan (2002) "Why Do You Think They Call It CAPITAL Punishment? Reading the Killing State," 36 *Law and Society Review* 783–812.

Schiff Berman, Paul (2002) "The Cultural Life of Capital Punishment: Surveying the Benefits of a Cultural Analysis of Law," 102 *Columbia Law Review* 1129–77.

Szumski, Jerzy (1997) "Dzieje polskiego abolicjonizmu" (The Activities of the Polish Abolition Movement), 1 *Państwo i Prawo* 80–90.

Titkow, Anna (1993) *Stres i życie społeczne: polskie doświaidczenia* (Stress and Social Life: The Polish Experience). Warsaw: Państowy Instytut Badawczy.

Toranska, Teresa (1987) *"Them": Stalin's Polish Puppets*. New York: Harper & Row.

Uitz, Renata (2002) "Eine Verkettung glücklicher Umstände: Das ungarische Verfassungsgericht und die Todesstrafe" (A Chance of Luck: The Hungarian Constitutional Court and the Death Penalty), in C. Boulanger, P. Hanfling, and V. Heyes, eds., *Zur Aktualität der Todesstrafe*. Berlin: Berlin Verlag Arno Spitz.

Utrat-Milecki, Jarosław (1996) "Więziennictwo w Polsce w latach 1944–1956" (Prisons in Poland in the Years 1944–1956), in *Studia: materiały badawcze*. Wrocław: Uniwersytet Wrocławski.

Voslensky, Michael (1983) *Nomenklatura*. London: Bodley Head.

Weber, Max (1978) *Economy and Society*, Vol. I. Berkley, CA: University of California Press.

Wolczuk, Katarzyna (2002) "The Constitutional Court in Ukraine," in W. Sadurski, ed. (337–38), *Constitutional Justice, East and West*. The Hague: Kluwer Law International.

Wolter, W. (1956) "Znieść karę śmierć" (Abolish the Death Penalty), 30 *Nowa Kultura*. As quoted in Zubik (1998: 101), notes 29 and 30.

Zimring, Franklin (2002) *The Contradictions of American Capital Punishment*. Oxford: Oxford University Press.

"Zniesienie przypieczętowane" (A Sealed Abolition) (2000) *Rzeczpospolita*, 15 April, http://www.rzeczpospolita.pl.

Zoll, Andrzej (1998) "The New Polish Criminal Law Codification in Light of the Constitution," nos. 1–4 *Polish Contemporary Law* 89–99.

Zubik, Marek (1998) "Kara śmierci w Polsce" (Capital Punishment in Poland), in M. Mitera and M. Zubik, eds., *Kara śmierć w świetle doświadczeń wspołczesnych systemów prawnych* (The Death Penalty in Light of the Findings from Contemporary Legal Systems). Warsaw: Helsińska Fundacja Praw Człowieka.

Statutes Cited

Dziennik Ustaw (1944) No. 5, item 46.

Dziennik Ustaw (1946) No. 30, item 192.

Dziennik Ustaw (1950) No. 69, item 377.

Dziennik Ustaw (1998) No. 88, item 5.

PART II

State Killing and State Violence in Central and South Asia and the Middle East

CHAPTER EIGHT

Capital Punishment in Kyrgyzstan

Between the Past, "Other" State Killings and Social Demands

BOTAGOZ KASSYMBEKOVA

Introduction

For a country in transition that claims to institutionalize democracy, a functioning legal system can play an important role not just in state building, but also in rethinking the past in relation to the present. This is true of Kyrgyzstan, one of the poorest of the Central Asian republics, now undergoing an involuntary transition from seventy years of Soviet experience to become a newly independent secular state. The sudden break-up of the previous Soviet rule, followed by numerous political and economic changes in society, made people reassess their values of political and economic stability. Though post-Soviet governments claimed to break with the "cruel Soviet past," the actual break, as it turned out, was a change from one authoritarian rule to another.

Given the long and depressing history of cruel Soviet penal practices and dictatorial state authority, it is interesting for social scientists to see how this affected penal culture. The idea of legal structuring of society is essential for Western democracies. The idea of social contract, rule of law and/or *Rechtstaat*, according to most Western development agencies in Central Asia, is a foundation of a functioning state. Rule of law in democratic states, however, is possible when laws are seen as legitimate by society. Thus, according to Max Weber's theory, rule of law or legal domination is possible when individuals in a society find legitimacy in the belief in the "legality of enacted rules and the right of those elevated to authority under these rules to issue commands" (cited in Morrison 1995: 291). Under rule of law everyone, including the leaders of the state or community, is subject to the same laws and should behave according to legal norms of that society (ibid.).

In such systems, then, punishment should be seen as part of a rational legal domain. Legal punishment should also be legitimate since it passes with due process and therefore is rational. Moreover legal punishment has its cultural sensibilities as legality and culture are tied to each other (Garland 1990). Thus, *legal punishment* is not only political but also *cultural*, it is communicative and symbolic, it communicates the criminal and normal in society, it points out the order and the danger. According to Garland, penalty projects should be able to say what society is and the way individuals are and ought to be. Laws ought to communicate stability and regularity, codify, prescribe, and determine (Peter Fitzpatrick 1999: 121). This means that penal practices and discourses structure people's social worlds, norms, and categories and can therefore tell us something about people's wider cultures.

The idea of looking at penal practices and discourses as the politics of "normalization" is based on the idea of a binary opposition of normal and abnormal, where normality is expressed in the law and the outer realm is usually conceived of as deviant. This opposition is not constant and what is abnormal now can become "normal" in the future. What is important to notice is that this way of looking at norms of society *through* laws, which are supposed to reflect social values, is based on an assumption that legal structures are democratic and do more or less reflect public sentiment. This insight—that punishment is not just a functional practice of social or political control, but a very specific kind of "cultural artefact" (Garland 1990: 193)—has been extremely powerful in directing attention toward the culturally embedded meanings of punishment. However, Garland's position, which rests on an assumption about the relationship between penal discourse and popular attitudes to punishment itself, deserves to be examined. It assumes that penal discourse does, more or less accurately, reflect attitudes about the appropriate definition and response to the "deviant" that are circulating more broadly in society. But what about situations where the assumption that those imprisoned are necessarily guilty, or that penal practice really *does* act as an effective tool for determining guilt or innocence, or where rules have been profoundly ruptured, or where such a correlation of penal practice and popular penal attitudes could never have been said to have existed in the first place? Kyrgyzstan presents a powerful case study for the exploration of such a possibility. The combined legacy of Soviet penal practice and recent legal policy demonstrate that penal practice may be very remote from the "cultural forms" relating to punishment that are circulating more generally in a society.

In this chapter I suggest that if we are to look at "penal cultures" and, more concretely for the purposes of this chapter, the culture of capital punishment in Kyrgyzstan, we must set ourselves outside the box of legality and look at the wider meaning of death and individual life in society. My approach to the culture of the death penalty differs from that of David Garland only in that it looks at culture not simply through laws (i.e., laws as discursive significations of norms and values), but takes into account other factors to understand a web of human relationships and meanings in a community. Studies of capital punishment should be more than a legal or moral debate. If we care about the practice of capital punishment in societies because we are concerned with the organization of these societies in regard to human beings, their lives, and rights, then our inquiries into this question should transcend more spheres of society, since the question of the death penalty is not so much the philosophy of death, but the philosophy and practice of *life*. The abolishment of the death penalty should signify a humanization of society and its structures, not simply of the legal domain.

The Setting

As in many other post-Soviet states, the government of Kyrgyzstan proclaimed itself a new democratic country with respect to human rights and thus made a radical break with the authoritarian past. However, President Askar Akaev has not left office since his first presidential election in 1991, remaining in office for a third term, a pattern resembling the rest of Central Asia. Unlike its neighbors, Kyrgyzstan is poor in natural resources; it is primarily a rural country of four and a half million people that was left with an inefficient infrastructure, which resulted in the fall of the economy, standards of living, and levels of education; it has also experienced the growth of AIDS, alcoholism, and poverty and a wider gap between the poor and rich. Nevertheless, despite the general growth of human rights abuses since the country's independence, the president of Kyrgyzstan was the first Central Asian leader to announce a moratorium on the death penalty in 1998, which has been subsequently prolonged through December 2004. The moratorium is not a reflection of great "cultural" changes in Kyrgyzstani society, which has not truly engaged in public debates about the issue in the mass media, education, or research. The very fact that there is no systematic analysis of attitudes toward capital punishment is indicative of the fact that people feel the issue of the death penalty is irrelevant. The few who try to raise the issue are usually human rights activists who work with other human rights organizations in the West.

The question of whether to leave capital punishment in the Criminal Code, prolong the moratorium on it, or abolish it is one which I think embodies the larger realities of political, legal, and social "developments" in the republic. The Kyrgyzstani regime, one of the poorest of the five Central Asian states, highly dependent on international assistance, is both attempting to *please* international organizations that donate money and ask for democratic reforms, and trying to *keep* centralized, authoritarian control inside the state. As donor states and organizations expect Kyrgyzstan to increase respect for human rights and abolish the death penalty, most people *inside* the country either are not interested in the issue or seem to accept or be in favor of this penal measure. Since its independence, Kyrgyzstan has had an international image as an "island of democracy," which was surrounded by authoritarian and dictatorial regimes in Kazakhstan, Uzbekistan, and Turkmenistan. This image has been shattered in the past few years by rising corruption, the oppression of independent media, the falsification of election results, and President Askar Akaev's decision to accept a third term. As Kyrgyzstan grew more authoritarian, the president took few steps to sustain the image of Kyrgyzstan as the most democratic country in the region.

The moratorium on the death penalty was one of the steps to show the international community Akaev's adherence to the principles of human rights and respect for individual life. The moratorium, however, was *not* the abolition of capital punishment. Thus, it has been reported that some 160 men were on death row by the end of 2002 (Amnesty International Report 2003). It is virtually impossible to obtain official statistics on the number of people who have been sentenced or executed in previous years. As during the Soviet times, institutions and practices of punishment in Kyrgyzstan are not discussed, publicized, or seriously questioned.

In this chapter, I discuss the reasons for this general silence about the death penalty in the country. People's approval or disapproval of the death penalty is connected to their understanding of the state, its function, and its responsibilities. In periods of "transition," the public perception of the new state involves comparing it to the previous one. Exploring people's narratives of the Soviet state helps us to understand their expectations of the role of the state and the social order that the Kyrgyz state should bring. Oral narratives about the past can illustrate people's political imagination: how they view the state and its functions and what they expect from it. More concretely, I will look at the social demands that are interwoven into people's narratives of the state. By looking at the memory of the Soviet past, I will discuss how the death penalty and extra-judicial state killings were and are discoursed as a form of nation building in the Soviet years and how those discourses were interpreted and accepted by people. Then, by looking at different kinds of "deaths" (legal, state, structural) I will reflect on the role of structural violence in the public indifference toward capital punishment. Lastly, I will address the issue of external legal authorities and their influence on the legitimacy and practice of capital punishment and human rights protection in Kyrgyzstan.

Criminality, Chaos, and the Need/Hope for Order

People in post-Soviet Kyrgyzstan and post-Soviet states more generally criticize and denounce the absence of order and economic stability, rising criminality, and chaos. Order, however, in this case has a particular meaning: autocratic governance with economic equality and growth. If we compare this with the Russian Federation, according to recent polls more than a decade after the collapse of the Soviet Union, a majority of people in Russia think that Stalin brought more positive than negative influences to Soviet society (Dubin 2003). The image of Stalin as a positive great leader, however, became popular only in the late 1990s. The rhetoric of "stability and order" in a chaotic and criminal society gained weight through the popularization of the symbol of Stalin as the promises of the new government turned out to be untrue (ibid.). An analogous situation can be seen in the south of Kyrgyzstan, where for the large Uzbek population the Uzbek president Islam Karimov was seen at the time as a "Khan figure in the sense of a wise and ruthless paternal despot whose harsh ways work for the good of his people" (Lui 2003: 204). The "order" and central control that President Karimov installed in Uzbekistan, with a centrally planned economy resembling that of the Soviet state in the early 1990s, were envied not only by the people of southern Kyrgyzstan, but also those living in southern Kazakhstan. Although these two areas particularly suffered from economic backwardness and criminality, the somewhat "Soviet" order on the other side of the border in Uzbekistan, was admired. Today, however, as Uzbekistani politics seem more and more disastrous, the Soviet past seems to have become the source of admiration. Still, it is not uncommon to hear people say, "it would be better if the Soviet Union lost World War II, so that Hitler developed the country; so at least we would have a German order. Look, we would all drive Mercedeses now." Such comments and outcries for order must not be understood literally as they demonstrate not so much the real desires of people, but their criticism of the contemporary situation. It is not likely that these people seriously think they would feel good under totalitarianism, since many of them sympathize with people in the states of Turkmenistan and Uzbekistan. However, it tells us what *kind* of authority—centralized and one that brings *order*—is in their political imagination; what kind of authority, in their desires, is more or less acceptable.

The need for order is due to the increased criminality on the streets, distrust in militia and legal institutions, the corruption of court personnel, and the portrayal of criminality in the media. Chaos and criminality make people desire cruel punishment for criminals and all those who destabilize the social order. Capital punishment then is not seen as an illegitimate way to "fight" with the chaos of the everyday. Paradoxically, strict punishment and control of the streets are not problematic and are even desired despite the general distrust of the courts and the legal structure. Thus, it is not simply the lack of state or court legitimacy that is the basis for people's indifference to the issue of the death penalty. The desire for social order and a strong state and at the same time skepticism toward the contemporary state that cannot satisfy economic, safety, and social needs of its citizens produces apathy toward engagement in political debates of penal practices in relation to rights of the prisoners. People's social downward mobility and rising insecurity about their and their relatives' future is a massive blow to their dignity, identity, and well-being. Thus it is relevant to look at why debates about retribution are so much about social demands, rather than the individual human rights of prisoners.

(In)Equality and Downward Mobility

Hence, equality is another concern which, although less significant, nevertheless adds to the discourse of harsh penal policies. Concern about equality is usually the concern of a large portion of the population who has experienced extreme downward economic and social mobility. There is no clear-cut link between capital punishment and the concern for equality. But there is perhaps a link between the *memory* of moral and economic equality that was pronounced by the Soviet government, and the contemporary rise in inequality that compels people to seek legitimacy in the previous Soviet government. The memory of equality does not mean that people blindly believe there was no inequality during the Soviet years; this would be a simple overestimation. The popularity and nostalgia of the "good old days" in many post-Soviet states is not so much a sign of absolute satisfaction with past politics and everyday life but, again, more a comparison with the past and a critique of the present situation.

In recollecting Soviet times, one of the most important issues is equality. This includes the intelligentsia and members of the Communist Party, as they often suffered no less than "ordinary" citizens. Shootings, state killing without trial, and the investigation of "important" people equalized them with ordinary people in death. In that regard, death signified equality. This is not an unusual phenomenon; for example, in the case of the French Revolution, Anne Norton suggested that "the guillotine put the institution of capital punishment in accord with the principle of equality manifest in a common mortality" (1999: 28). Although not as open and not as explicit, the Stalinist purges and other state killings of the Soviet period symbolize (at least today) this too, as not even high-ranking people were absolutely immune from being shot by order of the state.

Rising inequality and poverty, instability, and the absence of social, legal, and economic protection from the government make it easier for people to feel sympathetic toward the previous purges and killing of people in the higher echelons of the hierarchy. Those who face downward mobility, rising inequality, and poverty desire that justice be done to those who are in power. The desire to punish those who hold high positions in the government makes it more possible for them to be in favor of violent penal measures. People who suffer from economic and social depression look to avenge the dashing of their hopes for the future—a future that seemed quite promising before the collapse of the Soviet Union.

The cruelty of the Soviet regime and the sweet ideology of "equality" are legacies which, for better or for worse, constitute one dimension of the culture of capital punishment in Kyrgyzstan and in most post-Soviet arenas. I do not want to suggest that people in post-Soviet Kyrgyzstan (and other Central Asian states) are "not ready for democracy" or that order and economy come first, as Kazakh President Nursultan Nazarbaev stated in his speech to the nation (Nazarbaev 2003), but that these are the very arguments that are "taken for granted" and used to justify oppressive regimes and approval for harsh criminal penalties. I do, however, want to understand where they come from and what their consequences are. By supporting, or at least not opposing, cruel punishment, people strive for *equality* and *justice* in their understanding of these terms, and their position expresses a critique of the present social and political situation from which they often do not see a way out. My interpretative analysis of general attitudes toward capital punishment—the need for order and hope for equality, as well as displaced feelings of revenge—an interpretation of these attitudes and not an endorsement of them.

It has been suggested that authoritarianism and the death penalty are related phenomena. On the other hand, favoring the death penalty is not necessarily evidence that people who are accustomed to or favor violence are essentially undemocratic, but, as in the case of Kyrgyzstan, rather an expression of dissatisfaction toward the contemporary state or changes that have occurred in recent decades. Paradoxically, there is the image of the right, correct, and good state as all-powerful, giving, just, and successful authoritarian state. I remember talking to a Kyrgyz taxi driver about his service in the Soviet army (Bishkek, private communication, June 2003). Unexpectedly he cheerfully and at the same time sadly recollected that service in the army for him, a young man from a Kyrgyz village, was one of his happiest memories. I asked why. He answered that in the army he was taken care of, given food and clothes; he served and traveled to another country, something he would never have been able to do without the Soviet government. He said that he would love to hide from "real" life in the army today, if just someone called him to go to the Soviet army.

Is this the "authoritarian mind"? Yes and no. I think that it reflects a natural quest for economic and social stability. It is exhaustion with poverty and instability and the desire for a "normal/better" life. I am reluctant to call this mind authoritarian for the reason that it does not praise the present government, but in fact condemns it. It is and at the same time *it is not* the lack of the culture of human rights that influences the people's unwillingness to debate the issue of capital punishment. On the contrary, a distinctive outcry for rights can be seen in the lethargy about the present, and apathy toward the future makes this person look back to the authoritarianism of the past.

Between Past and Present Violence

If many postsocialist Eastern European societies have been actively dealing with their communist past by publicizing the wrong-doings of the state and state agents, Central Asian *societies*, as opposed to governments, have not hurried to denounce the violence of the Soviet state. Although the Kyrgyzstani government did criticize the previous government after declaring its independence, thus proclaiming a new, truly democratic government, today it is more likely to accept public *nostalgia* toward the Soviet past.[1] For example, a decade after its independence the Kyrgyzstani government restored the celebration of the October Revolution and therefore the Bolshevik legitimacy, and it still celebrates the May parade which commemorates the victory of World War II, the history and politics of which have not fully been questioned. After hundreds of thousands of people were killed under the Soviet regime, the violence of yesterday is not condemned and most ordinary people whose relatives were purged or killed do not seek justice.

Bluntly speaking, people in Kyrgyzstan would not go out onto the streets and shout that they or their relatives suffered. Some are even ashamed or simply fail to acknowledge that their relatives or neighbors were unjustly persecuted by and suffered from state killings. It is an honor to say that your relative was killed in World War II, but almost impossible to hear about purges. They are unknown, forgotten, or "never happened." Hundreds of thousands of ethnic Russians, Germans, Tatars, Meshitins, Chechens, Greeks, Jews, Ukrainians,

Koreans, and many others who were exiled to Central Asia during Soviet years from their homelands died or were killed on their way (Zemtsov 1991: 83). Their deaths are often not recognized as state killings, as often the new generation of these "punished" groups never questioned the Soviet rule. Neither archives nor memory allows people to rethink or be critical of the past regime. Although there are some criticisms toward the nationalities policies of the Communist Party (i.e., many Russians were first-class citizens), there is no general dissatis-faction with the history of Soviet repressions and deaths.

One interesting case is the "discovery" of a concentration camp where several dozen prominent men of various ethnic backgrounds were killed on "grounds of treachery" in a Stalinist purge in 1937 near Bishkek, the capital of Kyrgyzstan. A security guard who worked in the holiday villa of the Soviet Kyrgyz Central Committee, parts of which were used as the concentration camp, decided to reveal the secret of the state killings of 1937 to his daughter be-fore his death. The daughter was afraid to share the secret during Soviet years, even after de-Stalinization and *perestroika*. She told authorities about it only af-ter Kyrgyzstan gained independence, when it was safe to talk about the purges (interview with a memorial worker in Bishkek 2003; Khelimskaya 1994: 3). What is interesting is that there *were* other ways to find out about these killings after de-Stalinization and during *perestroika*, not just through this woman, but through archives and other people who also knew about the killings. They, however, did nothing to present the information to the public. Ironically, the father of one of the best-known people in Kyrgyzstan—writer Chingiz Aitma-tov—was shot and buried in this camp. The truth was revealed by the daughter of a security guard.

After independence, when the site was discovered almost by accident, the case was used in the creation of a new national identity, for nation building. The government publicized the case, since it fit the discourse well: Stalinist purges of Kyrgyzstani intelligentsia, particularly as they included people of dif-ferent ethnicities, offered a space for an ideological rupture with the Soviet past. Such a finding made it easier to condemn Soviet rule and pronounce the intro-duction of a new, supposedly democratic government.

The Kyrgyzstani government has since built a monument and museum to commemorate the victims of Stalinist killings, and archives of the persecutions were discovered immediately and shown to the public. Interestingly, although the men shot outside Frunze in 1937 had not been tried, there were legal documents about their cases and most were officially shot for being "enemies" or "traitors of the People." Was it capital punishment, or a state killing? If we agree that a state killing is murder in the name of the state and by state agents, but define capital punishment as the execution of a court's decision, then the 1937 killings—a deliberated killing in the name of the state, by state agents—present a puzzle. We have some legal documents and the "official" reasons why these people were killed; however, there was no trial and relatives of the killed were not told that their fathers, brothers, and husbands had been executed. The boundary between state and capital punishment in this specific case is virtually nonexistent. The Kyrgyzstani government did not address the issue in terms of the debate on capital punishment, but rather addressed it from the standpoint of the state killing, which for the present government seems to be two distinct things.

Although the Kyrgyzstani government has built a monument to commemorate the victims of Stalinist purges and, softly put, the wrongdoings of the Soviet regime are not denied, Soviet rule is still more positively than negatively regarded by the general public. This is not to say that people think Stalin was right to kill so many people, but that they think everyday life during the Soviet period was better, where "life" means economic well-being, stability, and social security. The question then arises: if people still consider the Soviet years as the best, even after the number of purges and cases of torture and hunger have been revealed, how can a few dozen annual cases of the death penalty in the country raise concern? How can there be a debate on capital punishment and respect for individual life and human rights if there are many people who proclaim that the country needs a second Stalin to put everything back in order, or that it would be better if Hitler had won World War II so people had the same standards of living as in Germany today, or that Mikhail Gorbachev ruined their lives?

It would be unjust to say that people in Kyrgyzstan do not see the negative side of authoritarianism and dictatorship. Collecting oral histories is particularly helpful in looking at people's understanding of repression. One popular memory in Bishkek is that under Stalin's rule if one was caught wrapping food or something else in a newspaper on which a picture of Stalin was printed, one would almost surely be exiled to Siberia or receive the death penalty.[2] Another common memory of Soviet oppression is the so-called law of the three, under which two persons could calumniate against a third, thus sending him or her to either a death sentence or to Siberia.[3] A good reason for denouncing a friend was a political joke or pronunciation of Stalin's name. One folk story, told to me by an eighty-year-old pensioner in Bishkek (March 2003) suggests that there is an interesting pattern in the two previous accounts. His story is that in Soviet times, there was a person who had been sentenced to death. However, just before he was supposed to be shot, the man tore his shirt and showed that he had "Stalin" tattooed on his breast. According to the pensioner, this tattoo saved the man's life since no one wanted or dared to shoot the Soviet leader. Such memories demonstrate that people do see the bad side of the previous regime, but they also portray a political imagination of the previous regime. At one point they define the personal authority of the leader and personalized punishment as cruel, at another moment it is kind because it saves you from death.

There is an interesting pattern of the personalization of authority and punishment in the memories and imaginations of people in Kyrgyzstan. This is not only personalization in the face of one leader, but also in neighbors and society, where one's neighbors can punish you for "inappropriate" behavior. It would be wrong to suggest that there was absolutely no principle of justice or legal norms in Soviet Kyrgyzstan, but rather that the principle of self-protection was and perhaps is still rather strong (S. Fitzpatrick 1999: 116). The decision not to execute a person with "Stalin" tattooed on his chest was not simply a matter of justice but also one of self-protection. How it would be reported or interpreted by others who might denounce you was thought and rethought. To be denounced, to be an outcast in Soviet society, was dangerous not only for that person, but also for his or her family and friends. It is thus not surprising that to talk about the previous terror would involve more than looking only at Soviet leaders—it would also entail examining yourself, your own community, community leaders, and so on.

Personalization of punishment is the result of the history of Soviet punitive structures, which need to be examined and considered. Particularly, there should be demystification of punishment. In many nondemocratic states, particularly in the Soviet state, *who* controlled the legal norms was clarified, but punishment was mystified. That is what makes the discussion about the culture of capital punishment in post-Soviet states difficult. Thus, in the Soviet past control belonged solely to the Communist Party, but the punishment delivered by that Party very often was not clear.

If democratic states implement punishment through legal structures, the control of this process is not clear, it is implied. In Western states there is great discussion about who controls the society. Is it people, governments, the elite, capitalism, history, laws, and/or cultures that control societies? There is no clear answer of who or what controls the state, the society, and the laws by which society is supposed to be governed. There are constellations of power, culture, traditions, and so on. Thus, where laws are being clarified as a means of control, control is somehow mystified. Although saying that control is mystified, I do not suggest that someone mystifies control on purpose. I am also not interested who or what exactly controls the society, since it is the synthesis of power.

Throughout the Soviet years often the identity of the "enemy of the people" or "traitor" was never clarified and was not explained in laws. "Enemy of the people" was an overloaded label that could be used as an excuse for punishing any crime or deed by the death sentence. Penal practices were used arbitrarily, often without trials, resulting in the imprisonment of thousands of innocent people. It is here that the legal prescription and societal values and norms have a ruptured relationship. Terror, rather than social norms and culture, dictated the penal discourse and practice. No one was secure from being labeled a traitor, the people's enemy, or a counter-revolutionary. Penal practices were often confusing and terrifying. Research by some historians during the Soviet years demonstrates that even those who were imprisoned believed that their imprisonment was an awkward mistake that the party was unaware of (see Khubova 1992; Sherbakova 1992). It is in these ways that the punishment was mystified.

For the society to develop its functioning and legitimate system, punishment should be constantly justified, articulated, challenged, and debated. Penal practices are as much discursive practices as they are physical and practical. Where there is silence or lack of clarity toward the practices, that is, penal practices, where social order is concerned, articulation is needed. Kyrgyzstani society should decide that the dilemma of capital punishment and state killing is a serious issue: should those be synonymous with one underlying logic or used as different things? A good example for such an analytical framework would be recent events when militiamen shot and killed several antigovernment protesters in March 2001 (see below). Was it a crime, capital punishment, or a state killing? This issue was, ironically, mystified; however, it should be clarified.

It has been suggested that memory depends upon comprehension and interest (Thompson 2000: 172). Memory is not just a passive collector of past events but is an active process in that it changes according to an individual's desires and identity. Thus, memory is not only an individual but also a social phenomenon. When people recall, they get into an active process of creating identities, be those of community, generation, civil society, gender, and so on. Second, memory can "equally convey the individual and collective consciousness" (ibid.) and the "variety of forms through which cultural communities imagine themselves in diverse representational modes" (Kritzman cited in David-Fox 2001: 611). Oral narratives, or "reflective insights of retrospection" are "precisely this historical perspective which allows us to assess long-term meaning in history" (Thompson 2000: 172). Since memories and many issues from the past are often rather sensitive, it can be argued that it is better to forget the past than remember or try to restore memories. Thus, as suggested earlier, questioning the Soviet past and the post-Soviet present raises nationality problems. The Russian and Kyrgyz urban populations blame each other for the failures of the past and of the present accordingly. What unites them, however, is common positive memory of the past.

The forgetting and lack of acknowledgment of previous crimes and even the celebration of the previous era raise a very difficult question. If social memory is an active process of construction of identities and meanings through the past, what should be done for the past to be reconsidered and memory to change? How, to use the words of Applebaum (2003), is it possible to make the past a burden, obligation, and bad consciousness by which to judge the past, present, and the future? There should be many answers. Further democratic transformations in the present society are preconditions for the respect of individual life and full recognition of the past atrocities, just as recognition of the past is necessary for the rethinking of the present.

By analyzing discourses about punishments from the past, I propose that the issue of capital punishment or state killing has to do with reconsidering the past as a larger phenomenon. If the violent, crude past state killings are not questioned by the people, how can a less violent contemporary government be questioned? Taking into consideration this historical legacy of "mystified" punitive measures, the absence of debates about it, and the nostalgic memory of the past that is due to the uncertain present, I believe it is still useful to look at the "structural" violence of the everyday to understand the social demands of the people. My refusal to think of the people as having purely "authoritarian minds" forces me to look at other issues, which I think are connected to the question of capital punishment. Therefore, I believe it is important to look at the constellation of death/state/society on a broader scale. How does the relationship between state, death, and society make the debate of capital punishment without consideration of "other deaths" in society superficial?

Capital Punishment, State Killing, and Other Deaths

Although for Austin Sarat (1999) there seems to be no difference between state killing and capital punishment, this difference was very important to the Soviet state and has now become important in many post-Soviet states. The idea of the legal structuring of society is essential for Western democracies. Rule of law, according to most Western development agencies in Central Asia, is a foundation of a functioning state. Rule of law in democratic states, however, should be possible when laws are seen as legitimate by society. In nondemocratic states, however, to look at the issue of capital punishment does not mean looking deeply at the issue of death, society, and the political/economic structure. Death exists outside legal structures but is still connected to the penal and state institutions that I suggest also contribute to people's disinterest in the issue of the death penalty in Kyrgyzstan and other post-Soviet states. The fact that government is responsible for more deaths, not simply those of capital punishment, makes debate on capital punishment in Central Asia, and perhaps other states, as the only state killing at times somewhat superficial.

The Kyrgyzstani government is not as oppressive as those in neighboring countries. The last state killing, which occurred in Kyrgyzstan in March 2001, was probably the only *public* state killing in its short history, when militiamen shot and killed six peaceful protesters in southern Kyrgyzstan. The protest movement had been asking officials to free a jailed opposition leader, called a political prisoner by human rights organizations. On the day of his trial, protesters staged a demonstration, and six men were killed. The militiamen and those officials who ordered them to fire in to the crowd are today receiving amnesty from the government and will not be put on trial. This state killing was not capital punishment; it was without trial. Still, the public by and large remained silent.[4]

To understand extra-judicial killings in post-Soviet Kyrgyzstan, it is not enough to understand people's social worlds and pessimism toward the issue of capital punishment. Open state killings such as those that took place in March 2001 in Kyrgyzstan are not a frequent event, even for the whole of Central Asia. Death and dying in Kyrgyzstan and other countries of Central Asia, as it is associated with the modern state, has to be understood in terms of institutionalized violence. If we want to comprehend the culture and therefore the meaning of capital punishment for people in Kyrgyzstan, it is important to look not only at what kind of authority people look to for preserving what is, in their understanding, "social order." It is also important to look at the understanding of death itself in a larger context. Thus, when thinking about state-assigned death, capital punishment would probably not be the first thing people would think about. Many believe that going to jail can often mean being killed: by being tortured to death by prison staff[5] or contracting a fatal illness such as tuberculosis. Going to jail is a real threat for many of the poor: Penal Reform International counts Kyrgyzstan among the twenty countries with the highest prison population (Aslanbekova 2003). This is one of the reasons a group of researchers, health professionals, and prison administrators ask why prisoners in Eastern Europe and Central Asia are sentenced to death since conditions in the prisons kill many of them (Stern 1999).

The daily expense for one prisoner in Kyrgyzstan is equal to ten to sixteen soms ($0.25–0.30) (Galunichev 2003). That would amount to 500–700 grams of bread and not even a liter of milk. The Kyrgyzstani Ministry of Justice reports that about 20 percent of prisoners die from illnesses such as tuberculosis, HIV, cholera, and dysentery. This in turn is caused by the rising number of imprisonments (International Centre for Prison Studies 2003; see Stern 1999), overcrowding, "poor sanitary and hygienic conditions, insufficient nutrition, and poor medical treatment in prisons" (Aslanbekova 2003). Deaths are prevalent not only in penal institutions such as prisons. To die in the army is a real danger too. Paying off your service in the army is not cheap, but people believe the price is worth paying for keeping your physical and mental health. Inhumane conditions in these state institutions (prisons and armies) are not capital punishment or state killings per se. They do, however, add to the culture of "state" death in Kyrgyzstan, where merely serving in the army can end in suicide or mental problems. To be more precise, although there is a higher possibility of dying while serving in the army either through suicide or torture in Turkmenistan and Kazakhstan, in Kyrgyzstan, illnesses, poor nutrition, recent war in the southern region, and torture make serving in the army unsafe.

In everyday life as well, widespread alcoholism, rising suicide and homicide rates (Lester 1998; UNDP 2002), and drug addiction in the villages keeps the possibility of death relatively high. The lack of medicines and money to buy them, unequipped hospitals, and poor medical services make the possibility of death ever-present. These and other similar possibilities of death are tied to the state, to its inadequate social services, the absence of care, and widespread corruption at all levels of executive institutions. These are not accidents or "natural" deaths, though they might be labeled as such, but deaths related to the state and the economic and political structure.

The link between the latter, institutionalized forms of "other deaths" and capital punishment is not clear-cut. However, if we are interested in looking at the social and cultural conditions of capital punishment, I think the analysis offers a certain insight: the political and social relationship between death and society lives not only in the legal domain. Therefore, if we are to address the issue of death, law, and society we should look at the possibilities of death outside the legal box since the death in the legal context does not necessarily mean something different from death outside. To challenge state violence in a purely legal context will not challenge its treatment of individual life.

To return to the fact that president Askar Akaev has proclaimed a moratorium on the death penalty, despite the general public's approval of it and the government's authoritarian trends, requires us to look beyond "internal" or national conditions surrounding the issue of the death penalty in Kyrgyzstan. The moratorium extends the culture of capital punishment outside Kyrgyzstan's borders, an issue I address in the next section.

The State from Outside, the State from Within

In his case study of legal process in three different cultures, David M. Engel explores the construction of injury, remedy, and identity and what the production of meaning in particular time and space can tell us about the making of social order. By looking at court cases that took place in Tibet in the 1940s, the United States in the 1880s, and Thailand in the 1960s the author tries to understand how court decisions and process reflect larger realities within these "local" social milieus. Engel concludes that the "[l]aw transforms symbols and images drawn from local settings and redeploys them as authoritative pronouncements that can potentially change the very settings from which they are drawn" (2001: 17). Engel suggests that law is not static and neutral, but that it is betwixt and between the local and the outside authority. Through courts, judges and groups are more broadly able to express their understanding of time and space, community and justice.

Although Engel warns those who attempt to understand laws in terms of social cultures not to overgeneralize these situations to other societies, in the case of capital punishment, I think it can tell us about how elites and societies try to construct *national* identities. In the case of Kyrgyzstan I suggest that the moratorium on capital punishment is not the expression of how the Kyrgyzstani community sees itself, or even how elites construct new identities. It says less about the understanding of justice, remedy, and injury in twenty-first-century Kyrgyzstan than it does about understandings of the relationship between Kyrgyzstan and "the West." The moratorium is not a result of "ordinary" people's understanding of themselves or the value of life and the notion of justice, but rather the elites' understanding of the particular relationship that the Kyrgyzstani government has with other states.

As an expert on legal transformations Barrister Charles Foster who worked in Central Asia has said of penal reform, "it is undoubtedly true that both [Kazakh and Kyrgyz] governments understand that western investment and donation are to some extent conditional on continuing reform, and I have no doubt that this is a big factor in legal reforms throughout Central Asia."[6] Although it would be an overestimation to say that all domestic laws are products of Kyrgyzstani government efforts to please foreign donors, this is the case with regard to capital punishment. Interestingly, the moratorium on the death penalty by government officials was not deliberately oriented toward the Kyrgyzstani *society,* for which the moratorium is supposed to be a step in securing human rights, but rather toward the international community and its attitude toward the Kyrgyzstani government. Thus, the ombudsman of the country commented, "I think if we prolong its [the moratorium's] term, the world community [and] our donor countries in Europe would welcome it" (Eshanova 2002). The state killings of the past and current human rights debate have thus far been only tools for the official nation-state ideology, not actual nation-state building.

David Garland has argued that "penal laws and institutions are always proposed, discussed, legislated, and operated within definite cultural codes" and that is why we should look at punishment "as a complex cultural artefact, encoding the signs and symbols of the wider culture in its own practices" (1990: 198). In the case of Kyrgyzstan one is forced to look at a global penal culture that transcends the boundary of the sovereign state. Conditionality by Western organizations, which by and large come from the United States, reflects the view of modern states on a more global scale. Having not fully abolished the death penalty in the United States it is able to influence other states to abolish it. What are global legal regimes if not bargains between the supra-national powers and "weak" states? I am not arguing that the moratorium on capital punishment is negative, but rather suggesting that in view of everyday attitudes toward the issue, or more correctly, everyday silences toward it, it is important not to overestimate "democratic" developments within the country. If abolishing the death penalty in order to please international donors allows a corrupt government to continue being supported with loans and donations, then the conditions for more humane and democratic governance are more likely to be ignored in a situation where rising poverty and corruption contribute to problems of overall violence and criminality. In other words, if we address only the question of capital punishment and capital power (the state), while believing that the authoritarianism of the state is expressed in state killings, then even if the international community deals with the issue of capital punishment through its abolition in Kyrgyzstan, the issue of authoritarianism will not be addressed. State killings can live on in other ways, which are much harder to trace, prove, and attribute responsibility for. David Garland aptly noticed that "any external force or determinant which seeks to transform penal practice—whether it be a law, a policy directive, or some economic or cultural rationality—must first transform this penal culture if it is to become effective" (1990: 210). This condition was not practiced in what is now Kyrgyzstan for the past century. Penal norms and practices were arbitrarily imposed and practiced. If before it was the imposition of the death penalty, today it is its abolition. Past legacies and memories, social norms and values, and structural predispositions are not taken into account.

In trying to understand popular sensibilities of the death penalty in Kyrgyzstan I am not defending popular justice or a return to capital punishment, but rather calling for a lesser gap between laws and society. The relationship between the latter should be reflective and therefore in some ways connected. This connection can be achieved if we address the issues of past penal practices, memory, institutional violence, and public concerns, which are part of a penal culture that contributes to particular understandings of authority, order, and justice. Changing laws without taking the wider context of these laws into consideration will not necessarily increase the respect for human life and rights. In its thrust for stability, order, and equality Kyrgyzstani society is not different from most other human communities; however, its historical legacies differ. By highlighting the influence of international organizations I do not defend Kyrgyzstani sovereignty. Instead I want to suggest that the current moratorium is used as a tool for international relations, not for penal reform. Penality should at least try to be more than the politics of officials; it should address the rights of individuals and groups, democracy, and rule of law. By addressing the issues of death, law, society, stability and order, the past and its memory, I believe we address not only death but the value of life.

Conclusion

Garland concluded that punishment is not simply a legal-administrative entity but also "an expression of state power, a statement of collective morality, a vehicle for emotional expression, an economically conditioned social policy, an embodiment of current sensibilities, and a set of symbols which display a cultural ethos and help create a social identity" (1990: 287). How much all these definitions or forces are "at work" varies from one context another. What we need to understand is that the policy of punishment—that "necessary evil"—involves more than one dimension of power.

For Kyrgyzstan, a newly independent secular state of four and a half million people with seventy years of Soviet experience, the issue of capital punishment is serious. The death penalty is accepted in the popular culture and is not yet outlawed in the Penal Code. Since the moratorium on the death penalty was *not* proclaimed for the genuine attempts to "humanize" the society, but rather to please the international community, more legal death sentences are possible, especially in the case of a change of political power. Furthermore, people are being "executed" even though there is a moratorium on the death penalty. Simple attempts to outlaw the death penalty will not solve the problem because the death penalty and capital punishment (strictly defined) is actually only one part of a larger, interconnected problem, which consists of the following four dimensions: (1) international subservience to an international donor community rather than a politics of deep-rooted social change, (2) a legacy of the past where penal practices were imposed without deliberation of the norms upon which they were imposed, (3) an authoritarian social and political culture in which average people actually value social order and stability over human life, and (4) the role of the state in death is actually much larger than capital punishment or state killings, as people can be "sentenced to death" simply by joining the army or checking into a hospital.

In order to increase respect for human rights (in society) and the institutionalization of laws that protect human rights (by the state), it is important to understand the discourses that both state and society (people) use to make sense out of capital punishment and make their own decisions about what is right and wrong. We can draw this understanding from a variety of sources: archival evidence, archaeological evidence, official statistics, and oral history.

These discourses are important for what they teach us about conceptions of the nature and role of the state (particularly an authoritarian, but "good and just" state); memories, real or imagined, of the Soviet past; and how people value social order and human life. Intervention must occur at the level of these discourses and not simply at the level of international politics.

Notes

I thank Julia Eckert, Tursunaly Asakeevich, Sarah Amsler, Madeleine Reeves, and Christian Boulanger for the comments on the drafts for this chapter.

1. Shortly before the submission of this chapter, the monument of Lenin was replaced with the new Liberty statute on the main square of Bishkek, the capital of Kyrgyzstan. Kyrgyzstan was the last country among the Commonwealth of Independent States to remove the monument of Lenin from its main square. The government decided

to replace the monument as part of its celebration of 2,200 years of Kyrgyzstani "state-hood." Lenin did not fit the newborn ideology of the "ancient" Kyrgyz statehood. The replacement of Lenin forged a political battle with demands for the resignation of the Kyrgyz prime minister.

2. Popular memories recorded in Bishkek, Kyrgyzstan, while conducting the oral history project on riots of 1967 in Frunze, 2002–3.

3. Ibid.

4. This is partly due to the fact that today in Kyrgyzstan opposition and human rights activists are portrayed by the pro-government mass media as a crowd of hooligans who want revolution, to bring more chaos, and do not let people work peacefully. President Askar Akaev stated that "a small group of provocateurs and demagogues" had tried to undermine public order by worming their way into the local people's confidence, but that the government managed to keep order (RFE/RL 2002). Keeping public order, just as in the Soviet years, by means of legal or extra-judicial killings again did not and does not make a difference. But, in contrast to the state killings of 1937, these were not condemned. Thrust for public order is what "unites" capital punishment and state killings in discourses of the past and the present. Despite widespread uncertaintly about Askar Akaev's rule, many consider him a better alternative than what has been portrayed as "a group of provocateurs." Moreover, the protesters were not seen as being punished by the state for their actions, but killed by mistake, just like thousands during the 1930s.

5. As I edit this chapter, another prisoner in a Kyrgyz jail has been killed by the prison staff. The official reason given was that it was to stop the mass riot against the prison staff inside the prison. Officials reported that they were thuse able to "restore the order." From "Prison riot," *Vechernyi Bishkek*, 20 October 20 2003.

6. Charles Foster—personal communication (via e-mail), June 2003.

References

Amnesty International (2003) "Kyrgyzstan," in *Amnesty International Report 2003*. London: Amnesty International. http://web.amnesty.org/report2003/kgz-summary-eng (accessed 4 June 2004).

Applebaum, Anne (2003) *Gulag: A History of the Soviet Camps*. London: Allen Lange.

Aslanbekova, Aisha (2003) "Desperate Conditions in Kyrgyz Prisons," *Central Asia—Caucusus Analyst*. http://www.cacianalyst.org/view_article.php?articleid=1681 (accessed 15 October 2003).

David-Fox, Michael (2001) "Cultural Memory in the Century of Upheaval: Big Pictures and Snapshots," 2 *Kritika: Explorations in Russian and Eurasian History* 601 (No. 3, Summer).

Dubin, B. (2003) "Stalin jil, Stalin jiv, Stalin budet jit" (Stalin Lived, Stalin Lives, Stalin Will Live), http://www.http://polit.ru/docs/585074.html (accessed 29 March 2003).

Engel, David M. (2001). "Injury and Identity: The Damaged Self in Three Cultures," in D. T. Goldberg et al., eds., *Between Law and Culture*. Minneapolis: University of Minnesota Press.

Eshanova, Zamira (2002) "Kyrgyzstan: Rights Groups Urge Bishkek to Extend Death Penalty Moratorium, Outlaw Executions," *Radio Free Europe/Radio Liberty* (12 December), http://www.rferl.org/nca/features/2002/12/20122002181802.asp (accessed 30 September 2003).

Fitzpatrick, Peter (1999) "'Always More to Do': Capital Punishment and the DeComposition of Law," in A. Sarat, ed., *The Killing State: Capital Punishment in Law, Politics and Culture*. Oxford: Oxford University Press.

Fitzpatrick, Sheila (1999) *Everyday Stalinism. Ordinary Life in Extraordinary Times: Soviet Russia in the 1930's*. Oxford: Oxford University Press.

Galunichev, A. (2003) "Legka li jizn' na narah?" (Is Life Easy in Prisons?), *Slovo Kyrgyzstana*, http://www.sk.kg/2003/n41/obch.html (accessed 15 October 2003).

Garland, David (1990) *Punishment and Modern Society: A Study in Social Theory*. Oxford: Clarendon Press.

International Centre for Prison Studies (2003) "Prison Brief for Kyrgyzstan," *International Center for Prison Studies*. http://www.prisonstudies.org/ (accessed 3 October 2003).

Khelimskaya, Regina (1994) *Taina Chon-Tasha*. Bishkek: Illim.

Khubova, Daria et al. (1992) "After Glasnost: Oral History in the Soviet Union," in L. Passerini, ed., *Memory and Totalitarianism* (International Yearbook of Oral History and Life Stories, vol. 1). New York: Oxford University Press.

Lester, David (1998) "Suicide in Post-Soviet Central Asia," 18 *Central Asian Survey* 121–24.

Lui, Morgan (2003) "Recognizing the Khan: Authority, Space, and Political Imagination among Uzbek Men in Osh." Ph.D. dissertation, Department of Social Anthropology, University of Michigan.

Morrison, Ken (1995) *Marx, Durkheim, Weber: Formations of Modern Social Thought*. London: Sage Publications.

Nazarbaev, Nursultan (2003) "The Message of the President of the Country to the People of Kazakhstan" (4 April). http://www.president.kz/main/mainframe.asp?lng=ru (accessed 24 September 2003).

Norton, Anne (1999) "After the Terror: Mortality, Equality, Fraternity," in A. Sarat, ed., *The Killing State: Capital Punishment in Law, Politics and Culture*. Oxford: Oxford University Press.

RFE/RL Kyrgyz News (2002) "Victims of the Kyrgyz Clashes Buried" (21 March), http://www.hri.org/news/balkans/rferl/2002/02-03-21.rferl.html (accessed 4 June 2004).

Sarat, Austin, ed. (1999) *The Killing State: Capital Punishment in Law, Politics and Culture*. Oxford: Oxford University Press.

Sherbakova, Irina (1992) "Gulag in Memory," in L. Passerini, ed., *Memory and Totalitarianism* (International Yearbook of Oral History and Life stories, vol. 1). New York: Oxford University Press.

Stern, Vivien, ed. (1999) *Sentenced to Die?: The Problem of TB in Prisons in Eastern Europe and Central Asia*. London: International Centre for Prison Studies.

Thompson, Paul (2000) *The Voice of the Past: Oral History*. Oxford: Oxford University Press.

UNDP (United Nations Development Program) (2002) *National Human Development Report*. Bishkek: Author.

Zemtsov, Ilya (1991) *Encyclopedia of Soviet Life*. New Brunswick, NJ: Transaction Publishers.

CHAPTER NINE

Death and the Nation

State Killing in India

JULIA ECKERT

> No person shall be deprived of his life or personal liberty except according to procedure established by law.
>
> Constitution of India, Article 21

> Of what use is the law which cannot protect the citizens?
>
> Satya—The Other Side of Truth;
directed by Ram Gopal Verma, 1999

> Fie upon the law that does not protect us.
>
> Saamna, mouthpiece of the
Hindu-nationalist party Shivsena, 9 January 1993

> This law can't give justice to the people.
>
> Bal Thackeray, leader of the Shivsena[1]

Civilized Killing

Indian doctrine states that in only the rarest of rare cases is the death penalty to be imposed.[2] Under the Indian Penal Code (IPC) the death penalty can be imposed for murder; waging war against the government; abetting the suicide of a child or an insane person; fabricating false evidence with the intent to secure a conviction for another person for a capital offense; kidnapping for ransom; gang robbery involving murder; and other offenses related to the above. Recently the use of the death penalty has been extended through antiterrorist legislation as well as antinarcotic trade legislation, and it has also been warranted for the abetment of *Sati* (the immolation of widows) (SAHRDC 2000: 12–13).[3] Judges have referred to the accused's heinous motive—the brutal, cruel, diabolical, dastardly, and treacherous manner of a murder, particularly when it was committed against innocent and helpless victims—to the antisocial or abhorrent nature of the crime and its effect on society, and to other aggravating factors to justify the imposition of capital punishment (Combat Law 2003: 31).

Recently there have been several rarest of rare cases; their political contexts have been so varied as to confuse the line of argument of propagators and opponents of capital punishment. One case was that of the sentence on 17 December 2002 against three men allegedly connected to the attack by Muslim militants on the Indian Parliament on 13 December 2001. S. A. R. Gilani, one of the accused, has since been released and his sentence quashed because the evidence against him was thin, bordering on nonexistent. Another case was the sentence of 6 June 2003 against eight members of the Yadav caste sentenced to death by hanging for a massacre of nineteen Dalit villagers fifteen years earlier in 1988. The third case was the sentence against Dara Singh who in 1999 killed an Australian missionary, Graham Staines, and his two sons, setting their car on fire while they were asleep inside. Dara Singh announced that he would forgo an appeal since he wanted to become a martyr for the Hindutva (Hindu-ness) cause.

With these sentences the judiciary appeared supremely neutral, above the political divisions of Indian society: capital punishment was imposed for Muslim terrorism as much as for caste violence and murder inspired by Hindu-nationalism. But as human rights lawyers claim: "It is the poor, the sick, and the ignorant who are sent to the gallows."[4] Human rights activists stand largely alone in their opposition to capital punishment. More widespread are attitudes like that of Kiran Bedi, a prominent policewoman now serving as the Civilian Police Advisor to the UN peacekeeping operations, who felt that "The death penalty is necessary in certain cases to do justice to society's anger against the crime."[5]

This retaliatory reasoning is embedded in conceptions of crime and punishment, of guilt and justice, that conceive of crime as something that has to be avenged for justice to be restored. Justice and punishment are foremost in the defense of the death penalty, although official pronouncements stress mainly the factor of deterrence. However, today the rarest of rare cases is too rare for the likings of many. The death penalty in India, although it is regularly imposed and regularly executed,[6] is publicly marginal. Capital punishment appears as simply an acknowledged part of a criminal justice system that is constantly bemoaned as far too inefficient, far too cumbersome—and therefore inept at ful-filling its duties: to protect the citizen from the dangers of crime, and increas-ingly also from those of terrorism. The Malimath Committee (2003: 46), insti-tuted to find solutions for the reform of the criminal justice system, states: "The system devised more than a century back has become ineffective; a large num-ber of guilty go unpunished in a large number of cases; the system takes years to bring the guilty to justice; and has ceased to deter criminals. Crime is in-creasing rapidly every day and types of crimes are proliferating. The citizens live in constant fear."[7] Such summations are frequent: there is widespread de-spondency about the state of the judicial system of India. Politicians, jurists, and the police despair over what they see as a fundamental threat to the rule of law. In the public's perception too, the courts have lost their ability to ensure that the law prevails.

The Indian courts have always been held in high esteem; they are considered to be relatively independent and fair. In fact, they have often been attributed with a prominent and active role for the achievement of the promises of inde-pendence. High hopes were pinned on law as an instrument for social transfor-mation, and the higher judiciary took up the challenge that arose from the se-vere inequalities of Indian society.[8] However, at the same time Indian courts are considered inefficient to the degree that they become irrelevant. In India many legal suits—civil as well as criminal ones—take years to be concluded, ten years being the norm for any ordinary case. Procedural rules make frequent post-ponements and repeated appeals possible (Moog 1992). Partially because of the long duration of the cases, conviction rates are very low. They hover around 6 percent in cases regarding "heinous crimes," some of which legally warrant cap-ital punishment.[9] Former Union Minister of Law Arun Jaitly stated that "the low rate of conviction leads us to the conclusion that crime in India is a very high profit and a low risk proposition. You commit a heinous crime and there is a 93,5 percent possibility that you will get away with it."[10] This perception of the impunity of crime and the profit to be made from it triggers fears of a soci-ety lost to crime and corruption. Where deterrence is perceived as failing be-cause the institutions of deterrence are too slow, too ineffective, or simply too cautious in terms of sticking to the principles of the rule of law, society stands unguarded. The perception of the law as aloof from the woes of the common man gains yet another twist.

The Illegitimate Sibling of Capital Punishment

The public perception of the inefficiency of the judicial system has time and again triggered debates on the legitimacy of alternative methods of combating crime. For the protection of society from the threats of crime and terrorism, the use of extra-legal means by state agents appeared to be increasingly justified, lest the whole system would collapse. Since the tasks assigned to the judiciary, namely, punishment and deterrence, were to all appearances not adequately executed by the courts, other state agencies were legitimated in taking on those vital functions. This detachment of particular functions deemed essential for the functioning of society from the state institutions officially responsible for them is most pronounced in the realms of crime control and punishment, as crime is increasingly perceived as particularly destructive of the social fabric.[11] This detachment also concerns the control of and decision about state violence and about state killing. Since capital punishment is widely perceived as just punishment and as necessary deterrence, this is so even when it is taken out of the hands of the judiciary.

Encounter killing is the colloquial term for the (civilian) deaths that result from what in official nomenclature is termed an exchange of fire.[12] Such encounters are frequent. In 1999, official statistics (for what they are worth) counted about 650 civilians who died in such encounters (Crime in India 1999: 381).[13] However, the National Bureau of Statistics does not clearly distinguish between the different situations that warrant the use of firearms by the police. All use of firearms falls in the broad categories of "riot control," "anti-dacoity operations" (i.e. against armed bandits), "against extremists and terrorists," and "other events." Encounters will be the mode of killing particularly in anti-dacoity operations and against suspected extremists or terrorists. The latter category encompasses 52.5 percent of total deaths and is thus the most frequent occasion for state killing (Crime in India 1999: 379).[14] Bombay is the city where the most encounters occur. In 1999, according to official numbers eighty-three people died from police bullets in the city. But 1999 was a quiet year: statistics from 2000 observe a 12 percent rise in police use of firearms. This, the office explains, is due to the "growing violence by terrorists, insurgents and dacoits" (Crime in India 2000: 371). In Bombay alone 102 people were killed (373).[15]

Officially, the police shoot in self-defense. According to public statements and media accounts, they always shoot back. The usual story of an encounter is that in the wee hours of the night a white Maruti drives up to a location where the police have laid a trap. The expected criminals or terrorists open fire when they discover that they are about to be arrested. The police retaliate. All alleged criminals die on the spot or on their way to hospital. The policemen involved are hardly ever injured.[16]

Due to this rather routine manner of encounter procedures, i.e. the well-nigh identical sequence of events reported to the press every time, nearly every encounter killing is surrounded by the suspicion of being a *fake encounter*, that is, one that has been staged and does not involve an exchange of fire or the genuine necessity of self-defense on the side of the police. Such staged encounters are illegal. According to official statistics there was one "fake encounter" in 1999, as well as one in 2000 in the whole of India (Crime in India 1999: 400; 2000: 392). There have been several trials against police officers accused of staging an encounter, and some of them have been convicted. However, it is not always easy to distinguish a staged encounter from a "real" one. Certainly there are many occasions in India where the police are involved in exchanges of fire with militants or members of criminal gangs. But the suspicion is often that the police pick up a person whom they suspect to be a criminal and execute him—either because they simply need a culprit for a deed for which they cannot find the culprit, or because they cannot provide enough evidence against an accused and they fear that the judiciary will set him free, or because the victim is a thorn in somebody's side. Thus, the suspicion is—and depending on the public mood, this suspicion can turn into "public knowledge"—that encounters happen when the police need a culprit who, because he is dead, cannot be found innocent again.

The uncertain nature of the encounters introduces the first note of ambivalence toward their evaluation. Not that the "fake" nature of an encounter would necessarily make it less legitimate. As discussed above, due to the perceived inefficiency of the judiciary and its inability to protect society by effectively imposing punishments, the task of punishment, also by death, that is considered just and necessary is legitimately taken on by others. Until 1997 the National Human Rights Commission complained about frequent encounters,[17] and the police made no secret of "staging" them when necessary. A "top police official" is quoted as saying: "Encounters are an effective way of dealing with criminals specially [*sic*] when the courts are unable to provide speedy justice."[18] Beyond the right to self-defense guaranteed under Sections 97, 100, and 103 of the Indian Penal Code (IPC), police refer to Clause 46.3 of the Indian Criminal Procedure Code (CrPC) that states in a double negation policemen have *no* right to cause the death of a person that is "*not* accused of an offence punishable with death or imprisonment for life"; which they read as saying that if a person accused of a crime punishable by death or life imprisonment resists arrest or attempts to evade arrest, police do have the right to shoot to kill. They thereby claim not only the right to self-defense but also the duty to prevent those accused, or sometimes only suspected, of a heinous crime from escaping their rightful punishment.

Thus, when police refer to self-defense to explain and justify encounters, they imply not necessarily their own personal self-defense but a collective meaning of self-defense of which they are the bearers. Crime control is at the heart of the police's professional identity. Their professional duty is to protect society from the threats of crime and disorder. Police brag about the number of alleged criminals or alleged terrorists they have arrested, exiled, or "encountered." Those who have fought crime effectively are the heroes of the corps. There are the so-called super-cops: Julio Ribeiro, who is attributed as having introduced "encounters" into police practice in the early 1980s;[19] K. P. S. Gill, who squashed Khalistani terrorism in Punjab by introducing extremely harsh policing manners; or D. Shivanandan, whose efforts were eternalized in the Bollywood film *Company* that deals with the international networks of organized crime. And there are the so-called encounter specialists, those who have the most shoot-outs to their credit. They inspire awe and envy within the corps. The media, too, pays homage to their achievements: "Sharma, 38, has an enviable track record in checking crime. He has been involved in 72 encounter killings and has arrested 400 criminals in his 18-year career," states *The Week*,[20] speaking of Pradeep Sharma, one of the Bombay encounter specialists. *Times of India* calls the encounters by encounter specialist Daya Nayak "Nayak's Big Hits."[21]

There is on the one hand the professional, or career logic, that needs a culprit for any crime so that the statistics of policing do not get unfavorably imbalanced. While a low crime rate is good for police image, a low detection rate is disastrous. There is, however, on the other hand also the logic of "justice," or rather just punishment, at work here. Punishment must happen to the guilty, lest they profit from their evil-doing—this reasoning underlies the justification of capital punishment as well as extra-judicial practices of punishment.

Moreover, since the judiciary is perceived to be unable—and sometimes unwilling—to punish, the assumption is widespread that "the common man" can only be protected by resorting to extra-legal means of combating crime. "It is better in the larger interest of society to eliminate a known criminal than to allow him to roam free and kill 100 innocent persons. 'It is better to destroy evil than to allow it to nurture and spread in society,'" proclaimed police officer Satyapal Singh, acclaimed for many encounters in Bombay, citing the Bhagawat Gita.[22]

> The fact is that encounters are not the problem but merely a symptom of the collapsing system of justice and of the public demand for quick solutions to the law and order problem. . . . when the police take recourse to extra-legal tactics to make up for the deficiencies of law and legal procedures, they are trying to remedy the inadequacies that they did not create.[23]

This was stated shortly after the infamous encounter at Ansal Plaza in South Delhi which raised many questions.[24] The justification of encounter killing, with reference to the inefficiency of the criminal justice system in getting alleged criminals behind bars, in a way confirms the open secret that encounter killings do not necessarily occur because of an immediate need for self-defense but in the context of a larger conception of (self-) defense.

In *Satya*, a Bollywood film of 1999 that tells the tale of the battle between two gangs of organized crime in Bombay, and that was perceived by many viewers from the city as "so realistic," this reasoning is played out between the reluctant police commissioner and a desperate politician:

> *New Commissioner*: What happens is that we arrest them and they get released later. If they get arrested then they will operate from inside the jail. And if they escape, they will operate from abroad! And we cannot do a thing. The amount of money we spend on their extradition is not even asked for extortion by them! And then there are people like Bhau who operate openly. Because they know very well how to break this system! Sir, I think there is no solution to this problem.
>
> *Politician*: A law protector cannot have the attitude of a law breaker.
>
> *New Commissioner*: Then don't blame us. They can do anything because they transgress the law. And we cannot do a thing because it is the same law that stops us! Simple.

Politician 2: I admit the law must have bound your hands many a times. But the fault does not lie with the law. The framework of our democracy is such. Democracy has given our citizens some basic fundamental rights. Men like Bhau violate these rights and mock at democracy. But it's the limit now! Rampant squabbles, hooliganism, threats. The public is getting terrified now. Of what use is the law which cannot protect the citizens? Mr. Commissioner I give you a free hand. Do anything. But please, clean the city. (*Satya* 1999)

The police then go on to "clean the city," shooting dead many a criminal—until the criminal hero is vanquished and shot dead at the doorstep of his beloved.

In the light of the perception of a society corroded by crime, encounters won wide public legitimacy. This was not restricted to the urban middle classes who perceived their world as increasingly threatened by crime (rather than poverty, hunger, and inequality that were, besides Pakistan, for long considered to be the prime enemies of the Indian nation). Also in rural areas, where citizens are much more exposed to the other threats to life and welfare that India holds in store, encounters were considered a legitimate way of dealing with those who threatened the livelihoods of the "common man." As one IPS (Indian Police Service) officer who had been stationed in a rural district of Uttar Pradesh recounted: "Villagers always asked me: 'Why don't you encounter them!'"[25]

The Nexus

It is not only the inefficiency of the judiciary, however, that is, in the perception of many police and their contemporaries, the enemy of the righteous, but also some provisions of rights for the accused, and above all, it is "politics." An "encounter specialist" of the Bombay police states: "You cannot imagine under what pressure we work. Even when we arrest a local thug, there will be immense political pressure to release him."[26] In the self-perception of the police, police violence sometimes takes on the role of restoring order in a chaotic body politic; it is, for them, the rescue from "politics" and the last resort for a society corroded by corruption. Where corruption is perceived to reign, and where crime seems to have invaded politics by criminals turning into politicians and by politicians relying on criminals for their finances and other services, the killing police, by killing criminals, rescue society from the grips of the so-called *nexus*: the alliance between organized crime and politics.

India is a highly politicized society. Political organization is the means for articulation of interests for a growing number of Indian citizens. However, despite the active participation in the democratic process, particularly for those social groups that had long been excluded (the rural poor, women, and low castes), there is a widespread distrust in the political class. Many voters feel that "politics corrupts even the best." The infamous "criminalization of politics," that is, the entering of well-known personalities with criminal antecedents into the political game, as well as the increasing use of criminal means for political profit, is one of the favorite themes discussed from the tea stalls to the universities. What they observe is the perversions of democratic procedures (Kothari 2000); the blatancy of corruption pervading all spheres of public life (Chowdhury 1996; Gill 1998; Visvanathan and Sethi 1998); the apparent increase of political violence (Kohli 1990); and the evident fact that the majority of the Indian population is still, after fifty years of independence, among the poorest in the world, without access to clean water, electricity, health care, and education. It is a "failure of governance" (Sen Gupta 1996; Chopra 1996) that leads to the predatory use of public goods and public funds, of public office and of the state.

After it became obvious that the twelve bomb blasts that shook Bombay on 13 March 1993 (in the aftermath of and as the Muslim-led Mafia gangs' retaliation for the pogroms against Muslims that had ravaged the city in the previous winter), had involved the collaboration of a diffuse network of criminal gangs, police, and customs officials as well as their political patrons, a commission was instituted to investigate the so-called nexus. The report by N. N. Vohra found such deep involvement of politicians with organized crime all over India that it was barred from publication. Only its general conclusion was made publicly available and therein Vohra observes: "The various crime syndicates/Mafia organizations have developed significant muscle and money power and established linkages with governmental functionaries, political leaders and others to be able to operate with impunity" (Vohra Committee Report, n.d., 10).[27]

The perception of the criminalization of politics feeds into and is born of a sense of deep state crisis. The experience of state crisis is not new and has accompanied perceptions of the state for a long time, definitely ever since Indira Gandhi changed the institutional fabric through her emergency rule. It is often described as an acute sense of crisis, as a slide into the abyss, as a downward spiral that spins the body politic away from "the good old times," a golden age of

the Indian state. The historic location of the golden age differs according to political affinities; but for many, the precise onset of decline is connected with the
emergency rule from 1975 to 1977. Although there are many who consider the
years of the authoritarian rule by Indira Gandhi as those when "the trains were
running on time," many also reflect that the centralization of command and the
abolition of party-internal democracy produced an increasing dependence of
civil servants and the police on their direct political masters and the onset of
corruption of many kinds.

State killing in this situation becomes, in the self-perception of the police as
well as in the understanding of many a "common man," a last rescue from the
murky networks of politics and crime. In this understanding the criminalization of politics—often seen in connection with democratic competition—is
opposed to an authoritarian idea of order and of the state, to a "strong hand"
that is also expressed in the many versions of the longing for a philosopher
king, of *Ramraj*,[28] *Shivshahi*,[29] or a "benevolent dictatorship."[30] The equation of
politics with corruption (and crime) and violence with order and clarity per-
vades many debates about politics. It is particularly prominent not only among
the members of those political parties that favor more authoritarian political
orders, but also among police officers who consider the protection of order as
their responsibility. Police officer Jogesh Pratab Singh in 2003 published his angry novel *Carnage by Angels* in which he charges that corruption is the force of
evil, the true killer in society and the true violator of human rights.[31] Against
corruption, he implies, you have to be brutal—brutality and corruption here
are opposites: "He realized that the police had forfeited its brutish constitution
for worldly expediencies. For, many of its men had already gone into an easy life
given to pleasure, with so much money coming from the vice dens. . . . Physical
abuse was not a paying undertaking . . . human rights activists would spur
themselves to create a hype in the media, and even move the courts. . . . Police
knew that in torture was no money. But without it there was money all over"
(Singh 2003: 46). Brutality, as "an imperative to squelch discords" (ibid.) has
given way to corruption and exposed society (and particularly its defenseless
women) to the "death game." It is aided by the "featherbrained comprehension"
(ibid.) of human rights activists who do not understand where the true forces
of evil operate. His hero, IPS officer Raghu Kumar, however, is out to save society from the threats of corruption. He fails in the end, vanquished by the
nexus.[32]

So, just as the inefficiency of the judiciary (and its close adherence to the rule of law) exposes society to the threats of crime, so does corruption, and above all the nexus between crime and politics. Both instances serve as a justification for police violence. Police killing gains a vigilante role; it saves society and social order by breaking its laws. Such a vigilante role is professed also by the police commissioner in *Satya*.

> He explains to his wife: "Have you ever wondered where these people talking about Human Rights disappear when the mafia blatantly kills innocent people! Nobody holds placards then, saying policemen are murderers, butchers! Even a butcher slaughters a goat only because people eat it! Why do you point a finger to the butcher? And we do not enjoy slaying anybody! We do not make criminals, Jyoti, the system does. Until the system gets rectified, someone will have to clean this filth! And today, under the prevailing conditions, I am doing that job. That's it." (*Satya* 1999)

Contract Killings?

Although state failure or the corrosion of public office serves to justify police violence, it is precisely the widespread perception of a crisis of the state, of widespread corruption and of the criminalization of politics that introduces a considerable element of uncertainty and ambiguity into the perception of state violence. On the one hand, state violence is turned to as a solution to judicial inefficiency and a rescue from political corruption; on the other it is also perceived as a possible tool of this very corruption. Considering the intricate networks of the nexus, there is a disquieting reading of encounters that is equally widespread as the ones of rescue and order discussed above. This other reading contradicts the former but often coincides. According to this other reading "the police have become contract killers for the politicians," as one member of an elite police unit felt.[33] Police encounters in this interpretation are well-targeted killings of economic and sometimes political rivals of politicians and their networks in organized crime. The police are their hirelings, paid with posts and other favors.

The infamous "politicization" of the police is attributed to the provisions of the Indian Police Act (Section 3) that, by making the posting and sacking of police commissioners subject entirely to state governments, encourages the use of postings as a tool of party politics. The motives of such influencing are usually the protection of networks and allies and their potentially illegal activities, be they political or economic. Granting immunity to either illegal economic or unconstitutional political endeavors by directing the police not to interfere is a pillar of political might. "All seek to bring the police under their own control, to oversee their recruitment, their posting and their behaviour to insure that they act on one's behalf and not on the behalf of one's enemies" (Brass 1997: 274; see also Vohra Committee Report, n.d., 9).

Politicians award police who operate according to the interests of their networks with the posts that they might seek: prestigious posts, pleasant posts, or lucrative posts in areas where there is money to be made from the *Hafta*, the money that semi-legal or illegal enterprises pay to the police to be left in peace, protection money really. If police resist the demands of their political superiors they are often punished: transferred to posts that either mean hardship for their families (particularly the schooling of their children); ineffective posts, where they cannot interfere, like police training posts; or posts that have no potential for additional revenue, so that the incumbent has no way of accumulating the means to buy another posting.[34] Punishment postings are for those police who disturb the workings of the nexus, for police who uncover corrupt deals, or for those who work for rival factions.[35]

Police blame such "political interference" for the failures of their work: for their inconclusive investigations, their false allegations, and their corruption.[36] They put their hopes for rescue in the recommendations of the Police Commission of 1980. The implementation of these recommendations would grant the police greater autonomy—and to the belief of many police, greater autonomy would set things right. To them, the problem lies in the chain of command. Fear focuses on a "politicized" police, one that is contaminated by all the murky stuff of interests, dealings, and compromises that are associated with (parliamentary) politics. Since "politics" has gained a well-nigh synonymous connotation with corruption and dishonesty, its "other" is seen in a more authoritarian idea of order, of unambiguous decisions, and clear-cut solutions. It is also a vision of the purity of "disinterested" violence, violence that purely serves the production of order. An autonomous police would be a pure police; its violence would likewise be pure rather than "politically contaminated" and thus would serve the common good and common longing for order and security against politics. In the perception of many police officers, the recommendations have become all but a panacea for the ills that have befallen the force.[37]

Encounter killings are considered to be yet one of the most drastic services the police supply to their patrons among politicians and organized crime. Conspiracy theories run wide of how particular targets of encounters were connected with the interests of political networks. When in the summer of 1997 the entire leadership of the Arun Gowli gang was killed in encounters on the streets of Bombay, this was interpreted as a result of a political feud between Gowli and his erstwhile patron, the Shivsena Party, which had by then become the ruling party in the city and state of Maharashtra. Arun Gowli was the local Don, the only one usually residing in Mumbai, in his infamous *Dagdi chawl*—or in neighboring prisons which he once described as the place "where a person gets a chance to think clearly."[38] When he aspired to turn his criminal fiefdom into political power by launching the Akhil Bharatiya Sena (ABS), a political party competing in local elections, he was considered a rival of the Shivsena—and so, urban lore claims, they annihilated his gang.[39]

However, it is not only in the big gang wars that the police are suspected of partisan involvement, but also in more everyday encounters. Relatives of people who have died in encounters tell tales of how they saw the encounter being prepared by the police lodging allegations against the victims so that they would have a reason to claim that they had resisted arrest. They often point toward recent conflicts between the victims and their rivals and allege that the police acted on behalf of the latter. Some of them tell how they had petitioned with the local authorities and even wrote to the prime minister when they "saw the encounter coming" and went to register this fear with the police itself, to no avail.

Thus, the encounters that are seen as a rescue from the undermining of the body politic by corruption and crime suddenly are themselves a symptom of that very corruption, of the dissolution of public institutions and the sway of crime. The confusion and disquieting uncertainty about the nature of state violence, as rescue from or as symptom of pervasive crisis, produce the deep ambivalence toward state killing and state violence in general: there is at once the imagination of order ensured by an (authoritarian and paternalistic) "strong hand"; and there is at the same time the deep suspicion of politics and of the political class, in the highly politicized and politically active Indian society. State violence can become the tool of both, of order as well as of corruption. Politics becomes the source of corruption as well as of rights. Political activity—protest, organization, and the active assumption of rights—runs parallel with the long-ing for a strong man, who is associated with ideas of clarity, order, and the pu-rity of force (rather than the ambiguities of democratic deliberation). Both are visions of the Indian state: of a state that provides rights and the other that pro-vides order.

Killing for Civilization

The deep ambivalence toward state violence is today slowly giving way to a sense of urgent self-defense that returns to state violence an unambiguous aura of purity, honesty, and justness—at least for those parts of the Indian public who are not threatened to become its victims. State violence is reevaluated in light of the perception of a new prime threat to society: not corruption, not crime, but terrorism. The fact that the forms of recent incidents of terrorist vi-olence in India and their interpretations have located this threat "outside" soci-ety, as an external threat, contributes to a new evaluation of state violence. State violence against an external (or externalized) threat is defense, whereas state vi-olence against internal threats is seen as the reestablishment of order (through punishment and deterrence). Within this new evaluation of state violence as defense, the various modes of state killing—capital punishment as well as en-counters—are no longer seen as replacing each other but as reintegrated.

In the course of time, encounters have gained a new justification. "En-counter experts have reunion, set eyes on terrorists" announces the *Mumbai Age* on 4 April 2003. Bombay has recently been the target of several terrorist at-tacks. Between December 2002 and August 2003 there were five bomb attacks in various public places, local trains, bazaars, and train stations, killing over fifty people. Terrorism is not new in India. However, while it had for a long time been restricted to certain regions like the northeast, Punjab, and Kashmir and had been connected to specific claims and demands (mostly territorial auton-omy or independence), terrorism now is often of a different kind: it has no claims but that for justice or revenge (Eckert 2003b), and it has entered the po-litical and financial centers of the country. More important, the perception of terrorism has changed and also the perception of what it allegedly attacks. It is not so much the state, as above all the nation (and society as such), that are per-ceived to be threatened by it. As such, as an attack on the nation, terrorism is perceived as external to society to a new degree. Its causes, or its relation to the society that it targets, become secondary. It comes to be seen more as part of and identical to an unspecific but nonetheless concrete general global danger, the roots of which lie not so much in "causes" but in "culture" and essential enmity. Because of its externality, combating it appears less complex, although possibly technically more difficult than combating the ills intrinsic to society.

New ideologies of how to bring the nation forward have emerged in the past decades: There was, against the old socialist developmentalism and Nehru's aspiration to India's leadership of the nonaligned countries, the neoliberal vision of Nehru's grandson Rajiv Gandhi of India as a global player of a different kind. The opening of the economy,[40] the propagation of a new Indian information-technology identity, and the nuclear tests of the late 1990s, which demonstated the country's aspirations to equal status with the other nuclear powers as well as affirmed its ballistic strength against Pakistan, all established India as a country to be counted on. The newly voiced (middle-class) aspirations for membership in the global club that also involved questioning the images of "authentic India," hitherto propagated as the rural and the traditional, converged with the fantasy of national unity (Hansen 1996). Ever since the democratic process was pluralized by the assertion of the lower castes since the 1980s, Hindu-nationalism, politically represented by the BJP (Bharatiya Janata Party) and its urging for Hindu unity, had become more plausible. *Hindutva* responded to the diversification of (organized) political claims with the call to unity on the grounds of its construction of an existential opposition between Hindus and Muslims as homogeneous groups of common interest. A republican vision of the nation and of "unity in diversity" gave way to a more organic version of the nation and of "unity in diversity." New notions of order—of a harmonious Hindu society overcoming its internal fissures—went along with new notions of threat that lie now primarily in the "dangerous other." While earlier the ills of the system had been seen as something internal,[41] now Evil and Danger moved out of the system. The collusion between politics, corruption, and organized crime, that has definite correlations in the networks of operation, is now considered foremost as the Achilles' heel of the nation, the open door to its prime threat, namely (Muslim) terrorism and its abettors.[42] Corruption—and the Congress Party's "vote bank politics," its alleged "pampering of minorities," and sell-out of Hindu rights to India—in this view opened ways of exploitation of the open society of India and of Hindu tolerance. Within the Hindu-nationalist discourse, the "metaphorical femininity" (Inden 1990: 96), part of the orientalist construction of spiritual India as the "other" of the "rational" West, turns into the incapacity of the tolerant Hindu to defend himself (and his nation, women, and country) against those who are so utterly different: above all the Muslims, whose religion is allegedly aggressive, hegemonial, and intolerant. "The right to self-defence is bestowed upon every citizen by the constitution,"[43] claimed Bal Thackeray, leader of the Hindu-nationalist Shivsena Party on the occasion of the riots in Bombay in the winter of 1993. "Fie upon the law which does not protect us. . . . Why are police not given orders to shoot at sight? It is your duty to enforce law and order. Why should you be worried about the death of Muslims? The criminals of Pakistan and Bangladesh are dancing ferociously in front of the police, where is the authority and prestige of your law and order?"[44]

This identification of the prime threat to society as lying in the "dangerous other" succeeded from being a mobilization issue of the Hindu right to becoming a widespread interpretation of the state of affairs. Such a clearly identifiable, personified threat is in many ways more easily vanquished than a malaise that is intrinsic to society.

Although the "dangerous other" is seen mainly in terms of Hindu-Muslim (India-Pakistan) conflict, the externalization of the roots of crisis and danger is not confined to Muslims alone but generalized to the perception of crime. With the loss of the hopes for the promises of developmental ideology and its replacement by a new idea of how to save the nation, there also arose a new interpretation of what the causes of crime are. Poverty, inequality, and injustice were not its sources anymore, nor was it the lack of development, education, and "civilization" referred to by an older generation when developmental ideology still held sway. Says the old police officer to his young colleague in *Satya*:

> Encounters are not a solution. After all, we are officers. You are not a roadside ruffian. After all there has to be some difference between us and them. The problem is not of law and order, but of education. Ours is a huge country with a very vast population but the literacy level is so low! No, no, we must educate them. The problem will get solved on its own then. Very simple. What do you think? (*Satya* 1999)

But the young one, belonging to a new generation of police and equipped with a new interpretation of the ills that have befallen society, answers simply: "No, Sir." This simple "no" seems to imply that crime is not to be explained or understood but simply to be vanquished. It no longer has sources that can be remedied by development. This is also the time when the gangsters in the films from Bollywood lose most traces of being a Robin Hood. They also lose their personal histories of grievances and injustice. While their ancestors from the 1970s had been "angry young men" rebelling against social injustice, or, in the 1980s, godfathers setting up parallel states for those excluded from and maltreated by the "system," Satya and his contemporaries of the 1990s kill for profit. The main character in the film *Nayakan* (which was made in 1984)[45] was the son of a unionist who had been "encountered" by the police and takes revenge for the killing of his father. But Satya's history is shrouded in mystery—so that his decline into crime has no identifiable social reason. A new image of the criminal appears—and with it a new role for the police. Now the encounter specialists of Bombay gathered in a fancy hall, brought their wives for the dance and the buffet, and reconsidered their roles.[46] The delegitimization of encounters that occurred in 1997 when too many innocents had lost their lives now gave way to a renewed plausibility of their necessity and justification—particularly since the new prime enemies, the terrorists, seemed not only highly equipped and well connected but also determined unto death. "If you have foreigners armed to death being sent in by intelligence agencies of foreign countries what do you do?" answered K. P. S. Gill[47] to the question of whether encounters were the shortcuts of judicial verdicts.

It is thus not (only) punishment or deterrence, as in the earlier justifications for capital punishment, but security and self-defense that are foremost in the justifications of state killing now. They are accompanied by a (Hindu-nationalist) redefinition of the self that is to be protected. This new definition of the self, and the changed perception of what is threatened (not the state but the nation and its future), underlie new ideas of citizenship and implicit legitimation of restrictions of civil rights. When addressing the Asia Pacific Human Rights Convention in November 2002 Vajpayee announced that in the fight against terrorism "we have sometimes to take tough decisions, even infringing some of our freedoms and abridging some of our human rights temporarily . . . so that our future generations can live in peace and harmony."[48] The threat is perceived and treated as external to the national self: on one level, it is "foreigners" or persons who are allegedly foreign funded and allegedly loyal to other countries[49] that are assumed to be the threat. On another level, crime and criminals have lost their (causal) connection to the societal order; they have no history that is embedded in or connected to the history of society. Therefore, they lose, or forgo their rights as citizens in the nation that can bestow them.[50] The state thereby moves away from the "utopia" of development, distributive justice, and individual rights to a heightened sense of security; social security is exchanged for national security as the prime political aspiration and basis for the legitimacy of rule. The production of clarity by locating societal woes within a foe—who is without history or reason—potentially overcomes the deep ambivalence toward state killing.

India has entered the global war on terror with, as its political representatives claim, a specific knowledge of the threats to civilization that arise from Islamic terrorism. They played out the Indian version of the Huntingtonian clash of civilization and are affirmed by the global discourse on the war on (Islamic) terror, of the distribution of Good and Evil in the world, and the need for the self-defense of "a civilization." Local state killing, as in encounters, therein became a part of enduring freedom.[51]

The discourses of security that accompany it have intertwined with and focused the ways India deals with and reperceives its domestic conflicts. They have affirmed the reconceptualization of crime and of terrorism, the new criminologies that locate the sources of crime and evil outside the community to be protected. Ideas about the relation between individual (personal) and national security have changed, and with them the ideas of (and expectations toward) the state have changed. With the (public) conflation of individual security with national security, state killing—whether police encounters or capital punishment—gains a new legitimacy, and a new urgency.

Notes

1. Quoted in Purandare (1999: 56).
2. Bachan Singh v. State of Punjab, AIR, 1980 SC 898.
3. Home minister Advani recently started a debate on whether the death penalty should also be given to rapists.
4. Rajeev Dhawan quoted in *Orbit* 71, http://www.vso.org.uk/publications/orbit/71/justice.htm.
5. Ibid.
6. Official statistics on the imposition of capital punishment, the number of execu-

tions each year, and the number of people on death row are not easy to come by. The Indian Express (30 January 1998) estimated an average of fifty persons executed (hanged) each year. A study by Asim Sarode found fifty-six cases of capital punishment imposed and executed between the years 1950 to 1998 at Pune and Nagpur Central Prison alone (Combat Law 2003: 32). The mode of execution in India is hanging.

7. World Bank programs have come up with suggestions for legal reforms that are to speed up adjudication in the spheres relevant to economic transaction. In the sphere of criminal law, express courts have been introduced and the Malimath Commission is suggesting measures to ease the persecution of crime.

8. On the history of the judiciary and its role for promises of development, welfare, and justice in independent India, see Baxi (1987) and Sathe (2002).

9. The judiciary holds that their frequent acquittals of accused are due partly to shoddy investigations by the police that make it impossible to prove someone's guilt "beyond reasonable doubt" as law demands. The police counter that their investigations are hampered by the long duration of trials, and that due to the long duration of the trials their cases against the accused are weakened: witnesses withdraw their statements simply to be rid of the endless duties at court; they move and are not to be found again; evidential material disappears or rots away in the humid air; but most dangerously they say, the accused who are free on bail use the opportunity to destroy evidence, intimidate witnesses, and force them to "turn hostile" or pay the police, the judge, or the witness to change the evidence. The police feel shortchanged by law itself. They detest the fact that confessions to the police are not admissible in court; they detest the rules of evidence and proof that to them seem to suggest mistrust in their work and their integrity. Moreover, they detest the fact that, to their mind, "the common man" suffers while those that corrode the social fabric with their criminal deeds enjoy the protection of the law in that their crimes have to be proven beyond reasonable doubt. The Malimath Committee, set up to suggest reforms for the criminal justice system, has largely adopted the reasoning of the police and has suggested, for example, to make confessions before the police admissible as well as to change the condition of evidence of one "beyond reasonable doubt" to one of the court being convinced of its truth (Malimath Committee Report 2003: 48).

10. Arun Jaitly quoted in "Justice Denied," *The Hindu*, 10 November 2002.

11. This is not necessarily connected to an increase in the crime rate or in violent crime. Rather, it is related to a stronger focus on crime (and terrorism) as public threats, and a lesser focus on societal problems such as poverty and social inequality; as well as a perception of vulnerability that is due to the experience of the corruption of politics and public office.

12. In 2002 then police commissioner of Mumbai M. N. Singh changed the official expression to "operation."

13. This seems a conservative estimate. The office counts 175 killed in the state of Andra Pradesh, 135 killed in Jammu and Kashmir, and 113 killed in Maharashtra.

14. Custodial deaths are also very frequent. Most occur in judicial custody rather than in police custody. Maharashtra, with the highest rate of custodial deaths, counted 104 deaths in judicial custody and 19 deaths in police custody in the year 1999–2000 (Menon 2002: 56).

15. Newsline published a comparison of the numbers of people killed in Bombay by the police, and those killed by the "underworld" and came up with the following numbers: in 1998 fifty-two people were shot in encounters by the police, forty-eight died from the bullets of the gangs; in 1999 the police killed sixty and the underworld killed sixty-five; in 2000 the police got the upper hand again, killing forty-nine while the underworld murdered only fifteen; in 2001 the police shot dead ninety-eight persons while thirty-five fell victim to the bullets of the Dons (*Sunday Newsline*, 31 March 2002).

16. Crime of India reports the death of 790 police personnel in the year 2000; most of them died in antiterrorist operations in the states of Jammu and Kashmir, as well as those states, like Bihar and Madhya Pradesh with a strong presence of Naxalite groups. In Maharashtra two were killed by "criminals" and six by dacoits. In Bombay, despite 102 civilians killed in encounters, no policemen were killed (Crime in India 2000: 378).

17. The Complaint of the National Human Rights Commission followed the death of two businessmen in Delhi who had been mistaken for criminals and shot point blank after being pulled from their car. In 1997, too, a peanut vendor, Abu Sayama, was abducted and killed by the police, again a case of mistaken identity. The cases threw light on the methods of encounter killings, and although the judge sitting in the writ petition against the policemen responsible for the death of Sayama set them free, the incidents sent a note of caution to the police headquarters in terms of justifying the encounters. Public perception of the legitimacy of the encounters changed for some time.

18. *Times of India*, 18 April 1997.

19. Ribeiro today rejects encounters as a valid means of crime control. He openly criticized former deputy chief minister of Maharashtra, Gopinath Munde, for publicly endorsing them.

20. "Living on the Edge," *The Week*, 10 February 2002.

21. *ToI*, 15 February 2003.

22. Quoted in *Asian Age*, 15 March 1997. The Bhagawat Gita is, in short, that part of the Indian epic, the Mahabharata, in which Krishna talks to Arjuna of his Dharmic duty to go into battle.

23. "Police Encounters," *The Statesman*, 19 November 2002.

24. The Ansal Plaza encounter became famous because of one doctor's struggle to give testimony about the event. He claimed to have witnessed the encounter and stated that the victims had been unarmed, and that the shooting had been a fake encounter.

The government and the police department employed several strategies to undermine his testimony and his credibility.

25. Personal interview, November 2002.

26. "Living on the Edge," *The Week*, 10 February 2002.

27. On 2 June 2002 the Supreme Court of India passed a judgment granting the rule of the Election Commission, that election candidates had to declare their assets and assert their criminal convictions, if any, of constitutional validity. All political parties protested the ruling.

28. Ramraj is the rule of Ram, the god-like king from the epic Ramayana: Gandhi used the term to denote an independent India and a society free of exploitation. Today it is employed mainly by Hindu-nationalist organizations to advocate a Hindu India.

29. Shivshahi is the rule established by the legendary Maratha king Shivaji, who is considered by many the first nationalist of India for his successful fight against the Mogul armies.

30. Benevolent dictatorship is frequently advocated and offered by the Hindu-nationalist leader Bal Thackeray (Eckert 2003a: 59–61).

31. He tells the story of a faithful wife who burns herself to death because her husband has gambled away even her jewels to the profit of the gambling dens and the police who take their share.

32. The novel has such close similarities to living persons as to warrant an angry letter of Maharashtra's Home Minister Chhagan Bhujpal to Singh, who had been posted already to a "punishment posting" in a training camp. Super-cop Julio Ribeiro supported Singh in the publication.

33. The interviewee demanded anonymity.

34. Posts in the Indian Police Service (IPS) as well as in the Indian Administrative Service (IAS) are frequently sold. Compare Wade (1982).

35. Such punitive transfers have also been employed against police officers who intervened decisively and impartially against Hindu-Muslim riots. Three police officers who put down the anti-Muslim pogroms that ravaged Gujarat in 2002 in their wards were immediately transferred by the state government under BJP chief minister Narendra Modi to posts where they could not disturb the violence (Combat Communalism Report 2003: 608–9).

36. Increasingly police officers question the apologetic reference of their colleagues to "political interference." Particularly after the unprecedented degree of police collusion in the Gujarat pogroms, police officers say that transfers are part of a police career and fear of transfers cannot be used as an excuse to act against ones legal duties.

37. Retired police officers in 1996 therefore entered a writ petition at the Supreme Court of India to implement the recommendation of the police commission of 1980. They expected the Supreme Court to decide upon the matter in 2003—but until now no

decision has been taken. The hopes put on the implementation of the recommendations are evidence of the debate that rages within the police corps on the state of the service.

38. *Mid Day*, 18 February 1997.

39. Arun Gowli's lieutenant Sada Pawle was shot by encounter specialist Salaskar. In 1996 Salaskar had shot dead Amar Naik, a Don assumed to be an affiliate of the Shivsena party. Salaskar thus was not associated with the Shivsena's interest for good. The many witnesses who initially claimed that the shooting of Sada Pawle had been a staged encounter all turned hostile.

40. Liberalization legislation restricted the opening of the Indian economy to foreign investment largely to the consumer goods sector, keeping many of the protections of the industrial, agricultural, and administrative sectors. The consumer goods sector expanded vastly, not only causing an explosion in the availability of such goods, but also business opportunities and jobs in the many joint venture projects which were initiated in the early 1990s. This sectorial economic growth, largely restricted to the emerging technology centers of Mumbai, Ahmedabad, Hyderabad, and Bangalore, brought with it a relative increase in prosperity of the growing middle classes in these areas.

41. (Academic) conceptions of the root of the crisis reasoned that the persistence of political forms that are governed by severe dependence and inequality; by violence ranging from electoral booth capturing, to the clashes of private and insurgent armies, to caste violence, and by the predatory use of public goods and public funds, was due to the fact that modernity had not worked in India. Because Indian society stuck to its traditional modes of organization—caste and kinship—so many assumed, the separation of private person and public office had failed (e.g., Gill 1998). However, others saw the root of the malaise in the unsuitability of modern secular institutions to the deeply spiritual society of India (Nandy 1990; Madan 1997). The perversions of the democratic process as well as the ever increasing political violence resulted from the homogenizing force of the modern nation-state (Nandy and Seth 1996). The (modern bureaucratic) state had been an alien project of a postcolonial elite that proceeded with the colonial endeavor of modernization (Chatterjee 1995: 55, 74). The modernist utopia governing India, in their view, was an impossibility.

42. Under various anti-terrorism laws of India, both corruption and organized crime were subsumed under those acts that potentially further and support terrorism.

43. *Saamna* 9 January 1993.

44. *Saamna* 9 January 1993.

45. The film *Nayakan* is based on the life of the Don Vardarajan who built up a smuggling empire in the Tamil-dominated enclaves of "Asia's biggest slum," Dharavi in Bombay. In the film he flees to the city after he murders the police killer of his father, when he is still a child. He becomes a godfather of the maltreated. Nayakan's adversary

from the police in the film concedes that "There is no difference between what you do and I do. Only that I wear a uniform," referring to Nayakan's role as peacemaker and adjudicator and the one who ensures law and order among his dependents.

46. *Mumbai Age*, 4 April 2003.

47. Quoted in *Hindustan Times*, 10 November 2002.

48. Quoted in *The Hindu*, 12 November 2002.

49. Hindu-nationalism has always held that only those for whom India was not only the fatherland but also the holy land, that is those whose holy places lay on Indian soil, were true and legitimate Indians. Christians and Muslims whose holy places lie elsewhere therefore have only a tolerated status of citizenship in this construction. Furthermore, Indian Muslims have been blamed for loyalties with Pakistan ever since the partition of the subcontinent in 1947.

50. Restrictions of civil rights in criminal procedure, as suggested by the Malimath Committee, were included in the antiterrorism law Prevention of Terrorism Act (POTA) of 2002 and the new regional laws for combating organized crime. POTA was repealed in 2005 by the United Front (UF) government that came to power in 2004.

51. The Indian government, headed by the BJP until October 2004, opposed the war on Iraq. Hindu-nationalist organizations, however, claimed that "the way to Ayodhya (the site where Hindu-nationalist organizations claim that Ram was born, because they destroyed the Babri mosque and plan to built a temple in its stead) goes via Baghdad," thus clearly aligning the Hindutva cause with the United States's bellicose strategies, and assuming a common goal for both.

References

Baxi, Upendra (1987) "Taking Suffering Seriously: Social Action Litigation in the Supreme Court of India," in N. Tiruchalvam and R. Coomaraswamy, eds., *The Role of the Judiciary in Plural Societies*. London: Pinto.

Brass, Paul (1997) *Theft of an Idol: Text and Context in the Representation of Collective Violence*. Princeton, NJ: Princeton University Press.

Chatterjee, Partha (1995) *The Nation and Its Fragments*. Delhi: Oxford University Press.

Chopra, Vir (1996) "The Mirage of Good Governance," *Politics India* (November) 24–28.

Chowdhury, T. H. (1996) "420 Parties and Governments," *Politics India* (November) 34–35.

Combat Communalism Report (2003), in J. Dayal, ed., *Gujarat 2002: Untold and Retold Stories of the Hindutva Lab* (425–680). Delhi: Media House.

Combat Law (2003) *Death Penalty, June–July*. Mumbai: Combat Law Publications.

Crime in India (1999) *National Crime Records Bureau*. Delhi: Ministry of Home Affairs.

Crime in India (2000) *National Crime Records Bureau*. Delhi: Ministry of Home Affairs.

Eckert, Julia (2003a) *Charisma of Direct Action; Power, Politics and the Shivsena*. Delhi: Oxford University Press.

Eckert, Julia (2003b) "Rache und Nation," 14 *Berliner Debatte Initial* 28–36.

Gill, S. S. (1998) *The Pathology of Corruption*. New Delhi: HarperCollins Publishers India.

Hansen, Thomas Blom (1996) "Becoming a Light onto Itself: Nationalist Phantasies in the Age of Globalisation," 10 *Economic and Political Weekly* (March 9) 603–16.

Inden, Ronald (1990) *Imagining India*. Cambridge, MA: Basil Blackwell.

Kohli, Atul (1990) *Democracy and Discontent*. Cambridge, MA: Cambridge University Press.

Kothari, Rajni (2000 [1983]) "The Crisis of the Moderate State and the Decline of Democracy," in Z. Hasan, ed., *Politics and the State in India*. Delhi: Sage Publications.

Madan, Triloki N. (1997) "Secularism in Its Place," in S. Kaviraj, ed., *Politics in India*. Delhi: Oxford University Press.

Malimath Committee Report (2003) 2 *Combat Law* 46–58.

Menon, Madhava, ed. (2002) *Criminal Justice India Series*, Vol. 4, Maharashtra, New Delhi: Allied Publishers in collaboration with National University of Juridical Sciences Kolkata.

Moog, Robert (1992) "Delays in the Indian Courts: Why the Judges Don't Take Control," 16 *Justice System Journal* 19–35.

Nandy, Ashis (1990) "The Politics of Secularism and the Recovery of Religious Tolerance," in V. Das, ed., *Mirrors of Violence: Communities, Riots and Survivors in South Asia*. Delhi: Oxford University Press.

Nandy, Ashis, and D. L. Sheth, eds. (1996) *The Multiverse of Democracy*. New Delhi: Sage.

Purandare, Vaibhav (1999) *The Sena Story*. Mumbai: Business Publications Inc.

SAHRDC (South Asia Human Rights Documentation Center) (2000) *Abolition of the Death Penalty*. Delhi: SAHRDC.

Sathe, Satyaranjan Purushottam (2002) *Judicial Activism in India: Transgressing Borders and Enforcing Limits*. Delhi: Oxford University Press.

Satya (Truth) (1999) Directed by Ram Gopal Varma, in India.

Sen Gupta, Bhabani (1996) *Problems of Governance*. New Delhi: Konark Publishers.

Singh, Jogesh Pratab (2003) *Carnage by Angels*. Mumbai: Samarpushp Books.

Visvanathan, Shiv, and Harsh Sethi (1998) *Foul Play: Chronicles of Corruption 1947–97*. New Delhi: Banyan Books.

Vohra Committee Report (n.d.) Delhi: Government of India, Ministry of Home Affairs.

Wade, Robert (1982) "The System of Administrative and Political Corruption: Canal Irrigation in South India," 18 *Journal of Development Studies* 287–328.

CHAPTER TEN

Imagining the Death Penalty in Israel

Punishment, Violence, Vengeance, and Revenge

SHAI J. LAVI

This study begins with a simple question: Why has the death penalty, with the notable exception of Adolf Eichmann,[1] never been applied in Israel, not even to terrorists?[2] How should one understand the absence of the death penalty, given the accumulation of nonjudicial killings of terrorists?[3] Why has the punishment of death been kept in confinement? What, in the collective memory of Israeli lawmakers, security experts, and the general public, raises the fear of the gallows? What ghosts are still haunting the guillotine?

To be sure, a comprehensive answer to these questions lies beyond the scope of this chapter. My focus here is on one aspect of the problem that has not been sufficiently examined in existing literature. Many scholars of the death penalty have emphasized its "extreme," "irreversible," "ultimate," "supra-human" characteristics, all of which belong to the death penalty qua death. This study takes a different point of departure and examines the death penalty qua penalty. The question is not, Why has the State of Israel refrained from the intentional killing of terrorists? (which it clearly has never ceased to do), but rather, Why has the State been reluctant to inflict death on terrorists *as punishment*? To hint at one possible answer to this more narrowly defined question, this chapter traces the history of the death penalty back to the times of the British mandate, exploring one formative moment, through which the death penalty became a dangerous spectacle.

On 31 July 1947, a small group of British soldiers, Jewish residents, and newspaper reporters was making its way through a thicket of eucalyptus trees on the outskirts of Netanya, a small town north of Tel-Aviv (Bell 1977: 237–38; Eshel 1990: 188–89; Evron 2001: 278–79). They were searching the woods to find the dead bodies of two British sergeants, Clifford Martin and Marvyn Paice, who had been killed several days earlier by the "Etzel," the National Military Organization (NMO), a dissident Zionist underground movement. As they approached their target, a horrifying sight appeared. The corpses of the two soldiers were hanging from a tree, their shirts covering their heads, dry blood that had dripped from their open mouths staining their clothes, and a short statement attached to their chests. The note explained that the two were executed after an NMO court had heard them testify to their crimes and added that the two had asked for pardon but the court rejected their plea. The note neither mentioned nor tried to hide the vengeful character of the deed. The execution of three NMO members several days earlier by a British military court left little room for doubt (Eshel 1990: 166–69; Evron 2001: 278–89; Kanaan 1976: 92–93).

These were the last days of the British Empire. In less than a year, the United Nations would revoke the British mandate in Palestine, divide the land between its Jewish and Arab inhabitants, and recognize the new Zionist state, along with the independence of India and Egypt. Although the British Empire was destined, as most empires are, to collapse internally rather than be vanquished, the British would not disappear from the land before a fierce struggle for independence, a struggle that created a zone of indistinction between four forms of force: violence, punishment, vengeance, and revenge.

The study that follows is devoted to the understanding of this single event in the history of British colonialization and Zionist militant resistance: the hanging of the two British sergeants. It is an inquiry into the fading distinction between punishment and revenge in times of political contestation, which turns the death penalty into a dubious mark of power. It begins with a paradoxical hypothesis regarding the nature of revenge: revenge is that which is unjust yet justifiable.[4] By this I mean, first, that revenge differs both from violence and from punishment, the former being unjust and unjustifiable, the latter being just and justifiable. It is this both liminal and hybrid character of revenge which places it between the "unjust" and the "justifiable" and lends it a transformative power to *present* violence as justifiable punishment and *represent* just punishment as brute force. Second, revenge bears an inverse relation to vengeance—or to what Benjamin calls divine violence (1978: 277–300), which may be defined as just yet unjustifiable. Due to this affinity between vengeance and revenge, the latter can disguise itself as the former, presenting itself as an act of ultimate justice that requires no justification.

My use of the attributes "just" and "justifiable" should be understood primarily in phenomenological rather than moralistic terms. Just force stands for the idea of completion—the power or at least the desire to bring the use of force to an end. This is true, albeit in different ways, of both punishment and divine vengeance (or its human *imitatio dei*). Conversely, injustice stands for the notion of incompletion, of opening up the future for new possibilities of force, as in the work of revenge and brute violence.

In a similar vein, justifiability should be understood phenomenologically. What makes force justifiable is its responsive character, which allows it to justify itself as a reaction to a forceful act that preceded it. Revenge and punishment are in this sense reactionary and thus justifiable, whereas violence and vengeance are unjustifiable primary acts of force.

Since the 1930s, and especially after the end of World War II, the Jewish community in Palestine was divided in its relation to British rule. The mainstream Zionist organization Ha'histadrut Ha'Zionit was determined to replace the British rule and found a Jewish state, but limited its struggle to diplomacy rather than combat. Military force was used, at least in theory, only for defense against Arab attacks, as the name of the organization's military unit the Hagana, literally "the Defense," suggests.

The NMO, a dissident organization which broke off from the Hagana as early as 1931, took a more militant approach. Its members, especially following the end of the war, believed that the Jews should take control over their lives and political destiny. Thus, the NMO refused to accept the Hagana's "Restrain Policy" (*mediniut havlaga*) and declared "open season" on all British military forces in the land. In addition, the NMO made use of more extreme "terrorist" measures in its struggle with the Arabs. The Zionist establishment viewed the NMO's actions as a threat to the delicate relation it had developed with the British government. They feared that those actions might jeopardize the Zionist plan to receive, upon British departure, the "keys" to the land. This implicit agreement between the British and the Jews was based on the close ties Zionist leaders had forged with the British authorities, despite mutual suspicion and at times manifest conflict. Thus, the Zionist establishment discouraged any direct assault against the British, and was not hesitant to use force against the dissenting underground movements when it saw fit. Expectedly, the NMO kidnapping and killing of two unarmed British soldiers drew from the establishment unequivocal opposition. The act of revenge was presented as an unacceptable act of violence, a horrifying crime.

Less than an hour after the corpses of the dead sergeants were found, Ben-Ami, the mayor of Netanya, distributed the following declaration to the press: "Of all the crimes that took place till this day on this land, this is the most grievous and disgusting one and will stain the purity of our peoples struggle for freedom. May this act of hanging remain as a sign of Cain on the doers of this disgraceful deed! The heavens and the earth are my witnesses," continued the mayor, "that most of our population took desperate measures to free the hostages and prevent this shame" (Kanaan 1976: 93–94). Ben-Ami was expressing the mainstream response of the Yishuv (the Zionist establishment), which opposed the terrorist attacks of the NMO not least out of fear for British retaliation.

For the NMO, the killing of the two British sergeants had a different significance. It was clearly not an extraordinary crime of violence, nor was it an ordinary attack against British military targets. The British soldiers were kidnapped in an attempt to deter the British authorities from executing three NMO members who had been caught during a previous operation—the break-in to the most guarded prison in Akko and the release of its Jewish inmates.

The NMO had good reason to hope that the British would yield to their demand to commute the death penalty, as they had done in the past, when a similar threat was posed. One such case involved the planned execution of Michael Eshbal and Yosef Simchon, who were sentenced to death by a military court on 13 June 1946. Although the Zionist establishment, both local and international, headed by Haim Weizmann, turned to the authorities for clemency, the NMO had a different plan. The underground radio station "The Voice of Combative Zion" announced, "Do not hang our captive soldiers. By God, we will shatter your gallows. We will respond to a scaffold with a scaffold" (Eshel 1990: 30).

Five days after the death verdict was given, the NMO kidnapped, in broad daylight, five British officers from a hotel in Tel-Aviv, and the following day another officer was kidnapped in Jerusalem. They were held as hostages to secure the life of the Jewish prisoners. According to the NMO the kidnapping of the British officers was not seen as an attack against the British forces, but rather was aimed to save the lives of the two death row prisoners. The leaders of the NMO explained: "On this matter we will be willing to go all the way to the end, literally: to the end. But there will be no need for this. You will see that the pressure will bring our men down from the scaffold" (Eshel 1990: 191). The British indeed succumbed to the pressure and entered a negotiation process, which led to a commuted sentence of life imprisonment. The following day, as promised, the kidnapped officers were released (Eshel 1990: 191–92).

Six months later a similar incident occurred in the case of Dov Gruner, who was brought to trial and during his "day in court" (literally!) was sentenced to be hanged. Again the NMO threatened that if the sentence was executed, British would also be hanged. And yet, unlike the previous case of Eshbal and Simchon, they did not kidnap soldiers. Some public officials convinced them that such an act would endanger the life of Gruner even more (since not all of the legal procedures were exhausted). But by 23 January it became clear that the execution would take place at the end of the month (Begin 1977: 190). Time was short, and the British, who had learned their lesson from the former kidnapping of hostages, were especially cautious. Soldiers and policemen were prohibited from leaving their safety zones and mingling with the population, except in the performance of their duties, and even then only in well-armed groups. Nevertheless, on the eve of 26 January, the NMO succeeded in kidnapping a retired major by breaking into his home in Jerusalem, and on the following day no less than the president of the district court in Tel-Aviv, Justice Ralph Windham from the courtroom itself. The kidnapping of a high-ranking British judge of noble descent from his seat in the middle of a trial took place only twenty hours before the time set for the hanging of Dov Gruner. The execution was postponed and Gruner was granted theright to appeal, which did not previously exist under British rule. The major and judge were later released (Bell 1977).

The kidnapping of the two British sergeants, however, did not have the expected impact. The reason is not fully clear, but it would seem that the British believed that the situation in Palestine was gradually getting out of control, and that they had to show a firm hand. The NMO captives were thus executed despite the threat, and Martin and Paice were allowed to pay the price. The NMO's leadership was now faced with a grave decision , but it did not hesitate; the execution of the sergeants must clearly take place (Begin 1977; Kanaan 1976).

What was the status of the kidnapped sergeants in Netanya, and what was the significance of their executions? The world saw them simply as the hostages of a terrorist organization, and their deaths as the expected outcome of violence run amok. But the leaders of the NMO had a different view of their killing, a view that may shed light on the phenomenology of revenge, that is, on how revenge is understood by its executors.

Five years after the episode Menachem Begin, the head of the NMO at the time and later Israel's first right-wing prime minister, explained how he understood the kidnapping and hanging in Netanya.

> None of the British that were caught, up to that point, and there were many British prisoners along the years, was used for the purpose of revenge. We have never executed the method of revenge against the British in response to the death of one of our warriors in battle during combat. We have taught our men that they have the role of warriors, which might lead to their imminent death. Only in one single case did we announce in advance that we would use that cruel rule, which is part of the laws of war the name of which is retaliation. We have proclaimed that if the British will not treat our soldiers as war-prisoners but rather treat them as criminal offenders and hang them, we will respond with a guillotine for a guillotine. (Kanaan 1976: 56–57)

To what extent should we take at face value this self-proclaimed sensitivity to the rule of law? After all, the NMO was not known for its moderate ways and was responsible, among other militant activities, for the later massacre of the inhabitants of the Arab village Dir Yasin.[5] It is also clear that Begin's memory, as we shall later see, failed him; the hanging of the sergeants was not the only act of revenge that took place under his leadership. We may nevertheless still wish to take seriously the specific justifications offered for this act of revenge.

In the passage quoted above, Begin lays out the basic structure of revenge as an unjust but justifiable act. The tone is apologetic precisely because it is clear to the leader of the NMO that it is unjust to kill an unarmed soldier outside of the battlefield. He nevertheless attempts to justify the action, distinguishing it from a brute act of violence. To do so he first suggests that the act of revenge was merely a response to an already established act of violence. The British are those who started the cycle of noncombative violence when they decided to put prisoners of war on trial as if they were criminals. This violent act of injustice called for a response in kind. Thus revenge appears as an unjust act of violence, which can nevertheless be justified as retaliation for a similar unjust act of violence.

It is significant, however, that the NMO did not simply avenge the death of their brothers-in-arm by killing two British soldiers. Rather, they set a formal judicial process: pressed charges, tried the two soldiers according to procedure, and only then ordered their execution. Moreover, it was important for the NMO to turn the execution into a public spectacle. So much so that the Jewish establishment feared that the corpses of the two would be hung for display on an electric pole in one of the busy streets of Netanya (Eshel 1990: 176).

Approximately twenty-four hours after the sergeants' execution, the NMO broadcasting station, the Combative Voice of Zion, delivered the following announcement:

> The two British spies, Martin and Paice, that were held in underground arrest since July 12th 1947, were put on trial after the completion of the investigation of their criminal anti-Hebrew activity. Martin and Paice were convicted on the following charges:
>
> A. Illegal entrance to our homeland.
> B. Membership in the British criminal-terrorist organization know as "The British Occupation Army in the Land of Israel" which is responsible for negating the right of life from our people, acts of repression and cruelty, torture, the murder of men, women and children, the murder of war prisoners, the murder of wounded prisoners and the expulsion of Jewish citizens from their homeland.
> C. Illegally holding weapons designed to uphold oppression and tyranny. (Eshel 1990: 186–88)

These charges should be understood first as a conscious parody of the criminal trials that the British organized against the NMO members. Parody, here as elsewhere, works through mimicry.[6] The legalistic language that the British military courts used against the NMO is reproduced against the British occupying forces themselves. The charges of illegality, criminality, and terrorism are reversed. But the parodic repetition of the trial should not be understood merely as political criticism, but rather as part of the structure of revenge.

Revenge, not unlike parody, has the structure of mimetic repetition, "an eye for an eye," a trial for a trial, a scaffold for a scaffold.[7] Here, however, the structure of revenge should also be understood through its political ambitions: not only to expose through parody the British system as arbitrary and unjust, but also to transform through revenge the system of punishment into an arbitrary violence. The power of revenge to transform punishment into violence is a result of its incomplete and open-ended use of force.

From Punishment to Revenge

Shortly after the hanging of the British sergeants became known, the leaders of the Yishuv dreaded the possibility of British retaliation. Tel-Aviv's Mayor Israel Rokach turned to the governor of the district for assurance. "There is nothing to fear, there will be no retaliation by the security forces," promised the governor and added, "One may count on the fair treatment of the British soldier" (Kanaan 1976: 95).

The truth—quite to the contrary—was soon discovered. The British response began at around 8:30 in the evening at the corner of Ben-Yehuda and Trumpeldor streets. Until that hour the people on the streets were relaxed as expected on a summer night in August. Some were seated in cafés, others were strolling or waiting for the late show at the cinema. This pastoral setting turned within minutes into a horrible site of violent gunfire. Dozens of soldiers and police officers, some wearing their uniforms but most dressed as civilians, carrying machine-guns, pistols, and heavy metal clubs, arrived at the place in three trucks escorted by a police armored vehicle. The police officers and soldiers attacked citizens with their clubs and indiscriminately battered men and women, old and young. When the streets eventually cleared of citizens, the "men of the law" began to break and shatter shop windows. Some policemen who were on duty at that time saw what was being done but did not intervene to prevent the outburst of terror. "These are not policemen, and we are not allowed to intervene, these are soldiers," answered the law officers on duty when citizens asked them to use their authority (Bell 1977: 237–38; Kanaan 1976: 97–98).

In unauthorized reports it was said that armored cars fired on Alenbi Street, and as a result a man on a bus was killed and a woman injured. It was reported that in Shkhunat Ha' Tikva shots were fired from an armored car, and a bomb was thrown out of it into a café. As a result three people were killed and several wounded. It was officially reported that all police vehicles on duty in Tel-Aviv were ordered to report back to their bases, their weapons were examined, and they were not in use (Eshel 1990: 195).

Conclusion

What does this exchange of force surrounding the hanging of the British sergeants suggest about the use of the death penalty in times of political strife? The NMO was determined to drive the British out of the land, but the use of military force was not its sole strategy. The NMO replied to military force with military force, but used revenge to respond to the forceful use of law. Unlike violence, which may destroy legality but cannot overcome it, revenge poses an effective threat to the rule of law.

Under the rule of law, only punishment and violence are recognized. Any force within the boundaries of the modern state which is not just and justifiable (i.e., punishment) is understood immediately and treated as unjust and unjustifiable (i.e., as violence). Legality acknowledges neither the unjust justifiability of revenge nor the unjustifiable justice of vengeance. And yet, in times of political strife, the acts of the state run the risk of being transformed through revenge into acts of violence. This outcome seems to characterize not only the NMO's perception of British legality, but also the response of the British who were forced to respond violently to revenge.

And yet, though revenge may wish to transform just and justifiable punishment into unjust and unjustifiable violence, it can never truly succeed in doing so. As the hanging of the British sergeants suggests, revenge can, at most, import the force of law into a cycle of revenge. Paradoxically, the NMO's act of revenge could only serve as proof of the need for the rule of law to bring the cycle of revenge to an end. Thus, revenge confronts the limits of its transformative powers. The law cannot be effectively challenged through the unjust use of revenge, nor through the just yet always-in-need-of-justification use of legality. Perhaps, one may suggest in conclusion that only vengeance as that which is just but is not in need of justification can serve that role. And thus the true power of the state is not its monopoly on the legitimate use of force, but rather a monopoly on the unjustifiable application of vengeance.

One may wonder if these general observations regarding the relation between violence, punishment, vengeance, and revenge bear any particular relation to the death penalty. It would seem that the same dynamics may play out
in relation to any kind of punishment. Indeed, only months before the hanging
of the British sergeants, Begin ordered an act of revenge against British soldiers
in response to the flogging of NMO fighters, leading the British to abandon the
practice (Begin 1977). It is important to note, however, that the NMO never
considered reacting in a similar way to the incarceration of its members. This
may suggest that what is special, though not unique, about the death penalty is
its manifestly punitive character, which it shares with flogging but not with imprisonment. Is it not possible that, because of its immediate and visible effects,
the punishment of the body belongs to a more originary order of punishment,
one dangerously closer to the orbit of violence, vengeance, and revenge?

Years after the event, and long after the establishment of the State of Israel,
the spectacle of the hanging bodies of Martin and Paice returns to haunt the Israeli public. This is how the former Israeli minister of justice explained his
reservations about enacting a death penalty for Palestinian terrorists:

> Every movement that sees itself as a freedom movement needs its martyrs that will
> set an example to the young generation of their people. Executed Palestinians will re-
> main in the conscious[ness] of their people as great heroes. . . . A verdict of death
> against a terrorist will inevitably lead to the kidnapping of Israelis to prevent the ex-
> ecution. . . . The affair will end in one of two possible ways: in the contempt of sur-
> rendering to terrorists and the abolition de-facto of the death penalty, or in a cycle of
> bloodshed of gallows and killing of hostages. One recalls the kidnapping of the two
> British sergeants by the NMO. The purpose of the kidnapping was to prevent the ex-
> ecution of NMO members which were sentenced to death by a British court. The
> British authorities were not deterred: the NMO members were executed and the two
> sergeants were killed. Since that episode the British stopped executing members of
> the NMO. The lesson is clear." (Zadok 1993)

Among the primary reasons still given for opposing the death penalty for
terrorists is the risk of drawing punishment into a cycle of revenge and of turning terrorists into martyrs. Since Israel has never executed terrorists, both concerns are based not on facts but on the equally compelling force of memory and
imagination. The memory of the NMO martyrs on the gallows and the frus-
trated violence of the occupying British forces are imagined as strong evidence
against the death penalty for Palestinian terrorists. Thus, the State of Israel has

forsaken its justifiable right to punish by death, only to maintain its monopoly on the unjustifiable force to take life by means of extra-judicial assassinations.

Notes

1. Eichmann v. State of Israel, Crim. App. 132/57, 11 *Piskei Din,* 1544.

2. Another, less famous exception is the trial and execution of Meir Tubyanski by a military court in 1948 for treason; see Gutman (1995). On the history of the death penalty in Israel, see Ben-Haim (1989), Inbar (1989), and Sanjero (2002).

3. Since October 2000, in response to the collapse of Clinton's peace initiative and to a second wave of Palestinian uprising, Israel has implemented a new assassination policy against terrorist leaders. Over 100 have been executed in this way. For a recent discussion of the legitimacy of targeted killing, see Gross (2003) and Statman (2003).

4. For a somewhat different though related understanding of revenge, see Hegel (1952).

5. For a somewhat apologetic account of the events that took place at Dir Yasin, see Gany (1977: 24–25).

6. For a discussion of mimicry in the context of colonialism, see Bhaba (1994).

7. "We repaid our enemy in kind . We had warned him again and again. He had callously disregarded our warnings. He forced us to answer gallows with gallows" (Begin 1977: 290).

References

Bhaba, Homi K. (1995) *The Location of Culture.* London: Routledge.

Begin, Menachem (1977) *The Revolt* (rev. ed.). New York: Nash Publishing.

Bell, J. Bowyer (1977) *Terror Out of Zion: Irgun Zvai Leumi, LEHI, and the Palestine Underground, 1929–1949.* New York: St. Martin's Press.

Ben-Haim, Ofer (1989) "Onesh Mavet B'Psikat Batei Ha'Mishpat Ha'Zvaiim B'Israel U'Baezorim Ha'Muchzakim [The Death Penalty in the Ruling of the Military Courts in Israel and in the Occupied Territories]," *Mishpat u'Zava* 10.

Benjamin, Walter (1978) *Reflections: Essays, Aphorisms, Autobiographical Writings* (1st ed.). New York: Harcourt Brace Jovanovich.

Eshel, Arye (1990) *The Cheated Hangman.* Tel-Aviv: Zmora-Bitan.

Evron, Joseph (2001) *Gidi: The Jewish Insurgency Against the British in Palestine.* Jerusalem: Misrad Ha'Bitachon.

Gany, Pesach (1977) *The Irgun Zvai Leumi.* Tel-Aviv: Machon Zabotinsky.

Gross, Michael L. (2003) "Fighting by Other Means in the Mideast: A Critical Analysis of Israel's Assassination Policy," 51 *Political Studies* 350–68.

Gutman, Yechiel (1995) *A Storm in the G.S.S.* Tel-Aviv: Yediot Aharonot.

Hegel, Georg W. F. (1952) *Hegel's Philosophy of Right.* Oxford: Oxford University Press.

Inbar, Zvi (1989) "L'Hatalat Onesh Mavet Ba'Ezorim Ha'Muchzakim Bidei Israel L'inyan Ha'Basis Ha'History [A Note on the Statutory Basis for Enacting the Death Penalty in the Occupied Territories by Israel]," *Mishpat u'Zava* 10.

Kanaan, Haviv (1976) *Gallows in Nathania.* Tel-Aviv: Hadar.

Sanjero, Boaz (2002) "Al Onesh Mavet B'Chlal V'Al Onesh Mavet Begin Rezach B'Pulat Terror B'Frat [On the Death Penalty in General and on the Death Penalty for Murder in Terrorist Acts in Particular]," 2 *Alei Mishpat.*

Statman, Daniel (2003) "The Morality of Assassination: A Response to Gross," 51 *Political Studies* 775–79.

Zadok, Haim C. (1993) "And What If Death Penalty to Terrorists Would Be Executed," *Yediot Aharonot* (June 14).

CHAPTER ELEVEN

The Palestinian Culture of Death

Shariah and Siyasah—Justice, Political Power, and Capital Punishment in the Palestinian National Authority

JUDITH MENDELSOHN ROOD

I'm used to being in a place where death, blood and killing is something normal.

Suleiman Shafhe, Palestinian journalist[1]

Introduction

In 2002, Rajah Ibrahim and her sister, Ikhlas Khouli, were executed by the Al-Aqsa Martyr's Brigade for the crime of collaboration with Israel. Rajah Ibrahim's husband was also executed. The Al-Aqsa Martyr's Brigade, which reported to Yasser Arafat, videotaped the confession of Ikhlas Khouli, a widowed mother of seven children, before her execution. In it, Ikhlas "appears resigned as she details her actions in response to an invisible interrogator." "She did it, she says, because her brother threatened to kill her. 'Everything I say is of my own free will,' she says. She is asked, 'What else do you want to say to Palestinians?' 'I want to say[,] tell everyone, women and men, young and old, that even if you are threatened, don't get into this.'" She was shot in the head and legs and left in the street. A member of the Brigade agreed to an interview with *New York Times* reporter Serge Schemann, explaining that

> killing collaborators is not the policy of the group, that the collapse of the Palestinian Authority had imposed this task on them. He insisted that the militia had taken pains to make sure that their charges were substantiated.
>
> "The interrogators were experienced and qualified intelligence men from the Palestinian Authority, trained in Britain and the United States," he said. "I know about human rights," he continued, "But when we feel threatened, we need to react.

I am a wanted man, so I might face the same fate. This is self-defense. Thirteen men have been assassinated in Tulkarem alone," he said, "and more than 100 elsewhere in the West Bank and Gaza."

The spokesman insisted that the interrogators did not coerce the "confessions" of the women or their families—that they had volunteered their information. "But the black eye [of] Muyaser Ibrahim, Rajah and Ikhlas' mother, brought back from her three days of interrogation tell another story." . . . "So do the ugly welts on Bakir Khouli's back." He declined to talk about his interrogation, but after some prodding he raised his T-shirt. It was an electric cable, he says. Yes, it was during the interrogation. In earlier interviews, he said he would have confessed to anything to stop the pain. (Schemann 2002)

The Palestinian culture of death and the glorification of its suicide-bombing "martyrs" reveal a society mobilized to embrace death in the service of political liberation. The death penalty has been the primary tool for the Palestinian National Authority (PNA, or PA) for demonstrating and preserving its power. Judicial processes in Palestine have been subordinate to the political. Extra-judicial executions in Palestine typify this subordination of law to politics. Palestinian civil society, which had been developing since the final years of the Ottoman Empire, was almost totally destroyed as a result of the Al-Aqsa Intifada (October 2002) against the Oslo Peace Process. Under the regime of Yasser Arafat, legitimate political aspirations were used as a cover for crime and vendetta against Palestinians and Israelis. The draft Palestinian Constitution, in Article 39, states, "Arbitrariness in execution shall be punishable by law," an oblique reference to the extrajudicial nature of the death penalty in the absence of a strong civil society (Palestinian Center for Policy and Survey Research 2001). Under Arafat, the right to summarily execute defined the role of the Palestinian National Authority more than any other aspect of its governance.

An analysis of the culture of death that emerged in Palestine must incorporate several factors beyond the state of war that serves as its justification. Central to this analysis is the historical relationship of capital punishment to political authority in Islamic and Palestinian political thought. It is important to consider the history of the death penalty because of the overemphasis on Islamic law in the contemporary debate on the nature of government in the Middle East.

Indeed, the very definition of government has resided in the leader's authority to use capital punishment to preserve order. Sovereignty and the death penalty have been inextricably combined throughout history. However, how that has been worked out in each particular time and place has varied widely. The death penalty in Palestine is so entwined in the structures of power that any analysis of the instrument of judicial and extrajudicial execution and the political and social structures that wield it must be embedded in a critique of the legitimizing authority of those structures. Such a critique, in turn, must employ a critique of the sources of legitimacy—the law and the institutions of the society that rely upon the death penalty for their very survival.

In the first section of this chapter, we will take a brief look at the sources of Palestinian law relating to the death penalty today.

The Death Penalty in Palestine Today

Despite the current focus on Shariah (Islamic Law), the primary sources of authority in modern Arab thought for the death penalty historically include not only Islamic, but also European laws and ideologies. The ideas legitimizing political terror, so central to the ideology of Palestinian national liberation, come from the organizational and political strategies of the French Revolution, fascism, and European colonial rule. Since the fall of the Ottoman Empire, the emergence of the Arab state system has been shaped in large part by the imposition of law codes based upon European ideas, starting with the Napoleonic Code, introduced in the Middle East during the French invasion and occupation of Egypt in 1798. Although secular Arab Nationalism failed to deliver a revolutionary, secular Palestinian state, European factors continue to influence Palestinian culture by merging revolutionary, fascist, and Islamist rationales for the use of terror.

Fatah, Islamic Jihad, and Hamas, the three most important political actors in Palestine, have endorsed the current conceptions of the Islamic state put forward by the Saudi, the Iranian, Pakistani, and Taliban regimes (Israeli 2003). This Salafi (Revivalist) interpretation of Islamic Law is based upon the pernicious theories of Ibn Taymiyyah as interpreted by the Wahhabis, Sayyid Qutb, the Muslim Brotherhood, and most lately, by al-Qa'ida.[2] The preference for Ibn Taymiyyah's ahistorical and extreme views on the Shariah by these groups is a consequence of their direct repudiation of Ottoman law, which had permitted the development of positive law: a corpus of administrative law (*Qanun*) which was designed to complement the Shariah but legislate in areas which the Qur'an and Hadith (Reports of the Sayings and Actions of the Prophet) were silent.[3]

Today's Palestinian laws relating to capital punishment are derived in part from codes dating to the time of Muhammad 'Ali, who ruled Palestine from 1831 to 1839, Ottoman codes from the Tanzimat Period, and from the British, Jordanian, and Israeli eras, thus representing a complex mixture of laws and legal theories. Following the Israeli occupation of the West Bank and Gaza Strip in 1967, the Israeli army issued an order forbidding the imposition of the death penalty for any crimes, including murder. When the Palestinian National Authority gained control over parts of the West Bank and Gaza in 1994, Palestinian President Yasser Arafat issued a decree informing Palestinians that the laws predating the Israeli occupation would go back into effect. The laws regulating the death penalty before the Israeli occupation are based on British Mandate laws promulgated in 1936. The Jordanians, who ruled the West Bank after the end of the British Mandate, added their own laws to this, as did the Egyptians, who ruled Gaza after the 1948 Israeli War of Independence. The Oslo Accords stipulated that Israel must approve laws passed by the PNA's Legislative Council and approved by the president. In addition, Israel and the PNA signed the Gaza and Jericho Agreement in 1994, which stipulated that suspects extradited to the PNA might not face the death penalty. Until 1997, the civil courts in PNA-controlled territory continued to use Israeli military decrees in the civil courts, unless they had been specifically revoked, but in 1998 even the civil courts began to apply the death penalty.[4]

However, it is not the civil courts which are of primary interest to us here. It is the Palestinian Military Court, which, like the Iraqi Ba'athist regime, considers collaboration with the enemy a capital crime punishable by immediate execution. Tha'er Mahmoud Faris (accused of collaboration with the enemy, Israel) was the first to be sentenced to death and executed by firing squad in 1995, according to the Law of the Palestinian Revolution, approved by the Palestine Liberation Organization (PLO) in 1974. The PNA's State Security Courts (SSC), established in 1995, were designed to adjudicate cases against personnel employed or affiliated with the various "security forces" working under the umbrella of the PNA, and, more specifically, the PLO—which includes, for example, the militias known as the Tanzim and the Al-Aqsa Brigades, which have been responsible for many acts of terrorism and murder since September 29, 2000, when the Al-Aqsa Intifada was initiated by Arafat.[5] Hamas and Islamic Jihad have their own military courts dealing with collaborators, but much less is known about them. The evidence, however, proves that Hamas and the Al-Aqsa Brigade have themselves collaborated with the PLO, and therefore with the PNA itself in "military actions" against Israel; both of these organizations are known to execute extrajudicial justice against their Palestinian opponents.[6] The Palestinian Human Rights Monitor Group stated in 1997:

> In our opinion, the operation of the Palestinian legal system is far from perfect, and that of the military courts even worse. The widespread and routine defects in the justice system (civilian and military) are an additional reason for abolishing the death penalty, which would be wrong even if the courts were above reproach.... The laxity of the rule of law, in the courts, and the implementation of the death penalty, and even in the supposed commutation of all death penalties is not acceptable. (Palestinian Human Rights Monitoring Group 1997)

In 1997, the PNA considered imposing the death penalty on any Muslim or Christian Palestinian convicted of selling land to Jews. At that time, at least three Palestinian realtors or landowners who sold land to Jewish clients were murdered. Yasser Arafat indicated his support for such legislation. Ray Hanania, a Palestinian American journalist, expressed one Palestinian perspective, writing:

> Palestinians who sell their land to an Israel [sic] and when we talk about Israel, we are talking about a Jewish State and therefore, selling land to a "Jew," we are talking about potential treason.... Banning the sale of land is a legitimate position for the PNA to take. Employing the death penalty as the ultimate punishment is subject to much emotional debate. Personally, I oppose the death penalty. But I do support harsh punishments for land sales while the peace process remains unresolved. (Hanania 1997)

It is in this highly militarized context that executions and summary extrajudicial killings of Palestinians have occurred, resulting in the flight of many from the territories. Well-organized vigilantes have assassinated people for alleged collaboration: the Al-Aqsa Martyr's Brigade (Fatah), the Elimination Unit, the Revolutionary Security System/Al-Aqsa/Tanzim (now the Arafat) Brigade, the Storm Forces, the Izz al-Din Qassam wing of Hamas, and the Revolutionary

Justice Brigade all have claimed responsibility in leaflets warning others not to make the same mistake.[7] According to reports from Human Rights Watch, such executions are carried out without "any semblance of due process, completely outside the justice system, killings are carried out for criminal purposes, including personal vendetta."[8]

Under Arafat, murder became a norm on the Palestinian street. Despite warning Palestinians not to carry out these extrajudicial killings, Palestinian police investigations were "perfunctory at best," and the Palestinian Authority did not prosecute anyone for these crimes. Total numbers of accused collaborators killed by assassination during the Al-Aqsa Intifada are unknown; however, the death toll during the first Intifada (the Intifada of the Stones 1987–1993) was estimated by Human Rights Watch to be 822. In a letter to Arafat dated August 2, 2001, Hanny Megally, executive director of Human Rights Watch Middle East and North Africa Division, asked that persons accused of collaboration and treason be provided with the following internationally recognized rights: presumption of innocence; trial by a competent, impartial, and independent tribunal; information about the charges; time to prepare and present a defense and to call witnesses; legal representation, if necessary free of charge by the state; knowledge of the evidence and witnesses of the prosecution; freedom to decline to testify or confess guilt; appeal of the conviction and sentence to a higher court (Megally 2001). Human Rights Watch reported that:

> [m]any of the human rights abuses . . . derive from fundamental weaknesses in the Palestinian justice system that emerged within six months of the PA being established in 1994. . . . A thread running through these factors is the way that the PA executive—the president, ministers, and the police and security forces—have systematically disempowered and undermined the authority and independence of the judiciary and legal remedies. Under Arafat, the separation of powers was not respected. [The executive] created a situation in which ordinary Palestinians had neither the means to redress injustice, nor any protection against their abusers. (Human Rights Watch 2001)

Death Penalty, Palestinian National Authority, and Islamic Law

Until the Al-Aqsa Intifada, which began in October 2001, it was unthinkable that the legal culture of the Palestinian National Authority would become Is-

lamic in the twenty-first century. Previous attempts to Islamicize the Palestin-
ian-Israeli Conflict had failed. Most notably, in the 1930s, the "Grand Mufti of
Jerusalem" (an office created by the British Mandate to allow a leadership position for the Muslims of Palestine), Hajj Amin al-Hussayni, embraced the ideology of the Muslim Brotherhood's Sayyid Qutb (a disciple of Ibn Taymiyyah) in
his attempts to resist Jewish immigration. During this period the Muslim
Brotherhood, in collaboration with the Nazis, adapted fascist organization to
their Islamist doctrines. The radicalization of the Palestinian resistance during
this period served only to undercut its legitimate political aspirations, to mar-
ginalize liberal Palestinian politicians, and to contribute to the strengthening of
the cause of Zionism in international public opinion.[9] Yet Islamic legal history
does have a bearing on Palestinian law, although not in the sense that those
waging holy war on Israel would like.

Since the Islamic conquest of Palestine in 638 A.D., all of the Muslim regimes
have exercised political power based upon differing interpretations of Islamic
law.[10] These interpretations have been variously puritanical or tolerant, depending in part upon the international context. At times jihad, or holy war, typ-
ified the political culture. At other times, the desire for commercial and scientific ties led to moderate rule entailing great toleration and autonomy for their
non-Muslim subjects. The fall of the Ottoman Empire and the abolition of the
Caliphate brought an end to Islamic rule in many regions of the Middle East,
including Palestine. The secularizing philosophies of the Arab nationalists overshadowed the remaining Islamic institutions, which, however, continued to
govern the personal status issues of the Muslim population.

The Iranian Revolution of 1979 and the subsequent establishment of Islamist
republics in Pakistan, the Sudan, and Afghanistan and the reemergence of Islamist movements throughout the Arab world were aimed at the establishment
of Islamic regimes based upon a literal interpretation of the Qur'an.[11] These developments have led to the popular, common misperception the West that "Islamic law" has determined, among other issues, the laws governing capital punishment in Muslim societies. Today, even most Muslims themselves frequently
do not know, let alone understand, the historical development and application
of law in historical Islamic societies.[12] The Shariah, the theologically developed
body of law based upon the Qur'an and upon the tradition of classical Sunni
jurisprudence (fiqh), formulated in the ninth and tenth centuries, constituted a

source of law in Islamic polities, but it had never been the sole source of legal authority until the twentieth-century establishment of the Wahhabi state of Saudi Arabia. The political theory of these Islamist states results from their strenuous rejection of the multidimensional legal theories of the Ottoman Empire.

Classical Islamic Legal Theory of Capital Punishment

In classical Islamic legal theory there are two general categories of crime and punishment: those stipulated in the Qur'an (*hadd*) and those that are not. A subset of *hadd* laws (*qissas*) relate to the crimes of homicide and assault. Discretionary punishment (*ta'zir*), designed for offences not stipulated in the Qur'an, is available to the Islamic judge (*qadi*) using his discretion in punishing the transgressor. Neither the Qur'an nor the Sunni traditions about the Prophet (*Sunna*) mention this word, although a case has been made to show that the concept of discretionary punishment is present in these texts. Although according to one report (*hadith*), the Prophet stated, "he who extends the punishment of a non-*hadd* offense to that of a *hadd* is a transgressor," some Muslim countries allow the death sentence to be implemented for the category of *ta'zir* crimes. One of the four Sunni schools of Islamic law, the Hanafi, accepts capital punishment for *ta'zir* crimes "which they term 'killing as an act of punishment for the sake of upholding public order' (*al-qatl siyasatan*)."[13] Islamic law calls for the following kinds of execution, depending upon the offence and the category of the person tried: crucifixion, stoning, strangulation, and hanging are all Qur'anic punishments. Notably, execution by firing squad, or the slashing of the throat by box-cutter, sword, or knife are not permissible.

Ottoman Legal Theory: Shariah and Siyasah

The Ottomans, who ruled the region from 1517–1917, developed the most sophisticated Islamic legal system in history. Ottoman political culture aimed normatively at preserving the "tranquility and repose" of its taxpaying subjects (Rood 2004). When the Ottomans began to realize that the decentralization of their empire might be an indication of its impending demise, they turned to the great Muslim philosopher of history Ibn Khaldun (1332–1406) to find answers for the source of their weakness. Ibn Khaldun, unlike Ibn Taymiyyah, was steeped in Greek philosophy and had adapted an Aristotelian view of ethics and politics. His theory on the rise and fall of dynasties centered upon their ability to rule justly. He recognized that political power naturally degenerated into tyranny (*mulk*) without the restraint of law—law based on revelation and reason. Thus, he upheld the supremacy of law over the ruler, and he emphasized the common good as the purpose of civilization. Ibn Khaldun built his new science of culture within the context of the Muslim religion, but allowed for the use of reason to adapt laws to suit the needs and aspirations of society in a particular time and place. He did this by building upon the work of Ibn Sina (Avicenna d. 1037) and al-Ghazzali (d. 1111), who themselves based their work on Aristotle's *Nicomachean Ethics*. Ibn Khaldun used this framework to develop a practical jurisprudence that he imbedded in his understanding of world history. As Muhsin Mahdi explained, the purpose of the study of history for Ibn Khaldun was "prudent action" (Mahdi 1971: 12). Ottoman jurisprudence did not define "Islamic law" as the seventh-century code reified by Ibn Taymiyyah, but as a practical code of law that adapts to the needs of a society at a particular time and place, rooted in what may be called "natural law" recognizable through reason (Mahdi 1971: 9–13; Black 2001: 154–59, 165–82, 255–78).

The administration of law under the Ottomans was often characterized as venal, no less by the Ottomans themselves than by Western observers during the nineteenth-century reform period. The Ottomans justified their nineteenth-century centralization under the banner of legal reform, weeding out corruption and abuses of power as they implemented the Tanzimat. There is no question that many aspects of Ottoman law, particularly its administrative law code, were never perfectly implemented. Nevertheless, there was a strong normative ideal of justice at the center of the Ottoman state, an idea of justice that transcended Shariah law. The Ottoman conception of Shariah allowed for the ruler to legislate laws in response to specific societal issues. All administrative and military authority concerning criminal cases and violations of the Ottoman administrative code was exercised by the officials who represented the executive power of the sultan in all capital cases in an Ottoman province.[14] It was the provincial governor's duty to enforce the decisions of the judge according to Islamic law, implement the sultan's orders, maintain the public order, bring criminal offenders to justice, and punish opponents of the government.[15] The sultan delegated "that discretionary power of the sovereign which enables him, in theory, to apply and to complete the sacred law, and in practice, to reg-

ulate by virtually independent legislation matters of police, taxation, and criminal justice" (Ayalon 1973: 14–15). Halil Inalcik's early description of the governor's responsibilities is echoed in Bernard Lewis's contention that the term
Siyasah had a special meaning in Ottoman government:

> [S]iyâsa . . . means neither politics nor statecraft but punishment. More particularly
> it means punishment which is severe, physical, probably capital, and—this is the im-
> portant point—not provided for by the Shari'a [sic]. Thus Siyasa [sic] entailed the
> discretionary political power of the sovereign and his representatives to punish those
> who rebelled against the ruler—and such punishment invariably meant "severe
> physical punishment and frequently death." (Lewis 1984: 9)

Indeed, Siyasah comprised "the whole of administrative justice which is dis-
pensed by the sovereign and his political agents" (Lewis 1984: 9). These officials
included the Ottoman judiciary, which served to implement the sultan's orders
and to ensure his compliance with the law. The governor and his deputies in
each particular administrative district maintained de jure control over those
matters not covered specifically by Islamic law and which pertained specifically
to the protection of civil order.

Indeed, we can find here an Islamic source for the separation of powers. The
jurisdiction of the military governor-general at the regional level was thus parallel and complementary to that of the Islamic chief judge (mulla qadi). Both
were theoretically independent within the realm of their own authority, but at
the same time both were bound ultimately to uphold the authority of the sultan, who epitomized both the Shariah and the Siyasah. Although, in principle,
the chief judge and the imperial treasurer (mal daftardar) were independent of
the governor, they required him to enforce the law and to provide for public security so that they could carry out their duties. The chief judge had the right to
petition the sultan in the case of a despotic governor, which could, under ideal
conditions, check the broad powers of the governor.

The Revolt of Muhammad 'Ali and the Transformation
of Politics in the Nineteenth Century

Muhammad 'Ali was an Albanian Muslim who served in the Ottoman army
in Egypt, leading to the defeat of Napoleon. With this victory, the Ottomans
named him governor of Egypt, its most profitable province. In 1831, Muham-

mad 'Ali rebelled against the Ottomans and invaded and occupied Syria in 1831. He took over the Ottoman legal system in the region, including the areas currently defined by Israel and the Palestinian National Authority. Whereas in the Ottoman system Siyasah and Shariah were intermingled in the office of the sultan, the sovereign power, and transferred to his representatives, Muhammad 'Ali separated them into two distinct court systems: the Islamic law court (*al-mahkamah al-shar'iyyah*) and the consultative council (*majlis al-shura*), the latter handling administrative (military, political, and criminal law) and the former dealing primarily with family and specifically personal status law. The Islamic law court retained a connection to the Ottoman legal hierarchy in Istanbul, while the consultative council reported directly to Muhammad 'Ali through his deputies. Muhammad 'Ali made it his business to constrain the power of the religious authorities and to bring them under his control. This system is the direct predecessor of the political and legal systems in the Arab states that emerged at the end of the First World War.

Although French law influenced Muhammad 'Ali's legal codes, he designed his dual legal system on the basis of Ottoman jurisprudence. The important development was that political authority and military authority were separated from the inherently religious office of the Caliphate, the divinely sanctioned political authority personified by the sultan, conferred upon him by Islamic law. Although he achieved a form of separation of "state" and "mosque," the nature of this regime did not separate the "executive" from the "judicial," nor the "military" from the "civil." As such, Muhammad 'Ali's regime is the prototype of today's military regimes in Iraq and the Palestinian National Authority and the authoritarian regimes of the Gulf states.

Two Post-Ottoman Movements: Arab Nationalism and the Saudi-Wahhabi State

Throughout the late eighteenth and nineteenth centuries, the Ottomans faced national liberation movements in the Balkans inspired by the French Revolution. They also faced a dissident form of Islamic political and legal philosophy that was emerging in Arabia: Wahhabi theology. Based upon the political and legal philosophy of Ibn Taymiyyah, the Wahhabis asserted the illegitimacy of Ottoman rule and repudiated the Ottoman interpretation of Islamic law. It was Muhammad 'Ali who defeated the Wahhabis in Arabia for the Ottomans in the 1820s.

Following the disintegration of the Ottoman Empire in the First World War and the abolition of the Ottoman Caliphate in 1924, the Wahhabi rejection of Ottoman political and judicial philosophy found political expression in the establishment of the Saudi state. Over the past century, the Saudis have used their vast economic resources in *da'wa*—proselytizing—developing a network of schools (*madrasas*) indoctrinating Muslims around the world with Wahhabi legal and political positions. Over the past hundred years, the creation of an Arab state system began to redefine the politics of the Middle East. For a century, the significance of Wahhabi ideology had been overshadowed by the rise of Arab Nationalism. Until the Six Day War, Arab Nationalism, created to allow for the development of secular political culture that would unite Muslim and Christian Arabs against Western domination, focused on the tension between Pan-Arabism and the legitimacy of the post–World War II Arab state system. This tension was finally resolved after the 1973 October War and the conclusion of the Egypt-Israel peace treaty, which sealed the legitimacy of the independent Arab states.

Nevertheless, the inability of the Arabs to unify in order to defeat Israel and the ultimate acceptance of a territorial settlement of the conflict represented by the signing of the Egypt-Israel Peace Treaty drove the long-submerged Arab Islamic movement out of the shadows. Indeed, in the 1980s Israel itself fostered the Islamic movement as an alternative to the secular nationalism of the Palestinian Liberation Organization, allowing Saudi Arabia to build social welfare institutions in the occupied territories.

One of the most important results of this process has been the rejection of the Ottoman model of government by contemporary Muslims. The Wahhabi attack on the legitimacy of the Sunni Ottoman government and its interpretation of Islamic law has become institutionalized in Islamic universities and in European and American curricula in Islamic history and has become the dominant trope for studying and understanding Islamic legal history. The Wahhabi interpretation of jihad has increasingly replaced the revolutionary, secular, and socialist ideology of the PLO among many Palestinians, thanks to the Saudi funding of the Hamas movement in the disputed territories of the West Bank and Gaza, where the Israelis permitted them to build mosques, schools, clinics, and hospitals as an alternative to the PLO's institutions in the 1980s. The Wahhabi *da'wa* was joined to the Islamic revolutionary ideology spawned by the Iranian Revolution of 1979 to present an alternative to the failure of the PLO to liberate Palestine. Since the first Gulf War, Arafat was able to manipulate increasing support for Islamist rule to reinvigorate Palestinian opposition to Israel and to revivify the Palestinian struggle for liberation. He has done this even when he was ostensibly eschewing the use of violence to resolve the conflict with Israel.

Voices of Islamic Legal Reform

Few in the Arab world or the West understood the significance of Saudi support of the Islamist movement until 9/11. However, that moment of clarity allowed us to reconsider an alternate Islamic understanding of political and legal power, that of the Ottoman Empire. Indeed, this form of Sunni Islamic political theory underpinned Islamic society in the Middle East since the victory of Salah al-Din al-Ayyubi over the crusading states in the twelfth century—a period of over 800 years!

Mohammed Arkoun analyzed the use of Islamic law in its "Islamicized" or "sacralized" form to revive the "'authentic' Arabo-Islamic spirit" as a "reaction to the cultural invasion of imperialistic Western ideas into the Arab world" (Arkoun 1998: 143).[16] The Wahhabis have reified decisions made by Muslim judges and administrators between 670 and 730 into a body of teaching about Islamic law that is "historically false," a "theoretical fiction" stressing and affirming the divine and unchanging nature of that law (ibid.). Arkoun's bold characterization of the ahistoricism of today's interpretation of the Shariah is unusual. Rather, moderate Muslims take a different position on the role of the Shariah in modern times, asserting that "Islam repudiates its own laws on the basis of its eternal principles—it is unacceptable to kill or coerce a person to accept Islam, to kill, torture or imprison political dissidents, to attack non-Muslims for their faith, or to ill treat or oppress people" (143). Instead, in this view, Islam supports political freedom, peaceful conduct, restraint of enmity and hatred, restoration of natural rights, forgiveness of political opponents, mercy, and respect for human life. It leaves capital punishment and strict *hadd* punishments only in theory to demonstrate the wisdom and mercy of the restraints put on the exercise of these penalties, demonstrated by the difficult proofs for those crimes (Palestinian Human Rights Monitoring Group 1999: 5–6). Thus the debate among Muslims on the very nature of Islam and Islamic law draws upon different strands of thought—both the transcendental and the historical.

Conclusion: The Costs of Terror and Violence

Reflecting on the execution of Nazi collaborators in France following World War II and the Algierian War of Independence, Albert Camus wrote:

> The application of ethical criteria to regicide, terror, and torture disqualifies the regimes and theories that depend on these means, whatever story they tell of themselves and whatever Heavenly City they promise in the earthly hereafter. The moral measure that we bring to bear in condemning the death penalty or the violence of Fascist regimes is indivisible and has the same disqualifying effect upon the actions and regimes of the revolution and its children, however "progressive." (as cited in Judt 1998: 95)

The combination of revolutionary terror at the heart of the Palestinian National Authority, and the Islamist parties' ideology, constitutes it, in Ibn Khaldun's terminology, as *mulk*—naked power—legitimized by force, unbalanced by any transcendent principle of justice. History will not come to the service of the Palestinians and retrospectively justify past crimes. Instead, the crimes committed in the name of national liberation ultimately will invalidate Palestinian nationalism if the Palestinians fail to repudiate terror and violence. The culture of death threatens to abort the establishment of a state based upon a dual commitment to Islamic law and democracy (El-Fadl 2003).

Basing the new constitution in a political theory kindred to Ibn Khaldun's would free the Palestinians to develop an authentic law, a law cognizant of the moral teachings of the Shariah, but capable of protecting human rights by defining Palestinian citizenship in secular terms. Indeed, this was the aspiration of the failed legal reforms of the Ottoman Tanzimat in the nineteenth century.[17] Those Ottoman reforms foundered when the nationalist political ideologies inspired by the French Revolution redrew the map of the Middle East in the twentieth century. However, with the failure of Arab Nationalism to secure the tranquility and repose of the Palestinian people, a new premise for political action must be found. Ibn Khaldun's recognition of the validity of the ancients' assertion of universal principles and norms—principles and norms that are also at the foundation of the Western notion of natural law—would provide the writers of the new Palestinian constitution with a starting point which would allow for the protection of human rights and liberty, including a proper interpretation of the death penalty in civil and military courts.

Palestinians and those who care about their future, as well as that of their neighbors, must realize that the sources of this culture of death, a culture that cheapens human life and suppresses all freedom of expression, must be transformed. The reformulation of Palestinian political culture from a culture of death into a Palestinian culture of life will depend upon the transformation of its legal system. With the passing of Arafat, it is possible that judicial power may at last be centralized, separated from the executive power, rights individualized, rationalized, and "constitutionalized" (Novak 2002: 264). For Palestinians to continue to adapt laws willy-nilly from Western codes as they have so far done would be counterintuitive. By the same token, making the Shariah a basis of the new constitution to placate the Islamists in Palestine and their supporters would be disastrous.[18] Continuing to allow the death penalty to serve as a cover for political violence will abort the hope of the Palestinian people. Perhaps at last the time has come that culture of death ruling Palestinian society will be defeated, replaced by a vigorous, civil culture of life.

Notes

1. See Wilkenson (2002). Shahfe received death threats and was banned from Gaza after he obtained, "from a masked, secret source, a tape of the execution of an accused collaborator. Palestinian officials did not want to show such brutal, summary justice. Its appearance on Israeli TV, and then on networks everywhere, infuriated the Palestinian Authority and, reportedly, Arafat himself." The phrase "Culture of Death" comes from Pope John Paul II (Ioannes Paulus PP 1995).

2. Schwartz (2002), Gold (2003), and Kepel (2002) are the three best sources on this topic.

3. See Postawko (2002) for an excellent and detailed survey on the sources and jurisprudence of Islamic law and the unfortunate interpretations of that law by Islamists.

4. See Palestinian Human Rights Monitoring Group (2001) and Al-Haq and Mandela Institute (1998). All such sources are also available in Arabic.

5. More than twenty extrajudicial executions occurred in 2001. In that year twelve people were sentenced to death after "unfair and summary trials" in the High State Se-

curity or Military Courts. Three were executed, one by firing squad on January 13, 2001, on charges of collaboration with Israeli security forces. Three others died in custody following torture or attempted escape. See Amnesty International (2002).

6. The Israeli tactic of targeted assassinations against militia leaders and operatives falls into a more nebulous area of the rules of military engagement. See also Hammer (2003).

7. Human Rights Watch, "The Death Penalty and Street Injustice," in Human Rights Watch (2001).

8. Ibid.

9. A full discussion of the complex development of Palestinian Nationalism is impossible in such a limited paper. Hourani (1983) and Khalidi (1997) are foundational for understanding the topic. The political trajectory of the Palestine-Israel conflict is still profoundly disputed, and the academic discourse on the topic reflects this. The role of Amin al-Hussayni has not yet been satisfactorily treated in Palestinian historiography, yet it is clear that militias and guerilla movements throughout the Third World modeled their organization on the idea of cells refined in the Europe of the 1930s. See Mattar (1988).

10. The Islamic legal culture in Palestine and the Arab world developed in ten phases: the Caliphal, Ummayad, Abbasid/Hamdamid, Fatimid, Ayyubid, Mamluk, Ottoman (to 1831), Muhammad 'Ali's brief but critical occupation of Palestine from 1831–1839, the Ottoman Restoration, and Reform Period (the Tanzimat 1839–1924).

11. Space does not allow to trace Ayatollah Khomeini's reinterpretation of Shi'ite views of the role and nature of government; suffice it to say that the Iranian Revolution had a profound impact on Sunni Muslims.

12. The work of the Muslim legal scholar Khaled Abou El-Fadl is transforming this situation.

13. Mawil Y. Izzi Dien, "Ta'zir," in *Encyclopaedia of Islam* (2001).

14. Halil Inalcik, "Eyalet," in *Encyclopaedia of Islam* (2001). See also the following articles there: Y. Linant de Bellefonds, Claude Cahen, Halil Inalcik, "Kanun," and C. E. Bosworth, I. R. Netton, F. E. Vogel, "Siyasa," W. Heffening, "Murtadd."

15. Inalcik, "Eyalet," and Kunt (1983: 21).

16. I ought to add here that the revival of an authentic "Arabo-Islamic spirit" is what animated the Wahhabis of Arabia, and which led the British to support them against the Ottomans, whom the British and the Wahhabis saw as inauthentic and corrupt.

17. This reorganization of Ottoman political structures abolished the old system of *millet*, which identified people according to their religious affiliation and which granted superiority to Islam.

18. The Palestinians ought to regard the Iraqi Civil Code of 1953, a code that balanced European and Islamic laws to create "one of the most innovative and meticulously systematic codes of the Middle East" (El-Fadl 2003). See also Brown (2003).

References

Al-Haq and Mandela Institute (1998) "Capital Punishment . . . Cruel Punishment." Press Release 1 September 1998, http://alhaq.org/releases/pr_980901.html (accessed 27 October 2002).

Amnesty International (2002) *Palestinian Authority: 2001.* Amnesty International Report, http://web.amnesty.org/web/ar2002.nsf/mde/palestinian+authority!Open (accessed 23 October 2002).

Arkoun, Mohammad (1998) "The Death Penalty and Torture in Islamic Thought," in G. H. Stassen, ed., *Capital Punishment: A Reader.* Cleveland, OH: Pilgrim Press.

Ayalon, David (1973) "The Great Yasa of Chingiz Khan: A Reexamination," 38 *Studia Islamica* 97–140.

Black, Anthony (2001) *The History of Islamic Political Thought.* New York: Routledge.

Brown, Nathan J. (2003) "The Third Draft Constitution for a Palestinian State: Translation and Commentary," Palestinian Center for Policy and Survey Research, http://www.pcpsr.org/domestic/2003/nbrowne.pdf.

El-Fadl, Khaled Abou (2003) "Rebuilding the Law," *Wall Street Journal* 21 April: A21.

Encyclopaedia of Islam (2001) CD-ROM edition, Th. Bianquis, C. E. Bosworth, E. van Donzel and W. P. Heinrichs, eds. Leiden: Brill.

Gold, Dore (2003) *Hatred's Kingdom.* Washington, DC: Regnery Publishing.

Hammer, Joshua (2003) *A Season in Bethlehem: Unholy War in a Sacred Place.* New York: Free Press.

Hanania, Ray (1997) "The Issue of Palestinian Land Sales to Jews," http://www.al-bushra.org/temp/hanania.htm (accessed 27 October 2002).

Hourani, Albert (1983) *Arabic Thought in the Liberal Age: 1789–1939.* Cambridge: Cambridge University Press.

Human Rights Watch (2001) "Justice Undermined: Balancing Security and Human Rights in the Palestinian Justice System," http://www.hrw.org/reports/2001/pa/index.htm (accessed 23 October 2002).

Ioannes Paulus PP. II (Pope John Paul II) (1995) "EvangeliumVitae" (On the Value and Inviolability of Human Life), http://www.vatican.va/holy_father/john_paul_ii/encyclicals/documents/hf_jp-ii_enc_25031995_evangelium-vitae_en.html (accessed 5 June 2004).

Israeli, Raphael (2003) "State and Religion in the Emerging Palestinian Entity," 44 (Spring) *Journal of Church and State* 229–49.

Judt, Tony (1998) "Albert Camus: The Reluctant Moralist," in *The Burden of Responsibility.* Chicago: University of Chicago Press.

Kepel, Gilles (2002) *Jihad: The Trail of Political Islam.* Cambridge: Belknap Press.

Khalidi, Rashid (1997) *Palestinian Identity: The Construction of Modern National Consciousness.* New York: Columbia University Press.

Kunt, Metin (1983) *The Sultan's Servants*. New York: Columbia University Press.

Lewis, Bernard (1984) "Siyasa," in Arnold H. Green, ed., *Quest for an Islamic Humanism: Arabic and Islamic Studies in Memory of Mohamed Al-Nowaihi*. Cairo: American University in Cairo Press.

Mahdi, Muhsin (1971) *Ibn Khaldun's Philosophy of History*. Chicago: University of Chicago Press.

Mattar, Philip (1988) *The Mufti of Jerusalem*. New York: Columbia University Press.

Megally, Hanny (2001) "Letter to Palestinian Authority President Yasser Arafat," Human Rights Watch Press Release 2 August 2001, http://www.hrw.org/press/2001/08/arafat-0802-ltr.htm (accessed 23 October 2002).

Novak, William J. (2002) "The Legal Origins of the Modern American State," in A. Sarat, Bryant Garth, and Robert A. Kagan, eds., *Looking Back at Law's Century*. Ithaca, NY: Cornell University Press.

Palestinian Center for Policy and Survey Research (2001) "Palestinian Constitution," http://www.pcpsr.org/domestic/2001/conste1.html (accessed 30 May 2003).

Palestinian Human Rights Monitoring Group (1997) "Death Penalties in Palestine: 1995–1997," http://www.phrmg.org/monitor1997/apr97–6.htm (accessed 30 October 2002).

Palestinian Human Rights Monitoring Group (1999) "Publication and Reports: Capital Punishment," *Palestinian Human Rights Monitor*, http://www.phrmg.org/monitor1999/jan99-capital.htm (accessed 27 October 2002).

Palestinian Human Rights Monitoring Group (2001) "Capital Punishment," http://www.phrmg.org/monitor1999/jan99-capital.htm (accessed 27 October 2002).

Postawko, Robert (2002) "Towards an Islamic Critique of Capital Punishment," 1 (Spring–Summer) *UCLA Journal of Islamic and Near Eastern Law* 269.

Rood, Judith Mendelsohn (2004) *Sacred Law in the Holy City*. Leiden: Brill.

Schemann, Serge (2002) "For Arab Informers, Death; For the Executioners, Justice," *New York Times* 2 September.

Schwartz, Stephen (2002) *The Two Faces of Islam: The House of Sa'ud from Tradition to Terror*. New York: Doubleday.

Wilkenson, Tracy (2002) "Reports from a Tightrope," *Los Angeles Times* 14 November: A1, A5.

PART III

Paternal States, "Asian Values," and Visions of Social Order

Capital Punishment in East and Southeast Asia

CHAPTER TWELVE

The Death Penalty in Japan

Secrecy, Silence, and Salience

DAVID T. JOHNSON

[Capital punishment may be] the most contentious social issue in America today.

> Donald A. Cabana, former Mississippi prison warden, in Bohm (2003)

Capital punishment is simply not a social issue in Japan.

> Former Japanese Minister of Justice Hideo Usui, in Struck (2001)

The Japanese state kills at a rate that is seven times lower than the United States and thirty-four to thirty-eight times lower than high-rate American states such as Texas, Oklahoma, and Virginia (Hood 2002: 92). Still, Japan is the only fully developed nation besides the United States that regularly uses capital punishment (Zimring 2003: 38). Since its surrender in 1945, the country has executed at least one person every year except 1964 (when the summer Olympics were held in Tokyo), 1968 (the year of the next summer games), and a forty-month period from 1989 to 1993 when four consecutive Ministers of Justice refused to sign execution warrants (see Tables 12.1 and 12.2). Although the Japanese government remains "firmly committed" to capital punishment (Hood 2002: 49), its scale resembles death penalty practice in other low-use democracies, such as India and South Korea, more than it does capital punishment in the United States.[1]

While Japan and the United States are the only two rich democracies in the world that remain committed to capital punishment, the Japanese state kills in a markedly different manner than the many American states that engage in executions. This chapter explores that difference and some of the other things that are distinctive and problematic about the death penalty in Japan. The first section shows how the secrecy and silence that shroud capital punishment both

TABLE 12.1

Death Sentences and Executions in Postwar Japan, 1945–2002

Year	Death sentences	Executions	Year	Death sentences	Executions
1945	17	8	1974	2	4
1946	15	11	1975	3	17
1947	39	12	1976	1	12
1948	49	33	1977	3	4
1949	79	33	1978	4	3
1950	25	31	1979	4	1
1951	32	24	1980	7	1
1952	41	18	1981	3	1
1953	25	24	1982	1	1
1954	21	30	1983	1	1
1955	14	32	1984	3	1
1956	24	11	1985	2	3
1957	27	39	1986	0	2
1958	21	7	1987	8	2
1959	12	30	1988	11	2
1960	33	39	1989	5	1
1961	24	6	1990	6	0
1962	13	26	1991	5	0
1963	17	12	1992	5	0
1964	9	0	1993	7	7
1965	7	4	1994	3	2
1966	13	4	1995	3	6
1967	14	23	1996	4	6
1968	11	0	1997	3	4
1969	10	18	1998	7	6
1970	14	26	1999	4	5
1971	7	17	2000	6	3
1972	7	7	2001	4	2
1973	5	3	2002	3	2

NOTE: "Death sentence" means "newly finalized capital sentence" (*shinkakuteishu*), that is, a death sentence that has been confirmed by the Supreme Court.

SOURCE: Shikei Haishi Henshu Iinkai (2003).

TABLE 12.2

Average Number of Executions in Japan, 1868–2002

Years	Executions per year
1868–1907	200.0 (Meiji era under old Penal Code; max = 1,246 in 1871)
1908–1945	39.0 (prewar & war under new Penal Code; max = 94 in 1915)
1945–1952	21.3 (American Occupation; max = 33 in 1948 and 1949)
1950–1959	24.6 (max = 39 in 1957)
1960–1969	13.2 (max = 39 in 1960)
1970–1979	9.4 (max = 26 in 1970)
1980–1989	1.5 (max = 3 in 1985)
1990–2002	3.3 (max = 7 in 1993)

SOURCES: Murano (1992); Shikei Haishi Henshu Iinkai (2003).

reflect and explain its low salience. Section two argues that while the law of capital punishment "fails" in both the United States and Japan, the failures are of markedly different kinds. In America, death penalty law fails to fulfill most of its many promises. In Japan, by contrast, the law fails to make many promises at all. The conclusion looks forward in order to discern the likely trajectory of capital punishment in twenty-first-century Japan. Although that future is foggy, when Japan abolishes it probably will do so as a "follower" of either the United States or South Korea.

Secrecy, Silence, and Salience

[In Japan,] prisoners are told of their execution only moments before their hanging, and are given only enough time to clean their cells, write a final letter and receive last rites. Relatives are told of the execution only after the fact and are given a mere 24 hours to collect the body. . . . Justice Ministry officials, for their part, insist that their system of secret executions is the most humane form of capital punishment.

New York Times (June 24, 2002)

Between 8:00 and 8:30 in the morning was the most critical time, because that was generally when prisoners were notified of their execution. . . . You begin to feel the most terrible anxiety, because you don't know if they are going to stop in front of your cell. It is impossible to express how awful a feeling this was. I would have shivers down my spine. It was absolutely unbearable.

Menda Sakae, who was exonerated and released in 1983 after spending thirty-four years on death row

The death penalty is more than a mechanism for punishing criminals and controlling crime, for it also expresses and exposes important values and assumptions (Garland 1990). In Japan, too, capital punishment reveals much that is significant, but decoding the messages can be difficult because the practice speaks in a highly taciturn way.

Unlike the United States, where capital punishment is a hotly contested issue (Zimring 2003: 119), the death penalty in Japan is characterized by low levels of public interest, debate, and conflict. This low salience is neither natural nor inevitable. It is in large part the result of the state's deliberate policy to keep the public uninformed about how, when, and why it kills. One consequence of this policy is that "the average Japanese knows nothing about capital punishment, and is not really interested in this subject" (Schmidt 2002: 195). In turn, public apathy serves the state's interest in avoiding scrutiny and opposition.

The secrecy that surrounds capital punishment can be seen at two different stages. First, after a death sentence has been finalized by an appellate court, the condemned offender is socially extinguished through the state's imposition of severe restrictions on meetings and correspondence. These constraints are so broad that if one is not the condemned's close relative or defense lawyer, contact with the inmate is all but impossible. What is more, even if one fits in one of the two permitted categories, strict limitations are placed on the frequency, duration, and content of contacts. The state's stated reason for this policy is to "promote stable feelings" in the inmate so as to help the condemned "prepare" for death. However, if humans are inherently "social animals," and if the Japanese are especially likely to have identities that are defined by their location in social networks (Hamilton and Sanders 1992; Nisbett 2003), then the effect of the state's post-conviction policy is to kill socially before killing physically.

Conditions on death row are harsh, especially for the condemned who have had their sentences finalized. In addition to being detained in almost total isolation, death row inmates are not permitted to stand up, lie down, or move without permission; they must sit in an approved posture; they are not allowed to receive letters from anyone except family members; they are given only five to ten minutes to eat each meal; they may exercise outside of their cells (by themselves) just two or three times a week for fifteen minutes per session; they may not choose which newspaper to read, and foreign books and all calendars are prohibited; their cells are constantly lit; and so on (Kikuta 1999: 298; Asian Political News 2003). Death row cells vary in design and size, but most measure around forty-six square feet, which is about 15 percent smaller than a typical cell on Florida's decrepit death row (Dowling 1994; von Drehle 1995).

The second stage of secrecy surrounds the moment of execution. No private citizens are permitted to attend executions, and the condemned learns of the time of hanging only an hour or two before he[2] is killed. The Ministry of Justice makes no public announcements until after the hanging. The condemned, therefore, has no chance to contact family or an attorney, and members of the public who might protest an imminent execution have insufficient information to do so.

After the condemned has been killed, the state typically sends news agencies a notification by fax. A typical announcement reads as follows: "Today in Tokyo, two death-row convicts were executed." That is all. The names of the deceased are not revealed (though journalists can learn who they were through backstage conversations), and the faxed notice may not even indicate who is making the announcement. Until 1999, the government did not make any post-execution announcements at all (Sato 2001). Journalists learned about hangings only when the condemned's attorney or family told them that a client or loved one had been killed. In some cases death was discovered only after mail addressed to the deceased was returned to the sender unopened.

Japan's Ministry of Justice argues that stage-two secrecy is also in the inmate's interest. As one prosecutor put it, "We have to consider the feelings of the criminal who gets the death penalty. It's such a disgrace against his honor. I don't think he surrenders his honor or his privacy just because he surrenders his life" (Struck 2001). Another prosecutor claims that "it would be more cruel if we notified the inmates of their execution beforehand because it would inflict a major pain on them. They would lose themselves to despair. They might even try to commit suicide or escape" (French 2002). Prosecutors also contend that secrecy protects the reputations of the condemned's relatives because, in Japanese society where the role of shame is powerful, "the taint of any serious crime can blight an entire household for generations" (French 2002). Relatives of the deceased are told about the execution after the fact. They are given twenty-four hours to collect the body, but most corpses go uncollected because the families have already dissociated themselves from the criminal. As a result, many of the bodies are buried in prison graveyards or are donated to hospitals for medical research (Connell 2002). In Japanese culture, where the living are expected to aid the spirits of the dead in making their transition to "the next world," the consequences of capital punishment can have eternal significance because the condemned are often "disposed of" without the requisite rituals for making the final journey.

Capital punishment in Japan was not always shrouded in so much secrecy. For two decades after World War II, death row inmates were notified a day or two in advance of the execution date and were given opportunities to arrange final meetings with family and friends, worship in a group with other inmates on death row, receive spiritual counseling, order last meals, and otherwise put their final affairs in order (Murano 1992: 10). Until 1975, the condemned were allowed to play softball together and to talk with inmates in adjacent cells (Connell 2002). In 1963, the Ministry of Justice's Corrections Bureau issued a circular (*tsutatsu*) declaring its authority to tighten restrictions on death row (Murano 1992: 74). This decision to strengthen restrictions may have been inspired by a desire to prevent suicides such as one that had recently been committed by a condemned inmate. The wardens and guards who conducted executions in that more open era also came to know the condemned as people. Their memoirs express ambivalence and regret about the roles they played in killing for the state (Murano 1992: 38). The historical record does not reveal whether secrecy and "social executions" were *intended* to protect death penalty operators from the emotional turmoil they felt when the process was more public, but the changes may have had that effect.[3] In the 1980s, the state's drive toward secrecy accelerated following the exoneration and release of four death row inmates (Foote 1992, 1993; Kikuta 1999).

There is no government power greater than the power of life and death and no government intrusion more invasive than the death penalty (von Drehle 1995: 178). There is, therefore, no government action in greater need of public oversight. If transparency and accountability are two hallmarks of democracy, then the secretive way in which the Japanese state kills seems decidedly undemocratic.

Of course, some advocates of secrecy contend that democratic values such as transparency and accountability are incompatible with the value of human dignity. Indeed, this is the position taken by the prosecutors who promulgate Japan's secrecy policy. One way to test their view is to ask the condemned whose dignity is ostensibly at issue. Some death row inmates have called the anxiety they feel—the "excruciating uncertainty" of not knowing whether the current day will be their last—"absolutely unbearable" (French 2002; Shimizu 2002b; Mugi no Kai 1990). On the other hand, at least one person exonerated from death row said he "would have gone mad" if he had known in advance when he would be hanged (Struck 2001). My own interviews of Japanese citizens suggest that if they were to end up on death row, most would want to know in advance the date they would die. That sentiment, however, is not universal.[4]

Western literature also suggests that knowing the day of one's death can be agonizing. In *The Idiot*, for example, Fyodor Dostoevsky (1998: 20), who himself was stood up to be executed by firing squad before being released, said that "The chief and worst pain may not be in the bodily suffering but in one's knowing for certain that in an hour, and then in ten minutes, and then in half a minute, and then now, at the very moment, the soul will leave the body and that one will cease to be a man and that's bound to happen." Similarly, in his tale of a boy adrift at sea in a lifeboat with a Bengal tiger, the Canadian novelist Yann Martel (2001: 147) said that

> Oncoming death is terrible enough, but worse still is oncoming death with time to spare, time in which all the happiness that was yours and all the happiness that might have been yours becomes clear to you. You see with utter lucidity all that you are losing. The sight brings on an oppressive sadness that no car about to hit you or water about to drown you can match. The feeling is truly unbearable.

This question—whether it is "more humane" to withhold information from death row inmates about the date of execution—admits no easy answer. What is clear is that the secretive way in which the Japanese state kills reflects and reinforces a contradiction, because even if killing secretly is "more humane" than a more publicized manner of execution, it is also less democratic.

The secrecy of capital punishment in Japan suggests an irony as well. For the last decade or so, governments in Japan have become substantially more transparent. In particular, bureaucracies have been required, by information disclosure statutes and by judicial interpretation, to expose more of their operations to the public eye (Marshall 2002). In the midst of this opening there is (in capital punishment) a countervailing movement toward increased information concealment in precisely the area of government where the state is at its most powerful. If information is "the currency of democracy," then when the state kills in Japan the public lacks a key to the treasury (Dando 2000).

Secrecy also means that capital punishment in Japan "speaks" more by invoking impressions and associations than by conveying information in a linear way. Without texts, events, and press conferences to interpret, Japanese observers invest special significance in the *timing* of executions and the *selection* of inmates for execution. Moreover, because the state kills so rarely, and because it neither explains nor justifies the executions it performs, *Why him?* and *Why now?* are questions that attract considerable attention in abolitionist circles.

The answers can be overdetermined. For instance, after Shinji Mukai was executed in Osaka on 12 September 2003, observers offered three overlapping answers to the *Why him?* and *Why now?* questions. First, because of the time difference between Japan and the United States, September 12 marked Japan's second-year anniversary of the 9/11 terrorist attacks. That morning, the nation's newspapers displayed large, color photographs of grieving victims at ground zero in New York City. Hours later, the evening editions carried news of Mukai's execution. By its temporal association with 9/11, this story told a twofold tale: that evil exists in the world, and that capital punishment is one way Japan deals with it.

The second answer conveys a similar message through a different temporal association. Two weeks before Mukai's execution, the Osaka District Court sentenced Mamoru Takuma, one of Japan's most notorious murderers, to death. The public thus had "murder on its mind" more than it usually does. In addition, Mukai's homicides resembled Takuma's in at least three respects: both occurred in Osaka, both involved death by stabbing, and both resulted in the deaths of young children (Sato 2001: 147). By holding Mukai's execution soon after Takuma's death sentence was imposed, the Ministry of Justice—the main agent of execution in Japan—appears to have engaged in a strategy of "justification by association."

Finally, Mukai was executed just eight days before an election was held to choose the president of Japan's ruling Liberal Democratic Party. It was understood that after the election was decided, a new cabinet—and a new Minister of Justice—would be installed by the Prime Minister. Since Japan's forty-month moratorium on capital punishment ended in 1993, prosecutors in the Ministry of Justice have taken pains to ensure that at least one execution occurs every year lest a de facto moratorium again gain momentum.[5] Prior to Mukai's hanging in September 2003, there had been no executions in that year. His hanging thus "kept the streak going" and avoided the "risk" of a zero-execution year. Hence, even if the new Minister of Justice turned out to be more reluctant to sign death warrants than his predecessor had been, moratorium momentum was forestalled for at least another year.

It seems, then, that the Japanese state chooses execution dates strategically. Sometimes (as in Mukai's hanging) the date seems selected to foster support for capital punishment through a strategy of "justification by association." This is also what happened in August 1997, when Norio Nagayama, a prolific author and Japan's most well-known death row inmate, was hanged less than two months after a Kobe juvenile was arrested for murdering an elementary school child and placing the victim's severed head on the school's front gate. The Kobe killer was fourteen years old. Nagayama, who spent twenty-nine years on death row, committed four homicides in 1968 when he was a nineteen-year-old minor. Many commentators contend that prosecutors chose Nagayama for execution at this time in order to foster support for legislation that would "get tougher" on juvenile offenders (Sato 2001: 13). Indeed, in 2000 Japan's Juvenile Law was revised to make it easier to transfer minors to adult court. In other cases, execution dates have been set for times when citizens are distracted or critics have difficulty voicing dissent. For example, executions often occur while Parliament is in recess, and the executions prior to Mukai's hanging occurred while the mass media were absorbed with Prime Minister Junichiro Koizumi's historic visit to North Korea (Amnesty International 1997).

States that practice capital punishment have a legitimacy problem: they need to distinguish how their killing differs from the criminal killing they aim to condemn. In the United States, one major legitimation strategy has been the effort to kill ever more "softly" and "humanely" (Sarat 2001: 60). This strategy, to give the condemned a "kinder and gentler" death, helps explain many of the transformations in execution method that America has experienced in the twentieth century—from hanging to electrocution to the gas chamber to lethal injection (Banner 2002; Gillespie 2003; Essig 2003). The quest by states to kill without imposing more pain than is "necessary" is not so much about sparing the condemned from suffering, it is about convincing the administrators and spectators of death that capital punishment is "civilized."

While the Japanese state faces a similar legitimacy challenge, it answers the call in a markedly different manner. In fact, Japan has experienced no significant changes in execution method since 1873, when a new type of gallows was introduced after an old-fashioned hanging had been botched (Murano 1992: 44). Hanging remains the only permitted method in each of Japan's seven execution centers, and there has been almost no discussion of other methods of execution such as lethal injection.[6] The absence of debate is not because the Japanese way of hanging is humane. There, as elsewhere, the point of a hanging is to crush or lacerate the spinal cord and to tear it from the brain stem. If the initial shock of the drop is not fatal, death is completed by strangulation (Gillespie 2003: 55). Hangings are botched in Japan as they are everywhere else.[7] When mistakes have occurred, some executioners apparently used strangleholds to "finish the job" by choking the condemned to death (Otsuka 1988: 135; Schmetzer 2000).

Thus, the secrecy that surrounds capital punishment helps explain the absence of controversy about the method of execution. In effect, "killing secretly" instead of "killing softly" is the Japanese state's main legitimation strategy. In the United States, lethal injection is now the sole or principal method of state killing in all but one executing jurisdiction (Bohm 2003: 95), and in the 1990s fully 83 percent of all American executions were conducted in this way (Zimring 2003: 51).[8] If one purpose of lethal injection is to show that "state killing is different from murder because it is done humanely," the message conveyed by the Japanese state is that "state killing is state business." A corollary truth is that capital punishment in Japan has not been "degovernmentalized" or "symbolically transformed" into a "victim-service program" as thoroughly as it has in the United States (Zimring 2003: 42). The strenuous effort to "degovernmentalize" the American death penalty—to present capital punishment as a means of obtaining "closure" for victims—has been called a "signal that many citizens feel *uncomfortable* watching governments kill to achieve solely governmental purposes" (Zimring 2003: 63). In Japan, by contrast, the state keeps citizens "comfortable" not so much by satisfying victims as by keeping them—and everyone else—in the dark.[9]

As described above, several justifications have been given for the secrecy and silence that shroud Japan's death penalty. None is convincing. If isolation helps the condemned to "accept the inevitable" and "prepare for death," it does so by killing twice: first socially and then physically. If secrecy is designed to protect the "honor and privacy" of the offender's family, it does so by sacrificing democratic values—transparency, accountability, and openness—at precisely those times when they ought to be most operative. And if silence helps maintain "stability" on death row, it does so through a mechanism of terror that profoundly destabilizes the psyches of many condemned persons. "Am I next?" and "Is today the day?" are questions that naturally preoccupy the people on Japan's death row. The uncertainty which surrounds them is meant to make them easier to govern, for those inmates know that misbehavior may hasten their appointment with the hangman (Watts 2001).

The generation of secrecy is not only a modern event, it is one without contemporary justification. Because it demands the total submission of the individual to the requirements of the state, Japan's policy of secrecy is nothing so much as totalitarian. Arguing that secrecy is a favor to the condemned is mostly a ruse rooted in self-interest, and to the extent that there may be a dilemma of notice for the prisoner, there is none for his family. Indeed, there is little evidence of concern for the offender's family in Japan's death penalty history (Sato 1994).

Power is inclined to blur the dividing line between rationality and rationalization (Flybjerg 1998: 227). When it comes to capital punishment in Japan, that line should be kept clear. The Japanese state's policy of secrecy and silence prevents capital punishment from becoming a salient issue (Schmidt 2002). It minimizes public interest and protest by blinding citizens to the barbarities of the institution (Murano 1995). It reinforces complacency about public policy that many Japanese consider perverse (*Daily Yomiuri* 2003b). It subordinates the interests of civil society to the needs of the state (Schwartz and Pharr 2003). It prevents judicial oversight of acts that involve the maximum use of state power (Kikuta 1999). It terrorizes inmates on death row (Kikuchi 2003). It undermines deterrence (Kamei 2002). In the end, the secrecy that shrouds capital punishment amounts to a "rule of silent violence" that causes more harm than good (Ishizuka 1997). From every perspective except the one taken by the prosecutors who have designed and promulgated this policy in order to save state face, it is an "absurd" and "senseless" strategy (Hermann 2002).

Two Ways Law Can Fail

> [Is] the [American] system delivering on its promise? . . . The purpose of capital sentencing is to select the few who must die from the many who will not. . . . Twenty men have been sentenced to die under Florida's modern death penalty laws for every one who has been executed. Nothing but chance has separated those who live from those who die.
>
> David Von Drehle, *Among the Lowest of the Dead*

> The Japanese Penal Code . . . does not offer any criteria to guide the judge in deciding what punishment to impose. . . . The principal question is whether relying on unwritten rules and standards rather than on legal provisions is in conformity with modern constitutional law and constitutional theory.
>
> Joachim Herrmann, "The Death Penalty in Japan: An 'Absurd' Punishment"

One way in which law can fail is by proving itself unable to keep its commitments. In states that kill, the primary purpose of the death penalty process is to select the few offenders who ought to die from the many who should not. American law promises that such choices will be made in a manner that is rational, consistent, and fair. Among other pledges is this: like cases will be treated alike and different cases differently.[10] It is an empty promise. When American states kill, the only constants have been inconsistency, confusion, contradiction, and chaos (von Drehle 1995: 402; Zimring 2003: 71). Indeed, the imposition of the death penalty in America is like being struck by lightning: it is unpredictable and arbitrary in its selective fury. As Supreme Justice Harry Blackmun wrote in 1994, because capital punishment cannot be administered in a manner that is consistent with constitutional promises, it is time to admit that the American "death penalty experiment has failed" (as cited in Bohm 2003: 55).

Death penalty law fails in Japan too, but in a markedly different manner. There, law cannot fail to live up to its promises because it hardly makes any in the first place. Capital punishment in Japan thus lacks the pretense that afflicts its American counterpart, but the corollary truth is that law in Japan is characterized by conspicuously low aspirations. Indeed, if the Japanese state had a motto it might be "Aim low, say nothing, and no one will be disappointed."

The failure of aspiration in Japanese law afflicts three stages of the death penalty process. First, the law provides little direction for the prosecutors who have to decide which cases to charge capital. As a statutory matter, there are no aggravating or mitigating circumstances for them to take into account, and beyond that there is only a meager body of judicial opinion to help shape their choices. Second, legislation give judges no guidance about whether and when to choose death. The penal code simply says that in homicide cases judges may impose anything from three years imprisonment to death by hanging, and within those parameters judges exercise their discretion as they see fit. Here, too, judicial precedent does little to fill the legislative void, for capital sentencing has not been "constitutionalized" as it has in the United States. Third, law in Japan does not attempt to regulate decisions about which condemned inmates to select for hanging. Formally, the Minister of Justice must sign a death warrant before an execution can occur, but in practice such warrants are prepared backstage by prosecutors—the Minister's subordinates—before being presented for approval to their titular head. The process by which this occurs remains impervious to judicial supervision, and the "check" exercised by the Minister is superficial in the extreme.

Some Japanese defense lawyers (including critics of capital punishment) admit that the death penalty is "lawless" while insisting that it is administered in a predictable way. One attorney claims he can predict the outcome of murder trials in the following way:

1. If you kill only one person, the prosecutor will never ask for the death penalty and a judge will not sentence you to death, unless you have a previous conviction for murder.

2. If you kill three persons or more, the prosecutor will definitely seek the death penalty and the judge will certainly impose it.

3. If you kill two persons and this is your first murder charge, it is difficult but not impossible to get life imprisonment instead of death.

The death penalty in Japan is not that predictable. For one thing, since executions resumed in 1993, forty-three people have been hanged. Of those, thirteen (30 percent) killed "only" one person (Sakamoto 2003: 240). In 2002, the most recent year for which data are available, prosecutors sought the death penalty in twenty-nine cases, of which death sentences were imposed in twenty. Courts imposed death in nine out of nine cases involving three or more victims, nine out fourteen cases involving two victims, and two out of six cases involving a single victim—and only one of the two had no prior conviction for murder (Shikei Haishi Henshu Iinkai 2003: 292). In the same year, two men were selected for execution from the fifty-six people on death row whose sentences had been finalized and who were, therefore, "eligible" for hanging. In previous years the Ministry of Justice usually chose for hanging those condemned inmates who had been on death row for the longest time. In 2002, however, the Ministry embarked on a new strategy of "terror through uncertainty" by choosing inmates who ranked, respectively, thirty-sixth and thirty-seventh in death row longevity (Sakamoto 2003: 249). Though this strategy has the effect of imposing "great stress and suffering" upon the people who remain on death row, the conscious pursuit of unpredictability seems designed to make it more difficult for abolitionists and support groups to buy time for death row "veterans" by filing petitions for retrial (Yasuda 2003: 259).

However predictable Japan's death penalty is, its lawlessness is a problem in several senses. First, claims to be governed by "the rule of law" ring hollow because that aspiration implies "government by law" and "government under law," and because capital punishment in Japan fails to fulfill both requisites. At the same time, the informal standards used by judicial and prosecutorial bureaucrats to regulate death-related decisions fail two other critical tests: the *nulla poena* principle that there should be no punishment without prior legislation, and the democratic principle that citizens and their elected representatives (not unelected bureaucrats) should decide matters of major importance (Hermann 2002: 832). The elusiveness of informal standards also makes it difficult for defendants, defense lawyers, and the condemned to know on what legal grounds to argue the merits of their cases. As one defense lawyer sees it, "You don't really know where to aim because there is no target." Missing targets help explain why one common capital defense strategy is to assist state officials in extracting remorse from their clients—the accused and the condemned—in order to elicit mercy and leniency from the sentencing and appellate judges.[11] Hence, without a clear legal framework to help focus the defense, attorneys employ in capital cases the same strategy they routinely use in more mundane trials. That "priestly" role sometimes inhibits effective advocacy (Otani 1999).

It has been said that in Japanese criminal justice consistency is "routinely aspired to and often achieved" (Johnson 2002: 160). Capital punishment remains one realm where law in Japan neither aspires to nor achieves consistency or, for that matter, many of the other values that American death penalty law promises in abundance. This is not because those values are unimportant in Japan. Indeed, consistency, legality, individualization, rationality, and fairness are as much a part of Japanese sensibilities as they are of American ones. Rather, the silence of Japanese law is part of a larger strategy of silence that is consciously pursued by some actors in the system and is tolerated by most of the rest. When law remains mute, prosecutors and judges cannot be found to have broken any promises, and here lies another reason why there is little push for reform. In the classroom, students often learn that if they say nothing they cannot be proven wrong. In capital punishment, the speechlessness of Japanese law reflects an analogous fear of failure. Silence is safe.

The Future

> If we save one person on death row, the fire will just jump to another condemned inmate. This does not mean that we should not save the first person. It does mean, however, that at the same time that we save him, if we do not do something else in addition to what we are doing now, we will be unable to stop the administration of death.
>
> Yoshihiro Yasuda, lawyer and leader of Forum 90, Japan's largest abolitionist organization

It has been said that those who love the law must hate capital punishment (Sarat 2001). The Japanese case illustrates another way this rings true. The death penalty in Japan is administered at least as arbitrarily and capriciously as it is in America, but the secrecy and lawlessness that pervade Japanese practice mean there is little public or juridical anxiety over the failures. When the trap door of the gallows falls and there is nobody there to hear it, it does not make a sound.

Since there is no government power greater than the power of life and death, the silence that shrouds capital punishment speaks volumes about the quality of Japan's polity. In this democracy, bureaucratic authorities often make decisions "affecting the lives of large numbers of people after little or no public debate" (French 1999; Van Wolferen 1989; Upham 1987). That message is no cause for celebration.

In many of the world's killing states it is customary to put a hood over the head of the condemned before he is executed. Since "the soul of the person, the spirit, is in the eyes," hiding the face enables observers to "watch without seeing" what really happens when the state kills (von Drehle 1995: 399). Japan does hood the condemned, but it also casts a much larger hood over the entire death penalty process, from the time a suspect is arrested, detained, and interrogated *incommunicado* (which is standard practice in potentially capital cases), to the morning of the execution when the condemned learns his life will be over in an hour. The process ends when prosecutors make a perfunctory post-hanging pronouncement that some anonymous someone was killed in Tokyo or Osaka. The Ministry of Justice contends that killing silently "is the best we can do at present" (Shimizu 2002a). In most cases, the press duly registers the execution event—more as an official gazette than a critical watchdog—the public quietly acquiesces, and the state continues business as usual.

Silence, secrecy, passivity, and public opinion: these facts may suggest that the death penalty will not disappear from Japan anytime soon. Furthermore, research suggests that "the strength of death penalty support and opposition appears to be both a psychological barometer of the level of dread and angst in a society and a symbolic marker of the social landscape" (Bohm 2003: 270). If this conclusion also characterizes Japan, a country in which fear and insecurity are at postwar highs, then abolition seems all the more unlikely. The Japanese state has taken a beating in recent years, for corruption, for failing to deliver economic growth, and for failing to enact necessary reforms. In these circumstances, the death penalty remains one way that the state can prove it is neither weak nor ineffective (Simon 2002).

On the other hand, some observers believe that capital punishment in Japan is "a matter only of government policy," not of deeply held cultural traditions as in the southern United States (Zimring 2003: 136). On this view, since the death penalty in Japan receives little *intense* support, and since the normative consensus in Europe is fast becoming the world's moral orthodoxy, there is reason to believe that "Japan will stop its hanging very soon indeed" (Zimring 2001: 217).

Time will tell, though I am not sanguine about the prospects for speedy abolition. In the long run, however, Japan will probably have to abolish capital punishment[12] even if it is difficult to predict when the next step toward "civilization and enlightenment" will occur. One harbinger of change will be seen when the Japanese state is forced (and it will be) to open the death penalty process to more public scrutiny. Over time, the interaction of international and domestic pressures seems bound to break down some of the walls of silence, for capital punishment is too important a practice to evince so little transparency. Pressure from Europe, creative use of the new freedom of information laws, and the maturation of Japan's civil society will eventually converge on this issue. Once that happens, increased openness will be only a matter of time (Shikei Haishi Henshu Iinkai 1999).

A more vital sign of change will be visible if South Korea, which has not executed anyone for more than seven years, abolishes the death penalty. Some Japanese abolitionists believe that executives in the Liberal Democratic Party will not stand idly by if the neighbor that Japan once colonized abolishes first; that would be too much of a blow to their self-image as leaders of the premier regime in Asia. For this reason, many abolitionists in Japan pay attention to events in South Korea, remaining ever ready to use developments in their neighbor's case to advance the Japanese cause (Cha 2003).

Although South Korea is one country Japan could emulate, if the United States abolishes first the effect would be even more powerful. Predictions differ about the future of American state killing. Some commentators contend that the United States "is still a long way from bringing an end to capital punishment" (Sarat 2001: 259), while others claim that "the end game in the effort to purge the United States of the death penalty has already been launched" (Zimring 2003: 205). My own view is that South Korea is likely to abolish before America does, and I therefore think the Korean case could be especially crucial for Japan. In any event, when Japan abolishes capital punishment it will probably do so as "a follower."

As for the domestic agent of abolition, capital punishment could cease in three different ways—though they are not equally probable routes to abolition. *Judicial abolition* is most improbable because Japan's Supreme Court is unlikely to rule that capital punishment (or any other policy) is unconstitutional (Schmidt 2002: 90). Similarly, *administrative abolition* of the kind seen from 1989 to 1993 seems doubtful because the willingness to sign death warrants appears to have become a qualification for becoming Minister of Justice, and because prosecutors have grown adept at making allies with other actors and institutions that want to retain the present system (Fukuda 2002).

Thus, if abolition comes to Japan the most likely proximate cause will be an *act of Parliament*, where there is more support for abolition than in society at large (Kikuta 1999: 41). In 1990, a coalition of anti–death-penalty groups (including Amnesty International's Japan chapter) coalesced to create "Forum 90," Japan's largest abolitionist organization (Kikuchi 2003). With a membership of about 5,000, Forum 90 holds a national congress on capital punishment each year in addition to publishing a regular newsletter and sponsoring a variety of meetings, lectures, and seminars. In 1994, Forum 90 helped stimulate the creation of the Diet Members League for the Abolition of Capital Punishment (*shikei haishi o sokushin suru giin renmeikai*). As of May 2003, 122 of the 762 members of parliament (16 percent) had joined the DMLACP, and its chairman, Shizuka Kamei (a former police officer and a faction chief in the conservative ruling party) predicted that membership would increase in the years to come (Kamei 2002; see also Shimizu 2002c).[13] The abolitionist movement receives support from the West, where the European Union and the Council of Europe have passed resolutions condemning the practice of capital punishment in Japan and calling for a moratorium that would lead to abolition. In May 2002, the Council of Europe helped sponsor an abolition seminar in Tokyo, during which the chair of the relevant COE Committee visited the Tokyo Detention Center, where the largest number of executions occurs, and met with the Minister of Justice and with two former inmates who had been acquitted in retrials after spending decades on death row. In another resolution, the Council of Europe has threatened to remove Japan's "observer status" in its Parliamentary Assembly if the country does not make significant "progress" toward abolition. Through efforts such as these, activists in Europe are attempting to export abolition, and their main strategy is to frame capital punishment as a "violation of human rights that must be prohibited by civilized governments" (Zimring 2003: 40).

For the time being, the future of capital punishment in Japan seems as uncertain as the futures of the men and women on death row. I would like to believe that in the long run Japan's death penalty will become as obsolete as samurai-style self-execution (*hara-kiri*) is today. I do have to acknowledge, however, that in the long run we all will be dead.

Notes

1. Execution rates usually are expressed as the total number of executions per year per million population. For the five years from 1996 through 2000, Japan's rate was 0.04, while the rates for the United States and Virginia (the highest rate American state) were, respectively, 0.27 and 1.51 (Hood 2002: 92). When the propensity to use capital punishment is calculated in a different way, by comparing the number of death sentences as a percentage of the number of potentially capital cases, the United States and Japan look much more similar because (as of 2004) the homicide rate in Japan is about fourteen times lower than in America.

2. In Japan as in the United States, the vast majority of death sentences are imposed on men. As of October 2003, fifty-six people had received "finalized" death sentences, of which three were women. The last woman to be executed was Nobuko Hidaka, on 1 August 1997. She was hanged from the Sapporo gallows with her husband after being convicted of arson-homicide. Since executions resumed in 1993, the average age of the forty-three men and women who have been hanged is fifty-six; the youngest was thirty-six and the oldest seventy (Shikei Haishi Henshu Iinkai 2003: 366).

3. For example, Hideo Itazu (1991), a prison guard in Nagoya from 1948 to 1963, has written that working on death row was "really tough" because interacting with the condemned awakened uncomfortable "human feelings." When Itazu was a prison official, the Ministry of Justice held debates about capital punishment and published abolitionist articles in its own house journal. Times have changed.

4. Although the custom is changing, the impulse to withhold bad news can also be seen in medicine, where some Japanese doctors, patients, and families believe it is not a good idea to tell ill or dying persons too much about their condition (Soeda 2001).

5. Japan's forty-month moratorium (November 1989 to March 1993) resulted from the refusal of four successive Ministers of Justice to sign death warrants. The third of those Ministers (Megumu Sato) was a Buddhist priest who said executions violated his belief in the sanctity of life. The moratorium ended when Masaharu Gotoda, a new Minister of Justice (nicknamed "The Razor") signed warrants authorizing the hanging of three death row men. Years after those executions, Gotoda (1998) called capital pun-

ishment an "insoluble problem," and he offered three reasons for signing the warrants: his obligation as Minister of Justice to "protect law and order"; the "thorough" process of case review and consultation that prosecutors in the Ministry of Justice engage in before selecting a person for execution; and strong "public support" for capital punishment (as expressed in public opinion polls). In 2003, abolitionist activists sued Gotoda for misrepresenting the public opinion figures; as this chapter goes to press the trial is in progress. During the year after executions resumed, capital punishment was a more salient issue in Japan than it has been ever since (Domikova-Hashimoto 1996; Shimizu 2002c).

6. Meiji University instructor Isa Tsujimoto believes that "because hanging is cheap and can be done anywhere," it remains the preferred method of execution (Connell 2002).

7. Japan may execute the mentally ill (Hood 2002: 124). For example, on 26 March 1993, Tetsuo Kawanaka struggled for ten minutes at the end of a rope before finally strangling to death. According to his lawyer and other knoweldgeable sources, Kawanaka had been "exhibiting the symptoms of schizophrenia for over a decade" (author's interviews; Dowling 1994; Struck 2001).

8. In American history, more people—at least 70 percent of the total—have been executed by hanging than by any other method, but only three states (Delaware, New Hampshire, and Washington) still allow execution in this way, and all of them also authorize lethal injection. Between 1622 and 2002, at least 170 legal hangings were botched in the United States (Bohm 2003: 87), and according to one recent study, during the last three decades of the twentieth century approximately one in twenty-two American executions was botched (Borg and Radelet 2004). The secrecy that surrounds capital punishment in Japan makes it impossible to make comparative "error" estimates.

9. Although this contrast remains true, crime victims have moved closer to center stage of Japan's criminal process in recent years (Atarashi 2000).

10. In 1977, for example, the U.S. Supreme Court said that "because death is a different kind of punishment from any other which may be imposed in this country," it must "be, and appear to be, based on reason rather than caprice or emotion" (*Gardner v. Florida*, 420 U.S. 349). As a result of decisions like this, the death penalty in America requires special procedures to ensure its lawful application, though such procedures have not rendered capital punishment any more predictable or reasonable (Zimring 2003: 71).

11. If prosecutors or judges do not show mercy, the executive branch is highly unlikely to do so. No death sentence has been commuted in Japan since 1975 (Shimizu 2002c).

12. What one commentator says about America may also describe Japan: "The length and the intensity of the struggle necessary to end the death penalty are not yet known, but the ultimate outcome seems inevitable in any but the most pessimistic view of the American [or Japanese] future" (Zimring 2003: 205).

13.   Although more MPs may join the Diet League, Kamei apparently does not regard abolition as a cause that will win votes. Indeed, during his campaign against Prime Minister Junichiro Koizumi and two other candidates for the presidency of the Liberal Democratic Party in September 2003, Kamei never mentioned capital punishment even though his opponents were staunch retentionists. Some observers believe Kamei's abolitionist stance is less sincere than it is a calculated effort to soften his hawkish image.

References

Amnesty International (1997) "Japan: The Death Penalty: Summary of Concerns," ASA 22/001/1997, http://web.amnesty.org/library/Index/engASA220011997 (accessed 5 June 2004).

Asian Political News (2003) "Human Rights Group Slams Japan on Executions," 28 May, http://articles.findarticles.com/p/articles/mi_m0WDQ/is_2003_June_2/ai_102670138 (accessed 5 June 2004).

Atarashi, Eri (2000) *Hanzai Higaisha Shien.* Tokyo: Komichi Shobo.

Banner, Stuart (2002) *The Death Penalty: An American History.* Cambridge: Harvard University Press.

Bohm, Robert M. (2003) *Deathquest II: An Introduction to the Theory and Practice of Capital Punishment in the United States.* Cincinnati, OH: Anderson Publishing.

Borg, Marian J., and Michael L. Radelet (2004) "On Botched Executions," in Peter Hodgkinson and William A. Schabas, eds., *Capital Punishment: Strategies for Abolition.* New York: Cambridge University Press.

Cha, Hyon Gun (2003) "Kankoku—Roh Moo Hyun Seikenka no Shikei Haishiho no Yukue," in Shikei Haishi Henshu Iinkai, ed., *Shikei Haishi Hoan.* Tokyo: Impakuto Press.

Connell, Ryan (2002) "Life on Death Row Hangs by a Thread," *Mainichi Daily News,* 28 December.

Daily Yomiuri (2003a) "Parents: Takuma Death Sentence Won't Bring Our Children Back," 30 August: 2.

Daily Yomiuri (2003b) "Ozawa Implies Japanese Voters Retarded," 28 September: 3.

Dando, Shigemitsu (2000) *Shikei Haishiron,* 6th ed. Tokyo: Yuihaku.

Domikova-Hashimoto, Dana (1996) "Japan and Capital Punishment," 6 *Human Affairs* 77–93.

Dostoevsky, Fyodor (1998) *The Idiot.* New York: Oxford University Press.

Dowling, Peter (1994) "Killing Time," (March) *Tokyo Journal* 31–35.

Essig, Mark (2003) *Edison and the Electric Chair: The Story of Light and Death.* New York: Walker & Co.

Flybjerg, Bent (1998) *Rationality & Power: Democracy in Practice,* translated by Steven Sampson. Chicago: University of Chicago Press.

Foote, Daniel H. (1992) "From Japan's Death Row to Freedom," 1 (Winter) *Pacific Rim Law & Policy Journal* 11–103.

Foote, Daniel H. (2003). "'The Door that Never Opens'? Capital Punishment and Post-Conviction Review of Death Sentences in the United States and Japan," 19 *Brooklyn Journal of International Law* 367–521.

Fox, Michael (2002) "Sing or Swing," (March) *Kansai Time Out* 32–34.

French, Howard W. (1999) "Japan Carries Out Executions in Near-Secrecy," *New York Times*, 20 December.

French, Howard W. (2002) "Secrecy of Japan's Executions Is Criticized as Unduly Cruel," *New York Times*, 30 June.

Fukuda, Masaaki (2002). "Homu Daijin ni Shikei Shikko no Gimu wa Aruka," in M. Fukuda, ed., *Nihon no Shakai Bunka Kozo to Jinken*. Tokyo: Akashi Shoten.

Garland, David (1990) *Punishment and Modern Society: A Study in Social Theory*. Chicago: University of Chicago Press.

Gillespie, L. Kay (2003) *Inside the Death Chamber: Exploring Executions*. Boston: Allyn and Bacon.

Gotoda, Masaharu (1998) *Jo to Ri: Gotoda Masaharu no Kaikoroku*. Tokyo: Kodansha.

Hamilton, V. Lee, and Joseph Sanders (1992) *Everyday Justice: Responsibility and the Individual in Japan and the United States*. New Haven, CT: Yale University Press.

Hermann, Joachim (2002) "The Death Penalty in Japan: An 'Absurd' Punishment," 67 (Spring) *Brooklyn Law Review* 827–54.

Hood, Roger (2002) *The Death Penalty: A Worldwide Perspective*. New York: Oxford University Press.

Ishizuka, Shinichi (1997) "Shikei Kiroku no Etsuran to Shimin no Shiru Kenri," in Kikuta Koichi et al., eds., *Shikei: Sonchi to Haishi no Deai*. Tokyo: Impakuto Press.

Itazu, Hideo (1991) "Jo ga Utsutte ne, Honto ni Tsurai Desu yo," *Forum 90* 14 June: 2–3.

Johnson, David T. (2002) *The Japanese Way of Justice: Prosecuting Crime in Japan*. New York: Oxford University Press.

Kamei, Shizuka (2002) *Shikei Haishiron*. Tokyo: Kadensha.

Kikuchi, Sayoko (2003) "Shikei Haishi o Kangaeru." Unpublished lecture given at a meeting of Amnesty International Japan (in Tokyo), on the occasion of "World Abolition Day" (October 10).

Kikuta, Koichi (1999) *Shikei: Sono Kyoko to Fujori*. Tokyo: Meiseki Shoten.

Marshall, Jonathan (2002) "As Japanese as Baseball: Taxpayer Suits as a Late-Blooming American Transplant," paper presented at the 2002 annual meeting of the Law and Society Association, Vancouver, British Columbia (May 30–June 1).

Martel, Yann (2001) *Life of Pi*. New York: Harcourt Books.

Mugi no Kai, and Nihon Shikeishu Kaigi, eds. (1990) *Shikeishu kara Anata e: Kuni ni wa Korosaretaku Nai*, Vol. II. Tokyo: Impakuto Press.

Murano, Kaoru (1992) *Nihon no Shikei*. Tokyo: Soshoku Shobo.

Murano, Kaoru (1995) *Shikei Shikko*. Tokyo: Kyoeisha.

Nisbett, Richard E. (2003) *The Geography of Thought: How Asians and Westerners Think Differently . . . And Why*. New York: Free Press.

Otani, Kyoko (1999) *Shikei Jiken Bengonin*. Tokyo: Yuyusha.

Otsuka, Kimiko (1988) *Shikei Shikkonin no Kuno*. Tokyo: Sou Shuppansha.

Sakamoto, Toshio (2003) *Shikei wa Ika ni Shikko Sareru ka*. Tokyo: Nihon Bungeisha.

Sarat, Austin (2001) *When the State Kills: Capital Punishment and the American Condition*. Princeton, NJ: Princeton University Press.

Sato, Masako (2001) *Gyakutai Sareta Kodomotachi no Gyakushu: Okasan no Sei Desu ka*. Tokyo: Akashi Shoten.

Sato, Tomoyuki (1994) *Shikei no Nihonshi*. Tokyo: Sanichi Shobo.

Schmetzer, Uli (2000) "In Japan, Executions Marked by Secrecy and Perhaps Incompetence," *Chicago Tribune*, 4 August.

Schmidt, Petra (2002) *Capital Punishment in Japan*. Leiden: Brill.

Schwartz, Frank, and Susan Pharr, eds. (2003) *The State of Civil Society in Japan*. New York: Cambridge University Press.

Shikei Haishi Henshu Iinkai (1999) *Shikei to Joho Kokai*. Tokyo: Impakuto Press.

Shikei Haishi Henshu Iinkai (2003) *Shikei Haishi Hoan*. Tokyo: Impakuto Press.

Shimizu, Kaho (2002a) "Ministry Secrecy Draws Spotlight: Even Victimized Divided on Death Penalty," *Japan Times*, 3 October.

Shimizu, Kaho (2002b) "Death Row Is Not Knowing When: Inmates Wake Up Every Day Wondering if It's Their Last," *Japan Times*, 3 October.

Shimizu, Kaho (2002c) "Time Is Ripe: Diet Group Against Death Penalty to Make Its Move," *Japan Times*, 4 October.

Simon, Jonathan (2002) "Why Do You Think They Call It CAPITAL Punishment? Reading the Killing State," 36 *Law & Society Review* 783–812.

Soeda, Yoshiya (2001) *Shi no Shakaigaku*. Tokyo: Iwanami Shoten.

Struck, Doug (2001) "On Japan's Death Row, Uncertainty by Design," *Washington Post*, 3 May.

Upham, Frank (1987) *Law and Social Change in Postwar Japan*. Cambridge, MA: Harvard University Press.

Van Wolferen, Karel (1989) *The Enigma of Japanese Power: People and Politics in a Stateless Nation*. New York: Alfred A. Knopf.

Von Drehle, David (1995) *Among the Lowest of the Dead: The Culture of Death Row*. New York: Times Books.

Watts, Jonathan (2001) "Japan in Dock for 'Inhuman' Treatment on Death Row," *Guardian*, 26 February.

Yasuda, Yoshihiro (2003) "Nagoya—Fukuoka no Nimei Shikko ni Kogi Suru," in Shikei Haishi Henshu Iinkai, ed., *Shikei Haishi Hoan*. Tokyo: Impakuto Press.

Zimring, Franklin E. (2001) "Crime, Criminal Justice, and Criminology for a Smaller Planet: Some Notes on the 21st Century," 34 *Australian and New Zealand Journal of Criminology* 213–20.

Zimring, Franklin E. (2003) *The Contradictions of American Capital Punishment.* New York: Oxford University Press.

CHAPTER THIRTEEN

What Is Wrong with Capital Punishment?

Official and Unofficial Attitudes Toward Capital Punishment in Modern and Contemporary China

VIRGIL K. Y. HO

Imagined Pressure?

Conducting unofficial interviews with ordinary citizens in the People's Republic of China on the subject of the death penalty was no easy matter, since most of my respondents and informants were initially reluctant to express their views on the subject.[1] This reluctance was the result of three main considerations, which became apparent to me only after I had been acquainted with the informants for some time. First, the issue of the death penalty is generally regarded as something that concerns the State alone and hence is highly sensitive politically. Informants were afraid that any comment they made would contradict the State's position on the issue. Second, most informants were aware that China has been strongly criticized by many human rights groups in the West for her overuse and misuse of the death penalty. Human rights, in their view, was a sensitive issue since the concept of human rights had until recently been renounced by the State as bourgeoise—that is, unmaterialistic and unscientific and, hence, un-Marxist. But what was even more worrying to them was the much-publicized fact that the enemies of China exploit the issue of human rights as a pretext for interfering in the domestic affairs of China (Guo 1998: 695–96). Therefore, their instinctive reaction to any unofficial or unsolicited inquiry on the subject was to treat it with suspicion. Third, death has never been a popular topic of conversation in China; it was, and to a large extent still is, a culturally taboo subject and therefore is to be avoided if possible.

The respondents' fears and caution, however, were actually groundless and unnecessary. Although the Chinese authorities may not endorse the kind of activity promoted by foreign human rights organizations in China, they do not penalize anyone who holds a different view over the issue of capital punishment, as long as s/he does not transform thoughts into organized collective action or public opinion that challenges the political supremacy of the State. More important, when informants hesitated to express their views on the matter, they were unaware of how similar their opinions actually were to that of their own government.

Among the hesitant informants were a number of mid- and low-ranking government officials and Party cadres. Their initial reticence, as they later explained, was mainly out of a natural instinct for self-protection: it seemed wise to refrain from responding to my inquiries so as to avoid making an ill-judged comment. Their reticence also reflected a failure of communication between the government and its people over the issue. Had the informants been better acquainted with the official position, they might have been more vocal. Their silence signaled more a distrust of the State than a challenge to the official view on the subject.

Official Perspective

Until recently, the social relevance and legal appropriateness of capital punishment have never been seriously questioned in China (including Taiwan). This is most strikingly reflected in the fact that between 1950 and 1985 only about forty, superficial essays were published in China on the subject of capital punishment. Serious writing and academic discourse on the subject only began after 1986, and the subject has become a lively topic of discussion in the field of legal studies only since the early 1990s (Hu 1995: 2–3).[2] A number of these post-1980s publications are similar in terms of argument and even narrative style. Nearly all have been published either by conservative university presses, such as the People's University of China and China's University of Politics and Law, or by official/semi-official publishing houses, such as the People's Publisher and the People's Public Security University of China, and their views mirror those of the Chinese authorities.[3]

So what is the position of today's Chinese government on the issue of capital punishment? The view expressed by a senior judge in Canton, Li Guo, in all likelihood represents the official view in present-day China. According to Judge Li, the death penalty is recognized in China for its commendable function as an effective deterrent to crime of the serious kind, which has risen dramatically in recent years as a result of rapid structural changes in the country. Li, like all other legal specialists in China who have written on the subject, reiterates an important official directive endorsed by the National People's Congress on the issue of capital punishment: that China must not abolish capital punishment at the present moment, though she should minimize its use. Underlying this basic policy are two politico-legal principles. First, capital punishment, in accordance with the Marxist materialist interpretation of history, will eventually and inevitably be made redundant in the final stage of historical development, in which all superstructures will be abolished. However, China needn't rush to abolish the death penalty, because the time for a country to discontinue this form of punishment must be determined solely by that country's "current practical necessity" and by the "situation of that country's national security, historical tradition, concept of values and so on." For China, Judge Li argues, keeping capital punishment is not an end in itself, but a means to its eventual abolishment. To retain capital punishment in China is a wise decision for the government for three important reasons: it fits perfectly well with didactical materialism and hence is ideationally scientific, it suits the current socio-political situation of the nation, and it brings progress to and helps civilize the country. This is, Li explains, what the people in China have been longing for (Li Guo 1995: 34–35, 37).

The second principle is that the passing of a death sentence and its frequency in China are always under close scrutiny and are regulated by the People's courts. To ensure the proper functioning of these legal safeguards, Judge Li explains, the Chinese State enforces a series of measures to govern the proper use of this form of penalty. They include the application of the death sentence to an increasingly smaller category of offenses, the exclusion of certain groups of convicts from death row (such as youngsters and pregnant women), the imposition of stricter legal review procedures, and the adoption of the sentence of *sihuan* (a suspended death sentence with a two-year reprieve and forced labor, followed by either execution or commutation of the death sentence), which has been hailed as a unique Chinese legal practice pertinent to the situation of China and displaying the government's flexibility and leniency toward convicts.[4] This view is widely shared by Chinese legal experts and academics, who have unreserved confidence in the impartiality of China's legal and judicial systems when sentencing a person to death or to a proportional sentence. The possibility of a miscarriage of justice, for these experts, is a remote one and, therefore, never a sound argument against the use of capital punishment in China. It is therefore not surprising to find in their writings lengthy descriptions (Li Wenyan 2002, for example, used over four hundred pages) of the elaborate judicial review process and the appeal mechanism that govern the passing of a death sentence (Chao 2001: chaps. 3–5; Hu 1995: 231–323; Li and Shen 1992: 136–75, 226–64; Li and Shen 1997: 246–73). The whole discourse is about constructing an image of a state that is caring, careful, impartial, and restrained when approaching the practice of capital punishment.

Along similar lines, most works on the subject published in China since the early 1980s begin with a historical survey of capital punishment in China from antiquity to the present. These historical narratives try to impress upon readers that China, like all other civilizations, has a long history of capital punishment, and that all the old forms of executions were gruesomely brutal. By describing cruel punishments such as slicing, burning alive, skinning, mincing, and consuming the flesh of a convict, they try to "prove" that today's China has come a long way from its "feudal" past in respect of the humaneness of capital punishment (Li and Shen 1992: 1–21; Hu 1995: 21–52).

Most experts of Chinese penal laws evoke and elaborate in their writings the "definitive" view of Chairman Mao on capital punishment to support theirs. According to them, Mao had ascertained the political usefulness and strategic importance of the death penalty, especially in consolidating the fragile power of the Chinese Communist Party in the early years of the Revolution (1924–27) and, later, in the People's Republic. On the other hand, Mao was also said to be an ardent supporter of the principles of "kill less" and "never kill mindlessly," for which he had initiated judicial reforms to ensure that the passing of a death sentence would be subject to a strict procedure of intensive re-examination so that its occurrence could be minimized. This dual policy is said to have been consistently upheld by Mao, the Chinese Communist Party, and the Chinese government (Li and Shen 1992: 71–75; Hu 1995: 169–76; Guo 1998: 269–79). The reason for bringing Chairman Mao into the discussion of the death penalty in contemporary China is, in all likelihood, a carefully calculated political one. As a cultic figure in modern China, Mao and his revered words bestow the Chinese State with both political legitimacy and the symbolic power of history over its policy toward capital punishment. Evoking Mao, who epitomizes modern China and the People's Republic, helps justify, in the name of history, the continuance of the death penalty.

Most writings on the death penalty emphasize that since China's judicial system effectively safeguards against miscarriage of justice, all convicts who are eventually put to death are, therefore, unmistakably wicked subhumans who commit unpardonable horrific crimes of the most serious kind and inflict great suffering on their victims, or who seriously disrupt law and order. Guo Daohui, a senior professor of law in China and a close acquaintance of former Premier Zhu Rongji, is an outspoken supporter of the death penalty in the country. In an article entitled "Death Penalty with Chinese Characteristics" (Juyou Zhongguo tese de sixing zhidu), he argues for capital punishment as a powerful deterrent to both counterrevolutionary and criminal activities. In support of his view, he writes that during the 1950s whenever "a group of counter-revolutionary [enemies] were [sentenced and] put to death, the people would be so delighted that their motivation for economic production was raised by leaps and bounds [and] their political power further strengthened, which brought over 50 years of peace and unity [to China]." With respect to the problem of the current crime wave in China, Guo firmly believes that by putting a number of convicted criminals to death, society can be cleansed of "trash" and the lives of the people protected. The death penalty is good for the well-being of the people and society and is therefore an "ultimate form of humanitarianism" (Guo 1998: 273–74).

Guo's words remind us of the rhetoric and the narrative adopted by the State-controlled media when broadcasting news about death sentences. The Chinese authorities occasionally publicize news about "criminals of the most wicked type" who are sentenced to death. These selectively publicized instances are unfailingly related to "crimes of the most serious kinds," and the convicts involved are as a rule portrayed as wicked by nature or cold-blooded perpetrators of violent crimes who show no respect for human life or public order (Ho 2000: 143–44). Through these narratives are constructed the stereotypes of the criminals and the unpardonable nature of the crimes they commit.[5] All the narratives are intended to justify the use of capital punishment in the eyes of the public. It must be added that the State-controlled media do not publicize all cases of a death penalty, especially those involving petty criminals who have committed relatively minor crimes. This is one of the reasons Amnesty International has criticized the Chinese government for keeping the number of executions a state secret (Amnesty International Annual Report/China 2000: 3, and 2001: 4–5). But in those cases which are publicized, the Chinese authorities always ensure that the convicts are portrayed in the mass media as "criminals of the most horrific and wicked type" so that their executions are justifiable and unregrettable—a choreographed practice with a long history (Ho 2000: 145–53). A dehumanized stereotypical image of convicts on death row is an important means to reinforce the position of the State on this matter—capital punishment is necessary and right because it protects the interest of the people, which is "the highest [principle] in law" (Guo 1998: 284–85). To highlight the symbolic importance of these executions and to celebrate the triumph of the State in the battle against serious crime, mass executions are frequently conducted prior to major political events or public holidays, such as the convening of National Congress, Labor Day, and, most symbolic of all, National Day (Amnesty International Annual Report 2000/China: 3; Amnesty International 1979: 75; BBC 2001b).

Many legal experts in China argue that it is wrong to assume that abolitionism is a trend among the world's nations, because there are at present more retentionist countries (130) than abolitionist (30) (Guo 1998: 270–71). It is, the experts opine, therefore unreasonable to measure a country's commitment to upholding the human rights of its countrymen, or the level of excellence of its civilization, by the arbitrary yardstick of whether or not capital punishment is still in use in that country. To justify China's retentionist stance over this matter, they emphasize that many countries that had earlier abolished the death penalty, including the leading critic of China's human rights record, the United States of America, have reinstated it after realizing its irreplaceable effectiveness as a deterrent against serious crime. China's choice, they hold, is lawful, justifiable, and cosmopolitan (Guo 1998: 270–71; Li and Shen 1992: 121; Hu 1995: 95–123; Zhao et al. 1992: 5–10; Gao et al. 1994: 139–40; Chao 2001: 75). The figures given in "evidence," however, are factually inaccurate[6]—an inaccuracy that is most likely intentional and represents a collective effort by Chinese academia and officialdom to refute criticisms of China by Western "adversaries." Accuracy has no place in these rhetorical narratives.

But are all these official and semi-official views mere rhetoric and self-rationalizing clichés that are not shared by the general public?

Popular Dimension

One reason for the initial reluctance of my respondents to discuss capital punishment is that death is still commonly considered a taboo topic, one that should especially be avoided in the weeks before an auspicious event such as Chinese New Year (symbolically associated with regeneration of life) when my survey was conducted.[7] This brings out an interesting aspect of the public's attitudes toward capital punishment—there is a cultural, even supernatural, dimension to their perception of the issue.

The respondents' initial reticence must not be taken as reluctance to make honest or pro-abolition comments on a sensitive issue. On the contrary, most of my respondents (73 out of 86) and informants insisted that China must keep the death penalty because they could not see why it should be abolished. Among these proponents were university students and middle-age professionals, including medical practitioners, university faculty, nurses, and businessmen—the social sector that seems to be most ardently supportive of an abolitionist stance in the West. Given the informal way my opinion survey was conducted, their positive attitude toward capital punishment was by and large spontaneous, and not in the least swayed by any fear of the State as one might have suspected.[8]

There are other reasons for doubting the influence of the State's ideological indoctrination on my respondents' and informants' views on the death penalty. First, Chinese scholarship on the death penalty, no matter how well articulated, is of no concern to these people, who, to my knowledge, have never read, and probably will never read, anything on such an inauspicious subject. They may, however, occasionally have watched reports on television about a "sentencing rally," which seems to have reinforced, rather than shaped, their own original beliefs and attitudes regarding the socio-cultural relevance of capital punishment, since many phrased their supportive comments in largely traditional parlance rather than that of the official media.[9] The influence of tradition is even more apparent when it comes to my observations in the field, where my peasant informants had never thought about the issue. They opined that since capital punishment has been a part of the Chinese penal system since time immemorial, its continuous existence is simply a matter of course. They don't need the State to educate them in recognizing the value of the death penalty.

Second, the Chinese State, to my knowledge, has never conducted any mass publicity campaign to "educate" its subjects in the official view of capital punishment. The "public discourse" on the death penalty is largely confined to a small circle of academics, legal experts, and senior officials; the general populace is both uninterested and uninvolved. It is not surprising, therefore, that the people don't always share the view of the State: seven respondents did argue for the abolishment of capital punishment in China, which they considered cruel and inhumane to the convicts and their families. Two of these seven abolitionists also argued that the death penalty is an uncivilized, open violation of the principles of humanitarianism and human freedom.

The overwhelming majority, however, held a highly affirmative view of the punishment. All of them expressed absolute confidence in the death penalty as an efficacious deterrent against crime, and they also regarded it as an effective way of safeguarding the well-being of society and the lives and the properties of law-abiding citizens like themselves, as well as of maintaining the people's confidence in the rule of law. A number of my respondents and informants described convicts on death row as "wicked criminals of the most horrible type," who, as a menace to the society, must be exterminated. One respondent, himself a senior professor at a medical school, compared the crimes committed by criminals punishable by death to cancer cells inside a human body, which would spread and cause fatal damage to its patient if left untreated, so that aggressive surgery was needed to have them eradicated. Capital punishment, according to many, must be employed to shock the populace, in particular the youngsters, who would then learn about the fatal consequence of committing serious crimes. Of the 73 retentionists, only 15 disapproved of public execution, which they favored because they believed it to be the best way to assuage the anger of a victim's family and of those good citizens who are appalled by the wickedness of the criminal. Although some years ago the State announced its intention to replace public execution by shooting with execution by lethal injection in the confines of a prison, this effort to "humanize" or "modernize" capital punishment has not been popularly received (*Ming pao*, May 2, 1998)—executing these criminals by lethal injection is regarded as unacceptably lenient. Three well-educated respondents even argued strongly for extracting organs from executed convicts for the purpose of transplant; only in this way, they said, could these bad social elements "make themselves useful to the society." My informants in the field, both urban and rural, had never doubted the validity of using an executed convict's organs for medical purposes.[10]

Underlying this approval of capital punishment is a common assumption that those who are sentenced to death must be the most wicked criminals whose crimes are of the most sinister type. In other words, these convicts deserve no pity and their death is an occasion for joy. People in China also have faith in the fairness and impartiality of the law and the judicial system, though their confidence is not unqualified. Over half the respondents supporting the death penalty admitted that they had worried about miscarriages of justice because of the common problem of corruption in Chinese officialdom. A few respondents learned about such injustice from an interesting source: a highly popular television drama series about the good deeds of the legendary Judge Bao (999–1062 A.D.), who is a household name for his incorruptible character and unswerving determination to redress countless cases of miscarriage of justice.[11] But in spite of their doubts about the integrity of the legal system, their faith in the efficacy and the ethical justifications of capital punishment remained unshaken. There was no shortage of people who had total trust in the State's legal and penal systems. Two respondents argued that the occasional occurrence of a false accusation must not be taken as evidence of a failure of the system as a whole. The death penalty, they argued, given all its advantages, must be enforced regardless of such "minor" shortcomings—nothing is perfect, and sacrifice must be made at times.

The reference to Judge Bao is interesting because it shows how people still think about the issue of capital punishment in terms of traditional cultural idioms, despite decades of rule by a totalitarian iconoclastic regime. The resurrection of the cult of Judge Bao since the 1990s, which was initiated unexpectedly by a Taiwanese TV melodrama series, not only reminded my respondents and informants of the potential danger of a false charge, but also reinforced their faith in the validity of a traditional religio-cultural tenet: the ultimate tri-

umph of good over evil. This conviction was important because it helped people construe the drama and the reality of capital punishment in ways determined by the story. In the historical dramas about Judge Bao, all the falsely accused eventually clear their names and are acquitted. Miscarriage of justice, as
"proven" in drama and perhaps even in real life, is at best only a remote possibility in the eyes of the viewers. Part of the reason for the huge success of the
TV show in South China may be that it helps people cope with their worries
about the possibility of sending an innocent man to death. It is interesting that
the five respondents who opined against the death penalty gave human rights
and compassion rather than a possible miscarriage of justice as the reasons for
their concern. Moreover, many respondents and informants questioned the validity of concerns about miscarriage of justice, dismissing them as ungrounded
and an overreaction. In their view, the legal and penal systems in China are sophisticated enough to have safeguards against false charges or miscarriage of
justice. Most important, they don't believe that a truly innocent person can be
easily framed, falsely charged, and sentenced to death without arousing the notice of the State and the legal authorities.

When conducting fieldwork in a cluster of villages in South China during
the late 1980s and the early 1990s, I was impressed with the huge popularity of
the Judge Bao series among the villagers. Five nights a week during months
when the program was broadcast, nearly all the villagers gathered in front of
their TV sets to follow the latest developments in the judge's investigation. Each
episode was followed closely and with great interest. Every time Judge Bao succeeded in clearing the name of a falsely accused character, or having the perpetrator of a sinister crime arrested and sent to execution, these rural audiences
all spontaneously clapped and bellowed with joy, apparently celebrating the triumph of good over evil, not only in the fictional world, but also in real life.[12]
The last episode in each story, though always predictable, always caused great
excitement among these rural audiences. Many empathetic viewers even "par-
ticipated" in such enactments of retributive justice by scolding the wicked characters in the drama from time to time, until the final apprehension or execution
of the guilty party brought them both relief and comfort. In the view of these
audiences, all criminals who are to be executed are unmistakably the most
wicked, evil, and unpardonable type of "trash." The public, they believe, not
only support their executions, but also wish that more criminals like them

could be executed so that law and order in China may be soundly maintained. In both dramatized and real-life versions of executions, these people see not only the triumph of Law and the power of the State, but also the delivery of retributive justice in a somewhat religious sense.[13] The perceived link between divine justice and capital punishment was, surprisingly, shared by a number of urban respondents and informants who were well-educated professionals. This popular attitude toward the death penalty resembles that of old-time theatergoers toward scenes of execution on stage (Ho 2000: 153).[14]

In the discourse of such retentionists, since China has a long history of capital punishment and an old popular belief in divine retributive justice, there is neither sound reason nor imminent need to uproot this aspect of Chinese cultural tradition. A foreign correspondent reported "that even the most sophisticated urbanites would shrink from the idea of abolishing capital punishment altogether. 'There is a Chinese saying that you should kill the chicken to scare the monkeys,' says [a] university graduate. . . . 'We need that threat to be there—it's part of our culture'" (BBC 2001a).

Capital punishment is popularly perceived and justified in the name of history, tradition, and Chinese culture. The combined effect of these popular perceptions of the death penalty apparently reinforces the impression that all those who are sentenced to death by the court must be criminals of the most wicked or sinister kind who deserve to be exterminated. The fact that those who sentenced to death include people who have committed more minor, nonviolent crimes, such as corruption, trafficking in women, robbery, negligence resulting in a fatal industrial accident, and so on,[15] doesn't seem to have bothered retentionists. Most respondents and informants maintained that since these criminals are wicked or evil, they must not be treated like ordinary people and in accordance with the principle of humanitarianism. These criminals, they opined, are themselves the violators of the principle of humanitarianism in their criminal acts. Accordingly, if these wicked criminals and murderers are not punished by death in public, the relatives of the victims of their crimes are not treated humanitarianly either. To some informants, even putting a "wicked criminal" of this type on trial was a waste of public resources and time; these "subhumans" should be "shot on the spot."[16]

The traditional attitude of "an eye to an eye" and retribution is commonly considered to be apt and fair and not at odds with the ideal or principle of humanitarianism. Although many informants were aware of criticisms of China's practice of capital punishment by Western human rights groups, most of those I spoke with did not support abolition in China. They argued that since crime in China shows no sign of abating in the current volatile socio-economic and political environments, the old Chinese wisdom that "severe penal codes are the answer to social disorder" (*zhi luanshi yong zhongdian*, a tenet of Chinese state-craft with a long history dating back at least to the time of Confucius, 511–479 B.C.) is still proper for China. They believed that since this tenet had helped China maintain a peaceful and orderly society in the past, its continuous relevance to the present-date China was undeniable. They also believed that since most people were for the death penalty, any abolitionist talk was a clear deviation from social responsibility, or what is commonly considered to be the right thing to do for maintaining a better society. On the day of the public execution of a former head of Jiangxi Province, who was convicted of embezzling public funds, many people were said to have felt a "festival-like" thrill—a pleasurable feeling arising from a sense of satisfaction with this "symbolical act of conquering a man [of evil]" (Qiu 2001: 17).[17]

⤙

This chapter set out to look for similarities and differences between the official and the popular attitudes toward capital punishment in modern China. My finding is that there are large areas of similarity, along with occasional areas of difference, in officials' and civilians' views of the death penalty. An insignificantly small number of officials and legal experts questioned the socio-political appropriateness of the death penalty. The majority of my informants and respondents supported capital punishment unreservedly, regarding it as essential for their country. The prevalence of this attitude is not necessarily to be attributed just to the ideological indoctrination imposed by the State upon its people; the regime hasn't launched any intensive publicity campaign in this respect, and the people need no such propaganda to shape their views of the socio-cultural and political meanings of the death penalty. My informants' opinions indicated that their feelings about capital punishment stemmed, not from the State's propaganda or from schools, but mainly from old cultural values embedded and disseminated through old history books or vernacular novels and theatrical and oral traditions. Somewhat ironically, history and tradition are thus utilized as twin towers to legitimize and justify China's continuous application of the death penalty in the modern age. Most of my respondents and informants did not see a contradiction between the practice of capital punishment and the ideals of humanitarianism, human rights, nonviolence, and modernization (or globalization). On the contrary, there seems to be a strong public consensus in China about the efficacy and desirability of capital punishment as a means of safeguarding these "modern," noble ideals, which are reserved only for law-abiding citizens. Such popular acceptance explains why the State's position on capital punishment is never seriously questioned; in the long history of capital punishment in China since antiquity, neither the elite nor the commoners have questioned its social, cultural, and political importance. The Chinese State has in the course of its history been concerned to abolish specific forms of cruel capital punishment, but the fundamental idea of the death penalty has never been challenged. It comes as no surprise, therefore, that even one of the most prolific and vocal abolitionists in China today, who is a law professor at a prestigious university, believes that "judging by the specific state of affairs of today's China, it is impossible to have capital punishment abolished in China in the near future. . . . What China at this moment can do is to adopt a policy of 'limiting [the kinds of crime to be punishable by the] death penalty'; this is a totally feasible target" (Qiu 2001: 97).

In the view of the majority, there is nothing ethically or socio-culturally wrong with the legal principle of capital punishment. For most Chinese in China (including Taiwan), the death penalty has served, and still serves, a meaningful purpose for their country and its people.

Notes

1. I use the term "respondents" in this chapter to refer to those who have responded to my opinion surveys, and "informants" to those whom I have spoken with in person.

2. Hu (1995: 324–29) includes a bibliography of some of these major works published since the early 1980s.

3. During the writing of this chapter, no official document containing a detailed elaboration on the present-day Chinese government's policy on capital punishment was available for analysis; such a document may not even exist. Secondary works are therefore important, and they are probably the only reliable sources of information about the government's conception of and position on this issue.

4. Guo (1998: 35–37) states that all judges in China are careful to differentiate be-

tween convicts who undoubtedly deserve to be punished by death and those who deserve the same sentence but show considerable potential for reformation and should therefore be given a chance to live behind bars.

5. Examples are abundant. For instance, a news report stresses, in strong emotional language as ever, the *wickedness* (my emphasis) of a woman who killed her father-in-law after a row over a *minor* domestic issue (again my emphasis). *Huashang bao*, Dec. 28, 2002. In another example, the journalist stresses the unrepentant attitude of a convicted serial killer who reportedly said that he did not feel anything when he killed. *Beijing qingnian bao*, Dec. 19, 2002.

6. According to Amnesty International, there were 99 abolitionist countries and 95 retentionist countries in 1966, 104 abolitionists and 91 retentionists in 1998, and 108 abolitionists and 87 retentionists in 2001 (http:/www.amnesty.org). My thanks to Christian Boulanger for drawing my attention to these figures.

7. A note on methodology is necessary. This paper is not intended to be a systematic survey of opinions in the whole of China, which is beyond my ability and resources; instead I conducted a small-scale opinion survey of 80+ people between November 2002 and February 2003, with the assistance of two research assistants in South China—one in Changsha in Hunan Province and the other in Foshan in Guangdong Province. To obtain honest feedback on a politically sensitive issue, questionnaires were distributed to people whom my research assistants knew personally, and their responses, which they wrote in private, were anonymous. At the end of the exercise, 86 responses were collected. Most of the respondents were middle-class professionals. To supplement the data, I utilized my past field-research materials in the form of interviews with local informants, most of them ordinary peasants, workers in cottage industries, and a few high-school students and small-business men I knew quite well, in various places in the Canton Delta area between 1989 and 1998.

8. In Taiwan, capital punishment, according to opinion polls, is also supported by a substantial majority (Zhang 1991: 14–65; "Zhichi baoliu sixing zhidu de linwai yihan liyou"; "Feichu sixing yantaohui").

9. Such as *yi bao yi bao* (lit., "violence for violence") and *sharen tianmin, qianzhai huanqian* (lit., "a killer must pay with his own life, just as a debtor must repay his loan to his lender").

10. For more details on this "trade," see Human Rights Watch/Asia (1994), Voice of America (1994), and Smith (2001).

11. For a traditional legal-cultural analysis of the folk stories about Judge Bao, see Xu Zhongming (2002).

12. Similar emotional reactions were also noticed in big cities such as Canton and Hong Kong.

13. I say only "in a somewhat religious sense" because most male informants, unlike

the female informants, were reluctant to admit their religiously inclined behavior publicly. Aijmer and Ho (2001: chap. 12).

14.   Popular obsession with execution scenes on the stage was vividly recorded by a Japanese traveler in Canton in the 1940s. At the end of a Cantonese opera performance when, in the usual manner, the villain was finally subdued and killed by the hero, realistic props were used: a pig's intestines and other internal organs, to the horror of the Japanese visitor. When the victor pretended to cut open the body of the slain villain, dragging out his internal organs and waved them around in the air to show the "certain death" of the force of evil, the audiences watched with amusement and excitement and rewarded the performance with thunderous applause (Kōsaka 1943: 38).

15.   This is a major concern of Amnesty International. In its 1995 annual report, for example, it wrote that "death sentences also were handed out for pornography, pimping, prostitution and theft. . . . Thirty three people were executed . . . for stealing cars in Guangdong. Embezzlement accounted for nine executions in Guangdong [and the] vice-president of a hospital in Henan was executed after being convicted of taking bribes to falsify 488 sterilisation certificates." *South China Morning Post*, May 1, 1995.

16.   Many people in today's Taiwan also hold a similar attitudes toward convicts apprehended for violent crimes (Zhang 1991: 28–29). According to an opinion poll conducted by the Taiwanese government in 1993, 71.7 percent of respondents were in favor of keeping the death penalty (Xu Chunjin 1994).

17.   This highly publicized case was eagerly followed and reported in official and semi-official Chinese mass media. After his execution, Hu's possessions and properties were auctioned; the occasion was a huge success and enjoyed by numerous enthusiastic bidders. "Hu Zhangqing zangwu paimai muji."

References

Aijmer, Göran, and Virgil Kit-yiu Ho (2001) *Cantonese Society in a Time of Change.* Hong Kong: The Chinese University of Hong Kong Press.

Amnesty International (1979) *The Death Penalty.* London: Amnesty International.

———— (1994–2002) Annual Report. London: Amnesty International.

Beijing qingnian bao (Beijing Youth Daily*).* Beijing.

Chao, Zuojun (2001) *Sixing xianzhilun* (On limiting [the handing out of] the death penalty). Wuhan: Wuhan daxue chubanshe.

BBC (2001a) "China Executions Part of Culture," July 6, 2001. http://news.bbc.co.uk/1/hi/world/asia-pacific/1426210.stm.

BBC (2001b) "China Tops Execution Tables," March 21, 2001. http://news.bb.co.uk/1/hi/world/asia-pacific/1234000.stm.

"Feichu sixing yantaohui" (Forum on the abolition of the death penalty [in Taiwan])
(2000) http://www/tahr.org.tw/death/dis20000527.

Gao, Mingxuan, et al. (1994) *Xingfaxue yuanli* (The principles of criminal law), vol. 3.
Beijing: Zhongguo renmin daxue chubanshe.

Guo, Daohui (1998) *Fa de shidai huhuan* (The call of the times of law). Beijing: Zhongguo fazhi chubanshe, Xinhua shudian.

Ho, Virgil Kit-yiu (2000) "Butchering Fish and Executing Criminals," in J. Abbink and
G. Aijmer, eds., *Meanings of Violence: A Cross Cultural Perspective.* Oxford: Berg.

Hu, Yunteng (1995) *Sixing tonglun* (A general discussion of the death penalty). Beijing:
Zhongguo zhengfa daxue chubanshe.

"Hu Zhangqing zangwu paimai muji" (Witnessing the auctioning of Hu Zhangqing's
booty). http://www.epochtimes.com/b5/2/5/13/n189544.htm, dated May 13, 2002.

Huashang bao (Chinese Business Daily). Shaanxi.

Human Rights Watch/Asia (1994) "Organ Procurement and Judicial Execution in
China," http://www.hrw.org/reports/1994/china1/china_948.htm.

Kōsaka, Junichi. (1943) "Kanton tsushin," 12.3 *Minzoku Taiwan* (Taiwanese Folklore).

Li, Guo (1995) "Lun sixing cailiang" (On the ruling and the penal measurement of death
sentence), in Jianqun Zhang and Chuanyang Li, eds., *Fanzui yu xingfa: Zhongguo
faguan lun xingshi shenpan* (Crime and punishment: criminal cases verdicts as seen
by judges in China). Beijing: Zhongguo zhengfa daxue chubanshe.

Li, Wenyan, ed. (2002) *Sixing anjian zhengju diaocha yu yunyong* (The use and investigation of evidence in cases leading to the ruling of the death penalty). Beijing: Zhongguo renmin gongan daxue chubanshe.

Li, Yunlong, and Deyong Shen (1992) *Sixing zhidu bijiao yanjiu* (A comparative study of
the penal systems of capital punishment). Beijing: Zhongguo renmin gongan daxue
chubanshe.

———— (1997) *Sixing zhuanlun* (Essays on the death penalty). Beijing: Zhongguo
zhengfa daxue chubanshe.

Qiu, Xinglong (2001) *Bijiao xingfa (diyi juan): Sixing zhuanhao* (Comparative penal
codes, vol. 1: special issue on the death penalty). Beijing: Zhongguo jiancha chubanshe.

Smith, Craig (2001) "China 'harvests' body organs of condemned after executions," *New
York Times*, March 12.

South China Morning Post. Hong Kong daily.

Voice of America (1994) "Executed prisoners organs used for transplant," cited in *World
Tibet Network News*, August 30. http://www.tibet.ca/en/wtnarchive/1994/8/30

Xu, Chunjin (1994) "Sixing cunfei zhi tantu" (An investigation into [the issue of] keeping or abolishing the death penalty). http://www.rdec.gov.tw/res/project/rdec69.htm.

Xu, Zhongming (2002) *Baogong gushi: yige kaocha Zhongguo falu wenhua de shijiao* (The story of Judge Bao: a perspective for understanding chinese legal culture). Beijing: Zhongguo zhengfa daxue chubanshe.

Zhang, Xianghua, ed. (1991) *Life or Death*. Taipei: Xingguang chubanshe.

Zhao Bingzhi et al. (1992) *Xiandai shijie sixing gaikuang* (The situation of the death penalty in the modern world). Beijing: Zhongguo renmin daxue chubanshe.

"Zhichi baoliu sixing zhidu de linwai yihan liyou" (Another reason for supporting the keeping of the death penalty). http://www.chinamonitor.org/view/support/blsxly. htm.

CHAPTER FOURTEEN

Capital Punishment and the Culture of Developmentalism in Singapore

ALFRED OEHLERS AND NICOLE TARULEVICZ

Introduction

Singapore is one of a number of countries where capital punishment is still practiced. An instrument bequeathed by the British colonial authorities, capital punishment was retained by the ruling Peoples' Action Party (PAP) when it led the country to self-government in 1959, and eventually, full independence in 1965. The exact number of times the sentence has been carried out since independence is difficult to estimate. No precise statistics on executions are publicly available, but judging by the number of occasions the sentence has been pronounced and the rarity of successful appeals, it would appear to be somewhat frequent. According to Amnesty International (2003), Singapore has the dubious distinction of having one of the highest execution rates in the world, relative to its population size. Since 1991, at least 369 executions have been carried out (ibid.)—a record that, when viewed together with the considerable material wealth and consumerist lifestyle enjoyed by citizens, contributes to a perception of the nation as a "theme park with the death sentence" (Clammer 1997: 142).

The frequency of the death penalty, and the secrecy surrounding it, has always been an issue of considerable sensitivity for the Singapore government. In early 2004, the issue again assumed prominence following the release of a highly critical report on Singapore by Amnesty International (2004). In response, the government issued a strongly worded statement to rebut the accusations leveled by Amnesty International, as well as to reject any suggestion that the administration of the death penalty could in any sense be questionable. Thus, according to a spokesman of the Ministry of Home Affairs:

> It is widely recognized that Singapore has one of the most fair and transparent legal systems in the world. All trials involving capital cases are tried in an open court and reported in the press. Even appeals heard by the Court of Appeal are held in an open court. Hence, all judicial decisions involving the death penalty are open to public scrutiny. All accused persons are also properly represented by lawyers. If the accused person is unable to afford a lawyer, the state will appoint him one, from a panel of private lawyers. Furthermore, no person is executed until all avenues of appeal for clemency have been exhausted. (Ministry of Home Affairs 2004)

While commanding international attention, within Singapore, the death penalty is very much taken as a given, evoking little discussion or debate. Thus, while Singaporean nongovernmental organizations such as the Think Centre, in conjunction with opposition politicians such as J. B. Jeyaretnam, have been vocal opponents, capital punishment remains something of a nonissue in much official and public discourse (Think Centre 2004). The death penalty only assumes significance when it becomes a thorn in the side of Singapore's international persona as an issue the West uses to criticize Singapore. For the government and most of the public, this is what causes outrage, controversy, and debate; not capital punishment per se.

In terms of its actual practice, capital punishment in Singapore is applicable in a fairly well-defined range of crimes. Premeditated murder, for example, is one crime where the death penalty is mandatory, as are robbery committed with the use of a firearm, drug trafficking, and treason (Amnesty International 2003). Conspicuously, despite its notoriety as a country with a highly authoritarian political system (Lingle 1996), capital punishment is not meted out in the case of political crimes or transgressions. This omission does not mean, however, that there is no political edge to capital punishment in Singapore. On the contrary, as this chapter will attempt to show, there is a very important political dimension to this form of punishment. The practice of capital punishment in Singapore was, and remains, an integral part of a wider effort to enforce a culture of developmentalism designed to underpin a postcolonial project of nation building. In this respect, capital punishment assumes considerable promi-

nence in defining the bounds of acceptable behavior or conduct. In criminaliz-
ing nonconformists and applying the ultimate sanction to their transgressions,
the state sends a powerful message about the limits of its tolerance and emphatically demonstrates its preparedness to eliminate those that do not submit
to its vision of the Singapore nation. Capital punishment, as such, plays a highly
significant role in instilling particular forms of compliance in Singapore as well
as in dealing with those malcontents who have no place in the idealized society.

To provide some background to this discussion, the emergence of a developmentalist state and culture in postcolonial Singapore will first be briefly
sketched in the following section. Using this as a backdrop, the discussion will
then move on to examine how criminality in Singapore is framed in the light of
this developmentalist ethic and nation-building effort. Building on this conception of criminality, consideration will then be given to how the practice of
capital punishment enforces these notions of criminality—and by extension—
the culture of developmentalism. This will largely be achieved by examining a
number of instances where capital punishment has been applied in the past and
the narratives that have been associated with these. A final section will conclude
the chapter and draw out some wider implications of the study.

Development and the Developmentalist State

When Singapore was granted self-government in 1959, its continued existence as a nation was far from certain. A tiny island of just 600 square kilome-
ters, it was virtually devoid of any natural resources, apart from a population of
around 1.5 million people. Historically, its existence had always rested on its role
as an entrepôt in the regional Southeast Asia trade and base for British naval fa-
cilities. However, rising nationalism in the region—and the consequent desire
to cut out Singapore's middleman role in trade—together with the closure of
British bases at this time, were beginning to pose serious threats to this livelihood. Already significant problems stemming from stagnating growth and a
lack of economic diversification—widespread unemployment, deteriorating
health, housing, education, and welfare, to name but a few—were set to inten-
sify considerably (see e.g. Deyo 1981; Rodan 1989).

These economic problems were compounded by an extremely tenuous political situation. Though an insurgency led by the Malayan Communist Party

had largely been suppressed by this time, communist subversion remained a significant threat, with strikes by pro-communist trade unions and politically motivated riots common occurrences. Exacerbating these ideological struggles, communal conflict was also a serious problem, with ethnic and religious tensions running high between the Chinese, Indian, and Malay communities on the island. These on occasion escalated dramatically, spilling over into bloody racial riots (see e.g. Chan 1971; Rodan 1989).

A temporary reprieve from these problems was gained in 1963 when Singapore became a state within the Federation of Malaysia. This merger, it was envisaged, would provide an economic lifeline to the tiny island as well as a more effective response to communist subversion and communal violence. Although there was much to recommend it, the merger, however, proved to be short-lived. Marked by controversy and acrimony from the outset, the relationship was eventually terminated just two years later in 1965. Singapore then found itself an independent sovereign nation, having to face a full suite of economic, social, and political problems entirely on its own (see e.g. Rodan 1989).

In seeking to overcome these challenges, the ruling PAP gradually evolved a unique approach to economic management in the island republic. Now dubbed the "Singapore model" (Huff 1995), the approach bore a strong resemblance to strategies being adopted in countries such as South Korea and Taiwan—contemporaries of Singapore then embarking upon a very similar path of development. In essence, this entailed a reorientation of economic strategy to focus on the promotion of export-oriented industries, with the state playing a leading role in fostering this process. The pervasiveness of this state role certainly stands out as one of the key distinguishing features of the approach and should not be underestimated. As others have pointed out, in the face of numerous internal as well as external impediments and handicaps, the success of the new strategy hinged critically on the state marshalling the necessary resources and deploying these to maximum effect in support of the effort (see Wade 1990; Deyo 1987; Perry, Kong, and Yeoh 1997). With such an extensive and dominant role in the process, the state in these countries—quite appropriately—is thus described as "developmental" in nature.

By all accounts, this form of state-led development was extremely successful in Singapore, lifting it from its origins as a colonial entrepôt into a major international center for trade, finance, and industry in the space of just a few short decades (see Huff 1994; Low 1998; Perry et al. 1997). As widely recognized, this rapid process of development owed much to the state employing an extensive range of instruments to influence the conduct and course of economic activity. Although definitely noteworthy, these economic initiatives should not be allowed to overshadow other state efforts, particularly on the social front. State interventions in this arena were equally—if not more—pervasive, with the state assuming a leading role in defining and inculcating in citizens what it deemed to be the appropriate social values to be subscribed to, the norms of public and private behavior, the languages spoken, and even citizens' outlooks on life (see e.g. Wilkinson 1988; Kuah 1990; Lingle 1996; Tamney 1996; Tremewan 1994).

In the literature examining Singapore's postcolonial development, these attempts at social engineering have been portrayed and understood in a variety of ways. Despite this diversity of opinion, however, it would be fair to suggest there is a broad consensus within discussions that these extensive social interventions were largely designed to sustain the process of rapid economic development then being pursued, as well as underpin the wider project of nation building. These social designs, in other words, were an effort to cultivate a distinct culture of developmentalism that would lend support to the economic and political initiatives simultaneously being implemented.

The precise contours of this culture of developmentalism may be variously defined. It appears, however, to have at least three key elements.

First, the culture insists on the subordination of the individual to the larger community or nation. Implicit within this is a surrender of individual rights and interests, as those of the community and nation take precedence and override those of individuals. This surrender and process of subordination should be understood in the broadest sense possible. At one level, it certainly involves political rights and interests. But it also goes much further than this to encompass even an individual's sense of social identity—and crucially, in a nation inhabited by a diversity of races and with a history of racial conflict, the individual's ethnicity. As part of this subordination process, unique and separate cultures, religions, languages, and values that fill individuals with a distinctive sense of identity are subsumed into a generic "Singaporeanness" and blurred. Individuals are—to use an oft-quoted term used by Lee Kuan Yew to describe this process—reduced to mere "digits," devoid of distinguishing characteristics (see e.g. Clammer 1985; Hill and Lian 1995; Tamney 1996).

Second, in tandem with this subordination to a broader social collective, the individual is also required to submit to an overriding national imperative of economic productivity. This preoccupation with productivity certainly manifests itself most strongly in the working environment, where citizens are continually exhorted to improve their performance and rise to new heights of efficiency. It is a logic, however, that is far reaching in its pervasiveness, going so far as to infect, in addition, wider social interaction in society and the very way citizens think. The overall conduct of citizen's lives is guided strongly by this calculus of efficiency, so much so that it is elevated to become the very raison d'etre of their existence. Striving to be the best and most efficient, and aspiring to ever higher levels of achievement, citizens are completely absorbed by the pursuit of economic development, much to the exclusion of anything else (Tamney 1996).

The third and final element in this culture of developmentalism involves the cultivation of a distinct nationalism and sense of national identity in citizens. In this, an attempt is made to distinguish Singapore and its citizens from regional neighbors by ascribing some universal traits that are supposedly quintessential and definitive of a unique Singapore character and ethos. In popular renditions, Singapore and Singaporeans are thus portrayed as rational, technocratic, and pragmatic, guided by reason rather than emotion and possessing a strong can-do attitude. Neighboring countries and citizens, by contrast, are variously described as emotive, unrealistic, unreasonable, and unpredictable, as well as lacking in initiative and drive. Through such sharp contrasts, a distinctive national identity is created affirming the "special" nature of Singaporeans and supportive of broader developmental goals. Crucially, it also establishes a significant "other," external to Singapore, comprising the nations and citizens in its immediate vicinity (see e.g. Yeoh and Willis 1999; Chua 1998, 2003; Ang and Stratton 1995).

To sum up this section, to complement its economic interventions, the state in Singapore also engaged in an extensive process of social engineering to create a culture of developmentalism to underpin its broader project of nation building. This culture was largely defined by three key elements: a subordination of the individual to the larger community or nation; the subordination of the individual to the pursuit of economic productivity; and finally, the cultivation of a nationalism that was heavily exclusive, affirming how "special" Singaporeans were, but excluding "others" in the immediate region. The following section will focus on how this culture of developmentalism informed the framing of criminality in Singapore.

The Construction of Criminality

According to John Clammer, crime in Singapore is "not just an assault on private property or the person." Nor is it simply a form of social "disorder" (1997: 142). In Singapore, crime takes on a far deeper meaning. It is "*ingratitude*, a perverse *unwillingness to co-operate* in bringing about the utopia that the government is so painstakingly building [and a] *foolishness* of refusing to accept a reality that everybody else can so clearly see" (145, emphasis added).

Given the centrality of the state in orchestrating the successful development of Singapore, the "ingratitude" Clammer refers to may be quite easily understood. As chief architect of the miracle that *is* Singapore, the ruling PAP believes the citizenry should be thankful for all the comforts it now enjoys—and while some dissension is tolerated—it should remain wholeheartedly supportive of the wider national project being pursued. Antisocial behavior in the form of criminal activity is likened to a spoiled child rebelling against well-to-do parents—a perhaps apt parallel given the highly paternalistic nature of the state in Singapore. It is an expression of ungratefulness, spurning the largesse that has so generously been made possible (see e.g. Heng and Devan 1991).

But that is not all there is to crime. Crime is also construed as an "unwillingness to co-operate" and a "foolishness of refusing to accept a reality." To understand why crime is posed in such terms, it may be useful to recall the culture of developmentalism discussed earlier. In many respects, the "reality" that is referred to here by Clammer is none other than a reality defined by this very culture of developmentalism. It is a reality that insists on the subordination of the individual to the whole; the relentless pursuit of economic productivity; the special and unique status of Singaporeans as rational beings guided wholly by reason. The "unwillingness to co-operate" is a refusal to submit to these requirements of the culture of developmentalism—the "reality" of life in contemporary Singapore as defined by the ruling PAP. The "foolishness," in turn, is a reckless disregard of this cultural imperative as an overarching given, resistance against which is ultimately futile.

Posed in these terms, crime is seen as a form of social deviance—a rebellion against and rejection of norms established by the culture of developmentalism. Bearing this in mind, it should not be surprising to see some specific themes figuring prominently in the portrayal and understanding of crime in Singapore. Though couched in different ways over time, these nevertheless have strong connections with the overarching culture of developmentalism, drawing on the central pillars of this culture to generate powerful images of criminality and the dangers posed to the nation.

First, criminality is often portrayed by both the government and Singaporean media as misguided attempts by individuals to rebel against the larger community or nation. In this guise, criminality is seen as an attempt to "reclaim" the individuality lost through the subordination of individuals to the larger collectivity. Typically, it is believed, these attempts involve potentially disruptive and destructive actions, both for the individuals concerned as well as the larger society. The catalogue of misdemeanors here is extensive and includes actions such as engaging in "alternative" lifestyles; experimenting with "alternative" forms of social organization; participation in "extreme" religious sects; and possibly most dangerous of all, the resuscitation of race, ethnicity, and religion as defining characteristics of individuals and groups. Such "extremism," it is suggested, erodes and distorts individuals' morals and values, setting them apart in their own society. In so doing, it upsets a delicate equilibrium and may potentially cause an unraveling of social order. Individuals engaging in such activity, as such, deserve censure and punishment.

Second, criminality is also seen as an attempt to avoid confronting the hard realities and facts of life. Posed in this manner, it is viewed particularly as a desperate attempt to escape the effort and responsibility of work, as well as the associated commitment to pursue productivity relentlessly. The "escapism" that is typically criminalized here may include the actions discussed in the previous paragraph. Hence, the pursuit of "alternative" lifestyles, rejecting the commercialism of life, and singular pursuit of economic development can equally be situated in this category of criminal activity. What is usually identified as gravest, however, is the escapism that is associated with drug consumption, which if left unchecked, could potentially undermine the strength of human resources in the country, compromising the pursuit of economic development. Drug abuse, moreover, could seriously erode the social fabric, creating tensions and stresses that could prove dysfunctional to the nation-building effort. Individuals connected with the drug trade, as such, should be viewed as threats to society as a whole and dealt with accordingly.

Third, criminality is seen as something typically committed by "outsiders." Implicit in this understanding of criminality is a notion that Singaporeans are somehow above committing crime, given their rationality, pragmatism, and other positive attributes. As a desperate act, crime is an activity that only the emotive and weak succumb to, and by definition, these are traits that Singaporeans do not possess. Foreigners, by implication, must be primarily responsible for such acts. On the occasion such crimes are actually committed by Singaporeans, this treatment of crime is rendered problematic. In such circumstances, however, attention is typically then focused on the characteristics, personal history, and innate attributes of the individuals concerned in order to highlight any deficiencies. In the course of doing so, it is implicitly suggested such individuals are atypical low-achievers suffering some form of infirmity, dependence, or affliction. With perpetrators thus cast as somehow aberrant and *un*-Singaporean, the notion of crime being committed primarily by "outsiders" remains intact.

In conclusion, the framing of criminality in Singapore largely rests on a notion of crime as social deviance, with criminal activity seen as a rebellion against norms of behavior established by an overarching culture of developmentalism. The next section will focus on how capital punishment has been used in the past to enforce such norms and entrench this culture of developmentalism.

Criminality, Punishment, and the Culture of Developmentalism

Since crime is perceived as a form of deviance involving the rejection of norms pivotal to the developmental effort, its occurrence in Singapore is viewed as a matter of grave concern. As John Clammer has insightfully pointed out, crime is considered "the first sign of the unraveling of the carefully constructed and managed social fabric of Singapore" (1997: 145); an indication that society is well on the slippery slope of succumbing to "the dark forces of chaos lying just beyond the tightly maintained boundaries of the state" (142). Thus

posed as a clear and present danger to order within Singapore, it logically follows that crime must be dealt with severely and in a decidedly uncompromis-
ing fashion: "like a germ or a virus [crime] must be stamped out before it begins to infect even wider ranges of the social order" (ibid.).

As David Garland (2001) notes, it has only been lately that a shift from a re-
habilitative to retributive system of punishment has occurred in countries such
as the United States and United Kingdom. In Singapore, however, in determined efforts to "stamp out" crime, punishment has historically always tended
to be punitive and retributive in orientation. High penalties are typically imposed for even minor transgressions in order to create a strong deterrent, making an example of those convicted and punished to serve as a warning to others. Sentencing, in addition, also exhibits a distinctly vengeful dimension,
seeking some form of redress on the part of victims as well as society as a
whole, for the wrongdoings that have been committed. In this retributive
mode, moreover, there is a clearly discernible strand in thinking that punishment should inflict some form of pain or discomfort on those convicted, as a
sign such retribution has indeed been exacted.

The infliction of such pain is achieved through an extensive array of punishments. By far the most frequently utilized are the monetary fines imposed
for transgressions ranging from the petty (jaywalking, littering, etc.) to the
more serious. The imposition of such monetary penalties—involving the forfeiture of monetary resources or income by the convicted—is seen as inflicting
a form of financial or material pain, condemning the convicted to a form of financial penury, transient as this may be. Imprisonment is yet another device
frequently resorted to. As a forfeiture of liberty, this inflicts a different type of
pain—isolation and the denial of social interaction—which, together with the
harsh conditions of internment, combine to exact a heavy toll on the convicted.
Discussion of criminal punishment in Singapore would not be complete without mention of caning—a punishment where actual physical pain is inflicted.
In this form of punishment, the convicted is strapped to a wooden trestle and
caned across the buttocks with a four-foot rattan rod. As graphically recalled by
those suffering this punishment, this is an excruciating experience, and one it
might be added, that results in the permanent scarring of the individual.

Last but not least, it should also be mentioned that in conjunction with all
the above, the sentencing of individuals in Singapore is also accompanied by an

extensive ritual of public shaming and humiliation. This practice, of course, also exists in other countries (Garland 2001). In Singapore, however, it assumes highly intrusive dimensions, with few parallels in the world. The convicted are subjected to intense media scrutiny, with personal details, photographs, and the minutiae of their lives paraded in public, together with graphic and detailed coverage of the crimes they have been found guilty of. As can well be imagined, this is an immensely stressful experience for those sentenced, and results in tremendous emotional and psychological distress (see e.g. Wilkinson 1988; Tremewan 1994; Tamney 1996).

Capital punishment, which entails the forfeiture of life itself, represents perhaps the ultimate pain that can be inflicted in this overall scheme of punitive and retributive punishment. In keeping with its British colonial heritage, execution is by way of hanging in Singapore, within the walls of the notorious Changi Prison. As in other countries and contexts where capital punishment is practiced, much may be read into the imposition of the death penalty upon an accused. In the light of the foregoing discussion on Singapore, however, the death sentence assumes significance in one special regard. Its pronouncement in effect signals a particular individual is unfit to be a member of civilized Singapore society. Perhaps more than that, the individual is designated as posing a serious enough threat that mere incarceration will not suffice. He or she must be eliminated entirely.

Precisely how an accused poses a threat, of course, is something that is very much socially constructed. Thus, in Singapore, though the crime committed may on the surface "fit" the punishment imposed (e.g., murder), the crime undergoes further reification and is given an additional twist such that it speaks to wider official concerns and anxieties. Given the developmentalist orientation of the state, these latter, unsurprisingly, are intimately connected with the enforcement of behavioral norms and patterns conducive to accelerated economic development in Singapore—in short, the culture of developmentalism previously sketched. It is quite normal, therefore, to see in official and popular commentaries on the death penalty, a grander story or narrative being woven in support of this culture of developmentalism. A parable is constructed, extolling the virtues of the culture, but also, warning that transgressions will invoke the ultimate penalty—death.

This is perhaps most clearly illustrated by cases involving the trafficking of

drugs. In official eyes, this is a heinous crime causing the pollution of bodies
with debilitating consequences. At a purely individual level, therefore, the seriousness of the crime—by effectively destroying a life—does appear to deserve
an equally stiff response in the shape of capital punishment. It is interesting,
however, that the justification for the death penalty goes one step further. In
particular, attention is drawn to the wider social implications of drug addiction
and trafficking, and the threats to society these pose. What is fascinating is that
in the construction of these threats, the deleterious impact addiction and trafficking have on matters economic seems to be heavily emphasized. Thus, for
addicts, it is suggested that with "the drug exerting a strong hold over his life, he
will not have the desire or will to pursue *worthwhile* interests" (Central Narcotics Bureau 2003, emphasis added). By this, of course, is meant *economically*
worthwhile interests, such as gainful employment, responsibility, and a commitment to constant improvement—the embrace of the culture of developmentalism. Further, it is suggested the crime carries distinct implications for
economic efficiency. As the Central Narcotics Bureau goes on to point out:
"Drug abuse inflicts a high *cost* on society as a whole. The Government has to
expend much effort and money to treat and rehabilitate addicts. *The number of
productive man-hours lost and the opportunity cost involved are enormous*" (ibid.,
emphasis added). The story about drug addiction and trafficking in Singapore
thus carries a much wider message. While definitely concerned with the most
immediate impacts of addiction and trafficking, it also speaks to concerns that
an escapist drug culture will erode the productionist ethic of the nation and
compromise the pursuit of economic efficiency. As a direct challenge to the culture of developmentalism as well as the wider nation-building project it under-
pins, the crime cannot be tolerated. As the Central Narcotics Bureau emphatically declares: "As *human resource* [*sic*] is Singapore's most precious asset, we
cannot allow drugs to take hold of our society. It is thus important to reinforce
the national consensus of zero tolerance towards drug abuse" (ibid., emphasis
added). An essential aspect of this "national consensus of zero tolerance," of
course, is the death penalty.

The significance of drugs, however, extends beyond its implications for productivity within the nation. It also bears relevance to another key pillar in the
culture of developmentalism—the cultivation of a unique Singaporean identity

and nationalism, juxtaposed against an "other" comprising peoples and nations in the immediate region. As it has been pointed out before, the majority of those who have been executed in Singapore for drug offences have been foreign nationals from the surrounding region (see e.g. *Economist* 1999). Of the 174 executions recorded by Amnesty International (2004) between 1993 and 2003, 93 were foreigners, primarily migrant workers. Another part of the story about drug trafficking, as such, relates to notions that crime is committed by "others," thereby affirming the special qualities and even superiority of Singaporeans. It is these "others," characterized by weakness or driven by a sense of malevolence against Singapore's achievements—"the dark forces waiting just outside the charmed circle of Singapore's boundaries" (Clammer 1997: 143)—who are largely to be blamed and should be punished. As "saboteurs" of the Singapore project, they too deserve the harshest punishment possible—death.

There have, of course, been other instances where this "other" has been identified, and in conjunction with capital punishment, utilized in the construction of a distinctly Singaporean identity. In this respect, one recent episode that drew considerable attention was the execution of a Filipino domestic worker, Flor Contemplacion, in 1995 (see e.g. Hilsdon 2000; Mules 1999). Contemplacion was hanged for the murder of another Filipino maid and the three-year-old Singaporean child under the latter's care. In her trial as well as in the accompanying popular reportage, much was made of her mental and emotional instability, her religiosity and superstition, irrationality, as well as her greed and envy (see e.g. Singapore High Court 1994). Thus, although Contemplacion was convicted and sentenced for the murders committed, her story was turned into something larger, providing a commentary on how Singaporeans were substantially different from "others." Looked at in this light, the execution of Contemplacion definitely served in the first instance as a warning to the sizable foreign worker community in Singapore that their eccentricities, weaknesses, and other *un*-Singaporean traits would not be tolerated. But an equally important part of the message in public commentaries was directed at Singaporeans themselves. Contemplacion's execution was a reminder of the dangers of succumbing to "backwardness." It signaled very emphatically the state's intolerance of such attributes that ran counter to Singaporean qualities supportive of the developmental effort.

Conclusion

In 2005, Singapore will be celebrating the fortieth anniversary of its emergence as an independent republic. There seems little doubt that its future existence is now assured, in contrast to the turbulent times of its birth. As a nation, it has made remarkable progress, in terms of both its material wealth and achievements and its social and political cohesion. Singapore is well on its way toward maturity, in nearly every sense of the word.

It is therefore reasonable to ask whether we can expect any fundamental change in the still highly authoritarian social and political order in the nation. On the surface, there are grounds to expect this may be forthcoming. Greater material wealth and security, combined with rising social and political expectations on the part of a better educated citizenry—all concomitant results of successful development—may conspire to push change along, delivering a more liberal order. With respect to the subject matter of this chapter—crime and capital punishment in Singapore—an optimistic reading of the future may even go so far as to foresee some relaxation in the understanding of crime and a movement away from the use of capital punishment.

In the light of the foregoing discussion, however, it may be suggested that these expectations are perhaps misplaced and overly optimistic. Capital punishment, and indeed, the entire system of criminal justice in Singapore, is oriented toward the preservation of order and the enforcement of a culture of developmentalism seeking to sustain the process of development and nation building. Although marginal changes are certainly possible, there exist definite limits to change under present circumstances. Indeed, to the extent that development and nation building remain the primary priorities under the prevailing political order, any significant relaxation in the approach to crime and its punishment will be most unlikely.

Hence, despite outward signs of dynamism, change, and progress, in terms of its social policies toward crime and punishment, little can realistically be expected to change in Singapore. In this sense, Clammer may be absolutely right in pointing out that Singapore, paradoxically, "is in many ways a *fossil*, despite, or disguised by, its economic dynamism and constant state of physical reconstruction" (1997: 150, emphasis added). Therein, however, lies a danger. For the only way it can continue to exist in such an ossified form is if a "society of fear" and paranoia is continually cultivated, buttressed by an extensive apparatus of control. As Clammer indicates, this may already exist, with the state effectively having "institutionalized the whole population, if not in a prison then certainly in a gigantic school: medicalized, sanitized and warned constantly of the degeneracy flourishing outside the walls and symbolized by the deviants within, those who will not 'play the game' and who consequently must be exposed, shamed and punished" (ibid.). Whether this is sustainable in the long run is an open question.

References

Amnesty International (2003) "Amnesty International Report 2003—Singapore," www.amnesty.org (accessed 27 November 2003).

Amnesty International (2004) "Singapore—The Death Penalty: A Hidden Toll of Executions," http://web.amnesty.org/library/Index/ENGASA360012004 (accessed 27 November 2003).

Ang, Ien, and Jon Stratton (1995) "The Singapore Way of Multiculturalism: Western Concepts/Asian Cultures," 10 *Sojourn: Journal of Social Issues in Southeast Asia* 65–89.

Central Narcotics Bureau, Singapore (2003) "Frequently Asked Questions About Drugs," http://www4.gov.sg/mha/cnb/education/faq.html#1 (accessed 27 November 2003).

Chan, Heng Chee (1971) *Singapore: The Politics of Survival 1965–71.* Singapore: Oxford University Press.

Chua, Beng Huat (1998) "Culture, Multiracialism and National Identity in Singapore," in Kuan-Hsing Chen, ed., *Trajectories: Inter-Asia Cultural Studies.* London: Routledge.

Chua, Beng Huat (2003) "'Multiculturalism in Singapore: An Instrument of Social Control," 44 *Race and Class* 58–77.

Clammer, John (1985) *Singapore: Ideology, Society, Culture.* Singapore: Chopmen.

Clammer, John (1997) "Framing the Other: Criminality, Social Exclusion and Social Engineering in Developing Singapore," 31 (December) *Social Policy and Administration* 136–53.

Deyo, Fred (1981) *Dependent Development and Industrial Order: An Asian Case Study.* New York: Praeger.

Deyo, Fred, ed. (1987) *The Political Economy of the New Asian Industrialism.* Ithaca, NY: Cornell University Press.

Economist (1999) "Singapore: World Execution Capital," 3–9 April: 25.

Garland, David W. (2001) *The Culture of Control: Crime and Social Order in Contemporary Society.* Oxford: Oxford University Press.

Heng, Geraldine, and Janadas Devan (1991) "State Fatherhood: The Politics of Nationalism, Sexuality, and Race in Singapore," in A. Parker, M. Russo, D. Sommer, and P. Yaeger, eds., *Nationalisms and Sexualities*. New York: Routledge.

Hill, Michael, and Kwen Fee Lian (1995) *The Politics of Nation Building and Citizenship in Singapore*. New York: Routledge.

Hilsdon, Anne-Marie (2000) "The Contemplacion Fiasco: The Hanging of a Filipino Domestic Worker in Singapore," in A.-M. Hilsdon, M. MacIntyre, V. Mackie, and M. Stivens, eds., *Human Rights and Gender Politics: Asia-Pacific Perspectives*. London: Routledge.

Huff, W. G. (1994) *The Economic Growth of Singapore: Trade and Development in the Twentieth Century*. Cambridge: Cambridge University Press.

Huff, W. G. (1995) "What Is the Singapore Model of Economic Development?," 19 *Cambridge Journal of Economics* 735–59.

Kuah, Khun Eng (1990) "Confucian Ideology and Social Engineering in Singapore," 20 *Journal of Contemporary Asia* 371–83.

Lingle, Christopher (1996) *Singapore's Authoritarian Capitalism: Asian Values, Free Market Illusions and Political Dependency*. Barcelona: Edicions Sirocco.

Low, Linda (1998) *The Political Economy of a City-State: Government-Made Singapore*. Singapore: Oxford University Press.

Ministry of Home Affairs, Singapore (2004) "Comments by Spokesman on Amnesty International's Criticism of Singapore's Use of the Death Penalty," 16 January.

Mules, Warwick (1999) "Globalizing Discourses: The Flor Contemplacion Affair," in P. G. L. Chew and A. Kramer-Dahl, eds., *Reading Culture: Textual Practices in Singapore*. Singapore: Times Academic Press.

Perry, Martin, Lily Kong, and Brenda Yeoh (1997) *Singapore: A Developmental City State*. Chichester: Wiley.

Rodan, Garry (1989) *The Political Economy of Singapore's Industrialization: Nation State and International Capital*. London: Macmillan.

Singapore High Court (1994) "Public Prosecutor vs. Flor Contemplacion, Judgment by Justice T. S. Sinnathuray," http://www.geocities.com/law4u2003/flor.htm (accessed 27 November 2003).

Tamney, Joseph (1996) *The Struggle Over Singapore's Soul: Western Modernization and Asian Culture*. New York: Walter de Gruyter.

Think Centre (Singapore) (2004) "Govt Criticized AI's Report on Death Penalty: J. B. Jeyaretnam Comments," http://www.thinkcentre.org/article.cfm?ArticleID=2288 (accessed 27 November 2003).

Tremewan, Christopher (1994) *The Political Economy of Social Control in Singapore*. New York: St. Martin's Press.

Wade, Robert (1990) *Governing the Market: Economic Theory and the Role of Government in East Asian Industrialization*. Princeton, NJ: Princeton University Press.

Wilkinson, Barry (1988) "Social Engineering in Singapore," 18 *Journal of Contemporary Asia* 165–88.

Yeoh, Brenda, and Katie Willis (1999) "'Heart' and 'Wing', Nation and Diaspora: Gendered Discourses in Singapore's Regionalization Process," 6 (December) *Gender, Place and Culture* 355–72.

CHAPTER FIFTEEN

Ending State Killing in South Korea

Challenging the Asian Capital Punishment Status Quo

SANGMIN BAE

In stark contrast to the worldwide trend toward the abolition of capital punishment, its practice remains most entrenched in Asia, where over 90 percent of all executions in the world take place. China is the world leader in the frequent and extensive use of the ultimate sanction. This country alone regularly accounts for more executions than the rest of the world combined, and applies the death penalty to as many as seventy crimes—ranging from counterrevolutionary sabotage to selling a panda skin, and from tax evasion to murder. The intentional spreading of the SARS virus was recently added to the list of capital crimes (*Xinhua News*, May 18, 2003). Although the government guidelines reserve the death sentence for extreme cases only, provincial courts apply it massively and inconsistently and without much regard for due process. Since the "Strike Hard" anticrime campaign was launched in April 2001, in particular, Chinese authorities have dramatically escalated the use of the death penalty. The official number of executions is a tightly held state secret each year. Yet Amnesty International reported that it had been able to determine 1,060 executions in China in 2002 and 2,468 the year before, with the actual figure believed to be much higher (Amnesty International 2002a, 2003).

China's enthusiasm for capital punishment finds an echo in other East Asian countries. After a three-year hiatus from 1990 to 1992, Japan has executed several people every year for the past decade. Executions took place in secrecy, usually when the Japanese Diet (parliament) was in recess, in order to avoid parliamentary debate and publicity. Taiwan has been one of the top ten executioners over the years: thirty-eight criminals were executed in 1997, thirty-two in 1998, twenty-four in 1999, and seventeen in 2000, which amounts to more executions per capita than in the United States despite a decrease in the number of executions in recent years (Death Penalty Issue Research Group 2000).[1] Singapore administers mandatory death sentences for murder, treason, firearm offenses, and drug trafficking. Despite a relatively low crime rate compared with other Asian nations, the use of the death penalty has increased for the past few years: twenty-one in 2000, twenty-seven in 2001, twenty-eight in 2002, and up to eighty in the first half of 2003, giving the small city-state by far the highest per capita rate of executions in the world (Agence France Presse 2003). According to a Singapore representative to the United Nations, the maintenance of capital punishment for the purpose of controlling drug trafficking is "an important precondition for the preservation of human dignity and the promotion and enjoyment of other human rights," and thereby "capital punishment itself is not a human rights issue" (UN Doc. A/C.3/49/SR.33, 6–7, and /SR.57, 4).[2] The ongoing executions in Asia confirm that the death penalty is far from dying out and the road that leads in the direction of complete abolition is still quite long.

Given the death penalty records in East Asia, the Republic of Korea (South Korea)[3] appears to have been taking a different path from its neighbors over the past few years, in terms of both the social attitude surrounding the death penalty and its actual practice. If Schabas (1998) is right in saying that the abolition of capital punishment is "generally considered to be an important element in democratic development for states for breaking with a past characterized by terror, injustice and repression," does the change in the death penalty practice in Korea have much to do with its democratic progress? In response to this question, two major issues are addressed in this chapter: First, the chapter begins with a brief overview of the current status of capital punishment in Korea. Second, in light of the persistent use of death sentences (despite the suspension of the actual executions), the chapter proposes a few reasons why Korea did not commit itself to abolishing the death penalty in a timely manner.

Efforts to Abolish Capital Punishment from Above

No death row inmate has been executed since President Kim Dae-Jung came to power in 1998, and thirteen death sentences have been commuted to life imprisonment in three separate special amnesties. Although a number of problems in the area of human rights remained unsolved during Kim's tenure from 1998 to 2002, the general improvement in human rights was commended by international and domestic human rights groups (Asian Human Rights Commission 2001; UN Economic and Social Council 2001; Amnesty International 2002b). The establishment of both the Presidential Truth Commission on Suspicious Deaths and the National Human Rights Commission was seen as an important step in increasing human rights protection and awareness in Korea.

Before he was elected, President Kim stated in an interview with the Seoul Catholic archdiocesan weekly *Pyonghwa Shinmun* (July 20, 1997) that the nation should gradually phase out capital punishment. Among his reasons were that it had proved to be ineffective in preventing crimes, and that the very existence of state killing of citizens contributed to the low value Koreans appear to place on human dignity and physical integrity. Kim's personal background, as a Roman Catholic and as someone who himself languished on death row under the military government, perhaps strengthened his belief in the abolitionist cause.

President Kim also took a different stance with regard to the cultural constraints of human rights. When leaders in many other Asian countries—notably Lee Kuan Yew of Singapore—advocated "Asian values," challenging international human rights norms as a Western ideological imposition, Kim staked out a position defending the universality of human rights (Zakaria 1994; Kim 1994; Han 1998; Lee 1998). In addition to defending the universal attribute of human rights, he has been very forthcoming regarding the internationally promoted human rights norm against state killing.

Along with the president's unwillingness to execute, the legislators also played a role in maintaining the moratorium status on the death penalty. A group of legislators jointly drafted a bill to abolish the death penalty that was submitted to the National Assembly in 1999 and 2001. Although both attempts failed because the bill was neither reviewed nor approved in the Legislative and Judiciary Committee before the end of its term, the proposal of the bills itself drew public attention. The legislators shared the view that it is a contradiction to take the life of a criminal in the name of justice, that it is at odds with the idea of human dignity and the right to life guaranteed by the Constitution. The following remark of a leading legislator indicates that the penal discourse has been reshaped in Korea. According to Chyung Dai-chul, who took the lead in introducing the anti–capital punishment bill in the National Assembly: "We now desire to abolish a system that allows one human being to take away the life of another in the name of law and, thus, effectuate a renewed sense of respect for life and human rights in this society."[4]

The perception of the death penalty system as a key state machinery for protecting national security from outside aggression changed to a perception of the system as a violation of basic human rights, at least at the elite level. In a seminar on the abolition of the death penalty, organized by the Parliamentary Assembly of the Council of Europe (PACE), held in the Japanese Diet in May 2002, Chyung Dai-chul stated that state executions in South Korea should be abandoned mainly because the abolition of capital punishment was a global trend, a hundred nations around the world having so far pursued abolition in their legal systems.[5] To abolish capital punishment, he implied, was to join an international human rights project.

Abolitionist Movements from Below

It has been argued that grassroots support does not seem to be a necessary condition for abolition (Hood 1996; Zimring and Hawkins 1986). At least this was not the case for Europe, where pro–capital punishment sentiment remained relatively high at the time of abolition. However, the fact that the majority of the general public support capital punishment does not necessarily mean that the anti–capital punishment movement stays underdeveloped. For instance, anti–capital punishment organizations in South Africa played a decisive role in expediting the process of abolitionism when the majority of the public backed the retention of capital punishment, invoking the unprecedented growth of violent crime in the postapartheid era (Abugre 1994; Mihalik 1991; van Rooyen 1993). In Korea, on the other hand, anti–death penalty activism remains immature compared to other areas in which human rights movements are active and well networked among civil groups. It is a mystery why no secular human rights groups—with the exception of Amnesty International's South Korean section—have capital punishment on their agenda.

The major human rights groups of Korea, such as the Citizen's Solidarity for Human Rights and Sarangbang Group for Human Rights, state that they oppose the death penalty because its system violates basic human dignity.[6] People's Solidarity for Participatory Democracy, a prominent civic group, also opposes capital punishment, arguing that it is not an effective deterrent (*Korea Herald* December 4, 2001). Except for their verbal opposition to the death penalty, however, this issue was never included in their campaign list. Failing to see the death penalty as one human rights violation among many that must be addressed, human rights groups did not contribute to placing the death penalty issues in public forums or establish horizontal networks to influence state penal policies. Leaders of some of the human rights civil groups openly stated that the death penalty agenda was not their priority.[7] The newly established National Human Rights Commission, the most prestigious human rights body in Korea, confessed that the death penalty was not discussed during the whole of the first year following its inauguration. When Amnesty International Korea asked for the Commission's stance on the death penalty system, the answer from this most influential Commission was "there is no official position about that issue."[8]

Two possible reasons for lack of anti–death penalty activism among human rights groups are the following: First, the death penalty, from the perspective of human rights groups, is very likely to be banned in Korea in a few years anyway so that extra work toward this outcome is unnecessary.[9] Second, human rights groups do not seem to wish to be involved in an issue most Koreans have strong reservations about. Since many Korean civic groups are still young and inexperienced, they prefer, perhaps until they feel they are entirely established, an agenda the public would widely support. When the abolition of the death penalty does not appear to be "the will of the people," it is considered risky for civil groups, let alone the political leadership, to work on this.

Although there was no demand for the reform of the death penalty from secular human rights groups, religious groups have so far led the anti–death penalty movement in Korea. There is no single dominant religion in South Korea. Shamanism, Buddhism, Confucianism, and Christianity coexist peacefully in Korea, "one of the most religiously pluralistic countries in the world" (A.

Kim 2000). Whereas Confucianism in Korea remains a set of overarching ethical codes rather than a religion, Buddhism, Protestantism, and Catholicism are
considered the three major religions. A plethora of churches and temples are
scattered across the nation. A foreign observer describes the Korean scenery as
follows: "Large Christian churches may be found in any city or town. At night,
one may look into a skyline and see numerous neon crosses lighting the night
sky in a single vista. . . . Buddhist temples are also abundant. Most neighbor-
hoods have at least one small temple; however, ancient temples, dating as far
back as the ninth century, may be found in many prefectural and national
parks" (Dwyer).

Religious groups are very important opinion leaders in Korean society. With
its social influence, the Catholic community, especially the Korean Bishops'
Committee for Justice and Peace, and the Social Correction Apostolate Committee of Seoul, plays a key role in raising public awareness on the death
penalty. Traditionally, Korean Christianity has greatly influenced the ousting of
the military rulers by putting a great deal of pressure on dictators to respect human rights and hold democratic elections. It is not an exaggeration that the
Catholic Church, during a time of fierce repression, was the only voice raised
on behalf of freedom and democracy. Myongdong Cathedral, the spiritual center of Catholicism located in downtown Seoul, often acted as a staging area for
protests and demonstrations against large corporations or the government.

The Catholic Church's activities for abolition included appealing to the public by releasing a petition titled "Cherish Life by Abolishing Capital Punishment," in December 1999, and conducting a campaign to collect signatures.
With the start of the "Year of Jubilee" in 2000, the Korean Catholic Church
named that year the "Year of Capital Punishment Abolition." Public response to
the campaign was fairly good, with more than 100,000 signatures within a year,
before other religious groups were asked to join the effort (*Chosun Ilbo*, May 24,
2001). In addition, the Catholic Church organized several symposiums on capital punishment, distributed videos and posters related to the death penalty,
and sent a petition calling for abolition of the death penalty to the United Nations (*Hankyoreh*, December 31, 2002).

The Catholic Church embraced other religious communities, mostly Protes-
tant, Buddhist, and Won Buddhist, in the abolitionist cause, and launched a nationwide coalition of major religious groups at the end of 2000. The "Panreli-

gious Anti–Death Penalty Campaign" aimed to enhance public support as well as lobby more efficiently for the repeal of death statutes. In their statement, the leaders of the coalition pointed out: "All life is sacred, including the lives of criminals who have committed heinous crimes. The campaign is inevitable as capital punishment undermines human dignity by taking state revenge on someone for their past mistakes" (*Chosun Ilbo*, January 26, 2001). As an alternative to what they called brutal executions, they proposed life imprisonment without parole should rehabilitation be unsuccessful. Their religious faith provided the most important source of the abolitionist sentiment, putting them on the frontline of the Korean abolitionist movement. Their past as "resistance groups" for many years before Korea's democratization meant that they were well trained to take the initiative to call for abolition of capital punishment, which other secular human rights groups have collectively ignored.

The abolition endeavor among religious groups as well as some legislators stimulated public debate on an issue which until recently had been almost entirely neglected in Korea. It is apparent that public attitudes toward capital punishment have become more relaxed. According to a nationwide survey co-conducted by a major Korean newspaper, *Chosun Ilbo,* and a mobile research institute, Mbizon, in November 2001, the number of South Koreans against the death penalty has grown: 36 percent of 838 respondents over age twenty opposed capital punishment, compared with 34 percent in 1999 and 20 percent in 1994 (*Korea Herald*, December 4, 2001). Similar results are found in other opinion polls. In a telephone survey in August 2002 conducted by Korea Survey Research Organization, 54.3 percent favored capital punishment, whereas 45.3 percent were against it and 0.3 percent did not respond. When the same questions were asked in May 1992, 66.5 percent favored capital punishment, while only 20.2 percent opposed it, and 13.3 percent had no opinion on the subject (Chyung 2002: 11). Similarly, Gallup Korea's survey shows that public opinion against capital punishment has increased over time from 20 percent in 1994 to 31.3 percent in 2001 and to 40.1 percent in 2003. Meanwhile, the number of people in favor of capital punishment dropped: 70 percent in 1994; 54.6 percent in 2001; and 52.3 percent in 2003 (Gallup Korea 2003).

Pro–death penalty public sentiment in South Korea grew suddenly after three consecutive gruesome murders took place in June 2003, and countless Internet articles called for immediate executions of death row prisoners. It happens worldwide that polls taken at the time of well-publicized violent crimes show a peak in support for capital punishment, perhaps distorting the true figures or perhaps suggesting that public support for the death penalty waxes and wanes in response to arbitrary events. Although supporters of capital punishment still form a majority in Korean society, a growing number favor its abolition. The efforts of the abolitionists for the past decade to put the death penalty on the social and political agenda seem to exert an influence on the people's views toward capital punishment. Given that one of the salient traits of sociopolitical culture in Korea is an orientation toward authoritarian values, this change seems significant.

Why Not Abolition Right Now?

Despite the various democratic reforms and institutional changes since the late 1980s, the penal system remained the same as before. Death sentences for ordinary or political crimes were imposed on a regular basis, whereas a succession of political events radically reshaped the political power structure of the democratically elected governments. For about a decade between 1987, the moment South Korea formally entered a new stage of democratic transition, and 1998, the last year executions were carried out, 101 people were put to death. During the Sixth Republic in Korea (1988–92), President Roh Tae Woo, the first democratically elected president, had thirty-nine people judicially killed. The Seventh Republic (1993–97) of Kim Young Sam, the country's first truly civilian leader since 1961, endorsed fifty-seven executions, including the execution of twenty-three convicts in a single day, which was the worst mass hanging in one day in the past twenty years.[10]

Though President Kim Dae-Jung's Eighth Republic (1998–2002) appeared very different from its predecessors in that it did not allow any prisoners to be put to death, Kim never officially addressed the topic let alone attempted to do anything for abolition during his presidency. Given that Korea's political institutions still remain shallow and immature, even though its democracy is in some minimal way consolidated (Im 2000: 32–35; Diamond and Kim 2000: 2), the temporary halting of executions can be lifted any time in accordance with a change in the political configuration. In this regard, it is vital to emphasize that a moratorium is simply a stage on the road to full abolition. A moratorium can never be an end in itself.

At least four arguments can be raised in explaining why the death penalty has not been abolished as soon as might be expected in democratic South Korea: (1) principal cultural values; (2) lack of regional enforcement; (3) authoritarian legacy; (4) contradiction of democracy.

The Impact of Cultural Values

Confucianism has been considered one of the central cultural traditions in East Asia. In spite of wide debates on the compatibility of Confucianism and democracy (Fukuyama 1995, 1997; Howard 1993; Huntington 1993; Kim 1997; Pollis 1996; Renteln 1990; Shils 1996), it is fair to say that Confucian values, placing a high value on harmony, consensus, order, and respect for hierarchy, were preferred over any central tenets of pluralist democracy such as individual freedom of expression, self-determination, disagreement, and competition.

In Korea, conformity, compliance with authority, and acceptance of a hierarchical social order have long characterized the patterns of political socialization, as was the case in neighboring countries. Importantly, the emphasis on the hierarchical social order helped shape the criminal justice system. The institutions of penalty were a major element in a generalized and concerted disciplinary strategy based on the ideological tenets of order and hierarchy. The state, like the head of the household, had supreme authority and control over the rest of its members. In the event of noncompliance, a variety of sanctions were enforced ranging from verbal warnings, ostracism, and expulsion from communities, to corporal punishment such as the death penalty. Ethical codes and punishment provided a regulatory and normative framework in which citizens respected politics of hierarchy. Punishment functioned as a weapon of the administration against those who were guilty of circumventing societal norms (Steinberg 2000: 218). Erich Fromm's reflection on the father's image of state-imposed killing is very relevant to this paternalistic society:

> The central factor in the father's power is the power to castrate, to cause serious bodily injury. It is no accident that the kaiser or the president is legally empowered to pardon those sentenced to death, that he therefore is allowed to make the final judgment about life or death. He is the symbolic embodiment of paternal authority, and

he proves himself as such through his right to decide about life and death. (2000 [1930]: 126)

Political leaders continued to propagate the state's dominant cultural ideology, which was manifested in a variety of ways, from the way they excused themselves from developing social policies for the elderly (Palley 1992) to the way they persisted in harsh punishment toward wrongdoers. For example, politicians promoted a cardinal virtue of the Confucian ethical and relational system, which requires the son's obligation and responsibility for his parents, for the purpose of minimizing a social welfare package for the elderly. The state's rhetoric was: "Government social service programs to assist the elderly would substitute for family care and, thus, undermine the Confucian culture" (Palley 1992: 796). The state's attitude might well entail social sanctions on those neglecting the "obligations" and family responsibilities. Unlike the way imperial Britain resolved a number of economic crises in the 1890s (i.e., expanding the range of penal sanctions while introducing a mass of social welfare legislation [Garland 1985]), penalty and welfare did not seem complementary strategies in Korea.

More important than the controversy as to whether the Confucian culture and democracy/human rights are compatible is the question whether, or to what extent, a certain group of people prefers to have a cultural status quo. Again, in order to justify or maintain the underdeveloped social welfare programs for the elderly, Korean political leaders emphasized the traditional family system, which holds the eldest son responsible for the care of his own parents. Yet Confucian virtues can be interpreted in a different way, which would argue for strong government intervention on behalf citizens' well-being: "This [Confucian] teaching is a political philosophy that emphasizes that role of government and stresses the ruling elite's moral obligation to strive to bring about peace under heaven (*pingtianxia*)" (Kim 1994: 195).

Under the impact of technological development, economic change, and social transformation, no culture remains the same. At the least, the traditional Confucian value of hierarchy has been challenged in Korea. The increase in juvenile delinquency perhaps indicates that the enforced cultural norms do not seem to reach some youths. Koreans are "no longer exclusively committed to the Confucian ethos extolling the virtues of authoritarian rule" (Shin and Shyu 1997: 117).

No Regional Human Rights Mechanism

Asia is the only continent with no regional human rights enforcement agency, and thus Korea has been relatively immune from direct influence of the international human rights injunctions against capital punishment. Except for the resolution of the Strasbourg-based European Parliament urging the abolition of capital punishment in Japan, South Korea, and Taiwan (European Parliament 2002; Chu 2002), Asia has never experienced significant peer group pressure toward advancing the abolitionist cause. In this regard, it is interesting how the European Union perceives "Asian values" on the issue of capital punishment. A member of the Labour Party of the European Parliament remarked in the 2002 session that "there is no Asian way to the rights of man. There is a universal way to the rights of man and democracy, and to win over the camp of the pro-abolition countries, of countries as important as Japan, South Korea and Taiwan, is essential to uphold the universal nature of the rights of man."

The Shadow of the Past

Given the geopolitical situation of Korea, the fear of (alleged) communist subversion provided the authoritarian governments with many excuses to deploy their forces against antigovernment protests. The dominant ideology had a profound impact on the promulgation and development of the legal apparatus. More than half of those executed up to 1987 had violated the National Security Law, the Anti-Communism Law, and the Special Law for Safeguarding the Nation. The various security-related legal measures meant that state killings occurred largely within the judicial framework. As Gibney remarked, the human rights situation in Korea under the authoritarian governments was a "legalized lawlessness," because "repression was justified by law, wherever possible." The authoritarian presidents knew how to keep up the appearance of a constitutional democracy (1992: 68).

Such times of political and social upheaval enhanced the role of cultural ideology such as social hierarchy, unanimous consent, and benevolent paternalism in shaping national consciousness. Like in the Confucian family system, where individual interests were sacrificed in the interests of the family as a whole, the Korean authorities emphasized that an essential obligation of all the people was to subordinate themselves to the state for its survival. For the survival of the nation, the most coercive judicial measure was considered a necessary evil. The Korean authoritarian regimes used the rhetoric of national security in urging coercive punishment as a rationale for restrictions on individual rights.[11]

The cultural values of social hierarchy and group orientation were also represented in the realm of labor relations. The transition from an agrarian to an industrialized society relied heavily on cheap labor and high productivity. Following the hierarchical philosophy, disputes against superiors were strongly discouraged. The trade union rights and the right to strike were held in check by harsh labor laws. In contrast to traditional modernization theory, which states that economic development tends to entail democracy (Rostow 1960; Lipset 1959; Huntington 1968), the success of modernization and the drastic economic growth of South Korea did not provide any corresponding political democracy. Instead, Korea's modernization process involved consistent gross violations of human rights, which, in turn, caused social disintegration. Owing mainly to the economic structural changes conducted as part of an International Monetary Fund reform package following the economic crisis in 1997 in particular, conflicts and tensions among labor unions, companies, and the government have only been growing. Hundreds of trade unionists have been arrested and harassed for organizing strikes. The state's excessive emphasis on economic success mandated political stability and efficiency for which the violation of individual rights was continuously justified.

The public's deep-rooted deference to authoritarian law and order hindered all requests for penal reform from below. A series of surveys found that public opinion in favor of capital punishment was still dominant even after democratization. Most citizens allow their politicians to lock up more and more offenders and to impose strict control upon behavior that should not be socially tolerated. The majority of the public favors the death penalty in most countries, however, so these survey results were not peculiar to the Korean case. The difference is that Koreans' respect of the hierarchical, authoritarian social order went as far as championing hard-core dictatorship. The survey statement "The dictatorial rule led by a strong leader like Park Chung Hee is much better than a democracy to tackle the various problems facing our country" was supported by a great majority of Koreans over many years (61 percent in 1994; 53 percent in 1996; 67 percent in 1997) (Shin 1999: 31). These political attitudes stem from long experience with undemocratic governance and its discipline, which have socialized the majority of Koreans to live under the false idea of security. As Shin and Shyu argue, this is comparable to the case in West Germany some decades ago when political ambivalence coexisted between democracy and order: "desiring freedom from political oppression while simultaneously wanting to be ruled by a strong leader" (Shin and Shyu 1997: 117). At any rate, it was more difficult for the abolitionist cause to gain wide support when most South Koreans generally favored strong authority. In other words, a key constraint to penal reform in Korea lies in the shadow of the past (i.e., the residual authoritarian mindset).

Dilemma of Democracy

Another key constraint is the weakness, or the conservative nature, of the democratic regime of South Korea. President Kim Dae-jung owed his election triumph to an alliance with Kim Jong Pil, one of the most conservative politicians in South Korea and the founder of the Korean Central Intelligence Agency under the military dictatorship. This determined in large measure the ideological spectrum of Kim's leadership, making any bold liberal initiatives toward penal reforms politically risky. Although the sixteenth South Korean president, Roh Moo-hyun, a former human rights lawyer and dissident, is known to be even more prone to reform than Kim Dae-jung, a similar pattern is found when Roh's progressive moves are consistently thwarted by the influential conservative camp including the majority Grand National Party (Hannara) and mainstream press. Governmental and legislative leaders therefore fear that such gestures may become a serious political liability for them, especially when all major domestic judicial bodies—the Constitutional Court, the Department of Justice, and even lawyers' groups—oppose the abolition of capital punishment (Shin 2002; Yi 2002).[12] When the leaders of the ruling party feel that they are in a politically weak position in domestic affairs, they are likely to maintain a cool attitude toward progressive policy reforms. Only a "tough on crime" and a security-priority attitude are seen to be "safe." The weakness of the regime means that the political leadership is also weak in its ability to advocate for penal reforms.

A civilian government is more sensitive to the policy preferences of the public than military dictators, who may feel freer to propose bold initiatives, partly because they do not have to worry about the legitimacy of their policy choices, and partly because their policies are likely to be interpreted as inherently conservative by virtue of the fact that the policies are initiated by dictators, no matter what the policies may be. Popularly elected governments are more constrained by the public constituency. This is why the stringent National Security Law still persists even under democratic civilian governments, and even when it appears to be at odds with the "sunshine policy" of engagement toward North Korea.[13]

Developments in the Judiciary

The South Korean judiciary was never autonomous, and the normative power of the Constitution was always weak (Neary 2002; Steinberg 2000). Although the Constitution is theoretically the supreme law of the state and sets the highest standards for the passing of government measures and laws, the Korean Constitution has been unable to preserve its dignity as the supreme law since its proclamation in 1948. It has been amended nine times so far, and all of these amendments were centered on the question of the method for electing the president, the length of the presidential term, and the structure of the state power. All the constitutional amendments, except for those of 1960 and the present Constitution of 1987, have been aimed at extending the term of office of the incumbent president or at providing ex post facto justifications of a military coup d'etat (1961 and 1980). The courts and the whole judicial process have been subservient to the executive branch (i.e., the judiciary was strongly influenced on important issues by the recommendations of the executive). In this Korean legal tradition, any active role on the part of the judiciary would seem to be difficult to establish. Despite democratic progress, Korea has experienced political continuity rather than drastic regime change, and previous legal or penal institutions are therefore unchanged, or incrementally changing at best. The death penalty has been abolished more quickly in many countries when they underwent radical changes of regime and thus could precipitate legal reforms that would have taken much longer to accomplish under stable governments.

At the same time, however, it is not impossible to expect judicial activism in South Korea that will, or will be willing to, take the lead in reshaping the previous authoritarian penal system that has infringed on human rights. Reflecting the change in the social and political atmosphere surrounding capital punishment, the Supreme Court, in February 2002, handed down a decision on a murder case in which the Military Court had twice ruled in favor of the death sentence. The justices ruled: "The death penalty was too severe as the crime was committed on impulse, and the defendant has had no trouble with the law in the past and had been faithful to his military duties before committing the criminal act . . . he has ample potential to correct himself" (*Hankyoreh*, February 23, 2002). It was unprecedented for the Supreme Court to overturn the lower court's judgment on the ground that the defendant had the potential to reform. This court case, along with a moratorium on executions for the past seven years, suggests that the country has been gradually moving toward a death penalty–free society.

Concluding Remarks

In her report following her participation in a death penalty symposium held in Korea in 2002, Sister Helen Prejean, author of *Dead Man Walking*, wrote, "I was deeply touched by the witness and good work for justice of the Catholic Church in Korea." She expected that Korea's example would exert a strong influence on other Asian countries, quoting Father Paul Lee's remark: "If the Korean National Assembly votes to abolish the death penalty, Japan will follow because they hate for Korea to surpass them in anything."[14] Even if we do not take into account the historic rivalry between Korea and Japan, the regional effects are likely to reflect the strategic nature of a normative social policy. As happened in Europe, the decisions on the death penalty abolition are often influenced, for whatever reason, by the actions taken in neighboring countries. If it is true that other governments follow suit when other countries in their region abolish the death penalty, Korea's final decision will have a great impact on the prospect of death penalty abolition in East Asia.

Notes

1.   At present, a significant change is occurring in Taiwan. In the face of public opinion polls that show 70 percent of Taiwanese favor the death penalty, President Chen Shui-bian has repeatedly remarked that death sentences are to be replaced by life sentences without parole. The Taiwanese presidential office and the cabinet have been

jointly drafting legislation to abolish the death penalty, resulting in the Criminal Code amendment in January 2005 that bans the execution of people under the age of 18 or over the age of 80. A major amendment to the entire death penalty section of the Criminal Code will take effect on July 1, 2006 (*Taipei Times*, September 8, 2003; September 10, 2003; October 3, 2003; October 28, 2003; January 8, 2005).

2.   U.N. General Assembly, 49th Session, 3rd Committee (November 16, 1994).

3.   The term "Korea" refers to the Republic of Korea or South Korea unless otherwise indicated. "North Korea" refers to the Democratic People's Republic of Korea.

4.   Chyung Dai-Chul, the member of the National Assembly and leader of capital punishment abolition campaign in South Korea (2002: 1).

5.   Personal interview, David Cupina, Parliamentary Assembly secretariat, Council of Europe (Strasbourg), June 11, 2002. Mr. Cupina, as a Council of Europe delegate, took part in that seminar as well.

6.   Personal interview, Oh Chang-ik, secretary general of the Citizens' Solidarity for Human Rights, Seoul, Korea, January 6, 2003; interview, Lyu Eun-sook, human rights activist at Sarangbang, Seoul, Korea, January 10, 2003.

7.   Interview, Oh Chang-ik, secretary general of the Citizens' Solidarity for Human Rights, Seoul, Korea, January 6, 2003.

8.   Interview, Kim Chulhyo, director of the Death Penalty Abolition Campaign, Amnesty International's South Korean section, Daegu, Korea, December 28, 2002; January 6, 2003. After receiving a number of letters from the AI Korean branch office that called for addressing the issue of capital punishment, in January 2003 the National Human Rights Commission added the death penalty to the list of "the 10 Facing Human Rights Agenda the New Governments Should Advance" (NHRC Press Release, January 28, 2003).

9.   Interview, Oh Chang-ik, secretary general of the Citizens' Solidarity for Human Rights, Seoul, Korea, January 6, 2003.

10.   To this date, this was the last execution to be carried out in South Korea.

11.   President Park Chung Hee's statements demonstrate the values considered most important in Korea in the mid-1970s: "If we wish to develop our democracy and to enhance the basic human rights of individuals, while also maintaining freedom and peace, we ought, first of all, to protect all such values from the threat of the North Korean communists.

Considering our relationship with the North Korean communists, we are under circumstances in which freedom of survival of the nation as such is threatened. . . . If we indiscreetly pursue freedom we will be deprived totally of the freedom of survival by the North Korean communists. We are doing our best to prevent this tragedy from occurring" (*Donga Ilbo*, December 5, 1974; quoted in Sohn 1989: 100).

12. The Capital Punishment Abolition Campaign Association, *Sapehyup*, filed petitions for the review of the constitutionality of the death penalty with the Constitutional Court in 1991, 1993, and 1996. All three petitions were turned down. The Court ruled that the current system of capital punishment was constitutionally legal.

13. The "Sunshine Policy" is a pro-engagement policy toward North Korea and includes an emphasis on greater business and civilian links with North Korea, including family contacts, rail and road links, tourist trips, and the importation of North Korean literature.

14. Sister Helen Prejean's official Web site, http://www.prejean.org (accessed 4 February 2005).

References

Abugre, Charles (1994) "NGOs, Institutional Development and Sustainable Development in Post-Apartheid South Africa," in Ken Cole, eds., *Sustainable Development for a Democratic South Africa.* New York: St. Martin's Press.

Agence France Presse (2003) "Capital Punishment Soars in Singapore" (September 24), http://www.singapore-window.org/sw03/030924a1.htm (accessed 4 February 2005).

Amnesty International (2002a) "China: Execution Is Not a solution. Amnesty International Condemns 46 Executions in Two Days," ASA 17/054/2002 (November 6), http://web.amnesty.org/library/Index/ENGASA170542002?open&of=ENG-2AS.(accessed 4 February 2005).

Amnesty International (2002b) "Republic of Korea (South Korea): Summary of Concerns and Recommendations to Candidates for the Presidential Elections in December 2002," ASA 25/007/2002 (June 11), http://web.amnesty.org/library/Index/ENGASA250072002?open&of=ENG-KOR (accessed 4 February 2005).

Amnesty International (2003) "1,526 Executed in 2002," ACT 50/007/2003 (April 11), http://web.amnesty.org/library/Index/ENGACT500072003 (accessed 4 February 2005).

Asian Human Rights Commission (2001) "Korea: South Korea Marks Human Rights Anniversary," *Asia Human Rights News* (11 December).

Chu, Monique (2002) "Europeans Want Taiwan to Scrap the Death Penalty," *Taipei Times* (22 June).

Chyung, Dai-Chul (2002) "Capital Punishment Abolition Campaign in Korea and Its Prospect." Unpublished manuscript on file with author.

Death Penalty Issue Research Group (2000) "The Taiwan Human Rights Report 2000: The Taiwan Death Penalty Issue in International Perspective," http://www.tahr.org.tw/data/report00/eng00/death.htm (accessed 4 February 2005).

Diamond, Larry, and Byung-Kook Kim (2000) "Introduction: Consolidating Democracy in South Korea," in L. Diamond and B.-K. Kim, eds., *Consolidating Democracy in South Korea*. Boulder, CO: Lynne Rienner.

Dwyer, Eric, "Teen Life in South Korea," http://www.fiu.edu/~dwyere/teenlifeinkorea.html (accessed 13 May 2003).

European Parliament (2002) "Debate on the Abolition of the Death Penalty in Japan, South Korea and Taiwan," News Release (13 June), http://www.coe.int.

Fromm, Erich (1930 [2000]) "The State as Educator: On the Psychology of Criminal Justice," in K. Anderson and R. Quinney, eds., *Erich Fromm and Critical Criminology: Beyond the Punitive Society* Urbana: University of Illinois Press.

Fukuyama, Francis (1995) "Confucianism and Democracy," 6 *Journal of Democracy* 20–33.

Fukuyama, Francis (1997) "The Illusion of Exceptionalism," 8 *Journal of Democracy* 146–49.

Gallup Korea (2003) "Should the Death Penalty Be Abolished?" http://www.gallup.co.kr/News/2003/release084.html (accessed on 1 October 2003).

Garland, David (1985) *Punishment and Welfare: A History of Penal Strategies*. Brookfield, VT: Gower.

Gibney, Frank (1992) *Korea's Quiet Revolution: From Garrison State to Democracy*. New York: Walker and Company.

Han, Sang-Jin ed. (1998) *Dongyangui Nooneuro Segeyrul Hyanghayoh* (Towards the World through an Eastern Eye). Seoul: Nanam.

Hood, Roger (1996) *The Death Penalty: A World-Wide Perspective*. Oxford: Oxford University Press.

Howard, Rhoda (1993) "Cultural Absolutism and the Nostalgia for community," 15 *Human Rights Quarterly* 315–38.

Huntington, Samuel (1968) *Political Order in Changing Societies*. New Haven, CT: Yale University Press.

Huntington, Samuel (1993) "The Clash of Civilizations?" 72 *Foreign Affairs* 22–49

Im, Hyug Baeg (2000) "South Korean Democratic Consolidation in Comparative Perspective," in L. Diamond and B.-K. Kim, eds., *Consolidating Democracy in South Korea*. Boulder, CO: Lynne Rienner.

Kim, Andrew Eungi (2000) "Christianity, Shamanism, and Modernization in South Korea," *Cross Currents* (Spring/Summer), http://articles.findarticles.com/p/articles/mi_m2096/is_2000_Spring-Summer/ai_63300897 (accessed 5 June 2004).

Kim, Byung-Kook (2000) "Electoral Politics and Economic Crisis, 1997–1998," in L. Diamond and B.-K. Kim, eds., *Consolidating Democracy in South Korea*. Boulder, CO: Lynne Rienner.

Kim, Dae Jung (1994) "A Response to Lee Kuan Yew: Is Culture Destiny? The Myth of Asia's Anti-Democratic Values," 73 *Foreign Affairs* 189–95.

Kim, Kyong-Dong (1997) "Confucianism, Economic Development, and Democracy," 21 *Asian Perspective* 77–97.

Lee, Kuan Yew (1998) *The Singapore Story.* Singapore: Times Edition.

Lipset, Seymour (1959) "Some Social Requisites of Democracy: Economic Development and Political Legitimacy," 53 *American Political Science Review* 69–105.

Mihalik, Janos (1991) "The Moratorium on Executions: Its Background and Implication," 108 *The South African Law Journal* 118–42.

Nearly, Ian (2002) *Human Rights in Japan, South Korea and Taiwan.* New York: Routledge.

Palley Howard (1992) "Social Policy and the Elderly in South Korea: Confucianism, Modernization, and Development," 32 *Asian Survey* 787–801.

Pollis, Adamanitia (1996) "Cultural Relativism Revisited: Through a State Prism," 18 *Human Rights Quarterly* 316–44.

Renteln, Alison Dundes (1990) *International Human Rights: Universalism Versus Relativism.* Newbury Park, CA: Sage.

Rostow, Walter W. (1960) *The Stages of Economic Growth.* New York: Cambridge University Press.

Schabas, William A. (1998) "International Law and Abolition of the Death Penalty: Recent Developments," 4 *ILSA Journal of International and Comparative Law* 535.

Shils, Edward (1996) "Reflections on the Civil Society and Civility in the Chinese Intellectual Tradition," in Tu Wei-ming, ed., *Confucian Traditions in East Asian Modernity.* Cambridge: Cambridge University Press.

Shin, Doh Chul (1999) *Mass Politics and Culture in Democratizing Korea.* Cambridge, UK: Cambridge University Press

Shin, Doh Chull, and Huoyan Shyu (1997) "Political Ambivalence in South Korea and Taiwan," 8 *Journal of Democracy* 109–24.

Shin, Uiki (2002) "Siljeongbub Kwanjeomesuh bon Sahyungjeido" [The Death Penalty from the Judicial Perspective], *Emerge* (March 1).

Sohn, Hak-kyu (1989) *Authoritarianism and Opposition in South Korea.* London: Routledge.

Steinberg, David I. (2000) "Continuing Democratic Reform: The Unfinished Symphony," in L. Diamond and B.-K. Kim, eds., *Consolidating Democracy in South Korea* Boulder, CO: Lynne Rienner.

United Nations Economic and Social Council (2001) "Consideration of Reports Submitted by States Parties under Articles 16 and 17 of the Covenant: Republic of Korea," reported by the Committee on Economic, Social and Cultural Rights, E/C.12/1/Add.59 (May 11).

van Rooyen, Jan H. (1993) "Toward a New South Africa Without the Death Penalty—Struggles, Strategies, and Hopes," 20 *Florida State University Law Review* 737–79.

Yi, Sang-don (2002) "Sahyung Pegi—Songsookhan Bubmoonwhaui Gwajei" [The Death Penalty Abolition—A Task of Maturing Legal Culture], *Emerge* (1 March): 60–69.

Zakaris, Fareed (1994) "A Conversation with Lee Kuan Yew," 73 *Foreign Affairs* 109–27.

Zimring, Franklin E., and Gordon Hawkins (1986) *Capital Punishment and the American Agenda.* New York: Cambridge University Press.

Index

In this index an "f" after a number indicates a separate reference on the next page, and an "ff" indicates separate references on the next two pages. A continuous discussion over two or more pages is indicated by a span of page numbers, e.g., "57–59."